THE OCEAN: HIGHWAY OF ALL NATIONS

Painted by Edward Moran

A
Navigation
Compendium

Naval Training Command

University Press of the Pacific
Honolulu, Hawaii

A Navigation Compendium

Prepared by
Naval Training Command

ISBN: 1-4102-2573-9

Reprinted from the 1972 edition

University Press of the Pacific
Honolulu, Hawaii
http://www.universitypressofthepacific.com

CREDITS

Source	Figure
Used by permission from United States Naval Institute, Dutton's Navigation and Piloting, 12th Edition, 1969	2-1, 3-13, 3-14, 8-1, 8-3, 8-5, 9-1
Sperry Rand Corp.	2-6. 3-5

PREFACE

This Compendium has been prepared for use in Navigation study at the Officer Candidate School, the various Naval ROTC Units, and within the fleet. Originally prepared and used by CAPT H. R. Moore, USN (ret.) when an instructor in the grade of LT at the Officer Candidate School, then published as a commercial text, it is now in a second edition as a naval text.

The material presented is intended to provide the essentials to the practice of navigation. Accordingly, the Compendium covers a wide and expanding subject area with brevity.

THE UNITED STATES NAVY

GUARDIAN OF OUR COUNTRY

The United States Navy is responsible for maintaining control of the sea and is a ready force on watch at home and overseas, capable of strong action to preserve the peace or of instant offensive action to win in war.

It is upon the maintenance of this control that our country's glorious future depends; the United States Navy exists to make it so.

WE SERVE WITH HONOR

Tradition, valor, and victory are the Navy's heritage from the past. To these may be added dedication, discipline, and vigilance as the watchwords of the present and the future.

At home or on distant stations we serve with pride, confident in the respect of our country, our shipmates, and our families.

Our responsibilities sober us; our adversities strengthen us.

Service to God and Country is our special privilege. We serve with honor.

THE FUTURE OF THE NAVY

The Navy will always employ new weapons, new techniques, and greater power to protect and defend the United States on the sea, under the sea, and in the air.

Now and in the future, control of the sea gives the United States her greatest advantage for the maintenance of peace and for victory in war.

Mobility, surprise, dispersal, and offensive power are the keynotes of the new Navy. The roots of the Navy lie in a strong belief in the future, in continued dedication to our tasks, and in reflection on our heritage from the past.

Never have our opportunities and our responsibilities been greater.

CONTENTS

CHAPTER 1

INTRODUCTION TO NAVIGATION

101. NAVIGATION DEFINED

According to John Hamilton Moore in his book The Practical Navigator, as revised by Joseph Dessiou and published in London in 1814, "The end and business of Navigation is to instruct the mariner how to conduct a ship through the wide and pathless oceans, to the remotest parts of the world, the safest and shortest way, in passages navigable." This definition as appearing over a century and a half ago in a manual which was to later have an important American counterpart, The American Practical Navigator by Nathaniel Bowditch, remains essentially valid and states the purpose of this compendium. Nevertheless, navigation as practiced today extends to the air and to outer space. It is deemed to be both an art and a science. With this as a point of departure, a modern definition follows.

Navigation is the art or science of determining the position of a ship or aircraft and of directing that ship or aircraft from one position to another. It can be regarded as an art because its application involves the exercise of special skills and fine techniques which can be perfected only by experience and careful practice. On the other hand, the subject with equal validity can be regarded as a science inasmuch as it is a branch of knowledge dealing with a body of facts and truths systematically arranged and showing the operation of general laws. Navigation has been practiced for thousands of years; however, modern methods date from the invention of the chronometer, a precision timepiece, in the 18th century. In our discussion we shall find it convenient to divide the subject into four categories as follows:

DEAD RECKONING. — A method of navigation by which the position of a ship is calculated from its last well determined position and its subsequent direction and rate of progress through the water.

PILOTING. — A near-shore navigation method by which the movements of a ship are directed by reference to landmarks, other navigational aids, and soundings.

ELECTRONIC NAVIGATION. — A method of navigation which employs the use of various electronic devices. Electronic navigation differs from piloting primarily in the manner of collecting information. Procedures involving display and evaluation are very similar.

CELESTIAL NAVIGATION. — The determination of position by the observation of celestial bodies (sun, moon, planets, and stars).

Navigation may be classified according to practice as: (1) marine navigation, (2) air navigation, and (3) space navigation. The first two are basically the same, differing slightly because of the speed extremes represented by aircraft and surface vessels. In aircraft it is impracticable to strive for marine standards of accuracy since it is more important to know your approximate present position than your exact position earlier. As air navigation is essentially an extension of marine navigation, space navigation is an extension of air navigation. Space navigation is developing as required for the operation of space vehicles. In anticipation of interplanetary travel, a body of theory is rapidly being expanded and applied to provide for navigation in the nearly limitless space of the universe.

102. BASIC DEFINITIONS

Elementary navigation terms are common to both navigation and geography. The following are basic:

EARTH. — The planet with which we are most familiar. Although it is approximately an oblate spheroid, for navigational purposes we assume

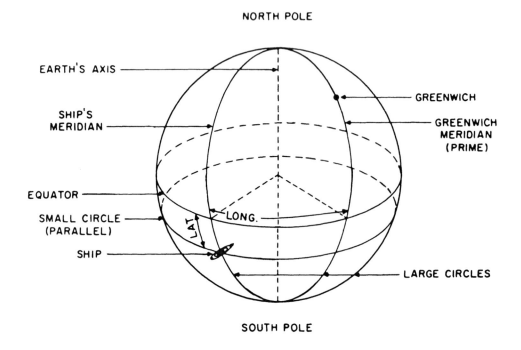

NORTH POLE

EARTH'S AXIS

SHIP'S MERIDIAN

GREENWICH

GREENWICH MERIDIAN (PRIME)

EQUATOR

SMALL CIRCLE (PARALLEL)

LONG.

LAT

SHIP

LARGE CIRCLES

SOUTH POLE

65.116(190)

Figure 1-1. — Earth's coordinate system.

it to be a true sphere about 21,600 nautical miles in circumference. (See fig. 1-1.)

AXIS. — The diameter upon which the earth rotates.

POLES. — The extremities of the earth's axis. One is called the north pole (Pn), and the other the south pole (Ps).

GREAT CIRCLE. — A circle on the surface of a sphere, the plane of which passes through the center of the sphere.

SMALL CIRCLE. — A circle on the surface of a sphere, the plane of which does not pass through the center of the sphere.

EQUATOR. — The great circle on the surface of the earth which is equidistant from the poles. The plane of the equator is perpendicular to the axis of the earth.

PARALLELS. — Small circles on the surface of the earth having planes parallel to the plane of the equator and perpendicular to the axis of the earth.

MERIDIANS. — Great circles on the earth's surface which pass through the poles. The plane of every meridian contains the axis of the earth. The poles bisect each meridian; this provides an upper branch and a lower branch. The upper branch of a meridian is the half between the poles which contains a given position. The lower branch is the opposite half. "Meridian" in common usage refers to the upper branch. When the lower branch is spoken of, it must be so specified.

PRIME MERIDIAN. — That meridian which passes through the original site of the Royal Observatory in Greenwich, England and is used as the origin of measurement of longitude. It is also referred to as the GREENWICH MERIDIAN.

LATITUDE. — The angular distance between a position (on the earth) and the equator measured northward or southward from the equator along a meridian and labeled as appropriate, "N" or "S." Latitude may be abbreviated as "L" or "Lat."

LONGITUDE. — The angular distance between a position (on the earth) and the prime meridian measured eastward or westward from the prime meridian along the arc of the equator to the meridian of the position, expressed in degrees from 0 to 180, and labeled as appropriate, "E" or "W." Longitude may be abbreviated as "Long." or with the Greek letter lambda (λ).

103. DIRECTION

The direction of a line is the angular inclination of that line to the meridian, measured right or clockwise from the north point of the meridian and expressed in three digits. Direction along a meridian itself is either north (000) or south (180). With direction defined, we may consider the following related terms:

COURSE.—The direction of travel as ordered to the helm for the ship's movement.

HEADING.—The direction a ship points at a given instant. Heading may differ from course.

COURSE MADE GOOD OR TRACK.—The direction of a point of arrival from the point of departure.

BEARING.—The direction of a terrestrial object from an observer. A true bearing is measured with reference to the true meridian. A magnetic bearing is measured with reference to the magnetic meridian. A compass bearing is measured with reference to the axis of the compass card. A relative bearing is measured with reference to the fore and aft axis of the ship. Relative bearing plus true heading equals true bearing. All bearings are converted to true bearings for plotting.

AZIMUTH.—The true direction of a celestial body from an observer.

RHUMB LINE.—A line on the surface of the earth which makes the same oblique angle with all intersected meridians.

104. BASIC UNITS

DISTANCE, which is the length of a line joining two places on the surface of the earth, is expressed in nautical miles. One nautical mile equals 6,080.2 feet and is by definition also equal to one minute of latitude, or one minute of arc along any great circle. Dividing the circumference of the earth by the number of degrees in a circle (360), we find that one degree of arc of a great circle (a circumference) is equal to sixty nautical miles. Dividing this value by the number of minutes in a degree (60), we conveniently find that one minute of arc of a great circle is equal to one nautical mile. Thus, arc can be converted to distance, and distance to arc. Distance refers to rhumb line distance unless otherwise specified. The shortest distance between two points on the surface of the earth is the great circle arc connecting them. For navigational convenience, it is common practice to treat the nautical mile as being 2000 yards in length.

SPEED is velocity of travel and is expressed in knots. One knot equals one nautical mile per hour.

ANGLES are expressed in degrees and tenths of degrees or in degrees, minutes, and tenths of minutes. Example: 349°.6 or 95°-14'.7.

DEPTH is expressed in either feet (ft) or fathoms (fm). One fathom is equal to six feet.

CHAPTER 2

THE COMPASS

201. INTRODUCTION

The measurement of direction is accomplished by means of the compass, of which there are two types, magnetic and gyro. The former utilizes the earth's magnetic field for directive force, while the latter, as addressed later in this chapter, employs the principles of gyroscopic inertia and precession, and the natural phenomena of the earth's rotation and gravitational field. The magnetic compass, one of the oldest of the navigator's instruments, is of unknown origin. It is believed that the Vikings used it in the eleventh century. Probably, the first magnetic compass was simply a magnetized needle thrust through a straw, resting in a container of water. The needle was probably magnetized using lodestone, an iron ore having magnetic qualities. Today, despite the rising importance and great convenience of the gyrocompass, the magnetic compass retains its importance because of its simplicity and reliability. A ship may be subjected to electrical power failure, fire, collision, grounding, or other hazard, and yet the magnetic compass will usually remain operative.

202. MAGNETISM

A magnet is any piece of metal having the property of attracting other pieces of metal. In its natural state, lodestone or magnetic oxide of iron, has this property. Ferrous metal and certain alloys become magnets by being subjected to the influence of strong magnets.

In any magnet, the power of attraction is concentrated at opposite ends or poles. At a point about midway between the poles the force of attraction of one pole equals the force of attraction of the other. The area of influence around a magnet is known as a magnetic field; at any given point within this magnetic field the force of magnetic attraction has both direction and intensity. The direction is the inclination of the line of magnetic force to some given reference. The intensity is a measure of the force of attraction and is inversely proportional to the square of the distance from the pole. A line of magnetic force, as mentioned above, is a line connecting two poles along which an isolated pole would move when acted upon by (the earth's) magnetism.

For the purposes of this discussion, magnetism may be thought of as being either permanent or induced, depending upon the magnetic properties of the materials involved and upon the manner in which the magnetism is acquired.

The magnetism of materials such as the high carbon steel alloys which have a high degree of magnetic retentivity is said to be permanent as it will continue to be a property of the material for a long time unless subjected to extreme heat or shock.

Some materials, for example, soft iron, which have a high degree of permeability, are capable of acquiring magnetism by being placed in a magnetic field. The magnetism produced in this manner is referred to as induced magnetism. When the influence of the original magnetic field is removed, the induced magnetism disappears.

203. EARTH'S MAGNETISM

As a result of its content of magnetic materials, the earth has magnetic properties and may be treated as a magnet. The magnetic poles are located approximately as follows (see fig. 2-1):

North magnetic pole — 74 N; 101 W.
South magnetic pole — 68 S; 144 E.

To avoid confusion when speaking of the action of poles, colors have been assigned. The earth's north magnetic pole is designated as "blue," and the south magnetic pole is designated as "red." A law of magnetism states that unlike poles attract each other while like poles repel. Thus the north seeking pole of a magnet is attracted to the earth's north magnetic pole and

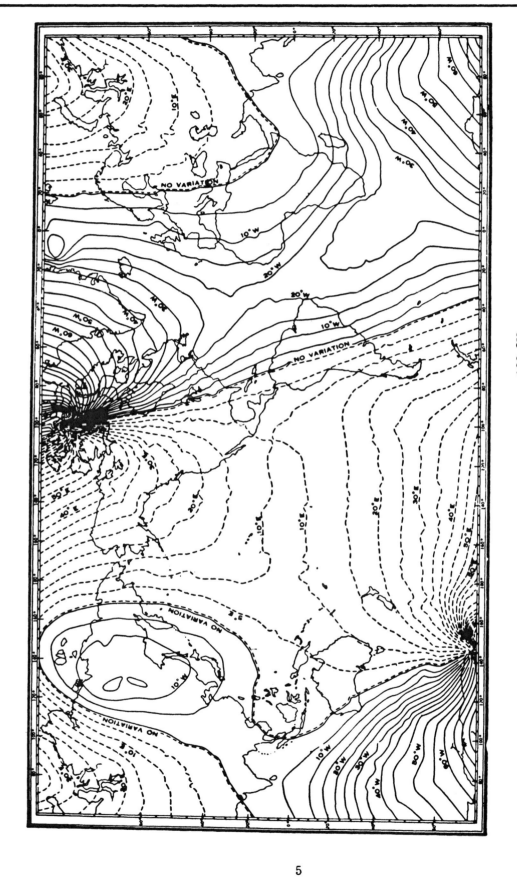

190.2X

Figure 2-1. — Magnetic variation.

is said to be "red" while the south seeking pole is attracted by the earth's south magnetic pole and is said to be "blue."

The magnetic lines of force which connect the magnetic poles may be called magnetic meridians. These meridians are not great circles. Because of the irregular distribution of magnetic material in the earth, the meridians are irregular, and the planes of the magnetic meridians do not necessarily pass through the center of the earth. Midway between the magnetic poles a circle called the magnetic equator crosses the magnetic meridians.

The earth's magnetism undergoes diurnal, annual, and secular changes. Diurnal changes are daily changes which are caused by the movement of the magnetic poles in an orbit having a diameter of about 50 miles. Annual changes simply represent the yearly permanent change in the earth's magnetic field. Secular changes are those which occur over a great period of years.

If a magnetic needle is freely suspended in both the horizontal and the vertical plane, it will seek to align itself with the magnetic meridian (a magnetic line of force). The vertical angle of inclination with the horizontal plane (plane perpendicular to force of gravity) made by the magnetic needle is called "dip" and the magnetic needle used to illustrate this vertical angle is called a dip needle. At the magnetic equator, dip is 0 degrees; with an increase in magnetic latitude, dip increases, reaching 90 degrees at the magnetic poles.

The direction and intensity of the earth's magnetic field may be resolved into horizontal and vertical components. At the magnetic equator the horizontal component is of maximum strength and at the magnetic poles the vertical component is of maximum strength. A magnetic compass actually reacts to the horizontal component of the earth's magnetic field and therefore its sensitivity reaches a maximum at the magnetic equator and decreases with increases in magnetic latitude. Dip, which indicates the comparative strength of components, may be found by consulting Oceanographic Office Chart number 30, for any position on the earth's surface.

204. VARIATION AND DEVIATION

Since the magnetic poles do not coincide with the true poles, and the magnetic meridians do not coincide with the true meridians, there are two lines of reference differing by a value called "variation." Variation may be defined as the inclination of the magnetic meridian to the true meridian; it must be labeled east or west. When from the observer's position facing north, the magnetic meridian is to the right or eastward, it is labeled east. Under the same circumstances, except with the magnetic meridian to the left or westward, it is labeled west. Variation changes with geographic locality and may be found on Oceanographic Office Chart 42. See figure 2-1.

The magnetic compass, being sensitive to magnetic materials, is affected by ferrous metal within its vicinity (for example the ship upon which it is mounted). This source of error, which causes the axis of the compass card to deviate from the magnetic meridian, is called "deviation." Deviation may be defined as the inclination of the axis of the compass card to the magnetic meridian; it is labeled east or west in the same manner as variation. The value of deviation changes with the ship's heading. This is due to the fact that the ship's induced magnetism varies as the ship changes its position relative to the earth's magnetic field.

205. COMPASS DESIGNATION

The magnetic compass on board ship may be classified or designated according to location or usage. The magnetic compass located in a position favorable for taking bearings and used in navigation is called the standard (STD) compass. The magnetic compass at the steering station used normally for steering, or as a standby when the steering gyro repeater fails, is called the steering (STG) compass. Direction from either of these instruments must be labeled as "per standard compass (PSC)" or "per steering compass (PStgC)," for identification. A magnetic compass located aft at a secondary steering station is called the after compass. A compass carried in a boat is properly called a boat compass.

206. COMPASS NOMENCLATURE

The following components make up a standard 7 1/2 inch Navy compass (7 1/2 inch refers to diameter as depicted in fig. 2-2):

MAGNETS. — Four (two in older compasses) cylindrical bundles of steel wire, with magnetic properties, or bar magnets, which are attached to the compass card to supply directive

45.595(69)
Figure 2-2. — U. S. Navy 7 1/2-inch compass.

force. Some newer compasses have a circular magnet made of a metallic alloy.

COMPASS CARD. — An aluminum disc graduated in degrees from 0 to 360 and also showing cardinal and intercardinal points. North is usually indicated by the fleur de lis figure in addition to the cardinal point. Being attached to the magnets, the compass card provides a means of reading direction.

COMPASS BOWL. — A bowl-shaped container of nonmagnetic material (brass) which serves to contain the magnetic element, a reference mark, and the fluid. Part of the bottom may be transparent (glass) to permit light to shine upward against the compass card.

FLUID. — A liquid surrounding the magnetic element. By a reduction of weight in accordance with Archimedes principle of buoyancy, friction is reduced making possible closer alignment of the compass needle with the magnetic meridian. Any friction present will tend to prevent complete alignment with the magnetic meridian. In older compasses the liquid may be a mixture of ethyl alcohol and water in approximately equal parts. The alcohol serves to lower the freezing point of the mixture. Newer compasses contain a highly refined petroleum distillate similar to varsol, which increases stability and efficiency and neither freezes nor becomes more viscous at low temperatures.

FLOAT. — An aluminum air-filled chamber in the center of the compass card which further reduces weight and friction at the pivot point.

EXPANSION BELLOWS. — A bellows arrangement in the bottom of the compass bowl which operates to keep the compass bowl completely filled with liquid, allowing for temperature changes. A filling screw facilitates addition of liquid which may become necessary notwithstanding the expansion bellows.

LUBBERS LINE. — A reference mark on the inside of the compass bowl which is aligned with the ship's fore and aft axis, or keel line of the ship. The lubbers line is a reference for the reading of direction from the compass card. The reading of the compass card on the lubbers line at any time is the ship's heading.

GIMBALS. — The compass bowl has two pivots which fit or rest in a metal ring also having two pivots which rest in the binnacle. This arrangement (gimbals) permits the compass to remain almost horizontal in spite of the motion of the ship. An important concept is that, regardless of the movement of the ship, the compass card remains fixed (unless some magnetic material is introduced to cause additional deviation from the magnetic meridian). The ship, the compass bowl, and the lubbers line move around the compass card. To the observer as he witnesses this relative motion, it appears that the compass card moves.

BINNACLE. — A nonmagnetic housing (fig. 2-3) which supports the magnetic compass and provides a means of inserting corrector magnets for compass adjustment as explained in art. 211. The binnacle also contains a light, usually below the compass bowl, to permit the reading of direction at night.

207. LIMITATIONS

The following characteristics of the magnetic compass limit its direction-finding ability:

(a) It is sensitive to any magnetic disturbance.

112.7
Figure 2-3. — Binnacle containing magnetic compass.

(b) It is useless at the magnetic poles and is sluggish and unreliable in areas near the poles.
(c) Deviation changes as the ship's magnetic properties change. The magnetic properties change with changes in the induced magnetism, changes in the ship's structure or magnetic cargo. Prolonged periods in dry dock, or alongside a dock, the heavy shock of gunfire or of riding out a heavy sea, and the vessel being struck by lightning, can alter the magnetic properties.
(d) Deviation changes with heading. The ship as well as the earth may be considered as a magnet. The effect of the induced magnetism upon the compass changes with the ship's heading.

(e) It does not point to true north.

(f) It requires adjustment annually, and more often if the ship is subjected to such influences as those described in (c) above.

208. COMPASS ERROR

Compass error, defined as the inclination of the axis of the compass card to the true meridian, may be easily computed since it is the algebraic sum of variation and deviation. Compass error (fig. 2-4) must be applied to compass direction to get true direction and must be applied to true direction, with reversal of sign, to arrive at compass direction. Variation is usually found recorded within the compass rose or direction reference of the chart in use, or by eye interpolation between isogonic lines of variation printed on the more recent editions of charts. Deviation is found by consulting the magnetic

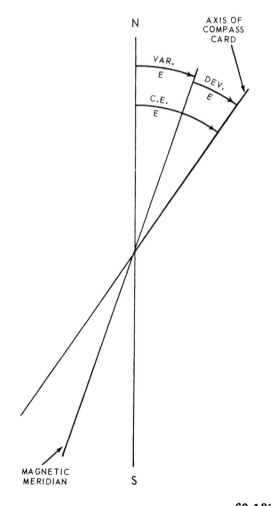

69.138

Figure 2-4.—Components of compass error.

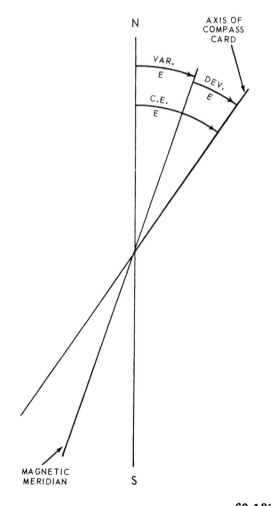

69.13

Figure 2-5.—Magnetic compass table.

compass table (fig. 2-5) which provides the deviation values for each 15 degrees of magnetic heading. If the ship has degaussing equipment installed, for protection against magnetic mines, a separate column must be provided on the magnetic compass table (deviation table) to take into account the effect of the degaussing equipment when energized.

209. COMPASS CORRECTION

Magnetic compass correction requires the understanding of the relationship between compass error, variation, and deviation. The difference between compass and magnetic direction is deviation. The difference between magnetic and true direction is variation. The difference between compass and true direction is compass error. (See fig. 2-4.) When correcting or working from magnetic to true or from compass to true, add easterly errors and subtract westerly errors. When uncorrecting, or working from true to magnetic or true to compass, subtract easterly errors and add westerly errors. Remembering the following line may help:

Can Dead Men Vote Twice At Elections

meaning

Compass Deviation Magnetic Variation True

Add East

For magnetic compass error, one may use equally well the rule as later given for gyro error: "Compass least, error east; compass best, error west."

For example, if compass direction is 068 and deviation is 2 E, then magnetic direction is 070. If variation is 3 W, then compass error is 1 W and true direction is 067.

If the sun is found to bear 105 by magnetic compass at a time which by computation the azimuth should have been 093 true, then compass error is 12 W. If the variation is 8 W, then the deviation must be 4 W.

210. SWINGING SHIP

The navigator computes deviation and prepares the magnetic compass table by an operation called swinging ship. Briefly, swinging ship consists of recording compass bearings on different headings and of comparing these compass bearings with true bearings obtained in some other manner, thus finding compass error. By applying variation to compass error, deviation is determined.

Five general techniques in determining deviation are in current practice, listed as follows:

(a) Comparison with gyrocompass. This technique is most common. It is essential that the gyro error, if any, be ascertained and applied.

(b) Comparison with other magnetic compass with known deviation.

(c) Reciprocal bearings from shore. A magnetic compass may be established on shore free from magnetic influence other than the earth's. The ship, on various headings, observes the bearing of a marker near the shore compass. By some means of communication, the bearing of the ship may be received from the shore station. The reciprocal of the received bearing is compared with the magnetic bearing in order to determine the deviation.

(d) Direction of distant objects. As a ship swings to a mooring buoy, a distant object of known true bearing may be observed. The radius of the circle of swing must be short in comparison to the distance in order that the true bearing does not change while the ship is at the extremes of its swing. A celestial body may be used for this as its azimuth can be precomputed and plotted as a function of time.

(e) Ranges. Any two objects on shore, when in line, provide direction and are referred to as a range. By observing a range with the ship on different headings, compass error is easily determined.

211. PRACTICAL COMPASS ADJUSTMENT

The purpose of compass adjustment is to reduce or eliminate deviation. Following adjustment, residual deviation must be measured.

Before adjustment, if the navigator lacks experience, he should consult H.O. 226 (Handbook of Magnetic Compass Adjustment and Compensation). This handbook contains a wealth of information; not only does it contain the theory of adjustment, but it contains a check-off list for adjustment and a guide in table form for the placing or movement of correctors. A summary of the order of procedure is as follows:

(a) Place all deck gear in the vicinity of the compass in its normal position. Secure degaussing coils. Check the alignment of the lubbers line with the ship's fore and aft axis. Check quadrantal spheres and Flinders bar for residual magnetism. The quadrantal spheres are spheres mounted on the arms of the binnacle. To check them, rotate them in place and note any effect upon the compass card. The Flinders bar is a cylindrical bar in segments, inserted in a tube usually located forward of the binnacle. Hold each segment horizontally near the north or south point of the compass card. If the compass card deviates more than two degrees as a result of residual magnetism in the quadrantal spheres or the Flinders bar, demagnetization of one or both by reannealing is appropriate.

(b) Place the Flinders bar by computation or estimate. The Flinders bar corrects deviation caused by induction in vertical soft iron.

(c) Place the quadrantal spheres by estimate. These spheres correct deviation caused by induction in symmetrically placed soft iron.

(d) Place the heeling magnet, red end up in north magnetic latitude, and lower to bottom of tube unless better information is available. This device corrects for errors due to the roll and pitch of the ship.

(e) Steam on two adjacent cardinal headings and correct all deviation from permanent magnetism using "fore and aft" magnets for east and west headings and "athwartship" magnets for north and south headings.

(f) Steam on the two remaining cardinal headings. Using athwartship and fore and aft magnets correct half of any remaining deviation resulting from permanent magnetism.

(g) Correct the position of the quadrantal spheres by removing all deviation on one intercardinal heading. Steam on an adjacent intercardinal heading and remove half of the remaining deviation.

(h) Record corrector positions and secure the binnacle.

(i) Swing ship and record residual deviation.

(j) Energize degaussing circuits (if installed). Repeat swing, record residual deviation and enter values in the magnetic compass table (see figure 2-5). With degaussing circuits energized, the residual deviation should not differ more than two degrees from that previously recorded. In addition to H.O. 226, the navigator should consult the Naval Ships Technical Manual, Chapters 9240 and 9810.

212. THE GYROCOMPASS

While the magnetic compass uses the earth's magnetic field, the gyrocompass uses the earth's gravitational field and rotation, and the inherent properties of a gyroscope known as gyroscopic inertia and precession, for directive force. The gyrocompass, unlike the magnetic compass, is essentially a modern device, although the basic theory of its operation had early antecedents. The ancient Egyptians understood something of the earth's rotation on its axis, and of precession.

Sir Isaac Newton's first law of motion which stated that "a body at rest or in motion will remain at rest or in uniform motion unless some external force is applied to it," (see Appendix B), has application to gyroscopic inertia. Newton's mathematical explanation of the earth's precession, a conical motion of the earth's axis caused by the gravitational pull of the sun, set the stage in the seventeenth century for the development of the gyroscope. Newton was followed by other British and German scientists whose experiments advanced the use of a rotor for direction reference. Based on these advances, the French physicist Foucault demonstrated the earth's rotation using a pendulum in 1851, and with a spinning wheel, which he named a "gyroscope," a year later. By 1908, gyrocompasses had been successfully tested in the German Navy, and in 1911, Dr. Elmer Sperry demonstrated his American model in the battleship U.S.S. Delaware. After World War I, gyrocompasses gained in usage, although the early concepts of gyrocompass design saw little change until mid-century. During the past two decades, gyrocompass design and usage have rapidly advanced.

213. PRINCIPLES OF GYROCOMPASS OPERATION

The gyroscope, a rapidly spinning body with three axes of angular movement, is increasingly used bogh for navigational reference and for providing stabilization data. One axis of the gyroscope is the spin axis; the other axes support inner and outer gimbals. Gyroscopic inertia tends to keep the gyroscope spinning in the same plane in which it is started. When a force is applied to the axis of a spinning gyrocompass, the axis rotates 90° from the direction in which the force applied. This, known as precession, is in accordance with Foucault's law which stated that "a spinning body tends to swing around so as to place its axis parallel to the axis of an impressed force, such that its direction of rotation is the same as that of the impressed force" (see Appendix B). Thus by the application of torques of the proper direction and magnitude, a gyroscope can be made to align its axis of rotation with the plane of the meridian, and provide direction as a compass. The pull of gravity provides the necessary torque, keeping the spinning axis parallel to the meridian, causing precession around a vertical axis at a rate and direction which cancels the effect of the earth's rotation, and causing the spinning axis to remain nearly level when parallel to the meridian. Oscillations across the meridian are reduced by a damping action to the force producing precession. Additionally, more precision is obtained by compensation of those errors introduced by a shipboard environment.

214. COMPARISON OF GYROCOMPASS AND MAGNETIC COMPASS

The gyrocompass has four important advantages over the magnetic compass, as follows:

(a) The gyrocompass seeks true north, whereas the magnetic compass seeks the direction of the magnetic north pole.

(b) The gyrocompass is not affected by proximity to the magnetic poles. The magnetic compass, on the other hand, is rendered useless near the magnetic poles because the directional force of the earth's magnetic field is almost vertical in these areas.

(c) The gyrocompass is not affected by magnetic material. It can therefore be located in a well protected place below decks. The magnetic compass is very sensitive to nearby magnetic material; hence it must be located topside in a relatively unprotected place. Even so, the magnetic compass is usually subject to errors due to the magnetic properties of the metal in the ship.

(d) The directional information provided by the gyrocompass can be transmitted electrically to remotely located indicators called gyro repeaters. The magnetic compass is not as readily adaptable to this type of remote indication.

Limiting features of the gyrocompass include:

(a) The gyrocompass is a complex mechanical device and hence is subject to mechanical failure. The magnetic compass, being a very simple instrument, is virtually immune to mechanical failure.

(b) The gyrocompass is dependent upon an uninterrupted supply of electrical power. In various types of emergency, it is not uncommon for the ship's main electrical power source to fail, and thus an alternate supply source is required. The magnetic compass would naturally be unaffected by a power failure.

(c) The gyrocompass requires the services of a skilled technician for maintenance and repair. Very little skill is required to keep the magnetic compass operating properly.

(d) The directive force, and hence the accuracy, of the gyrocompass decreases at higher latitudes, particularly above 75°, although newer precision models such as the Mark 19 have largely overcome this limitation.

(e) Older models of the gyrocompass must be adjusted to compensate for errors caused by change of latitude, change of speed, and acceleration. Furthermore, after these compensations have been made, a small residual error is not uncommon. However, the latest models, including the Mark 19, have automatic speed and latitude compensating devices.

(f) The gyrocompass should be started four hours prior to getting underway to ensure satisfactory operation. If it is expected that the ship will get underway on short notice, the gyrocompass should be kept running. In an emergency, the gyrocompass can be started and, while slightly less dependable, can generally be used after thirty minutes of operation.

In summing up the relative merits of the two compasses, it can be said that the magnetic compass is the most reliable while the gyrocompass is the most convenient.

215. GYRO ERROR

A modern gyrocompass, properly adjusted, generally has an error of only a fraction of a degree. Occasionally, an error of a degree or more may be present. In case of serious malfunction, the error may be as much as 180°. It is not a perfect compass, and it requires frequent checking. Usually, and particularly in naval ships, the accuracy of the gyrocompass is checked at least daily when underway. The prudent navigator checks his gyrocompass at every practical opportunity. This is done by celestial observation, by noting a range (two objects in line of known true direction), by routine comparison with the magnetic compass, and by trial and error as described in Chapter 7.

The difference between true direction and direction by gyrocompass is known as "gyro error." It is classified as "easterly" or "westerly." If the compass points to the east of true north, the error is easterly. Conversely, if the compass points to the west of north, the error is westerly. To convert gyrocompass direction to true direction when gyro error exists, add easterly and subtract westerly gyro error. To convert true direction to direction by gyrocompass, subtract easterly and add westerly gyro error. When the error is easterly, the gyrocompass reads low, and when westerly gyro error exists, the gyrocompass reads too high. "Compass least, error east: compass best, error west."

As an example, if the true bearing of two objects in a range is 075 and the gyro bearing is 076.5, the gyro error is 1.5 west. If the

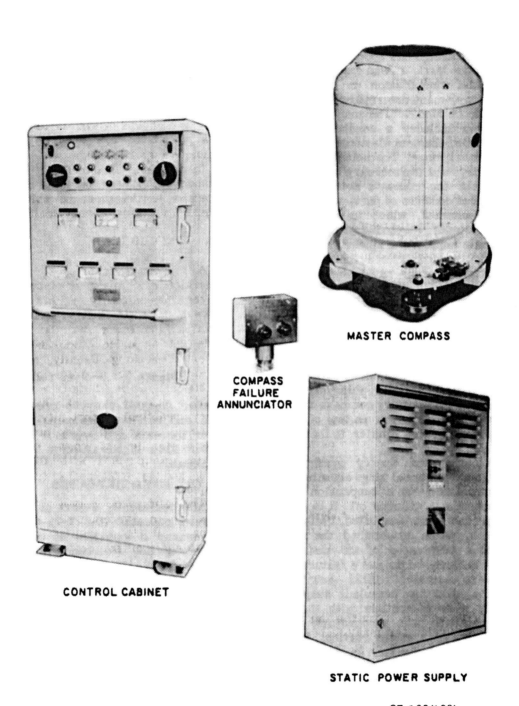

MASTER COMPASS

COMPASS
FAILURE
ANNUNCIATOR

CONTROL CABINET

STATIC POWER SUPPLY

27.169(190)
Figure 2-6.— Sperry Mark 19 Mod 3C Gyrocompass equipment.

azimuth of the sun is observed to be 164 when the computed true azimuth is 164.5, the gyro error is 0.5 east.

216. GYRO SYSTEMS

Gyrocompass design has seen many improvements since the Mark 1 was introduced after Sperry's initial installation in the U.S.S. Delaware. Today, many destroyers for example, have the Mark 11 Mod 6. The master compass in this system includes a sensitive element, mercury ballistic, phantom element, spider, binnacle and gimbal rings. The sensitive element is north seeking, and the mercury ballistic uses gravity to make the compass seek north. The phantom element consists of parts which support the sensitive element, which in turn is supported by the spider. Pivoted gimbals within the binnacle or case support the spider.

The Mark 19 Mod 3 (see figure 2-6), as used generally in larger naval ships, contains two gyroscopes which serve as a sensitive element. A meridian gyro aligns its spin axis with the meridian, and a slave gyro mounted on the same support, is oriented east and west. This system identifies the true vertical, as well as north, and thus is useful in fire control.

The Mark 23 Mod 0 is a small gyrocompass designed for use in smaller ships. It is also used as a second or auxiliary compass in larger vessels. Some features, such as that of sensing the force of gravity, are similar to those found in the Mark 19.

In the most recent Sperry gyrocompass, the Mark 27, outside gimbal rings are eliminated, and the conventional wire suspension is replaced by flotation in silicone oil. It is accordingly smaller and more simplified. Unlike older gyrocompasses, which established the vertical by a pendulous suspension of the instrument, the Mark 27 is designed to use a feature known as "deck-plane azimuth." This new insight eliminates the need for pendulous suspension. Nevertheless, it is compatible with the needs of the navigator who uses a coordinate system which is perpendicular to the vertical. Azimuth error with this new design, as compared to azimuth in the horizontal plane, is 0° on the cardinal headings (0°, 90°, 180°, and 270°) and maximum, but acceptable, on the intercardinal headings (45°, 135°, 225°, and 315°). The speed of the wheel, 12,000 rpm, is just half the speed in the Mark 19, and this alone reduces the power requirement and the generated heat. The advantages of the Mark 27 are that it is a highly

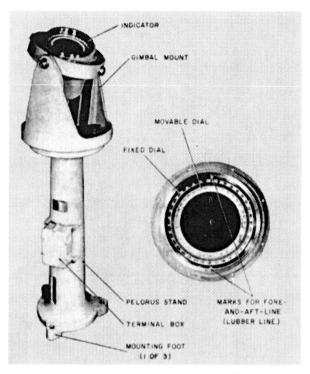

51.131
Figure 2-7.—Gyro repeater.

reliable, rugged, easy to operate, reasonably small, and relatively inexpensive, gyrocompass.

For the care and overhaul of gyro systems, Chapter 9240 of Naval Ships Technical Manual is applicable.

217. THE GYRO REPEATER

While technically a part of the gyro system, the gyro repeater (fig. 2-7) can be treated as a compass. It consists of a compass stand, a lubber's line (reference point aligned with fore and aft axis of the ship), and compass card graduated in 360 degrees. The compass card is driven through a synchro system which receives an electrical input from the master gyrocompass.

A gyro repeater mounted in the pilot house in the vicinity of the helm is known as a "steering repeater." If mounted on the wings of the bridge or elsewhere for the convenience of taking bearings or azimuths, a gyro repeater is simply called a "bearing repeater." Other repeaters in the gyro system are built into those instruments and devices which require the indication of direction, such as radar, fire control, and automatic dead reckoning equipment.

CHAPTER 3

NAVIGATIONAL INSTRUMENTS

301. GENERAL

In determining position, and in conducting a ship or aircraft from one position to another, the navigator must utilize certain instruments in addition to the compass as discussed in the preceding Chapter. These usually include bearing taking devices which are used in conjunction with the compass. Speed, distance, and depth measuring devices are essential. Plotting tools, automatic dead reckoning, relatively sophisticated electronic navigation equipment, timepieces, and celestial navigation instruments are also included.

Instructions for the care, custody, and replacement of navigational instruments in naval ships are contained in Naval Ships Technical Manual, Chapter 9240.

302. BEARING TAKING DEVICES

Instruments for observing azimuths and bearings consist of azimuth circles, bearing circles, telescopic alidades, self-synchronous alidades, and peloruses or dumb compasses. Their descriptions follow.

An AZIMUTH CIRCLE (fig. 3-1) is a nonmagnetic metal ring sized to fit upon a 7 1/2 inch compass bowl or upon a gyro repeater. The inner lip is graduated in degrees from 0 to 360 in a counterclockwise direction for the purpose of taking relative bearings. Two sighting vanes, the forward or far vane containing a vertical wire, and the after or near vane containing a peep sight, facilitate the observation of bearings and azimuths. Two finger lugs are used to position exactly the instrument while aligning the vanes. A hinged reflector vane mounted at the base and beyond the forward vane is used for reflecting stars and planets when observing azimuths. Beneath the forward vane a reflecting mirror and the extended vertical wire are

mounted, enabling the navigator to read the bearing or azimuth from the reflected portion of the compass card. For observing azimuths of the sun, an additional reflecting mirror and housing are mounted on the ring, each midway between the forward and after vanes. The sun's rays are reflected by the mirror to the housing where a vertical slit admits a line of light. This admitted light passes through a 45 degree reflecting prism and is projected on the compass card from which the azimuth is directly read. In observing both bearings and azimuths, two spirit levels, which are attached, must be used to level the instrument. An azimuth circle without the housing and spare mirror is called a BEARING CIRCLE.

A TELESCOPIC ALIDADE (fig. 3-2) is similar to a bearing circle, differing only in having a telescope attached to the metal ring in lieu of the forward and after sight vanes. A reticule within the telescope, together with a prism, facilitates the reading of bearings while the telescope lens magnifying power makes distant objects appear more visible to the observer. When looking through the telescope, the bearing may be read, since the appropriate part of the compass card is reflected by the prism in such a way as to appear in the lower part of the field of vision.

When a ship is yawing badly, it is easy to lose sight of an object using the telescopic alidade, the field of vision being very limited. To overcome this handicap, a telescope has been mounted on a compass card having an additional synchro motor driven by the master gyrocompass. It is possible with this development to set the alidade on a desired true bearing and observe an object without having the telescope deviate from the desired bearing because of the motion of the ship. This instrument is the SELF-SYNCHRONOUS ALIDADE. See figure 3-3.

The PELORUS (dumb compass) (fig. 3-4) consists of a compass stand, compass bowl

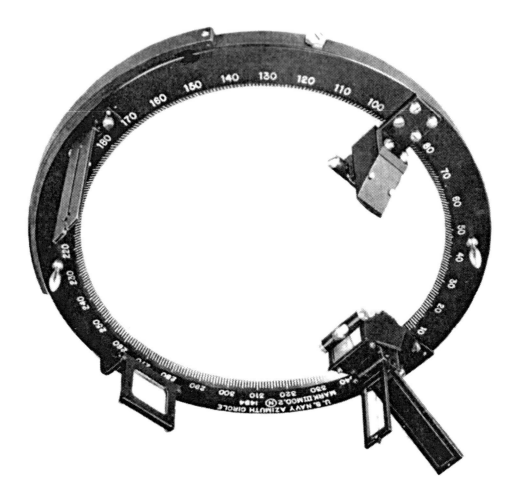

65.122
Figure 3-1.—Azimuth circle.

(containing lubber's line), and compass card. The compass card, which is graduated in 360 degrees, may be rotated using a knurled knob on the side of the compass bowl. To obtain a true bearing using the pelorus and bearing circle, the observer must match the ship's true course on the compass card, and the lubber's line on the compass bowl, using the knurled knob. After aligning the sight vanes with the object, he should call "Mark" and note the bearing from the reflected portion of the compass card. On "Mark" the helmsman should note the ship's heading. The observer should then apply the difference between course and heading as a correction to his bearing, taking care to apply the correction in the right direction. Another method is to read the relative bearing from the inner lip of the bearing circle at the lubber's line; then the relative bearing is added to the true heading noted at time of "Mark," to obtain the true bearing. For greater convenience, in modern installations the dumb compass has been generally replaced with a gyro repeater. In current usage, however, a gyro repeater mounted in a "pelorus" stand will be referred to as a "pelorus."

303. SPEED MEASURING DEVICES

Instruments for measuring speed or distance sailed are known as logs, and may be considered under six general types.

An old and simple type was the CHIP LOG which consisted of a piece of line containing

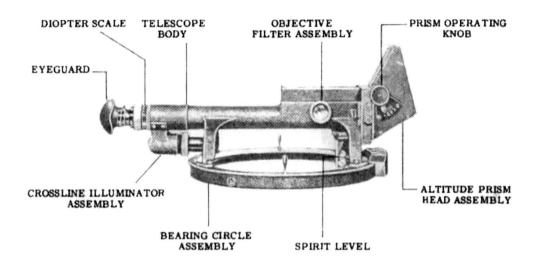

DIOPTER SCALE   TELESCOPE BODY   OBJECTIVE FILTER ASSEMBLY   PRISM OPERATING KNOB

EYEGUARD

CROSSLINE ILLUMINATOR ASSEMBLY

ALTITUDE PRISM HEAD ASSEMBLY

BEARING CIRCLE ASSEMBLY   SPIRIT LEVEL

MARK 2, MOD 3

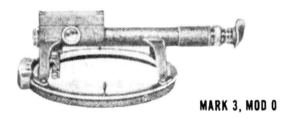

MARK 3, MOD 0

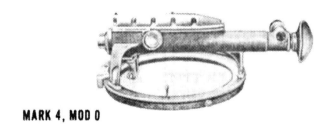

MARK 4, MOD 0

45.39
Figure 3-2.— Telescopic alidade.

equally spaced knots and terminated by a wood float. The log was paid out over the stern of a ship underway. By counting the knots paid out over a period of time, and considering the distance between knots, the navigator computed speed. A more accurate type of chip log consists simply of a chip of wood and a timepiece such as a stop watch. While the ship is in motion the chip is thrown into the water forward of the stem and to leeward. The relative motion of the chip is observed, and as it passes the stem of the ship the stop watch is started. As it passes the stern, the stop watch is stopped. From the elapsed time and the length of the ship, the navigator computes speed. Before stop watches were available, a sandglass was used for time measurement with all forms of chip logs.

More in general use is the Pitometer or PITO-STATIC type. Pitometer logs (pit logs)

17

45.39(69)B
Figure 3-3. — Self-synchronous alidade.

69.20
Figure 3-4. — Pelorus or "dumb compass."

have a three foot pitot tube extending through the hull, which contains two or more orifices, one of which measures dynamic pressure and the others static pressure. Through a system of bellows, mercury tubes, electromechanical linkages, or some combination thereof, the difference between dynamic and static pressure is measured. This difference, being proportional to speed, is recorded on a master indicator capable of transmitting readings to remote stations.

A log in general use is the IMPELLER TYPE Underwater Log System in which a water-driven propeller produces an electric impulse which in turn is used to indicate speed and distance traveled. A rodmeter, extending about two feet through the sea valve, contains the impeller in its head assembly. The frequency of the alternating current generated is amplified and passed to a master transmitter indicator, and is directly proportional to ship's speed.

Also in general use, and of high precision and accuracy, is the ELECTROMAGNETIC log. Calibrated for speeds of 0 to 40 knots, it consists of a rodmeter, which is generally retractable through a sea valve, and an induction device to produce a signal voltage. Its principle of operation is that any movement of a conductor across a magnetic field, or any movement of

a magnetic field with respect to a conductor, will induce a signal voltage that is measurable and transmittible. This voltage varies with the speed of the ship, thus providing an accurate indication of speed. Although pitching and rolling of the ship will also provide an incremental output signal, such is rejected by the transmitter indicator.

With pito-static and rodmeter types of logs, it is essential that the navigator at all times be aware of the ship's increased draft when the pitot tube (known also as the pit sword) or the rodmeter is lowered. When shallow water, or any endangering underwater obstruction, is approached, the pitot tube or rodmeter should be raised and housed.

A log less accurate but still in use, particularly in small craft, is the TAFFRAIL or PATENT log. It consists of a rotator and sinker attached to a line paid out astern and connected to a registering device located on an after rail or taffrail. Towed sufficiently far astern to avoid the wake effect, the rotator turns by the action of the water against its spiral fins. Through the log line, the register, which is calibrated to indicate miles and tenths of miles run, is driven. The taffrail or patent log should be frequently checked for accuracy. Importantly, the log tends to read slightly high in a head sea and slightly low in a following sea.

An important feature of the logs thus far described is that they are intended to measure the speed through the water. Coming into use is the Doppler sonar which provides an effective means for measuring speed over the bottom. This innovation in speed measurement has a great advantage in accuracy, making it particularly useful in piloting and specifically in anchoring and mooring. It is, however, limited to use in water depths of only a few hundred feet.

An example of the newest log is the Sperry Doppler Sonar Speed Log, Model SRD-301. It uses a pulse system at a frequency of 2 Megahertz and a single, extremely small, transducer. Because of its small size, the transducer is mounted flush with the bottom of the hull. This precludes fouling or damage by seaweed or other objects, and makes it unnecessary to install pneumatic or hydraulic retracting mechanisms. Digital data outputs provide data to radar and other navigation and collision avoidance systems. It has a speed range of 0 to 35 knots. See figure 3-5.

In addition to the use of logs we may compute the approximate speed knowing engine or shaft revolutions per minute (RPM). Within the engine room, a counter records either engine turns, shaft turns, or both. The ratio of engine turns to shaft turns is the reduction gear ratio and both are directly related to speed since speed is dependent upon the turning of the propellers and the pitch of the propeller blades (constant on most vessels). A ship may run a measured mile (a course of definite length established by ranges on shore) at various engine or shaft RPM settings and prepare a graph showing speed vs RPM, with RPM along the ordinate and speed in knots along the abscissa. From this graph a table may be prepared to provide a useful reference for both the officer of the deck and the navigator.

304. AUTOMATIC DEAD RECKONING
EQUIPMENT

This equipment consists of a DEAD RECKONING ANALYZER-INDICATOR (DRAI), (fig. 3-6) and a DEAD RECKONING TRACER (DRT) (fig. 3-7). Since dead reckoning requires the knowledge of the direction and the speed of the ship's progress, electrical inputs from the gyro and log are required to supply the DRAI with direction and speed respectively. The DRAI resolves

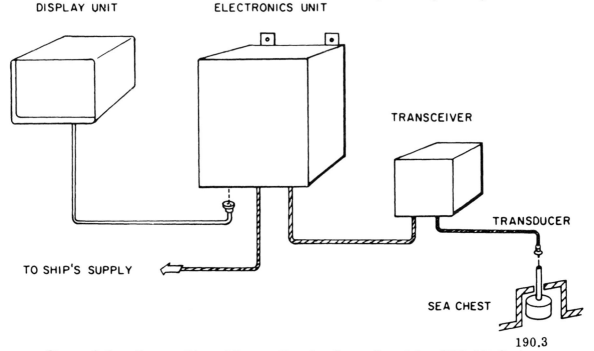

DISPLAY UNIT   ELECTRONICS UNIT

TRANSCEIVER

TRANSDUCER

TO SHIP'S SUPPLY

SEA CHEST

190.3

Figure 3-5.—Composition of Sperry Doppler Sonar Speed Log SRD-301 System.

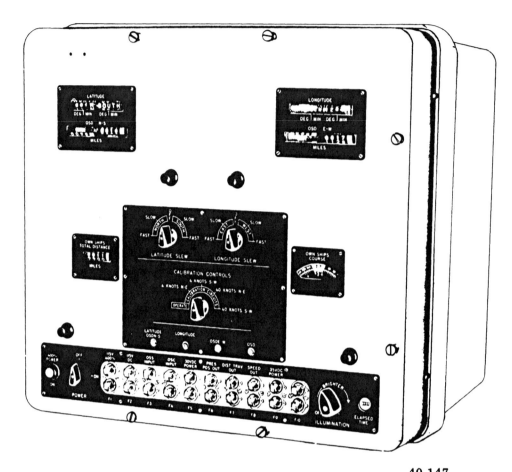

40.147

Figure 3-6.—Dead Reckoning Analyzer-Indicator Mark 9 Mod 0.

direction and speed into east-west and north-south components and sends these components as inputs to the DRT. On direct reading dials, the dead reckoned coordinates in latitude and longitude are generally given. These dials should be set to conform to the ship's position upon starting the dead reckoning equipment and reset upon fixing the ship's position. While the dials are convenient, the DRAI unfortunately cannot account for current effect. A scale setting for the DRT is selected and made, and this setting together with heading and speed inputs from the gyro and log respectively, after resolution by the DRAI into N-S and E-W components, enable the DRT to trace the ship's track. (See figure 3-8.)

The DRT may be used to produce either a geographical or a relative plot. For a geographical representation, a Mercator or a polar coordinate chart is used, with chart scale fully considered. The ship's progress is traced with

pencil as its position image moves across the chart. For a relative plot, used primarily in tactical situations on the high seas, blank plotting paper is used. Contacts or targets are plotted with respect to the ship, in addition to a trace of the ship's path. A type of DRT used largely in antisubmarine warfare ships is the NC-2 Mod 2 Plotting Table which conveniently projects by spots of light not only the ship's position but that of certain selected targets.

305. SHORT RANGE MEASURING INSTRUMENTS

For ranges of 200 to 10,000 yards the STADIMETER is utilized. The trigonometric principle employed is that in a right triangle, if one knows the length of one leg and the value of the opposite angle, the length of the other leg may be computed. On an index arm of a stadimeter the height of an object in feet is set;

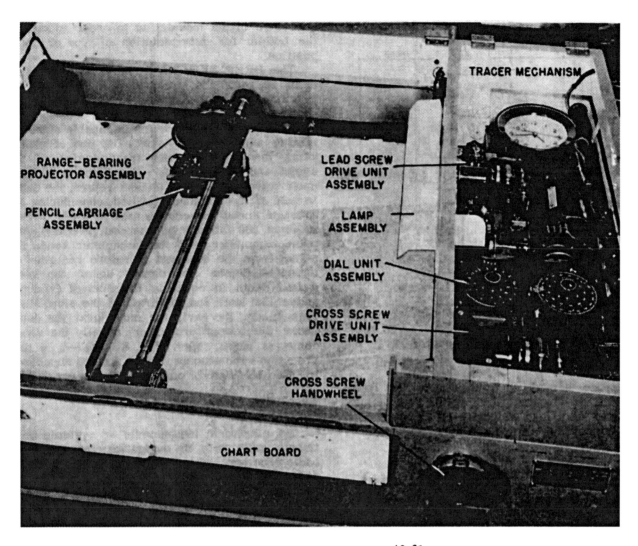

40.61
Figure 3-7.—DRT plotting table.

this moves an index mirror through a small arc and thus introduces one given value. Through a sighting telescope, two images of the object of known height may be viewed. A direct image appears on the left and a reflected image appears on the right (the reflected image is produced by the index mirror). By moving a micrometer drum, the top of the reflected image may be brought into coincidence with the bottom of the direct image. This movement of the micrometer drum measures the subtended arc (the second given value) and automatically solves the triangle for the length of the adjacent leg; from the drum, the range in yards (length of adjacent leg) may be read directly. Two types

of stadimeter, alike in principle of operation but differing in construction, are the Brandon sextant type (fig. 3-9) and the Fisk type (fig. 3-10).

306. DEPTH MEASURING DEVICES

Depth measuring devices may be classified as mechanical and electronic. The mechanical type is represented by the hand lead; the most common example of an electronic type is the fathometer.

The oldest and most reliable depth finding device for shallow depths is the HAND LEAD.

21

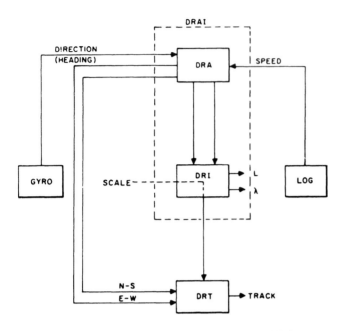

190.4
Figure 3-8.—Schematic of DRAI/DRT.

Reference is made to its use in the <u>New Testament</u> (27th Chapter, Acts of the Apostles). It consists of a lead weight (7-14 lb) attached to a 25 fathom line marked as follows:

2 fm	2 strips of leather
3 fm	3 strips of leather
5 fm	white rag
7 fm	red rag
10 fm	leather with hole
13 fm	same as 3 fm
15 fm	same as 5 fm
17 fm	same as 7 fm
20 fm	line with two knots
25 fm	line with one knot

The hand lead is heaved by using a pendulum motion to produce momentum for two complete turns, then let go at such time as to allow the lead to sink ahead of the chains (station on ship from which soundings are taken). The leadsmen call out depths referring to definite markings as "By the mark...." and other depth values as "By the deep....". Phraseology for fractions are "And a half," "And a quarter," or "A quarter less" as appropriate; for example, "And a half five" (5 1/2 fm) or "A quarter less four" (3 3/4 fm). The lead line should be measured and marked when wet. In the end of the lead a hollow indentation permits "arming," which is the application of tallow or other suitable substance to the indentation in order to sample the bottom for determination of type or composition.

The DEEP SEA LEAD is a lead weighing from 30 to 50 lbs. attached to about 100 fm of line for deep water sounding.

The FATHOMETER (fig. 3-11) or echo sounder is an electronic device which is capable of transmitting a sound signal vertically and of measuring the time between transmission of the signal and return of the echo. Since the signal must travel to the bottom and return, the depth is half of the distance traveled, considering the average speed of sound waves in water, which is about 800 fathoms per second. The navigator must remember that the fathometer sends the signal from the keel and therefore recorded or indicated depths are depths under the keel. Actual depth is equal to the sum of (1) depth under the keel and (2) draft of the ship. More importantly, the navigator must know the depth under the lowest projection, usually the sonar dome in naval ships. The AN/UQN-4, a new precision echo sounder, is the planned successor to the AN/UQN-1 currently in general use.

307. ELECTRONIC INSTRUMENTS

Six electronic instruments or systems contribute materially to navigation; these are the radio receiver, the radio direction finder, radar, sonar, loran, and Decca.

The RADIO RECEIVER provides a method of receiving time signals, weather, and hydrographic messages which advise the navigator of changes in navigational aids.

A RADIO DIRECTION FINDER (RDF) consists of a receiver and a loop antenna which is direction sensitive. The bearing of any station which transmits may be ascertained, and if it can be identified, a locus of position obtained. Also certain RDF stations, will upon request, receive a transmission and report the bearing.

RADAR (an abbreviation of the term "radio detecting and ranging") equipment sends out radio waves in a desired direction and measures the time delay between transmission of a signal and the receipt of its echo. Using the time delay and the speed of travel of radio waves in air, the equipment is capable of indicating range (distance).

SONAR (sonic ranging) equipment, although developed primarily for underwater detection, fulfills a navigational purpose by furnishing

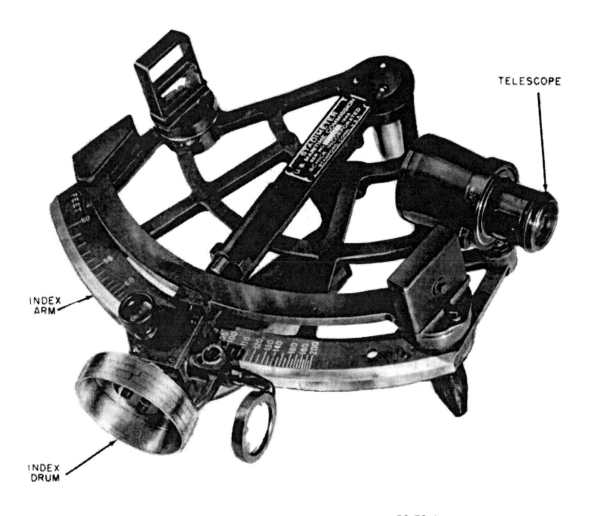

58.78.1
Figure 3-9. — Brandon sextant type stadimeter.

distances and bearings of underwater objects. Sonar transmits a sound wave in water in any desired direction; if an echo is received, it measures the time delay, takes into account the underwater speed of sound, and then indicates both the distance and the bearing of the reflecting object.

LORAN (an abbreviation of the term "long range navigation") equipment consists of a radio receiver on board ship and pairs of transmitting stations on shore. The radio receiver measures the time delay between receipt of signals from individual stations within each station pair; each time delay produces a hyperbolic locus of position.

DECCA is a British electronic navigation system in which the distances from transmitters are determined by phase comparison. Each master station is associated with three secondary stations; all transmit a continuous wave at a different frequency, making it possible for hyperbolic lines or loci of position to be determined.

Except for radio receivers, the above electronic instruments or sets are described in greater detail in Chapter 8. Newer electronic navigation systems now coming into use are described in Chapter 9.

308. CELESTIAL NAVIGATION
INSTRUMENTS

The primary celestial navigation instrument is the SEXTANT, so named because as originated it contained a metal frame which represented one sixth of a circle. Like the stadimeter (especially the Brandon sextant type), the field of

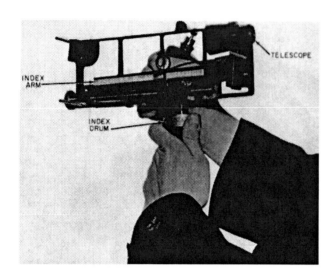

58.78.2
Figure 3-10. — Fisk-type stadimeter.

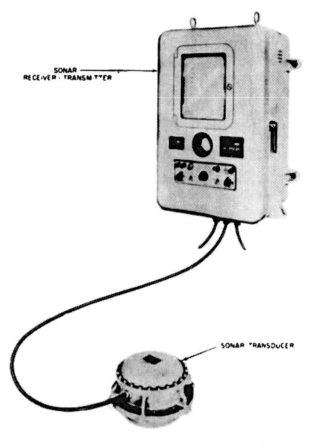

62.9
Figure 3-11. — AN/UQN-1 fathometer.

vision offered by the sextant provides a direct image on the left and a reflected image on the right. By moving the index arm along the limb of the instrument, an index mirror is rotated through a small angle, a celestial body is brought into coincidence with the horizon, and a vertical angle is measured. The value of this angle may be directly read from the limb and vernier. The instrument may also be held 90 degrees to normal and used to measure horizontal angles by bringing two objects into coincidence. The sextant is described in greater detail in Chapter 12.

309. TIMEPIECES

The knowledge of precise time is essential to the computation of longitude. Therefore, since a modern navigator must compute longitude as well as latitude to completely fix his position, he provides himself with accurate time through the use of chronometers. Ship's clocks, comparing watches, and stop watches, are also essential timepieces.

The CHRONOMETER is a high grade clock mounted in a nonmagnetic case supported by gimbals and resting in a padded wooden case. The chronometer is wound daily and frequently checked by radio time signal; it is initially set to keep the time of Greenwich, England (Greenwich mean time). Subsequent error is recorded as checked, without resetting of the chronometer.

SHIP'S CLOCKS are ordinary spring-powered clocks set to keep standard or zone time and located within a ship wherever essential. These clocks must be wound, checked, and reset (if necessary) every 6 days.

The COMPARING WATCH is a high grade pocket watch which the navigator uses for checking the exact time of observation of celestial bodies. Upon the navigator's "Mark," when observing a celestial body, the quartermaster records the time as read from the comparing watch. Later the quartermaster compares the watch with the chronometer and after applying any watch or chronometer error, provides the navigator with either the local zone time or the Greenwich mean time of the observation.

The STOP WATCH is useful in celestial navigation, and in piloting for the identification of lights. When observing celestial bodies, the watch is started on the first "Mark." On succeeding "Marks" the time in seconds is recorded.

4.16
Figure 3-12. — Parallel ruler.

After observation, the stop watch is compared (at a given instant) with the chronometer and the chronometer time of the first sight or observation is computed. Any chronometer error present is applied, providing the Greenwich mean time of the first observation. For the Greenwich time of subsequent observations, the recorded times in seconds are added to the Greenwich mean time of the first sight. Timepieces including newer quartz crystal oscillator clocks, are described in greater detail in chapter 11.

310. PLOTTING INSTRUMENTS

The most basic of plotting instruments is the PENCIL; navigators use No. 2 or No. 3 pencils, and keeping all lines short, write labels legibly, and lightly to facilitate easy erasure. Art gum erasers are normally used for erasure since in comparison with India red rubber erasers, art gum is less destructive to chart surfaces.

The NAVIGATOR'S CASE which contains drawing compass, dividers, and screw driver (for adjusting points) is an essential navigation instrument. Dividers are used to measure distance; the drawing compass is useful for constructing circles and arcs such as circular lines of position and arcs of visibility.

PARALLEL RULERS (fig. 3-12) are simple devices for plotting direction. The rulers consist of two parallel bars with cross braces of equal length which are so attached as to form equal opposite angles, thus keeping the bars parallel. The rulers are laid on the compass rose (direction reference of a chart) with the leading edge aligning the center of the rose and the desired direction on the periphery of the rose. Holding first one bar and moving the second, then holding the second and moving the first, parallel motion is insured. Lines representing direction may be plotted as desired upon the chart.

The ROLLER RULER consists of a rectangular frame with pivot points at two inside extremes holding a hexagonal roller. From any desired position this ruler may be rolled, thus transferring parallel lines of direction.

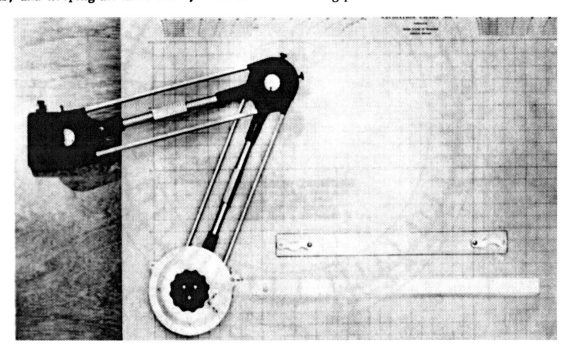

59.57(190)
Figure 3-13. — Universal drafting machine.

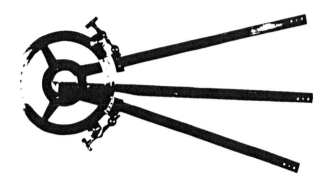

29.269(190)X

Figure 3-14.— Three-arm protractor.

The HOEY POSITION PLOTTER is a celluloid protractor with an attached drafting arm. The protractor has imprinted horizontal and vertical lines permitting alignment with parallels or meridians. After alignment, using the protractor

and drafting arm, desired angles which represent direction, may be drawn.

The UNIVERSAL DRAFTING MACHINE or PARALLEL MOTION PROTRACTOR (fig. 3-13) is a plotting device which is anchored to the chart table and consists of two links and a drafting arm. Between the two links an elbow permits unrestricted movement. Between the outboard link and the drafting arm a metal disc is graduated as a protractor. It permits orientation of the protractor with the chart. A set screw, usually on the inner edge, is loosened when in use, in order to set the drafting arm on any given direction, it is tightened before plotting. The advantage of the Universal drafting machine over other plotting instruments is speed.

A THREE-ARM PROTRACTOR (fig. 3-14) consists of a circular metal or celluloid disc graduated in degrees with a fixed arm at 000 and two movable arms, attached to the center. After a sextant observation of two horizontal angles defined by three objects with the observer at

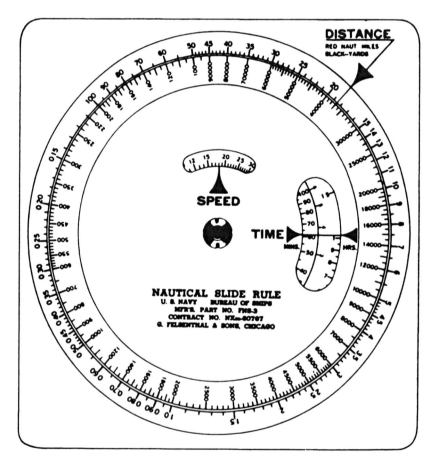

45.52(74)

Figure 3-15.— Nautical slide rule.

the vertex, the three-arm protractor may be set up to represent the two angles and the position of the observer. When the three-arm protractor has been thus set and oriented to the objects used for measurement, on the chart, the center of the protractor is the position of the observer.

Two right triangles may be used in conjunction with a compass rose as a means for plotting direction.

Although not a plotting instrument in a true sense, a useful plotting accessory is the nautical slide rule (fig. 3-15). Composed of plastic, and circular in shape, the nautical slide rule provides a quick solution for problems involving time, speed and distance. It solves the formula D = S x T in which D is distance in miles, S is speed in knots, and T is time in hours. Additionally, it provides distance in both miles and yards, and time both in hours and minutes.

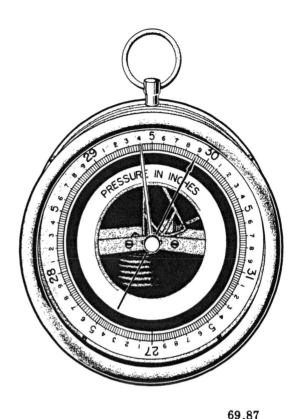

69.87
Figure 3-17.—Aneroid barometer.

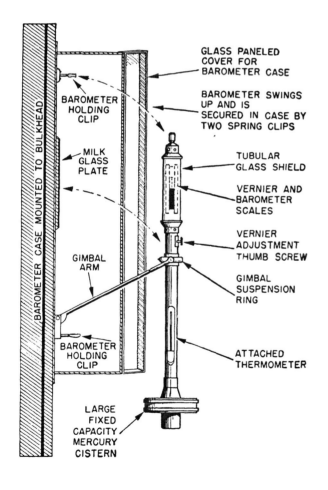

GLASS PANELED COVER FOR BAROMETER CASE

BAROMETER SWINGS UP AND IS SECURED IN CASE BY TWO SPRING CLIPS

TUBULAR GLASS SHIELD

VERNIER AND BAROMETER SCALES

VERNIER ADJUSTMENT THUMB SCREW

GIMBAL SUSPENSION RING

ATTACHED THERMOMETER

BAROMETER HOLDING CLIP

MILK GLASS PLATE

GIMBAL ARM

BAROMETER HOLDING CLIP

LARGE FIXED CAPACITY MERCURY CISTERN

BAROMETER CASE MOUNTED TO BULKHEAD

69.86
Figure 3-16.—Mercurial barometer.

311. WEATHER INSTRUMENTS

The basic weather instrument is the BAROMETER which measures atmospheric pressure in terms of inches of mercury. Two types, the mercurial (fig. 3-16) and the aneroid (fig. 3-17), are in use. The mercurial consists of a column of mercury acted upon at the lower surface by the atmospheric pressure which drives the mercury up into a vacuum tube calibrated for reading in inches. The aneroid barometer is more complicated mechanically and consists of a metal cylinder which contracts and expands with changes in atmospheric pressure. This change passes over a linkage to an indicator where the pressure, in inches of mercury, may be read. Standard atmospheric pressure is 29.92 inches. Fluctuations in pressure are indications of weather changes.

A THERMOMETER is a well known instrument for determining temperature (also useful in weather prediction), scarcely necessary to be described. Most Navy thermometers are calibrated in accordance with the Fahrenheit scale (freezing of water 32 degrees, boiling point 212). The Centigrade thermometer is generally used in experimental work (freezing point of water 0 degrees, boiling point 100).

The PSYCHROMETER consists of two thermometers mounted side by side in a wooden case. One conventional type thermometer is called the "dry bulb." The other, called the "wet bulb," has a small container of water connected to the outside surface of the bulb by a wick. The evaporation of water around the wet bulb lowers the temperature, bringing about a lower reading. By comparing the two thermometer readings and consulting a table contained in The American Practical Navigator (Bowditch), the relative humidity, which is useful in weather predicting, may be computed.

The ANEMOMETER measures wind velocity. It consists of a metal cross, having a small sphere at each extremity, which rotates in the horizontal plane as a result of wind force. It is mounted in an exposed location on the mast or yardarm and is equipped with an electrically operated indicating device which is calibrated in knots. When underway, the wind speed measured is that of the apparent wind, which is the resultant force of the following components: (1) the true wind and (2) ship's course and speed. Knowing the resultant and the second component,

the first component (true wind speed) may be computed.

312. MISCELLANEOUS INSTRUMENTS

Binoculars and flashlights serve useful purposes in the navigation department. Binoculars, because of their magnification, which ranges from about 7-power for handheld binoculars to 20-power for a larger ship mounted type, provide a means of early sighting and identification of navigational aids. The glass lenses used in binoculars are normally treated for reduction of glare, and additional filters are often available. Binoculars are delicate instruments and must be handled carefully and cleaned frequently. They should never be dropped nor subjected to sharp knocks. For cleaning, only lens paper should be used, otherwise the polished surface will be damaged and their usefulness as an optical aid will accordingly be reduced.

The FLASHLIGHT is useful during morning and evening twilight observations to provide light for reading the comparing or stop watch as well as the limb and vernier of the sextant. A red plastic disc should be inserted in the illuminant end to insure a red light in order not to disturb the navigator's night vision or unnecessarily illuminate the ship when steaming under wartime darken-ship conditions.

CHAPTER 4

CHARTS AND PUBLICATIONS

401. INTRODUCTION

Charts and publications constitute a source of information which the navigator constantly uses. A chart or a map is a representation of an area of the earth's surface. For example, the early charts devised and used by the natives of the South Sea islands were merely diagrammatic, being constructed of palm leaves and sea shells. The sea shells represented islands and the palm fronds represented currents and the angles of intersection of ocean swells. The Pacific natives still use their knowledge of these angles of intersection as a basis for a unique system of navigation which they successfully practice.

There is a difference between charts and maps. Maps, for the most part, show land areas, their political subdivision, and topography. A chart serves a navigation purpose; nautical charts show water or coastal areas and give a great deal of hydrographic information which is useful to the navigator. An air navigation chart may, like a map, portray mostly land, but it will provide the air navigator with elevations and locations of navigational aids. Usage is the basis for chart and map classification.

A chart projection is a method of representing a 3-dimensional object on a 2-dimensional surface. Cartographers (chart or map makers) employ various chart projection techniques to construct desired charts. However, it is impossible to project a 3-dimensional object upon a 2-dimensional surface without some distortion. The best type of chart projection depends upon the area to be represented and how the chart is to be used.

Publications are separately addressed in art. 412.

402. EARLY CHARTS

Ptolemy, the Alexandrian astronomer, mathematician and geographer, who lived in the second century A.D., made many charts and maps, some of which were used until the time of Columbus. Ptolemy, who was unequalled in astronomy until Copernicus in the sixteenth century, had based his charts on the theory that the world was round, with a circumference of 18,000 miles as computed by the Greek philosopher Posidonius, circa 130 to 51 B.C. It was unfortunate that Ptolemy based his cartography on the calculations of Posidonius, inasmuch as a more accurate circumference of 24,000 statute miles had been calculated in the third century B.C. by another Alexandrian, Eratosthenes. In fact, the computation of Eratosthenes was to remain as the most accurate until 1669. Important contributions of Ptolemy included the convention of making the top of a chart or map to be north in direction, and the listing of important places by latitude and longitude.

In the Middle Ages, using the knowledge acquired by seamen principally in the Mediterranean Sea, charts were constructed in Catalonia, known as Portolan charts. A distinguishing feature of these charts was the depiction of direction by thirty-two lines emanating from a point. These lines represented the thirty-two points of a compass, as was then in general usage, a point being the equivalent of 11 1/4 degrees (360/32). This depiction of direction was an antecedent of the modern compass rose.

403. MERCATOR PROJECTION

Modern cartography is indebted to the Flemish astronomer, geographer, and theologian, Gerardus Mercator, who in the sixteenth century made a world chart, based upon a cylindrical projection. Essentially, the chart, which has ever since borne his name, is projected by first placing a cylinder around the earth, tangent at the equator. (See fig. 4-1.) Planes are passed through the meridians and projected to the cylinder upon which they appear as parallel lines. Lines are drawn from the center of the

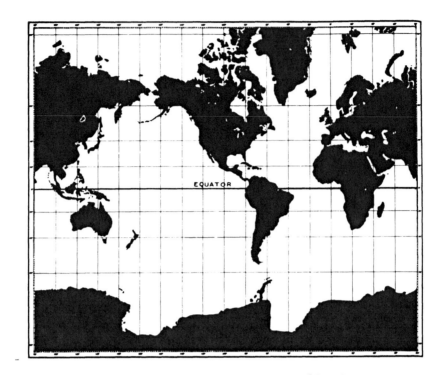

65.117
Figure 4-1.—Mercator chart of the world.

earth to the cylinder passing through the parallels; this locates the parallels on the cylinder. Next the cylinder is cut lengthwise and flattened out. The resulting graticule (horizontal and vertical lines of a chart) is representative of a Mercator projection, the important difference being that in the latter, parallels are spaced by mathematical formulae. In fact, both meridians and parallels are expanded with increased latitude, the expansion being equal to the secant of the latitude. Inasmuch as the secant of 90° is infinity, a Mercator projection based upon tangency with the equator, cannot include the poles.

To envision the linear relationship between parallels of latitude and meridians on a Mercator projection, it is helpful to remember that meridians are separated in distance in accordance with the cosine of the latitude. At the equator, or latitude 0°, the cosine of the latitude is 1 and one degree of longitude is equal in distance to one degree of latitude; at the equator, and only at the equator, the longitude scale can serve as a true distance scale. At latitude 60°, where the cosine is 0.5, one degree of longitude is equal in distance to one half of one degree of latitude, or 30 nautical miles. At the poles, or latitude 90°, the cosine is 0, and the meridians merge. Thus,

at any latitude, 1° of longitude is equal to 60 miles multiplied by the cosine of that latitude, and the relationship between latitude and longitude is found by the solution of the trigonometric equation $d^L o = d^L / \cos^L$ in which $d^L o$ is the difference in longitude and d^L is the difference in latitude, both in arc. Also, $p = d^L o \times \cos^L$ in which p is the length of an arc of a parallel; $d^L o = p \times \sec^L$. Thus, considering the trigonometric relationship of secants and cosines, it can be proved that inasmuch as the expansion of meridians is dependent upon the secant of the latitude, the separation of meridians is dependent upon the cosine of the latitude.

The advantage of a Mercator projection, also called an orthographic cylindrical projection, is that it is a conformal chart, showing true angles and true distance. A rhumb line plots as a straight line on a Mercator chart. By definition, a rhumb line is a line which makes the same oblique angle with all intersected meridians. On a Mercator chart meridians are parallel; therefore, any transversal fulfills the requirements of a rhumb line. A disadvantage of a Mercator chart is the distortion at high latitudes. On the earth the meridians actually converge at the poles while on the chart they are parallel; a conformal chart under these conditions can be had by expansion of the meridians. On a Mercator chart, because of the higher latitude, Greenland appears larger than the United States, although it is actually much smaller. Despite this distortion in high latitudes, the determining of true distance is not prevented. The expansion of the meridians, which is related trigonometrically to the latitude, makes areas appear larger, and changes at the same time the latitude (distance measuring) scale, thus permitting the navigator to measure true distance. Since the distortion varies with the latitude, whenever measuring distance on a Mercator chart of a large area, the navigator sets his dividers to the scale of the mid-latitude of the area in which he is making a measurement. See figure 4-2.

404. PLOTTING SHEETS

A plotting sheet is an incomplete chart with latitude and longitude lines, and generally a compass rose. It contains no information on land, water depth or navigational aids. Being less expensive than charts to produce, such sheets are used primarily for economy in plotting celestial fixes.

A small area plotting sheet (fig. 4-3) makes use of the fact that on a Mercator projection of a small area, the difference in spacing between successive parallels of latitude is nearly negligible. It thus approximates a Mercator projection by using equal spacing between the parallels represented. The relationship between latitude and longitude is found by solution of the trigonometric formula—Dlo equals p secL—where Dlo is the difference in longitude in arc, and p equals the linear distance between two meridians measured along an arc of a parallel. Given either the latitude scale or the longitude scale the other may be computed graphically as follows:

(a) Longitude scale specified. Any uniformly ruled paper may be used. Place the paper with

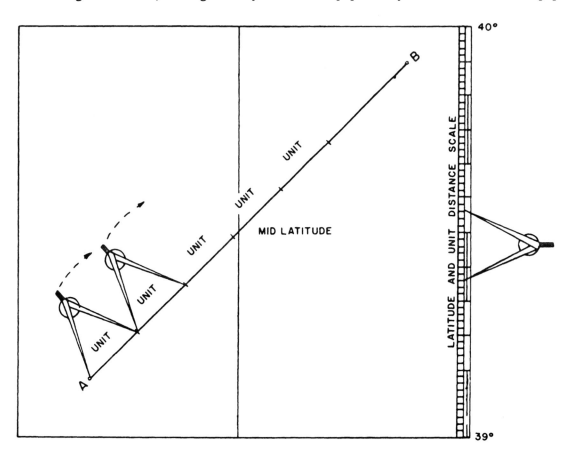

190.5

Figure 4-2.—Distance measured at mid-latitude of route on a mercator chart.

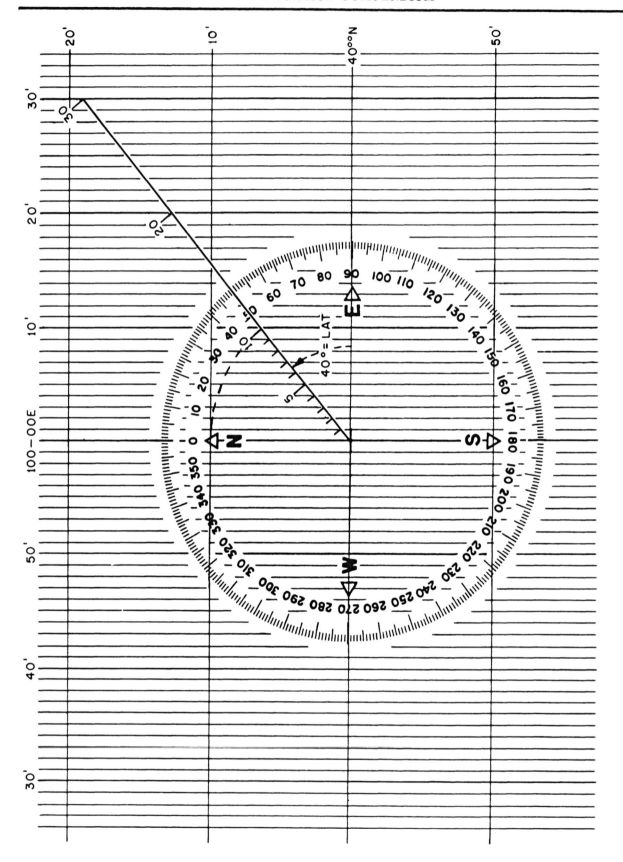

65.130(190)

Figure 4-3. — Small area plotting sheet, longitude scale specified.

the lines vertical; label meridians as desired. Construct a perpendicular to the meridians midway between the top and bottom of the plotting sheet. Label this perpendicular as a latitide line making it any desired mid-latitude. At the point of intersection of the mid-latitude line and the central meridian, construct an angle with the horzontal equal to the mid-latitude. The length of this transverse line between two meridians which are 1 degree apart in longitude, is 60 miles or 1 degree of latitude. The length of this transverse line between two meridians which are 10' apart in longitude is 10 nautical miles or 10' of latitude. Using these measurements, the remaining latitude lines may be plotted.

(b) Latitude scale specified. Any uniformly ruled paper may be used. Place the paper with the lines horizontal and label parallels as desired. Construct a perpendicular to the parallels, midway between the right and left edges of the sheet. Label this meridian as the central meridian. Using as a radius, the distance between the mid-latitude line and an adjacent latitude line, measured along the central meridian, draw a circle with the center at the point of intersection of the mid-latitude line and the central meridian. From the center of this circle construct a line which makes an angle with the horizontal equal to the mid-latitude. At the point of intersection of this line and the circle, drop a perpendicular to the mid-latitude line. The distance between this perpendicular and the central meridian, measured along the mid-latitude line, represents 1 degree of longitude if the latitude lines are 1 degree apart, and 10' of longitude if the latitude spacing is 10'.

A plotting sheet may also be constructed using "meridional parts" as given for each degree and minute of latitude in Table 5 of American Practical Navigator (Bowditch). Meridional parts, expressed in minutes of equatorial arc, provide a computed expansion of the meridian, based upon the secant of the latitude. Plotting sheets for large areas should be constructed using meridional parts.

Additionally, and more in use, are position plotting sheets printed by the Naval Oceanographic Office for various latitudes. These ready-made plotting sheets have numbered parallels, and unnumbered meridians which are spaced as appropriate for the latitude and thus may be numbered as convenient for the navigator.

405. GNOMONIC PROJECTION

The gnomonic projection actually predates Portolan and Mercator charts. It is credited to Thales of Miletus, Chief of the Seven Wise Men of ancient Greece, who founded Greek geometry, astronomy and philosophy, in addition to being a navigator and cartographer, circa the sixth century B.C. The value of this projection was little realized until the earth's circumference had been more accurately computed, if even then, and its usage appears to have been secondary to the later Portolan and Mercator charts.

The gnomonic or great circle projection is made by projecting the earth's features from its center to a plane tangent to its surface; the center of the plane (point of tangency) marks the center of the projected area. The gnomonic projection is advantageous in that great circles (the arcs of which represent the shortest distance between two points on a spherical surface) plot as straight lines. Known also as an azimuthal projection, all directions or azimuths from its center are true. The chief limitation, nevertheless, is that difficulty is encountered in finding both direction and distance. Also, there is some distortion which increases with distance from the point of tangency.

The gnomonic (great circle) chart (fig. 4-4) is normally used for planning long voyages since great circle courses are generally shorter than rhumb line courses. On a gnomonic chart, the navigator plots the departure point and the point of destination. These points are then connected with a straight line. Route points are marked each 5 degrees of longitude apart. The coordinates of these points are noted, transferred to a Mercator chart, and connected by straight lines. These lines in effect, are chords of the great circle course. The ship, in making the voyage, changes to a new course upon reaching each route point. This is more practical than changing course continuously, which would be required if an exact great circle were to be followed.

406. POLAR CHART PROJECTIONS

Obviously, because of extreme distortion in high latitudes, the ordinary and popular Mercator projection is unsatisfactory for polar navigation. There are five general types of projections which may be used. Two of these types are special forms of the Mercator and Gnomonic.

The polar gnomonic is a special gnomonic chart projected by placing the plane tangent to the surface of the earth at the pole. Meridians are shown as straight lines radiating from the poles. An interesting concept is that at the north pole all directions are south and at the south

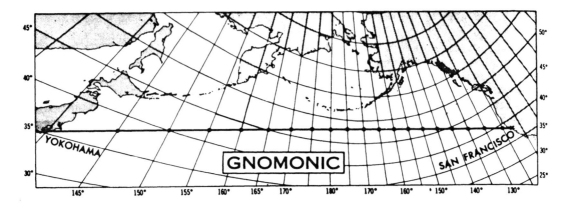

65.118(69)B
Figure 4-4.—Gnomonic chart.

pole all directions are north. Parallels are shown as concentric circles around the pole, spacing increasing with the distance from the pole.

The azimuthal equidistant projection is similar to the polar gnomonic except that parallels are uniformly spaced. The maneuvering board, although used primarily in solving problems in relative motion, is an example of an azimuthal equidistant projection.

The polar stereographic (azimuthal orthomorphic) projection is made by placing a plane tangent to the earth at the pole, and perpendicular to the earth's axis. The earth's features are projected from the opposite pole rather than from the center of the earth as in the case of the polar gnomonic projection.

The inverse Mercator is useful and preferred by many navigators because it is similar to the ordinary Mercator with which they are already familiar. The inverse and the oblique Mercator are types of transverse Mercator projections which are projected by placing the cylinder tangent to a great circle on the earth's surface other than the equator. When the great circle making the point of tangency is a meridian, the result is an inverse Mercator. If the point of tangency is not a meridian, then an oblique Mercator will be the result.

A recent innovation of use particularly to air navigation in the arctic regions is known as the polar grid system. It does not allow the conventional use of the geographical pole to become an encumbrance. The grid system for the north polar region, for example, consists of an overprinted chart depicting a grid of parallel lines in lieu of meridians. The center line corresponds to the meridian of Greenwich, and thus passes through the north pole and southward into the Pacific. The direction of this line is "grid north" and remains as such when technically, the aircraft is traveling southward from the pole. Inasmuch as direction never changes, polar navigation is greatly simplified. With this grid system, as shown in figure 4-5, a "Polar Path Gyro" is used. Built by Bendix Aviation Corporation, and housed in a sphere the size of an orange, this gyro when set in a given direction will continue to point in that direction. Additionally, the gyro may be used to steer an aircraft's automatic pilot. As a check upon position for additional navigational safety, celestial navigation procedures may be used.

407. CONIC PROJECTIONS

Ptolemy charted the Mediterranean using the first known conic projection. Conic type projections in use today are the Lambert Conformal, other conic, and polyconic projections. In all cases, one or more cones are placed on the earth's surface with the axis of the cone(s) coinciding or in alignment with the axis of the earth. The area of least distortion is near the apex of the cone.

The Lambert Conformal may be projected by making the cone not tangent to the earth but intersecting the earth through two parallels. Like the Mercator, however, it spaces parallels by computation, relating the separation of parallels to that of meridians, and thus providing a conformal chart. It was designed in the Eighteenth century by an Alsatian, Johann Lambert. It is used primarily in aeronautical charts.

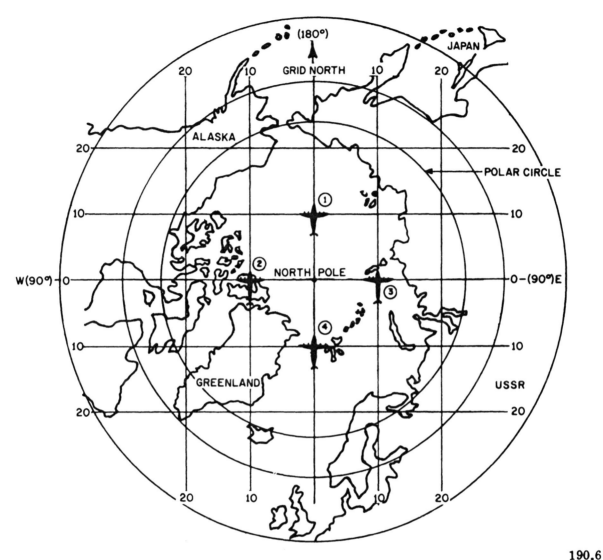

190.6

Figure 4-5.— Polar grid chart. Although all four planes are flying "grid north," the first plane is heading south, the second west, the third east, and the fourth north.

Although conic charts resemble Mercators, direction is less accurate. To obtain best results in measuring direction, the nearest compass rose, or the nearest meridian, should be used. The navigator cannot indiscriminately choose any compass rose, parallel, or meridian as a direction reference. A rhumb line on a Lambert Conformal chart is a curved line. A great circle on a Lambert Conformal chart approximates a straight line. For a long voyage, a straight line should be drawn on a Lambert Conformal chart, and the course noted at the intersection of each meridian. For distance, the nearest latitude scale should be utilized.

408. CHART SOURCES, IDENTIFICATION AND SCALE

There are two major chart issuing activities for U.S. vessels, the Naval Oceanographic Office, and the National Ocean Survey; both are situated in Washington, D.C., and conveniently have numerous branch offices. The Naval Oceanographic Office, by its own surveys and through liaison with foreign oceanographic agencies, prepares and publishes both nautical and aeronautical charts of the high seas and foreign waters. The National Ocean Survey within the

Department of Commerce prepares and publishes coastal and harbor charts of the United States and its possessions. Also, aeronautical charts of the United States are published by the National Ocean Survey, which was formerly known as the United States Coast and Geodetic Survey.

Minor sources for charts include:

(a) The U.S. Lake Survey Office, Army Engineer District, Detroit, Michigan, for charts of the Great Lakes (less Georgian Bay and Canadian Harbors), Lake Champlain, and the St. Lawrence River above St. Regis and Cornwall, Canada; and

(b) The Department of the Army, Corps of Engineers, Army Map Service, Washington, D.C., for topographical maps.

A chart is identified by number as well as by source. The numbers are related to geographical location and scale. The relationship to geographical area simplifies filing and retrieving, and permits the orderly arrangement of charts by portfolio. Charts are numbered with one to five digits as follows:

One — Oceanographic symbol sheets and flag charts (nine non-navigational and non-geographic charts).

Two & Three — Charts of the world's deep oceans divided in nine areas coinciding with ocean basins. The first digit indicates area, for example, "1" is a North Atlantic chart. The next one or two digits indicate scale. The scale range of a two digit chart is 1:9,000,000 and smaller; three digits indicate a scale between 1:2,000,000 and 1:9,000,000. See fig. 4-6.

Four — A special series of non-navigational charts, including wall charts, planning charts, magnetic, time zone and star charts. Scale is not involved.

Five — These charts are most used by navigators, and range in scale from 1:2,000,000 to larger. They consist mainly of coastal and harbor charts. Coastal areas are divided into nine regions, with each region having as many as nine sub-regions which are numbered counterclockwise around the continents. See fig. 4-7. All five numbers have a geographic meaning. The first two digits indicate the general geographic location by region and subregion. The final three numbers serve in placing the charts

in geographic sequence. Currently, there are gaps in the numbering sequence in anticipation of the issuance of additional large-scale charts.

This system of chart identification was established by the Naval Oceanographic Office on 1 March 1971, replacing a system which had been in effect for approximately 140 years. To accommodate the change in identification numbers, new editions of previously issued charts bear the new N.O. numbers in bold type and the former H.O. (Hydrographic Office) numbers in smaller and lighter type.

Charts which show features in large size and with great detail are "large-scale" charts. "Small-scale" charts show less detail, but cover a greater area, as they depict more miles per inch. It is important to remember that the larger the scale number, the smaller the scale.

409. CHART PROCUREMENT AND CORRECTION

Two types of chart catalogs provide information for chart ordering, chart coverage, and accounting. Each issuing activity compiles a chart catalog listing chart numbers and titles of charts which they have issued. Thus, the Naval Oceanographic Office publishes N.O. Pub. No. 1-N, in the form of a series of pamphlets. Additionally, that office publishes a "Portfolio Chart List," N.O. Pub. 1-PCL, which lists the charts of major issuing activities and provides instructions for their arrangement by portfolio. N.O. Pub. 1-PCL provides information as well on chart procurement and correction.

Charts may be ordered by Navy ships from Naval Oceanographic Distribution Centers. These are located at Philadelphia, Pa., and Clearfield, Utah, for support of Atlantic and Pacific Fleet ships respectively. DD Form 1149 is used for chart requisitions. Priority for delivery should be specified.

Corrections to charts are promulgated weekly in Notice to Mariners. The quartermaster maintains a 5 x 8 card (NHO5610/2) for each chart carried. This card contains the chart title, chart number, edition number, edition date, and the number of the last Notice to Mariners correction posted prior to receipt. Columns are provided for posting the reference numbers of corrections received in weekly Notice to Mariners. The navigator requires immediate correction of charts which cover areas the ship is expected to visit. Charts of remote areas which are not expected to be used or charts which will not be used until a distant future date

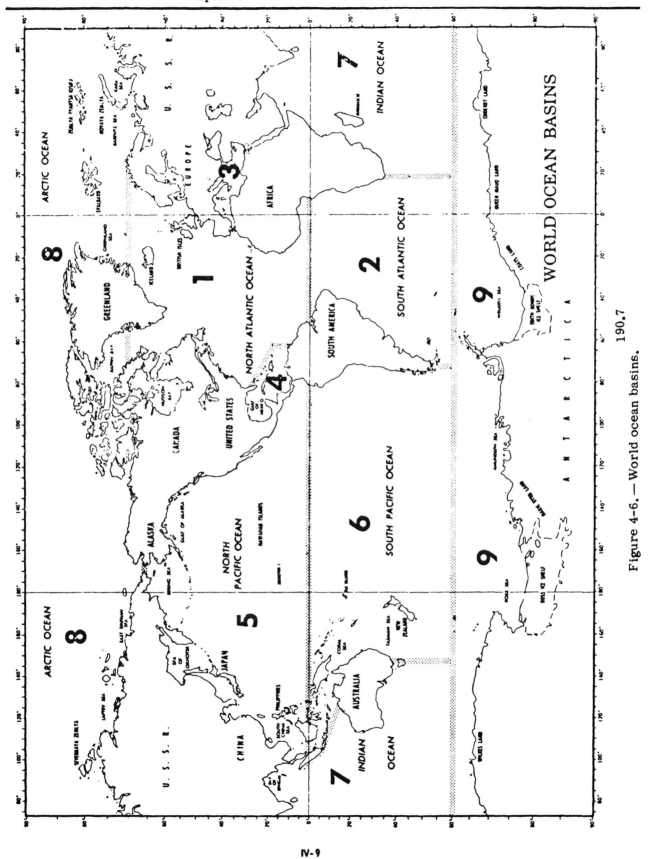

Figure 4-6. — World ocean basins.

190.7

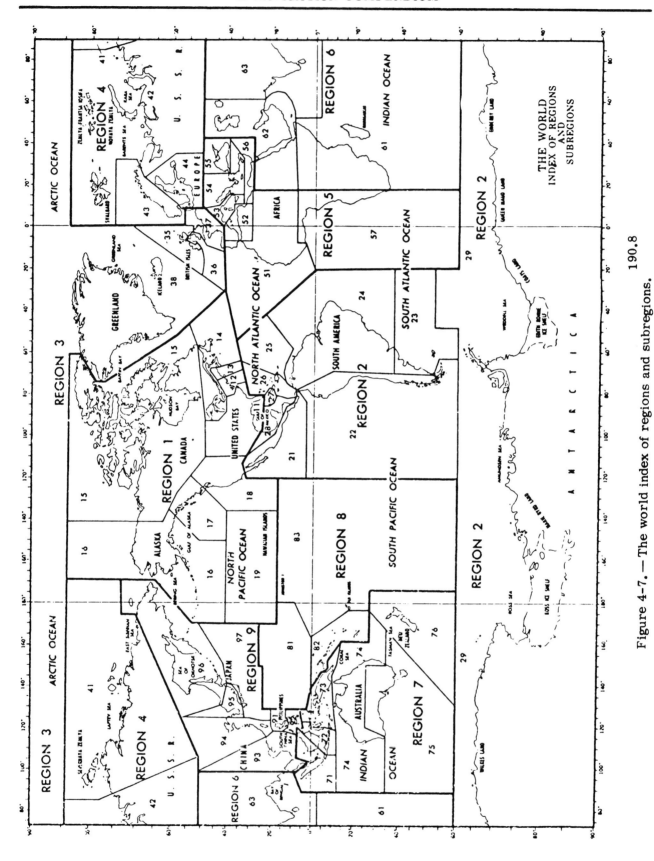

Figure 4-7. — The world index of regions and subregions.

190.8

are not corrected; posting of the correction is sufficient for the interim. Prior to using any chart, all posted corrections must be made, with card NHO5610/2 showing the date corrected and the initials of the corrector. This is an efficient way of making chart corrections, since one correction may cancel out another. Navy Regulations—Art. 0930, requires that every chart used for navigation be corrected before use, through the latest information that can be obtained, which is applicable to it. Corrections, other than temporary, are made with ink; the use of red ink, which is not readable under customary red night lights, should be avoided. Standard chart symbols are used in making corrections.

410. CHART ACCURACY

A chart is no more accurate than the survey upon which it is based. With this in mind the navigator is obligated to evaluate probable accuracy.

Guides to probable accuracy are as follows:

SURVEY.—Note the recency of survey, the number of surveys, and the surveying agency. Recent surveys, because of better instrumentation, are generally superior to those made in the distant past.

COMPLETENESS OF SOUNDINGS.—Blank spaces or sparse soundings may indicate an incomplete survey.

PRINTING.—Plate printed (black and white) charts have a considerable shrinkage error in comparison with lithographic (colored) charts.

SCALE.—Detailed information cannot be included on a small-scale chart of a large area.

411. CHART READING

Through chart reading a navigator translates symbols into a picture. As a qualification for chart reading he must then recognize standard abbreviations and conventions.

The lettering distinguishes topographic and hydrographic features. Vertical lettering is characteristic of land features which are always above water regardless of tide; leaning lettering is characteristic of hydrographic features such as reefs which may be above or below water depending upon the state of the tide.

Soundings may be recorded in either fathoms or feet, but in any case the chart will indicate within the legend the depth unit used and the datum or reference plane. Fathom curves connect points of equal depth, and, regardless of whether soundings are in fathoms or in feet, the curves are based upon soundings in fathoms. These are commonly shown for depths of 1, 2, 3, 6, 10, and multiples of 10 fathoms. Tide tables will refer to the datum plane of the chart. The newer chart editions may show bottom contours in great detail using color. Shoal areas may be emphasized by the use of different colors or shades. The type of lettering used to indicate depth is unimportant; it indicates the activity which reported the depth.

Bottom types are abbreviated using either capital or lower case lettering. A capital letter indicates composition; a lower case letter, color or texture.

Commonly used nautical chart symbols and abbreviations appear in Appendix A.

412. PUBLICATIONS

Publications used by the navigator may be classified as manuals, navigation tables, almanacs, and chart supplementary publications. These publications are usually obtained from the Naval Oceanographic Office, or Naval Oceanographic Distribution Centers, in the same manner as charts, certain manuals and almanacs, excepted. On board ship they are stowed on the navigator's publication shelf (generally located above, and in easy reach of, the navigator's chart desk). Corrections to oceanographic publications are promulgated by the Naval Oceanographic Office weekly; annual supplements are originated by the Naval Oceanographic Office which summarize the weekly corrections.

a. Some useful manuals used in navigation include:

H.O.-9 American Practical Navigator. Nathaniel Bowditch, near the end of the eighteenth century, discovered numerous errors in the principal navigation text then in use, which was titled, Practical Navigator, a British publication written by John Hamilton Moore. Bowditch then published a corrected version with additional information. In 1802 he completely revised his earlier work, included a new method for the determination of longitude, and published in simplified form his new American Practical Navigator. Through updating, it has remained as a most valuable text and reference. The navigational tables which it contains are particularly useful. The copyright was purchased in 1868 by the Hydrographic Office, the forerunner of the Oceanographic Office, which has published subsequent revised editions.

Dutton's Navigation and Piloting. Since 1926, when first prepared as a text for midshipmen at the U.S. Naval Academy by Commander Benjamin Dutton under the title Navigation and Nautical Astronomy, this through revision has remained as the basic navigation textbook for the U.S. Navy. Published by the U.S. Naval Institute, Annapolis, Maryland, it was significantly updated in its twelfth edition (1969).

Primer of Navigation. Written by Colonel George W. Mixter and initially published in 1940, this is an excellent navigation textbook. It is basic and non-technical, and thus useful to the beginner. Nonetheless, it is sufficiently thorough for the practicing navigator. Published by D. Van Nostrand Company, Inc. of Princeton, New Jersey, it has been periodically updated, its most recent revision (fifth edition) being published in 1967.

Air Navigation. (Department of the Air Force, AF Manual 51-40, Volume I). This manual, for use in air navigation, is basic and precise, and provides vital material for both students and air navigators. It is published by the Air Training Command, U.S. Air Force, and is sold by the Superintendent of Documents, U.S. Government Printing Office, Washington, D.C.

Space Navigation Handbook. (Department of the Navy, NavPers 92988). Published by the Chief of Naval Personnel, and based primarily upon the research, teaching, and inventive genius of Captain P. V. H. Weems, USN (Ret.), this text provides in brief form a simplified concept for the more difficult three-dimensional navigation in space, together with supporting background information.

b. Navigation tables which provide azimuths of the sun and other bodies, and solutions of the astronomical triangle for the determination of position without resort to difficult formulae, are as follow:

(1) Azimuth tables —
HO-66 Arctic Azimuth Tables. These tables provide values for azimuth angles of bodies with a declination of 0° to 23°, with declination of the same name as latitude, for latitudes of 70° to 88°. No longer in print.
HO-260 Azimuth Tables. These tables complement HO-66 for latitudes of 0° to 70°, and replace HO-71 which was referred to as the "red azimuth tables" and which is no longer in print.

HO-261 The Azimuths of Celestial Bodies. This volume is similar to HO-260 except that it provides azimuths for bodies with declination of 24° to 70°. It replaced HO-120 which is no longer in print.
(2) Tables for computation of position —
HO-208 Navigation Tables for Mariners and Aviators. (Dreisonstok).
HO-211 Dead Reckoning Altitude and Azimuth Tables. (Ageton)
HO-214 Tables of Computed Altitude and Azimuth. This set, developed by the Hydrographic Office, consists of nine volumes, one for each ten degrees of latitude, and has wide usage, for both the computation of lines of position and azimuth.
HO-218 Astronomical Navigation Tables. Consisting of 14 volumes, one for each five degrees of latitude from 0° to 69°, and with solutions for 22 stars, these tables are similar to HO-214, but are less accurate inasmuch as they are designed primarily for use in air navigation.
HO-229 Sight Reduction Tables for Marine Navigation. Prepared through a cooperative effort internationally between the U.S. Naval Oceanographic Office, the U.S. Naval Observatory, and Her Majesty's Nautical Almanac Office, and consisting of six volumes, one for each 15° of latitude, this set will eventually replace HO-214.
HO-249 Sight Reduction Tables for Air Navigation. Prepared cooperatively as in the case of HO-229 but earlier, through a combined British and American effort, and consisting of three volumes, HO-249 is the air counterpart of HO-229. Volume I provides solutions for selected stars, Volume II provides complete data for latitudes 0° to 39°, and Volume III provides complete data for latitudes 40° to 89°.

c. Almanacs have a relatively short but interesting background. Astronomical observations of the Danish astronomer Tycho Brahe in the late sixteenth century were the basis of Kepler's laws of motion which in turn became the foundation of modern astronomy and celestial navigation. The first almanac for mariners was the British Nautical Almanac which appeared in 1767. America entered the field in 1852 when the U.S. Navy Depot of Charts and Instruments, which preceded the Hydrographic Office, published the American Ephemeris and Nautical Almanac for the year 1855. Since 1858, an American Nautical Almanac has been published annually; it is similar to the American Ephemeris and Nautical Almanac except that it omits the Ephemeris which is of primary interest to astronomers. Thus, the Nautical Almanac is the principal almanac for the use of mariners today, although the Air Almanac, which was of more recent origin and which was prepared largely for use in air navigation, is also in general use. Almanacs should be requested either from the Superintendent, Naval Observatory, Washington, D.C., or in the case of commerical activities from the Superintendent of Documents.

The Nautical Almanac is now prepared jointly by the U.S. Naval Observatory in Washington, D.C. and H.M. Nautical Almanac Office, Royal Greenwich Observatory, to meet the requirements of the U.S. Navy and the British Admiralty. Printed separately and annually in the two countries, this almanac provides all necessary astronomical data for the practice of celestial navigation at sea.

The Air Almanac first appeared as an American publication in 1933. It is issued thrice yearly, each edition being prepared for a four-month period. The U.S. Naval Observatory and H.M. Royal Greenwich Observatory cooperate in its publication. While useful for both marine and air navigation, it is primarily used for the latter.

d. Chart supplementary publications are books used in conjunction with charts and include the following:

Coast Pilots — Edited by the National Ocean Survey, a Coast Pilot provides navigational and general interest information for the coasts of the United States and its possessions.

Sailing Directions — Edited by the Oceanographic Office, Sailing Directions provide navigational and general interest information for definite geographic areas beyond the coasts of the United States and U.S. possessions.

Tide, Tidal Current Tables, and Tidal Current Charts — Prepared by the National Ocean Survey, Tide, Tidal Current Tables and Tidal Current Charts, as discussed in the following chapter, provide predictions of tidal effect.

Light Lists — The Light List provides descriptive information concerning lights of the coasts of the United States and U.S. possessions in five lists which are printed by the U.S. Government Printing Office. The Oceanographic Office prepares for foreign waters a List of Lights in seven volumes.

Notice to Mariners — A weekly pamphlet from the Naval Oceanographic Office. Two copies are mailed to each addressee on the N.O. mailing list unless more are requested. One copy is used for chart correction and permanent file while the second copy is used for correcting Coast-Pilots, Sailing Directions, and Light Lists, being cut up as necessary (corrections may be "pen and ink" or "cut-out").

Daily Memoranda — Single sheets containing hydrographic information promulgated if urgent by radio from the Naval Oceanographic Office and later superseded by Notice to Mariners.

Monthly Information Bulletin. — This monthly bulletin from the Naval Oceanographic Office serves the purpose of updating index catalogs and the Portfolio Chart List,
e. Other:

HO-117 — Radio Navigational Aids, in two volumes, HO-117A and HO-117B by geographic location, contains information such as the time and frequency of hydrographic broadcasts, Naval Observatory radio time signals, distress traffic, radio beacons and direction-finder stations, loran coverage and stations, and radio regulations for territorial waters.

HO-118 — Radio Weather Aids, also in two volumes, HO-118A and HO-118B by geographic location, contains information concerning the making of weather reports, codes, report contents, and frequencies, and informs the navigator of available weather broadcasts.

HO-150 — World Port Index is a useful guide containing detailed information concerning specific ports and provides a cross reference of charts and publications applicable to a given port.

HO-151 — Table of Distances Between Ports — Useful in voyage planning, HO-151 lists distances between ports.

HO-220 — Navigation Dictionary — A useful reference for learning the meaning of various navigation terms and expressions.

HO-226 — Handbook of Magnetic Compass Adjustment and Compensation (Spencer and Kucera). This useful manual was described in art. 211.

HO-2102D — Star Finder and Identifier. This device, which is most useful in celestial navigation, is described in chapter 13.

CHAPTER 5

TIDES AND CURRENTS

501. INTRODUCTION

Johannes Kepler (1571-1630), a German who succeeded, and was familiar with the work of, the Danish Astronomer Brahe, developed three laws of motion which in turn led to the development of the almanac. In turn, Kepler's laws (Appendix B) led to the development of three laws of gravity and motion by the English mathematician and philosopher Sir Isaac Newton (1642-1727). From Kepler's laws and his own, Newton developed his famous universal law of gravitation (Appendix B) which states that "every particle of matter attracts every other particle with a force that varies directly as the product of their masses and inversely as the square of the distance between them."

Thus, gravitation, the force of attraction between bodies in the universe, depends upon the mass of the bodies concerned and their distance of separation. The moon, a satellite of the earth, is near enough and large enough to exert a sizable pull. The sun also exerts a force, which is inferior to that force exerted by the moon, because of the comparative distances. This gravitational force of attraction acts upon every particle within the earth; since different points on the earth are at varying distances from the moon, the force of attraction consists of components of varying values, depending upon distance. The point on the surface of the earth which lies on a line connecting the centers of the earth and the moon is acted upon with great relative force because of the comparatively short distance involved. This brings the water (the earth may be considered as a hard core surrounded by water) toward the moon, making the depth greater. Also the center of the earth is acted upon by a greater force than is a point on the side of the earth opposite the moon. For that reason, the center of the core tends to pull toward the moon making the depth of the water on the opposite side of the earth greater. The

end result is that as the moon transits a meridian, depth increases on both the upper branch and the lower branch of that meridian.

502. TIDE

Tide is the vertical rise and fall of the ocean level resulting from gravitational force. The following terms are associated with tide:

HIGH TIDE.—Highest water level normally reached during a cycle.

LOW TIDE.—Lowest water level normally reached during a cycle.

STAND.—A period within the cycle during which the water level appears not to change.

RANGE.—The difference between the height of high water (high tide) and the height of low water (low tide). Heights are reckoned from a reference plane.

DATUM PLANE.—A reference plane established which may or may not be sea level but in all cases may be converted to mean sea level.

MEAN LOW WATER.—A datum plane based upon the average of all low tides.

MEAN LOWER LOW WATER.—A datum plane based upon the average of the lower of two low tides which occur during a lunar day (a lunar day is a time measurement based upon one apparent revolution of the moon about the earth).

MEAN LOW WATER SPRINGS.—A datum plane based upon the average of extreme low tides called spring tides.

In some foreign countries, the datum plane may not correspond to those listed above. However, the tide tables are based upon the datum plane of the most detailed local chart. The datum plane is an arbitrary value. It must be understood that ACTUAL DEPTH OF WATER EQUALS CHARTED DEPTH PLUS HEIGHT OF TIDE. If the height of tide is a negative value, then the actual depth is less than the charted depth.

TIDAL CYCLE.—Since a high tide occurs at two longitudes simultaneously, in one lunar day (24 hours, 50 minutes) two high tides and two low tides occur. One high tide and one low tide constitute a tidal cycle which, in time is one half a lunar day or 12 hours and 25 minutes. The time difference between one high tide and one low tide is approximately 6 hours and 12 1/2 minutes (half a tidal cycle).

PRIMING.—When the gravitational effect of the sun leads the moon's effect, causing the time of high tide to be earlier than normal, we call the phenomenon "priming of the tide."

LAGGING.—When the gravitational effect of the sun trails the moon's effect, causing the time of high tide to be retarded, we speak of the phenomenon as the "lagging of the tide."

SPRING TIDE.—When the sun and moon are acting in conjunction, which occurs when we have either a new or a full moon, high tides are higher than usual and low tides are lower than usual. These extremes are called spring tides.

NEAP TIDE.—When the sun and moon are acting in opposition, tidal range is at a minimum and the tide is called neap tide.

503. TIDE TABLES

Tables are prepared annually for various areas by the National Ocean Survey of the Department of Commerce, which contain predictions of the state of the tide. Each volume consists of the following tables:

TABLE 1.—A list of reference stations for which the tide has been predicted. The time and heights of high and low tides are tabulated for each day in the year for each of these reference stations. Also, the position of the datum plane with reference to mean sea level is given for each reference station.

TABLE 2.—A list of subordinate stations for which the tidal differences have been predicted with respect to a reference station having nearly the same tidal cycle. Above groups of subordinate stations, the reference station for that group is listed. After the name of each subordinate station the latitude and longitude to

the nearest minute is given together with tidal difference. Tidal difference consists of a time correction (in hours and minutes) and a height correction (in feet), both preceded by either a plus or minus sign. There is generally a height correction for both high and low water. If the correction is omitted for low water height, it may be assumed that the height of low water at the subordinate station is the same as the height at the reference station. If for some reason, height differences at a given station would give an unsatisfactory prediction, height difference is omitted and ratios for high and/or low water are given, identified by asterisk. To find the heights of high and low water using ratios, multiply the heights at the reference station by their respective ratios. If a ratio is accompanied by a correction, multiply the heights of high and low water at the reference station by the ratio, then apply the correction. Table 2 also provides the mean range (difference in height between mean high water and mean low water), the spring range (average semidiurnal range occurring semi-monthly as a result of a new or full moon), and the mean tide level (a plane midway between mean low water and mean high water) with respect to chart datum.

TABLE 3.—Table 3 is a convenient means of interpolation which allows for the characteristics of the tidal cycle. While tables 1 and 2 provide time and heights of high and low tides, the state of the tide may be desired for a given time in between. The arguments for entering table 3 are duration of rise or fall of tide, time between that desired and the nearest tide, and range. From table 3 we obtain a correction. If the nearest tide is high tide, the correction is subtracted from the height of the high tide; if the nearest tide is low tide, the correction is added to the height of low tide. This provides the height of the tide at the desired time.

The height of the tide alone does not fully describe the state of the tide; it is desirable to know whether the tide is rising or falling. If the desired time is preceded by a high tide and is succeeded by a low tide, the tide is falling. If the desired time is preceded by a low tide and is succeeded by a high tide, the tide is rising.

The tide tables as published include three additional tables for the convenience of the mariner. Table 4 provides the local mean time of sunrise and sunset. Table 5 provides corrections for conversion of local mean time to standard time. Table 6 provides the time of moonrise and moonset as computed for key reference stations.

EXAMPLE 1 (Data from Appendix C):

What is the state of the tide at Mayport, Florida on 7 August 1970 at 1320?

Reference Station	High Tide	Height	Low Tide	Height
Mayport, Fla.	1124	4.3	1718	0.6

Duration of fall: 1718 - 1124 = 5 hrs., 54 min.

Time between desired time and nearest tide (high): 1320 - 1124 = 1 hr., 56 min.

Range of tide: 4.3 - 0.6 = 3.7 ft.

Correction (Table 3): 0.9 ft.

State: 4.3 - 0.9 = 3.4 ft.   The tide is falling.

Data was taken from the tables for the desired data, noting times and heights of the two nearest tides. Table 3 was entered using the arguments (1) duration of fall (5 hrs., 54 min.), (2) time interval between high and desired time (1 hr., 56 min.), and (3) range of tide (3.7 ft.). The correction (0.9) thus obtained was applied to the height of the nearest tide (4.3 ft.). During the period 1124 to 1718 the tide changes from high to low and therefore must be falling.

EXAMPLE 2 (Data from Appendix C):

What is the state of the tide at St. Augustine, Florida on 4 July 1970 at 0600?

Reference Station	High Tide	Height	Low Tide	Height
Mayport, Fla.	0848	3.7	0236	0.0
Corrections	+14	-0.3	+43	0.0
St. Augustine, Fla.	0902	3.4	0319	0.0

Duration of rise: 0902 - 0319 = 5 hrs., 43 min.

Time between desired time and nearest tide (low): 0600 - 0319 = 2 hrs., 41 min.

Range of tide: 3.4 - 0.0 = 3.4 ft.

Correction (Table 3): 1.6 ft.

State: 0.0 + 1.6 = 1.6 ft.   The tide is rising.

The appropriate reference station was found above the subordinate station in bold print, in Table 2. Subordinate station corrections applied to reference station values were also found in Table 2.

504. OCEAN CURRENTS

A current is the horizontal flow or movement of water. There are two general types, ocean currents and tidal currents. The ocean currents result from the effects of the wind above the sea, and effects of temperature and salinity differences within the sea. The following ocean currents are most noteworthy:

Atlantic North Equatorial . . . Westward from Cape Verde Islands and clockwise in North Atlantic

Atlantic South Equatorial . . . Westward from the African coast and counterclockwise in South Atlantic

Atlantic Equatorial Counter . . . Between the two currents described above and eastward from South America to Africa

Gulf Stream . . . . . Through Straits of Florida, extending northeast

Greenland . . . . . Southward along east coast of Greenland, thence northwestward and counterclockwise in Baffin Bay

Labrador . . . . . .Formed from the Greenland Current and flowing southward from Davis Straits along the Labrador coast.

Brazil. . . . . . . .Southwestward and counterclockwise in the South Atlantic as a branch of the Atlantic Equatorial Current, along South American coast

Pacific North . . . .Westward in North Pacific
Equatorial

Pacific South . . . .Westward and counterclockwise in South Pacific
Equatorial

Pacific . . . . . . .Between the two currents
Equatorial   described above and east-
Counter   ward in Pacific

Japan Stream . . . .Northeastward off shore of Japan; partially a branch of the Pacific North Equatorial Current

Oyashiwo . . . . . .Southeastward between Alaska and Siberia, along the Siberian coast

California. . . . . .Southeastward off Californian shore

Australia . . . . . .Southward between Australia and New Zealand; a branch of the Pacific South Equatorial Current

Peruvian . . . . . .Northward along west coast of South America

Indian South. . . . .Counterclockwise in Indian
Equatorial   Ocean

Agulhas . . . . . . .Southward between Africa and Madagascar

505. TIDAL CURRENTS

Tidal currents result from tidal changes; in order for the tide to rise and fall there must be some horizontal movement of water between the ocean and the coastal estuaries. During the rise in tide, while the current is standing toward the shore, we refer to the current as "flooding." When the current is standing away from the shore, it is "ebbing." When there is no detectable horizontal movement of water, we speak of the condition as "slack" or "slack water." The strength of the current at any time depends upon both the tidal cycle and the configuration of land. When high tide occurs in a bay having a small mouth, a great amount of water must flow through the mouth, and therefore a strong current may be expected. This current will at least be strong in comparison with a current entering a bay having a wide mouth or entrance.

506. TIDAL CURRENT TABLES

Like tide tables, tidal current tables are prepared annually for various areas by the National Ocean Survey of the Department of Commerce, to provide predictions of the state of the current. Each volume consists of the following tables:

TABLE 1.—A list of reference stations in geographical sequence, for which the current has been predicted. For each reference station the times of slack water, maximum current and the velocities of maximum current are tabulated for each day of the year. Also, table 1 tabulates flood and ebb direction.

TABLE 2.—A list of subordinate stations for which the difference between local current and current at a reference station has been predicted. Above groups of subordinate stations, the appropriate reference station is listed. After the name of each subordinate station, the latitude and longitude to the nearest minute is given. Following the geographical coordinates, the time difference and velocity ratio are tabulated. To find the time of a current at the subordinate station, apply the time correction according to sign, to a time of current at the reference station. To find the velocity of the current at any subordinate station, multiply the velocity at the reference station by the velocity ratio at the subordinate station. Among many current characteristics tabulated are the average velocity of flood and ebb currents.

TABLE 3. — Table 3 provides a means of interpolation for the state of the current at any time between tabulated times. It is divided into two parts, table 3A and table 3B. Table 3A is used for tidal currents while table 3B is used for hydraulic currents such as the man-caused currents found in the Cape Cod Canal and other listed reference stations or referred subordinate stations. The arguments for entering table 3 are the interval between slack and maximum current and the interval between slack and desired time.

Table 3 provides a factor which must be multiplied by the velocity at either the reference or the subordinate station, depending upon which is under consideration.

The state of the current is the velocity in knots, whether it is ebbing or flooding, and the direction toward which it flows.

The tidal current tables include two additional tabulations which are sometimes useful in the prediction of tidal current. Table 4 predicts the duration of slack water, the period in minutes when the velocity varies from zero to 0.5 kts., in 0.1 kt. increments. It is divided, like Table 3, into two parts, Tables 4A and 4B. The former applies to normal tidal currents while the latter applies to currents, such as those in the Cape Cod Canal, and at other listed reference stations or referred subordinate stations. Table 5 provides data on rotary tidal currents such as are found at Nantucket Shoals.

The tidal current tables also contain current diagrams for certain harbors. These diagrams provide a graphic table showing the velocities of flood and ebb and times of slack and its strength over a considerable length of channel in a tidal waterway. Additionally, the tidal current tables contain data for estimating the currents which are wind-driven and the combined effect of tidal and wind currents. Certain ocean currents, such as the Gulf Stream (in the Tidal Current Tables, Atlantic Coast of North America), are described.

EXAMPLE 1 (Data from Appendix D):

What is the state of the current at St. Johns River Entrance, Florida on 2 March 1970 at 1400?

Reference Station	Slack	Maximum Current	Velocity (flood/ebb)	Direction
St. Johns River Entrance, Fla.	1312	1506	1.2 f.	275(f)

Interval between slack and maximum current: 1506 - 1312 = 1 hr., 54 min.

Interval between slack and desired time: 1400 - 1312 = 48 min.

Factor (Table 3): 0.5

Velocity: 1.2 x 0.5 = 0.6 kts.

Direction: The current is flooding. Direction is 275.

In choosing current times, as in the tide tables, choose the two times which form the nearest bracket to the desired time. In some problems, particularly where the subordinate station time correction is large, the given time is seen to be bracketed by the selected reference station quantities, but when the time correction is applied the given time is not bracketed at the subordinate station. The bracketing times in tide and current subordinate station problems must bracket the desired time at the subordinate station; after the time correction has been applied, one time must immediately precede the desired time, and the other must immediately follow it. An easy way to take into account the correction is to add minus corrections to the desired time, then choose brackets at reference station, and conversely subtract plus corrections from the desired time before selecting brackets.

EXAMPLE 2 (Data from Appendix D):

What is the state of the current at Jacksonville, Florida, off Washington Street, on 12 April 1970 at 0720?

Reference Station	Slack	Maximum Current	Velocity (flood/ebb)	Direction
St. Johns River Entrance, Fla.	0300	0548	1.7 e.	-
Corrections	+220	+250	0.7 (Velocity ratio)	060 (e)
Jacksonville, Fla., off Washington St.	0520	0838	1.2	060 (e)

Interval between slack and maximum current: 0838 - 0520 = 3 hrs., 18 min.

Interval between slack and desired time: 0720 - 0520 = 2 hrs.

Factor (Table 3): 0.8

Velocity: 1.2 x 0.8 = 1.0 kt.

Direction: The current is ebbing. Direction is 060.

Tidal current charts are now available for certain major ports or seaways, to be used in conjunction with the Tidal Current Tables. These charts, prepared by the National Ocean Survey, show hourly directions and velocity of tidal currents. To select which chart to use from a booklet for a given port, determine from the tidal current tables the time difference between the desired time and the nearest preceding slack water; the chart that agrees most nearly with this time computation should be used.

507. CONSIDERATION OF TIDE AND CURRENT

The navigator must fully consider the state of the tide together with charted depth to insure that water is kept under the ship's keel. Tidal ranges may be such as to cause some basins to dry at low tide even though sufficient water is present for safe navigation at high tide. Occasionally the tidal range permits crossing of bars which would not otherwise be navigable.

Knowledge of ocean currents may be used to advantage, either to speed a voyage or to conserve fuel. When standing northeastward through the Straits of Florida, by following closely the axis of the Gulf Stream, the ship's speed may be increased without any increase in engine or shaft RPM. When rounding Florida enroute to the Gulf, the mean axis of the stream should be avoided in order not to slow the speed of advance; actually, a lesser countercurrent to the Gulf Stream may be experienced in close proximity to the Florida Keys, which will be of assistance.

Tidal currents affect a ship considerably when docking, undocking, and whenever underway in pilot waters. A current may be so strong as to prevent a partially disabled ship from making any headway.

The navigator may use both ocean currents and tidal currents to his advantage, and should always be fully conscious of the state of the current and of any expected changes, anticipating how the expected changes, in the state of the current will affect the maneuverability of his ship. As for reliance upon tidal current data, the navigator must expect conditions occasionally other than those predicted. Storm conditions, man-made currents from lock sluice gates or spillways, and currents developed in dredging operations, among others, tend to reduce the accuracy of tidal current data available to the navigator.

CHAPTER 6

DEAD RECKONING

601. INTRODUCTION

Dead reckoning has previously been defined as a method in navigation in which the position of a ship is calculated from the direction and the rate of progress through the water from the last well determined position. The direction and the rate of progress cannot always be measured exactly, and dead reckoning as a method may leave much to be desired. However, when either celestial navigation or piloting is used as a primary means of navigation, dead reckoning provides a check and serves the worthwhile purpose of indicating errors. When other means of navigation fail, the navigator must rely upon dead reckoning alone. Since the automatic dead reckoning equipment is subject to mechanical or electrical failure, the navigator with drafting instruments, and up to date information concerning the ship's movements, manually constructs the dead reckoned plot.

602. THE PLOT

Dead reckoning, as presently accomplished, is a graphic means of navigation. Decades ago, it was accomplished by computation using trigonometric formulae. A dead reckoning plot (fig. 6-1) originates with a well determined position (a fix or running fix as described in the following chapter). From the fix, a course line representing the ship's course is drawn, using the compass rose as a reference. The course line is actually a locus of successive DR positions. Predicted positions, called DR positions, are marked at intervals along the course line. These positions are determined by the speed of the ship, the time interval, and the scale of the chart. For example a ship making a speed of 10 knots would travel 2 1/2 nautical miles in 15 minutes. On a DR course line, using the chart scale, a navigator would set his divider points 2 1/2 nautical miles apart in order to measure from the last well determined position,

along the course line, to the predicted position 15 minutes in the future. The DR plot is first a prediction of the ship's travel and later a graphic history of the route the ship attempted to follow. The course line may be referred to as a DR track or trackline.

When using time and speed to compute distance in dead reckoning, it is often advantageous to use the three-minute rule. Easily proven, the rule merely notes that the distance traveled in yards in three minutes is 100 times the speed in knots. Thus, if a ship is making a speed of twenty knots, it will travel 2000 yards, or one nautical mile, in three minutes.

A well determined position is labeled with the time indicated in 4 digits followed by the word "Fix;" for example "0800 Fix." Above a course line, the letter "C" is placed, followed by the ship's true course in 3 digits, indicating the direction of travel; for example, "C090." Below the course line, the letter "S" followed by the ship's speed in knots indicates the rate of progress and determines the speed of generation of the trackline; for example, "S12." A dead reckoned position is labeled with the time followed by the letters "DR"; for example, "0900 DR." Symbols as well as labels can be used to distinguish a fix from a dead reckoned position. While both are normally indicated as a circle around a point, and are distinguished by the letters "fix" or "DR," some navigators follow a former practice of indicating a fix with a circle and a DR with an arc connecting the course lines, an approximate semi-circle.

DR positions are usually plotted for each hour. In in-shore navigation the DR should be plotted more frequently, perhaps as often as every 3 minutes, but always depending upon circumstances and proximity to danger. At sea on a steady course using a small scale chart, one DR position plotted each 4 hours is considered satisfactory.

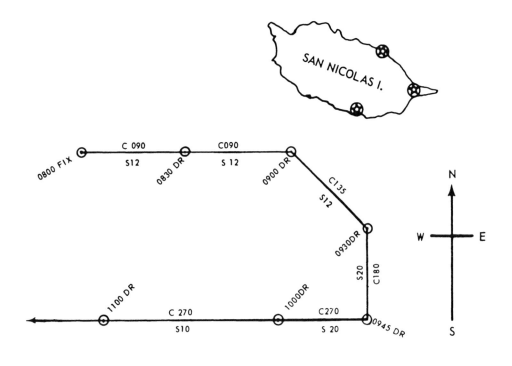

190.9
Figure 6-1. — Dead reckoning plot.

By the dead reckoning plot, the estimated time of arrival (ETA) at a destination is computed in advance. Similarly, the estimated time of departure (ETD) from a given point may be calculated unless the point marks the origin of the voyage in which case it is determined by operational planning.

603. CURRENT

We have previously thought of current as the horizontal movement of water; at this point we must define it for our future convenience, as the total effect of all forces causing a discrepancy between predicted and actual positions. Current when so broadly defined includes the horizontal movement of water, wind effect, steering errors, variations in engine speeds, and any momentary deviation from the basic course made by the conning officer.

Current can be described in terms of two qualities called set and drift. SET is the direction a current acts; DRIFT is the velocity in knots of a current.

To derive set and drift (fig. 6-2), a fix is compared with the DR position for the same time by connecting the DR and the fix with a broken line, terminated by an arrowhead at the fix. This line or vector represents current. The direction of the line (arrow) is the set. The length of the line in nautical miles divided by the hours the current has acted (time interval between last two fixes) is the drift.

The navigator consults current tables, the Coast Pilot or Sailing Directions as appropriate, and pilot charts and draws from his own experience to decide what caused an apparent current. If he decides that the apparent current represents an actual movement of water which can be expected to continue for some time, he may use the determined set and drift of the current to either compute the course and speed essential to making good a desired track or to predict the resultant track for any given course and speed. The accuracy of such computations depends upon the accuracy of the prediction of the set and drift and whether or not any change in the value of the current occurs.

To predict the track using (1) course and speed of the ship and (2) set and drift of the current, represent these basic values by vectors. The direction and length of the ship's vector are based respectively upon the ship's course and speed; the direction and length of the current

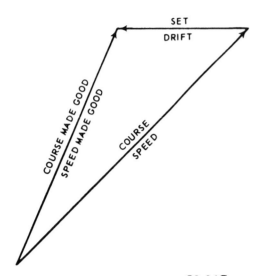

58.84C

Figure 6-2. — The current effect.

vector is based upon the current's set and drift. Draw the ship vector for an hour's effect. From the end of the ship's vector, draw the current vector for an hour's effect. The resultant, that is the line connecting the origin of the plot and the terminating end of the current vector, represents the probable track; by inspection of the direction and length of this resultant vector the navigator predicts course and speed made good. The vectors may be drawn in length to represent either an hour or a multiple of an

hour. When the navigator prefers the latter representation, and accordingly draws his vectors, then the length of the resultant track is a corresponding multiple of the speed made good.

When it is desired to make good a predetermined track, the first step is to construct the resultant which represents the desired track. From the termination of the desired track (point of destination), the current vector is drawn as the reciprocal of the set, with the length equal to the drift multipled by the time enroute in hours. By completing the triangle the ship's vector is determined; to compute the ship's course and speed respectively, determine the direction of the vector, and its length divided by the duration of the voyage in hours. This plot is of great practical use.

It is no more a safe practice to assume that a current will adhere to a predicted value than it is to assume that no current exists. The cautious navigator will construct on his chart both the DR track based upon course and speed and the predicted track taking current into account. He carefully checks all features between the two tracks, to detect dangers should the current be reduced. He checks features adjacent to and beyond each track to detect dangers should the effect of current either exceed or undergo a reversal in its predicted value. The navigator should assume that the most unfavorable condition of current exists and take appropriate action to insure the safety of his vessel.

CHAPTER 7

PILOTING

701. INTRODUCTION

Piloting has been previously defined as a method of directing the movements of a vessel by reference to landmarks, other navigational aids, and soundings. It is generally used as a primary means of navigation when entering or leaving port and in coastal navigation. It may be used at sea when the bottom contour makes the establishment of a fix by means of sounding possible. In piloting, the navigator (a) obtains warnings of danger, (b) fixes the position frequently and accurately, and (c) determines the appropriate navigational action.

702. LINES OF POSITION

Piloting involves the use of lines of position, which are loci of a ship's position. A line of position is determined with reference to a landmark; in order for a landmark to be useful for this purpose it must be correctly identified, and its position must be shown on the chart which is in use. There are three general types of lines of position (fig. 7-1), (a) ranges, (b) bearings including tangents, and (c) distance arcs.

A ship is on "range" when two landmarks are observed to be in line. This range is represented on a chart by means of a straight line, which if extended, would pass through the two related charts symbols. This line, labeled with the time expressed in four digits (above the line), is a locus of the ship's position. It should be noted that the word "range" in this context differs significantly from its use as a synonym of distance.

It is preferable to plot true bearings although either true or magnetic bearing may be plotted. Therefore, when the relative bearing of a landmark is observed, it should be converted to true bearing or direction by the addition of the ship's true heading. Since a bearing indicates the direction of a terrestrial object from the observer, in plotting, a line of position is drawn from the landmark in a reciprocal direction. For example, if a lighthouse bears 040, the ship bears 220 from the lighthouse. A bearing line of position is labeled with the time expressed in four digits above the line and the bearing in three digits below the line.

A special type of bearing is the tangent. When a bearing is observed of the right hand edge of a projection of land, the bearing is a right tangent. Similarly, a bearing on the left hand edge of a projection of land as viewed by the observer is a left tangent. A tangent provides an accurate line of position if the point of land is sufficiently abrupt to provide a definite point for measurement; it is inaccurate, for example, when the slope is so gradual that the point for measurement moves horizontally with the tide.

A distance arc is a circular line of position. When the distance from an observer to a landmark is known, the locus of the observer's position is a circle with the landmark as center having a radius equal to the distance. The entire circle need not be drawn, since in practice the navigator normally knows his position with sufficient accuracy as to require only the drawing of an arc of a circle. The arc is labeled with the time above expressed in four digits and the distance below in nautical miles (and tenths). The distance to a landmark may be measured using radar, the stadimeter, or the sextant in conjunction with tables 9 and 10 of the American Practical Navigator.

703. FIXES

A fix (fig. 7-2), previously thought of as a well determined position, may now be defined as the point of intersection of two or more simultaneously obtained lines of position. The symbol for a fix is a small circle around the point of intersection. It is labeled for better identification with the time expressed in four digits

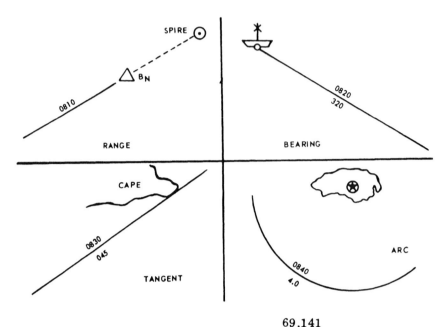

69.141

Figure 7-1.—Lines of position.

followed by the word "fix." Fixes may be obtained using the following combinations of lines of position:

(a) A line of bearing or tangent and a distance arc.
(b) Two or more lines of bearing or tangents.
(c) Two or more distance arcs.
(d) Two or more ranges.
(e) A range and a line of bearing or tangent.
(f) A range and a distance arc.

Since two circles may intersect at two points, two distance arcs used to obtain a fix are somewhat undesirable; the navigator in making his choice between two points of intersection may, however, consider an approximate bearing, sounding, or his DR position. When a distance arc of one landmark and a bearing of another are used, the navigator may again be faced by the problem of choosing between two points of intersection of loci.

704. SELECTING LANDMARKS

Three considerations in the selecting of landmarks or other aids for use in obtaining lines of position are: (a) angle of intersection, (b) number of objects, and (c) permanency.

Two lines of position crossing at nearly right angles will result in a fix with a small amount of

error as compared to two lines of position separated by less than 30 degrees of spread. If in both cases a small unknown compass error exists, or if a slight error is made in reading the bearings, the resulting discrepancy will be less in the case of the fix produced by widely separated lines of position than in that of the fix obtained from lines of position separated by a few degrees.

If only two landmarks are used, any error in observation or identification may not be apparent. By obtaining three or more lines of position, each line of position acts as a check. If all cross in a pinpoint or form a small triangle, the fix may generally be relied upon. Where three lines of position are used, a spread of 60 degrees would result in optimum accuracy.

When a choice of landmarks or other aids exists between permanent structures, such as lighthouses or other structural and natural features identifiable ashore or in shallow water, and less permanent aids such as buoys, the former should be given preference. The fact must be recognized that buoys, while very convenient, may drift from their charted position, because of weather and sea conditions, or through maritime accident.

The navigator oftentimes has no choice of landmarks, their permanency, number, or spread. In such cases he must use whatever is available, no matter how undesirable. In the evaluation of

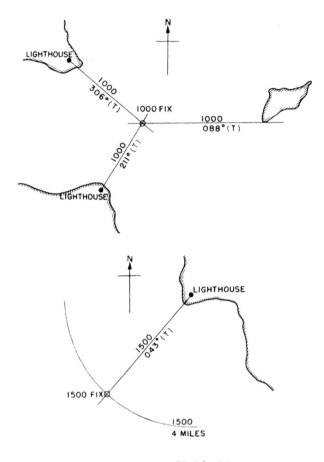

58.76:.77
Figure 7-2. — Fixes.

determine the correct error. If the error assumed is improperly identified (east or west), the triangle will plot larger. If the error proves to be properly identified but the triangle still exists, although reduced in size, the navigator should on the second trial, assume a larger error in the same direction.

706. RUNNING FIXES

It is not always possible for the navigator to observe lines of position simultaneously. Sometimes only one landmark is available; the navigator may make frequent observations of the one landmark, or he may, after one observation, lose sight of the available landmark only to sight a new navigational aid. During these observations, if the navigator is able to compute distance he may easily establish his fix. If not, or if for any reason his data consists of lines of position obtained at different times, then he may establish a position which only partially takes into account the current. This position is the running fix identified by the same symbol as the fix except that the time label is followed by the abbreviation "R. Fix." It is better than a DR position but less desirable than a fix.

A running fix is established by advancing the first line of position in the direction of travel of the ship (the course), a distance equal to the nautical miles the ship should have traveled during the interval between the time of the first line of position and the time of the second line of position. The point of intersection of the first line of position as advanced, and the second line of position, is the running fix. The advanced line of position is labeled with the times of the two lines of position (LOP's) separated by a dash, and the direction, above and below the line, respectively. See fig. 7-3.

To advance a line of bearing, a tangent, or a range, measure from the point of intersection of the LOP and the DR track line, along the track line, the distance the ship would have traveled at its given speed. This measurement provides a point on the DR track line, through which the earlier line of position is re-plotted without any change in its direction. (Fig. 7-3A.)

To advance a distance arc, draw the course line as a broken line on the chart from the landmark first observed. Along this broken course line, measure the distance the ship should have traveled, based upon the elapsed time between observations and the speed of the ship. At the point thus established, reconstruct the earlier distance arc. (Fig. 7-3B.)

his fix, the number of landmarks, their permanency, and their spread should receive consideration. When three lines of position cross forming a triangle, it is difficult to determine whether the triangle is the result of a compass error or an erroneous line of position. The plotting of four lines of position will usually indicate if a line of position is in error.

705. CHANGE IN COMPASS ERROR

When lines of position cross to form a small triangle, the fix is considered to be the center of the triangle, a point which is determined by eye. If the size of the triangle appears significant, it is possible that the value of the compass error has changed.

To compute the new compass error, without the benefit of a range or azimuth, assume an error, then by successive trials and assumptions

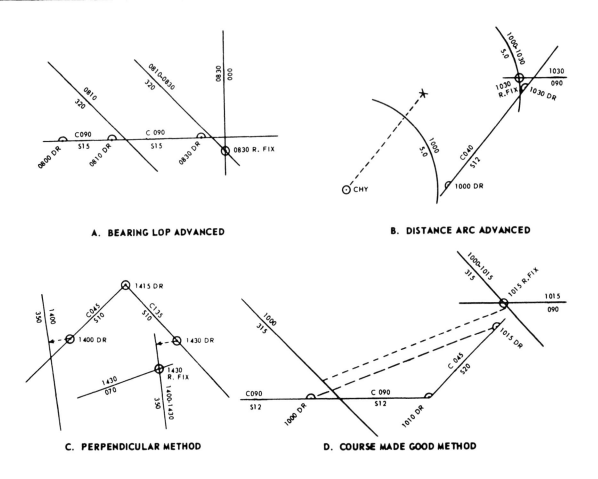

A. BEARING LOP ADVANCED

B. DISTANCE ARC ADVANCED

C. PERPENDICULAR METHOD

D. COURSE MADE GOOD METHOD

58.76(190)
Figure 7-3.—Running fixes.

If the ship changes course and/or speed between observations the problem is not so simple to solve, and one of the following methods should be used:

PERPENDICULAR METHOD.—After two lines of position are obtained, plot DR positions corresponding to the times of the LOPs. From the earlier DR, drop a perpendicular to the earlier LOP. At the second DR, construct a line having the same direction and length as the first perpendicular. At the termination of the latter line, construct a line parallel to the original LOP; this is the advanced LOP. The intersection of this advanced LOP and the last observed LOP establishes the running fix. The logic of the perpendicular method is that since the speed and course of the ship generates the DR track line, if the advanced LOP lies with respect to the second DR position as it previously lay with

respect to the old DR, then it has been advanced parallel to itself a distance and a direction consistent with the ship's movement during the intervening time. A variation of this method is to construct, instead of a perpendicular, a line of any direction between the first DR and LOP. This line is then duplicated at the second DR and the LOP advanced as before. In duplication, the line from the second DR must be of the same length and direction as the line connecting the first DR and LOP. (Fig. 7-3C.)

COURSE MADE GOOD METHOD. — As in the perpendicular method, plot DR positions to match the time labels of the LOP's. Connect the DR positions; the connecting line represents the course and distance which the ship should have made good. Advance the first LOP a distance and direction corresponding to the line connecting the two DR positions. (Fig. 7-3D.)

DRAI METHOD. — Since the DRAI resolves received inputs into components (N or S, E or W) the components for a given run may be plotted and connected by a line. The hypotenuse of the right triangle thus formed represents the direction and distance the first LOP should be advanced.

707. SPECIAL CASES

A special case of the running fix is the "bow and beam" situation. (See fig. 7-4.) When the bearing of a landmark diverges 45 degrees from the ship's heading, it is said to be broad on the bow. When the divergence increases to 90 degrees, it is on the beam. By noting the time a landmark is broad on the bow and the time it is on the beam, the distance passed abeam can be computed; the distance abeam will be equal to the distance run between bow and beam bearings which in turn will depend upon the elapsed time and the ship's speed. Knowing the distance abeam, when a beam bearing is observed, makes the plotting of the running fix quite simple. The true bearing will be the true heading plus or minus 90 degrees depending upon whether the landmark is abeam to starboard or abeam to port. The distance run equals the distance abeam because 45 and 90 degree angles provide a right isosceles triangle with equal sides.

Another special case, which is related to that of the bow and beam, is one known as "doubling the angle on the bow." The angle formed by the

course of the ship and a sight line in the direction of a navigationally useful object is observed and noted, together with the time. A second observation is made and the time noted when the angle on the bow is double that of the first observation. At that instant, the distance from the object is equal to the distance run between observations.

The triangle formed by two bearings and the course line is a right isosceles triangle in the special bow and beam case which we have seen. However, it can be easily proved that upon doubling the angle on the bow, the triangle thus formed is also an isosceles triangle, having two equal sides, although not usually a right triangle.

708. RUNNING FIX ERRORS

The running fix may be a well determined position and is usually considered as such. For this reason, the DR track is normally replotted using the running fix as a new point of origin.

However a running fix does not fully account for current, and the displacement of the running fix from the DR is not a true indication of current. If a head current is expected, extra allowance should be made for clearance of dangers to be passed abeam, because the plot of running fixes based upon any single landmark near the beam will indicate the ship to be farther from that danger than it actually is. If a following current is experienced, then the opposite condition exists. This occurs because the actual distance made good is less with a head current and greater with a following current than the distance the LOP is advanced based upon dead reckoning. Usually, a limitation of 30 minutes should be imposed on the elapsed time between lines of position in a running fix; this however, is not a hard rule because of other considerations.

709. ESTIMATED POSITION

While it may not be feasible for the navigator to obtain either a fix or a running fix, he may observe such data as to make possible the plotting of a position more probable than a DR. Such a position is called an estimated position. It is identified as a square with a dot in the center and labeled with the time in four digits followed by the letters "EP."

If the navigator has computed or knows the approximate strength of the current, this information may be applied to obtain an EP. At any DR position, construct the current vector; the direction of the vector will represent the set and

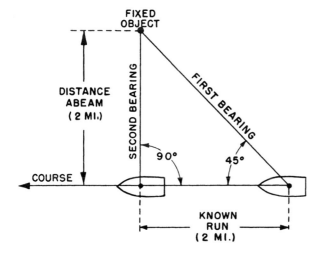

58.79

Figure 7-4. — Bow and beam bearings.

the length of the vector will depend upon the drift and the elapsed time since the last fix. The point of termination of this vector is the estimated position.

Occasionally in reduced visibility the navigator may sight an aid momentarily and establish an EP. An EP may identify a fix or running fix which, in the judgment of the navigator, has been inaccurately obtained, or a fix obtained using radio bearings.

When a vessel passes over a bottom having abrupt changes in depth or irregular contours, soundings may be utilized in the establishment of an EP. The navigator directs the recording of soundings at regular intervals. If these soundings are obtained using the fathometer then the draft of the ship is added to all values. His data then consists of depth recorded against time. A sheet of paper is graduated on one edge with the space between marks corresponding to the distance run (as measured on the scale of the chart in use) between the recording of soundings. These marks are labeled with time and depth. The navigator places the sheet on the chart with the labeled edge of the sheet in the general vicinity of the DR track. He moves the paper laterally in an effort to match the depths on the paper with charted depths (bottom contour). In lieu of the use of a sheet of paper on which the edge serves as the DR track, a sheet of flimsy paper with the DR track drawn anywhere on it, may be marked with soundings and used. If successful, the navigator may locate an estimated position by this procedure.

Whether the navigator considers the DR or the EP as the ship's actual position depends upon the proximity of danger to each position with the track extended ahead, whichever position and track is nearest danger should be considered as the actual position and track in order to provide the widest margin of safety.

710. FIXES BY SOUNDING

A new and rather unique piloting procedure has evolved whereby a fix instead of an EP can be obtained by soundings. This new procedure is characterized by the use of bottom contour lines as lines of position.

By this method, it is first necessary to record the time of crossing each bottom contour line, together with the sounding. Second, it is necessary to indicate on the DR track the DR positions for times that such soundings were taken. Third, on a sheet of flimsy paper a line is drawn with an arrow on one end to indicate the direction

of travel; a dot is placed approximately three inches back of the arrow point as a reference mark. Fourth, the flimsy paper is placed over the DR track with the reference dot over the DR position corresponding to the first recorded sounding and with the arrow in the direction of travel; the contour of the sounding recorded at that time is traced and labeled. Fifth, by moving the sheet in the direction of travel, and with the reference dot over successive DR positions, corresponding contour lines are identified by sounding and traced. Finally, after three or more contours are plotted, the intersection of contours may indicate a fix. It should be remembered that contour lines because of their irregularity may cross at more than one point, and thus several may need to be plotted to resolve possible ambiguity. The time of the fix corresponds to the time of the last plotted sounding.

EXAMPLE: Having noted the bottom contour lines on the chart in use, the following soundings were taken and recorded.

Time	Sounding
1000	110 fms.
1005	110 fms.
1007	120 fms.
1010	130 fms.
1015	140 fms.

Preparation:

Having recorded the time of crossing of each contour, as indicated by sounding, on the chart, place the ship's DR track on the chart and indicate the DR position for each of the times recorded. (Fig. 7-5.)

Take a sheet of flimsy paper, draw a line across the sheet, and place an arrow point on one end of the line to indicate the direction of travel. Place a reference dot approximately three inches behind the head of the arrow. (Fig. 7-6A.)

Plotting:

Step 1 — Place the flimsy paper over the chart with the dot over the first DR position and the arrow pointing in the direction of travel. Trace the contour of the sounding recorded at that time and label with sounding. (Fig. 7-6A.)

Step 2 — Move the flimsy sheet in the direction of travel until the dot is over the second DR

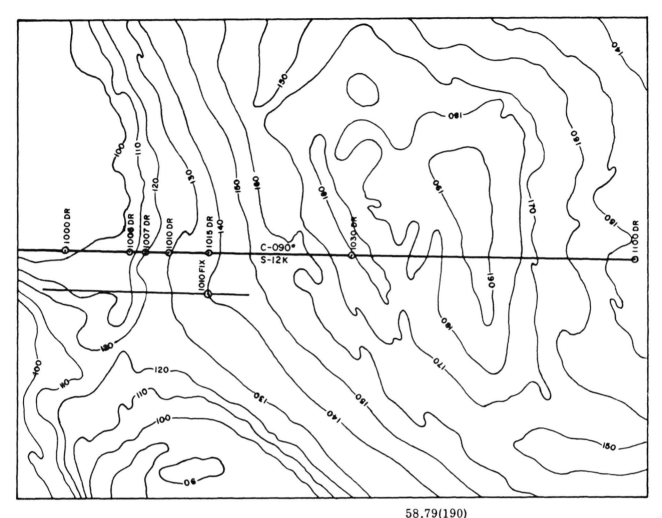

58.79(190)

Figure 7-5. — Fix determined by sounding.

position. Trace the contour of the sounding recorded for that time and label with the sounding. (Fig. 7-6B.)

Step 3 — Move the sheet in the direction of travel until the dot is over the third DR position. Trace the contour of the sounding recorded for that time and label with the sounding. Examine for possible fix results. (Fig. 7-6C.)

Step 4 — Move the sheet in the direction of travel and trace the next sounding as in steps 1 through 3. The position of the fix should be apparent. The time of the fix when located will be the recorded time for the sounding last used for fix information. (Fig. 7-6D.)

Step 5 — Since sounding contours are not usually straight lines and can cross in more than one place, the position must be checked by placing the DR, with both time and soundings,

on the flimsy paper. Place the last DR time over the newly obtained fix and check the times and soundings against the apparent track. (Figs. 7-6D and 7-5.)

It may be noted that the position obtained by this procedure is technically a running fix, rather than a fix. Dependent upon the amount of elapsed time and the correlation of track and soundings, the position obtained may be considered as a fix, a running fix, or an estimated position.

711. DANGER BEARINGS AND
DANGER ANGLES

It is possible to keep a ship in safe water without frequent fixes through the use of danger bearings and danger angles.

57

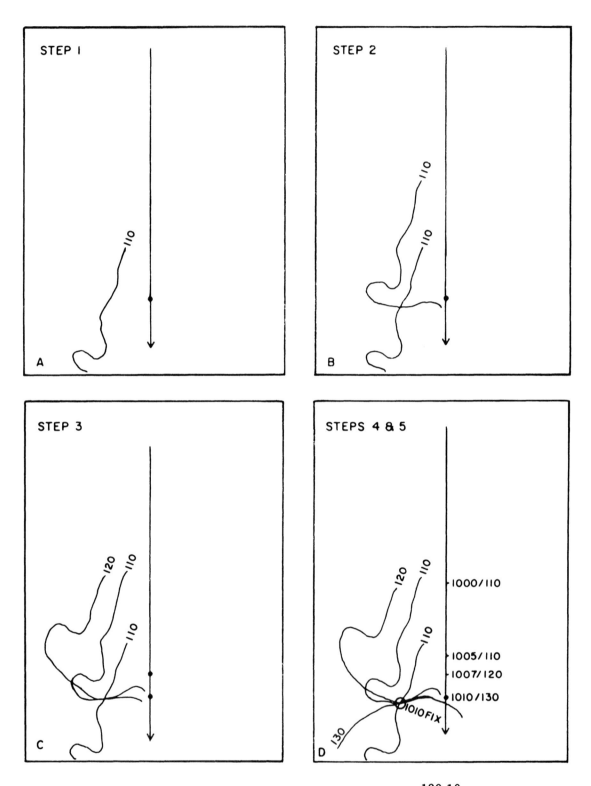

190.10
Figure 7-6.— LOP and fix determination by sounding.

If a ship must pass a dangerous area such as unmarked shoal water, draw a circle around the area on the chart. Check the chart for some prominent landmark in the general direction of travel (or the reciprocal). Draw a line from the landmark tangent to the danger circle and label the line with its direction. This direction is the danger bearing on the landmark from which it is drawn. With the danger bearing as a line of demarcation, the mariner can tell whether he is outside or inside of the danger area just by checking the bearing of the object.

Danger angles are of two types, horizontal and vertical. If two prominent landmarks are available, a horizontal angle is used. If only one prominent landmark is available then a vertical angle is used; however, this method requires that the height of the landmark be known. In either case the first step is to draw a circle around the danger area on the chart. For a horizontal angle, a circle is constructed passing through the two available prominent landmarks, and tangent to the danger circle. If it is desired to leave the danger area between the ship's track and the selected landmarks, the circle through the landmarks contains the danger circle; if it is wished to pass between the danger circle and the prominent landmarks, the danger circle although tangent, will lie outside the circle which passes through the selected landmarks. To construct two circles tangent to each other, it is necessary to make use of the fact that their diameters lie in a straight line. From the point of tangency of the two circles draw two chords, one to each landmark. These chords provide an inscribed angle the value of which is the danger angle. To leave the danger area between the track and the selected landmarks, the angle formed by the two landmarks with the ship's position as a vertex must not be allowed to become greater than the danger angle. To pass between the two prominent landmarks and the danger area, the angle must not be allowed to become smaller than the danger angle.

To use a vertical angle, construct a circle tangent to the danger circle, using the landmark of known height as the center. The vertical danger angle may be found by entering table 9 of the American Practical Navigator with the radius of the tangent circle and the height of the object.

To pass between two danger areas, the navigator computes an upper and a lower limitation for the value of the danger angle.

712. TACTICAL CHARACTERISTICS IN PILOTING

Thus far in this discourse upon piloting, the tactical characteristics of the ship have not been considered. It has been assumed that course and speed changes would be effected instantaneously. In actuality, such is not the case. At sea, when at great distance from navigational hazards, such an assumption can be made, inasmuch as the ship is in no immediate danger, and on a small scale chart the tactical characteristics will not alter the plot. However, most piloting is accomplished inshore, in close proximity to navigational hazards. Large scale charts enable the navigator to depict his position with greater accuracy as essential for ensuring safe passage. Accordingly, the largest scale, most detailed charts available are used when in restricted or pilot waters, and full allowance is made for the tactical characteristics of the ship.

Tactical characteristics vary with each ship. To effect either a course or a speed change requires varying amounts of time and space, dependent upon the ship, the magnitude of the change, sea and weather conditions. Particularly in effecting a course change, the ship may be expected to be offset some distance from the planned track unless the turning characteristics are considered. Failure to consider such characteristics can directly contribute to driving the ship into danger.

Tactical data is obtained and recorded for each ship to describe turning characteristics in terms of "advance" and "transfer" for varying rudder angles, usually every 15°. "Advance" is the distance gained along the original course extended, and "transfer" is the distance offset perpendicular to the original course; both are measured from the point at which the rudder is put over. Advance is maximum for a turn of 90°.

Other related terms include:

Angle of turn — The arc in degrees through which a ship turns.

Turning circle — The path followed by the pivot point of a ship turning 360°.

Tactical diameter — The distance offset right or left of the original course when a turn of 180° is made.

Final diameter — The distance perpendicular to the original course as measured between tangents to the turning circle at 180° and 360° points in the turn. Essentially, it is the diameter of the turning circle. The final diameter is always somewhat less than the tactical diameter.

Standard tactical diameter—A prescribed distance used by all ships in a formation as a tactical diameter for uniformity in maneuvering.

Standard rudder—That amount of rudder required for a ship to turn in its standard tactical diameter.

Tactical data also includes tables of acceleration and deceleration to accommodate the need for accurate calculation of a ship's progress along the planned track.

In restricted or pilot waters, the need for accuracy is generally so great, that advance and transfer must be considered before each course change. Accordingly, advance and transfer are estimated, and at that point on the chart where the course change is to be effected, it is plotted in reverse direction. This identifies the point at which the rudder should be put over to effect the course change in a timely fashion. Additionally, the bearing of a landmark or other aid to navigation, preferably close to the beam, should be noted, as measured from that point on the plot at which the rudder will be put over. This bearing, termed the "turn bearing," is used as one means of ascertaining the proper time for making the turn. However, it is always good practice to obtain a fix a minute or so before the turn, and an additional fix after the turn when the ship is steady on its new course.

In addition to allowing for advance and transfer in making a turn, the combined effect of wind and current should be considered. The wind can be observed, and the current can generally be predicted, as we have seen previously, from tables. Experience in ship handling and knowledge of local sea and weather conditions are most helpful, and provide reason for navigation being an art as well as a science.

713. PRECISION ANCHORING

For practical convenience, the Oceanographic Office publishes anchorage charts of principal U.S. ports. These are merely harbor charts with anchorage berths preselected and overprinted as colored circles of various diameters. Anchorage berths, with centers usually in a straight line, and with limiting circles usually tangent to those adjoining, are identified by letters and/or numbers for simplification of anchorage assignment. For anchorage in an area in which such berths are not readily available, it is the usual practice to specify or locate the anchorage in terms of bearing and distance from a prominent landmark.

The requirement for anchoring should be anticipated, and except in an emergency situation, deserves detailed preparation. The location must be studied, noting the depth of water, nature of bottom, and the navigational aids useful for accurately fixing the position during the approach, upon, and after anchoring. The proximity of navigational hazards, and the proximity of channels or fairways subject to ship traffic, should be considered. The nature or type of bottom is an indication of the holding qualities; for example, the anchor will hold better in mud or clay than in sand or rock, and will usually hold better in sand than on a rock bottom. The type of bottom, depth of water, and anticipated weather, should be considered in planning the scope of anchor chain, in addition to the proximity of other ships, underway or at anchor, and navigational dangers.

A planned track must be prepared to the anchorage, with careful consideration of all hydrographic features and the draft of the ship. Consideration must be given to the raising of the pit sword or rodmeter, if extended, and of the type which can be raised and housed. Wind and current must be considered. It is advantageous to approach the anchorage, when possible, by heading directly into the current, except when the wind effect exceeds that of the current, in which case it is advantageous to head into the wind. Such contributes to greater steering accuracy, which can be further improved by the ship maintaining a steady course for at least the last 500 yards to the anchorage. The location of navigational aids should be fully considered. If wind and current conditions will also permit approaching the anchorage with the ship "on range," which is the maintaining of two fixed objects in line with the direction of the line corresponding to heading, then even greater navigational accuracy can be achieved. The navigator can thereby practically eliminate the effect of compass error on steering. He can determine the ship's progress along the approach track merely by observing and plotting one cross bearing, although the plotting of two such cross bearings is more desirable.

In further preparation, the navigator should consider the distance from the bridge, where the bearings are to be taken, to the hawse pipe, at which point the anchor is to be dropped; this is known as "bridge-hawse distance." Converted to yards, and measured along the track from the anchorage in opposite direction of the approach, the bridge-hawse distance identifies that point which when reached by the bridge, places the hawse in the proper position for anchoring, assuming that the heading of the ship corresponds to the direction of the approach track. Appropriately, the bearings upon anchoring will normally be observed from the bridge, and when plotted should fix the ship's position that distance away from the desired anchorage as is equal to the bridge-hawse distance in a direction which is the reciprocal of heading. Also, the navigator should strike arcs of range circles, from the point established using bridge-hawse distance, so that the distance to anchorage can be directly read from the plot without resort to direct measurement. Arcs of range circles are usually drawn, crossing the approach track, using radii in 100 yard increments out to 1000 yards, with additional arcs at 1200, 1500, and 2000 yards. Labeling the point for letting go the anchor as 0,

the other arcs are labeled in accordance with their represented range from the anchorage. (See fig. 7-7.)

If turns are to be made in the approach, the navigator should note and record the "turn bearings" of suitable navigational aids. The immediate availability of turn bearings, together with an estimate of advance and transfer, will serve the navigator in effecting the turn with accuracy. Additionally, he will note and record the "drop bearing," that is, the bearing of a prominent landmark which is approximately perpendicular to the approach track. Allowance for the bridge-hawse distance is made in determining the drop bearing.

It is common practice for the navigator, well prior to anchoring, to inform the Commanding Officer, the Officer of the Deck, and the First

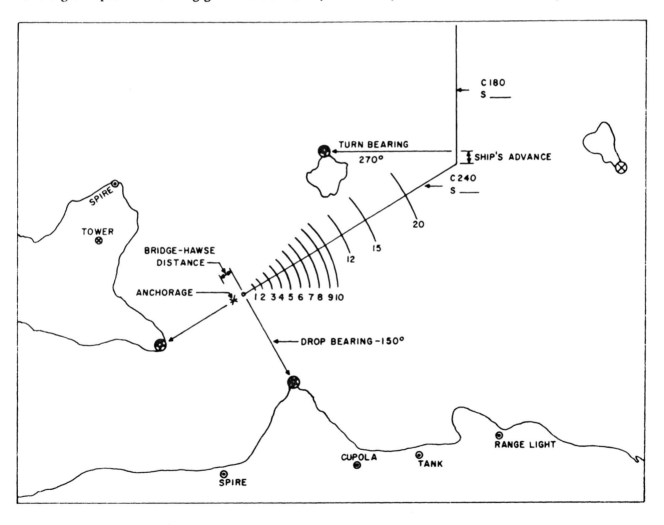

190.11

Figure 7-7. — Preparation for precision anchoring.

Lieutenant of the depth of water, the type of bottom, and the distance and location of shoal water or other navigational hazard in the vicinity of the planned anchorage. Before the approach, the navigator should show the Commanding Officer and Officer of the Deck the approach track and inform them of the principal landmarks to be used, of turn bearings if any, and of the drop bearing. Throughout the approach, the navigator will report the direction and distance to anchorage.

It is good seamanship practice under most conditions for the ship's headway to be reduced as it approaches the anchorage, and upon reaching the drop bearing, in anticipation of which propellers are reversed, to let go anchor with a small amount of sternway on. This generally makes it possible to set the anchor without its chain tending under the ship where it may endanger such appendages to the underwater body as the sonar transducer. By a careful combination of engine orders and the holding or veering of chain, the anchor can usually be safely set.

Upon anchoring, it is necessary to accurately fix the position by observing and plotting a round of bearings. As soon as the anchor is known to be holding, the position should again be fixed. Additionally, by using a sextant and a three-arm protractor as explained in art. 310, with sextant measurement of horizontal angles as observed from the forecastle (at the hawse, when the chain is nearly vertical), an accurate fix can be obtained. This can serve as a check upon the fix based upon bearings observed from the bridge. While at anchor, bearings are taken and recorded periodically for comparison with the established fix as a precaution against dragging.

Upon getting underway from anchor, the navigator must commence piloting procedures as soon as the heaving in of the anchor chain is commenced. The ship's position must be accurately known, particularly from the time the anchor breaks ground. During this crucial period in getting underway from anchor, accurate knowledge of the ship's position is necessary as a precaution against dragging or drifting into shoal water or other hazard.

714. BUOYAGE

Buoys are navigational aids which serve as markers. Some are so equipped as to be useful at night or during periods of reduced visibility; some are not so equipped and hence are useful only in daytime. Buoys are not fixed aids (they consist of a float, mooring, and anchor) and can

not be completely relied upon. Their service is chiefly that of warning the navigator of impending danger. The following are representative types (descriptive of the float, which identifies a buoy):

SPAR BUOY. — A trimmed log which resembles a stake at a distance.

CAN BUOY. — A cylindrical steel float.

NUN BUOY. — A steel float the shape of a truncated cone.

BELL BUOY. — A buoy with a skeleton tower which holds a bell generally actuated by the motion of the sea. Some bells are struck by the action of gas compressed in a cylinder.

GONG BUOY. — Similar to a bell buoy but equipped with gongs instead of a bell, which make sounds of different tones.

WHISTLE BUOY. — Similar to a bell buoy but equipped with a whistle (useful in low visibility) usually actuated by the motion of the sea. Some buoys are equipped with trumpets which are sounded mechanically.

LIGHTED BUOY. — Buoy which carries a light at the top of the skeleton with either acetylene gas or electric batteries for power. A lighted buoy may for some reason become extinguished and therefore is not completely reliable.

COMBINATION BUOY. — A buoy which combines a light signal with a sound signal. Examples are lighted whistle buoys, lighted bell buoys, and lighted gong buoys.

RADAR REFLECTOR BUOY. — A buoy which supports a screen and makes early detection by radar probable.

Buoys which mark turning points may be equipped with a ball, cage, or some other device.

Each maritime country has developed, and in most cases, standardized by law, the colors for its own particular buoyage system. These systems are described in appropriate Oceanographic Office Sailing Directions. The following colors represent U.S. buoys and, with the exception of white and yellow, indicate lateral significance:

RED. — Identifies buoys on starboard hand of a channel entering from seaward. A rule to remember is "3R's" meaning "Red-Right-Returning." These buoys are usually of any type except can, and bear even numbers commencing with 2 at the seaward end of a channel. They may carry a red or white light.

BLACK. — Identifies buoys on the port hand of a channel entering from seaward. These buoys are usually of any type except nun, and bear odd numbers commencing at the seaward end of the channel with 1. They may carry a green or white light.

RED AND BLACK HORIZONTALLY STRIPED. — Identifies an obstruction or junction and may be passed on either hand.

BLACK AND WHITE VERTICALLY STRIPED. — Identifies a fairway or midchannel buoy which should be passed close aboard. Only white lights are carried by this type of buoy.

WHITE. — Anchorage.

YELLOW. — Quarantine anchorage.

Beacons, stakes, and spindles may be erected in shallow water. Their color is in accord with the buoyage system but usually also provides a contrast with the background. These are fixed landmarks and are generally more reliable than buoys.

Representative lighted and unlighted buoys, as well as various beacons, are illustrated in Appendix A.

715. LIGHTS

Lighted aids consist of lightships, lighthouses, lighted beacons, and lighted buoys. These are listed in the light list to facilitate identification. Failure to correctly identify a light has often resulted in disaster; light identification requires corrected charts and publications, and warrants the use of a stop watch to check the period or cycle. Characteristics of lighted buoys are illustrated in Appendix A.

Light colors may be white (W), red (R), or green (G). If not indicated, the light is assumed to be white.

The period of a light is the time in seconds a light requires to complete a cycle, or endure a complete set of changes.

716. VISIBILITY OF LIGHTS

Light visibility is categorized by three types of ranges, geographic, nominal, and luminous.

The Geographic visibility of a light is the number of nautical miles a light may be seen by an observer at a height 15 ft. above sea level, under conditions of perfect visibility, and without regard

to candlepower. The geographic visibility and the height of a light may be found on the chart, adjacent to the light symbol, and in the Light List. The higher the light the greater the distance it should be seen; theoretically, the distance a light should be seen by an observer at sea level is the length of a beam measured from the light to its point of tangency with the earth's curved surface, assuming that the light is not restricted by candlepower or brilliancy.

The nominal range is the maximum distance at which a light may be seen in clear weather, which is meteorologically defined as a visibility of ten nautical miles. Nominal range is listed for only those lights having a computed nominal range of five nautical miles or greater. If the geographic range is greater than the listed nominal range, the latter will normally govern.

The luminous range is the maximum distance a light may be seen under existing conditions of visibility. The luminous range is determined from either the nominal range or the intensity, and the existing conditions of visibility. See Appendix E.

Intensity or candlepower of light given is approximate and is based upon the International Standard Candela.

The navigator is interested in the radius of visibility of a given light under existent conditions. Thus, the navigator normally determines luminous range, then computes that limitation imposed by the earth's curvature; by comparison, it can readily be seen which limitation is applicable, that determined by intensity or that imposed by the heights of the light and of the observer's platform.

Using the luminous range diagram (Appendix E), either the nominal range or the intensity, and the meteorological visibility, the luminous range can be found by inspection. Using the distance of visibility of objects at sea (Appendix E), the height of the light, and the navigator's height of eye, the distance a light can be seen as limited by earth's curvature can be computed; values as taken from the table of distance of visibility for each of the two heights are simply added. The radius of visibility of the light will equal the lesser of these two range limitations, luminous and earth's curvature.

The applicable Light List provides the heights of lights, and as appropriate, the nominal range and intensity. The navigator must know his own height of eye and the meteorological visibility.

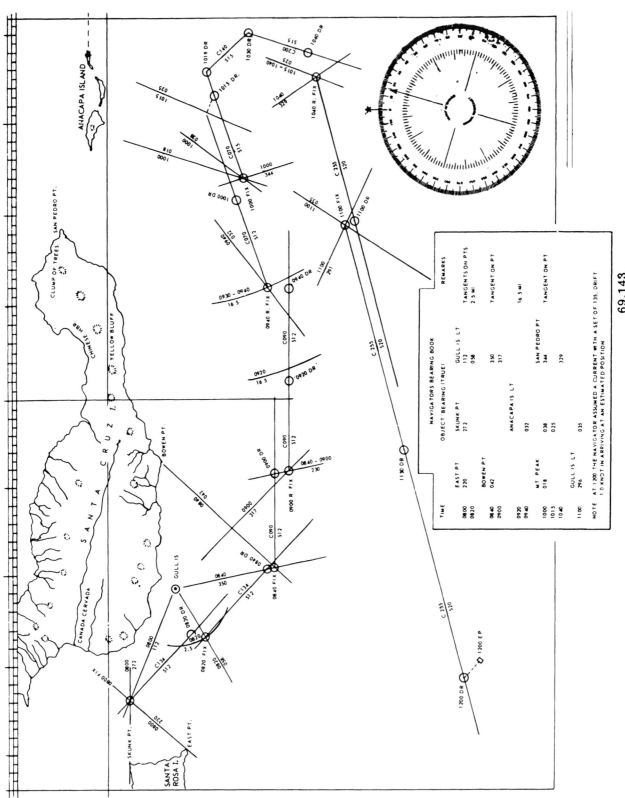

69.143

Figure 7-8. — Piloting plot and bearing book.

EXAMPLE 1:

Given: Light, 55 feet high, geographic range 13 miles, nominal range 11 miles, intensity 2,000 Candelas. Navigator's height of eye, 27 feet; visibility 5 miles.

To find: Radius of visibility.

Solution: Enter the luminous range diagram (Appendix E) with (1) either the nominal range or the intensity; and (2) the meteorological visibility. When both nominal range and intensity are given, it is preferable to enter the diagram with intensity. It may be determined that the luminous range is 7 miles. Since the navigator is at a greater height than that upon which geographic range is computed (15 feet), he should be able to see the light at least 13 miles away (its geographic range), unless limited by its intensity. Using the distance of visibility of objects at sea as tabulated in Appendix E, the distance visible as limited by the earth's curvature is computed as follows:

height of light, 55 feet - 8.5
height of eye, 27 feet - 6.0
Total - 14.5 nautical miles

However, since the light is limited by intensity and existing visibility, the luminous range is applicable, and the radius of visibility is 7 miles.

EXAMPLE 2:

Given: Light with same characteristics as in Example 1. Navigator's height of eye is 10 feet; visibility is 20 miles.

To find: Radius of visibility.

Solution: The luminous range based upon the diagram, is found to be 16 nautical miles. The range, based upon the earth's curvature, is determined as follows:

height of light, 55 feet - 8.5
height of eye, 10 feet - 3.6
Total - 12.1 nautical miles

Thus, the radius of visibility, in this case, as limited by the earth's curvature, is about 12 nautical miles.

It should be noted that if the characteristics of a light and the distance to it upon sighting are known, the luminous range diagram may be used to determine the meteorological condition of visibility.

717. PREDICTING THE SIGHTING OF A LIGHT

Having computed the radius of visibility, draw a circle using the computed radius with the light as center. The point of intersection of this circle and the DR track marks the point at which a light should be sighted. This time is computed by dead reckoning; the true bearing is the true direction of the light from the point of intersection of the DR track and the circle.

718. LIGHT SECTORS

Shield or colored glass shades may be fitted to lights making them obscure in one or more sectors or so that they will appear to be one color in certain sectors and a different color in other sectors. These sectors may be located on the chart by dotted lines and color indications. Such sectors are described using true direction in three digits for each sector boundary, and the direction given is as observed from seaward looking towards the light and clockwise. Many of our lights located along dangerous coastlines such as the Florida Keys have red and white sectors; when in the white sector the ship is usually in safe water but when in the red sector the ship is inside of a danger bearing and is in danger of running upon a reef.

719. BEARING BOOK

It is good practice to maintain a small book of convenient size for the recording of bearings and other desired piloting information, together with the identity of aids used and the time. Normally, the pages of such a record book are ruled so as to provide approximately six vertical columns. Each page, as used, is dated, and the first column on the left is used for the recording of time. In other columns, headed individually by the identity of aids, the bearings observed are accurately recorded, horizontally opposite to the recorded time. One column may be set aside for recording soundings for correlation with fixes as obtained. Bearings are true unless otherwise noted. If gyro bearings are recorded in lieu of true bearings, they must be so identified, together with the gyro error, if any. Because of the importance of such a record, as of other records having legal significance, erasures are not permissible. (See fig. 7-8.)

CHAPTER 8

BASIC ELECTRONIC NAVIGATION SYSTEMS

801. GENERAL

Electronic navigation is considered here as a definite division of navigation and one which will be further developed during the next few decades. As far as basic techniques are concerned, electronic navigation is an extension of piloting. It differs from piloting in the methods by which the data is collected.

Radio, radio direction finder, radar, sonar, loran and Decca, are examples of basic electronic navigation equipment. Radio, as used principally for obtaining time signals, weather, and hydrographic information, was briefly mentioned in art. 307. The other basic electronic instruments, together with related equipment such as radar beacons and Shoran, are addressed in greater detail in this chapter. More advanced electronic navigation systems are described in chapter 9.

802. MARINE RADIOBEACONS

Marine radiobeacons are important aids to electronic navigation and are described in H.O. 117 Radio Navigational Aids. The letters "RBn" denote their location on a nautical chart. They are particularly useful in piloting during periods of poor visibility. Transmitting in the medium frequency range, and identified by the dot and dash arrangement of their transmission, radiobeacons may be classified as directional, rotational, and circular. Directional radiobeacons simply transmit their signals in beams along a fixed bearing. Rotational radiobeacons revolve a beam of radio waves in a manner similar to the revolving beam of light of certain lighthouses. Circular radiobeacons, the most common type, send out waves in all directions for ship reception by radio direction finder as described in the following article.

803. RADIO DIRECTION FINDER

This is an azimuthal instrument, formerly called a radio compass, which upon receipt of a radio signal can determine the direction of the sending station. It is an important navigational aid because of its usefulness in search and rescue, or distress operations, and in homing aircraft.

Generally, the shipboard equipment consists of a receiver and two antennas. One antenna is a vertical stationary sense antenna, the other a rotatable loop antenna. The latter, in essence, is the "direction finder."

As the antenna is rotated, its output varies with the angle relative to the direction of the received signal. When it is perpendicular to the signal, signal strength is at a minimum or "null." The reading is taken at this point because a small change in the relative direction of the signal thus obtained causes a greater change in signal strength than does an equal change when the signal strength is at or near the maximum level.

Changes in the signal strength can be observed and related to bearings which are read from a dial. Bearings may be true or relative, depending upon the equipment. Since there are two "null" points for each complete revolution of the antenna, the sensing antenna works in conjunction with the loop antenna to resolve the ambiguity.

Variations of this antenna arrangement exist in the Automatic Direction Finder (ADF) in which two loops are rigidly mounted in such a manner that one is rotated 90° with respect to the other. The relative output of the two antennas is related to the orientation of each with respect to the direction of travel of the radio wave. Newer radio direction finders, often small, portable, and battery operated, have a ferrite rod coupled inductively to the receiver which serves in lieu of the loop antenna.

Radio bearings may be obtained from equipment other than the radio direction finder and if the source of the signal can be identified, such bearings may be used to establish or to confirm a navigational position. As primary sources, however, marine radio beacons and direction finder stations are regularly provided in many parts of the world. Their position can be determined from maritime charts and from HO Pub 117, Radio Navigational Aids. It is of the greatest importance in plotting radio bearings to keep in mind the fact that the reciprocal of the bearing represents the direction of the ship from the transmitting source. These bearings are great circle bearings and over long distances must be corrected, prior to plotting on a Mercator chart, by a method described in HO Pub 117, Radio Navigational Aids.

804. RADAR

The word "radar" is an abbreviation for "radio detection and ranging." Radar equipment generates a directional radio wave which travels at the speed of light and which upon striking an object, is reflected back at the same velocity. A radar set is so calibrated that the range (distance) of an object can be directly read; this is feasible since the equipment is designed to compute distance from speed and time (the fraction of a second required for the signal to travel to an object and return is divided by two). The direction of a generated signal depends upon the direction the antenna is trained; for continuous search in all directions the antenna is permitted to rotate at uniform speed.

The principal parts of a radar set and their functions are:

(a) Transmitter — Transmits electrical energy.
(b) Modulator — Cuts off transmitter periodically to convert signal to pulses.
(c) Antenna — Radiates signal and receives echo.
(d) Receiver — Receives echo via antenna.
(e) Indicator — Indicates the time interval between pulse transmission and pulse return as a measurement of distance to the reflecting object.

Part of the indicator is the cathode ray tube, the face of which is referred to as the "scope." There are two general types of scopes differing in presentation, the most common of which is the "PPI" or "plan position indicator." It is graduated in degrees for the direct reading of true and relative bearings; true direction is supplied by an input from the gyrocompass.

The center of the PPI scope represents the ship's position. Reflecting objects within range appear as shapes upon the scope. Range may be read from the PPI scope either approximately by the use of concentric range circles or more accurately by matching a "range bug" with a target pip and reading the range from a dial. (See fig. 8-1.)

805. ADVANTAGES AND LIMITATIONS OF RADAR

The usefulness of radar, a range-bearing device, is illustrated by the following advantages:

(a) Safety in fog piloting — Radar provides an extra pair of eyes when the ship operates in reduced visibility, and can penetrate darkness and fog in the interest of safety.
(b) Means of obtaining range and bearing — This information may be sufficient to establish a fix.
(c) Means for rapidly obtaining fixes — The radar may easily provide position information faster than can be obtained through any other means. The PPI actually provides a continuous fix.
(d) Accuracy — This depends upon skill of the operator and the adjustment of the equipment;

190.12X
Figure 8-1 — Radar PPI presentation.

however, an accuracy of a few yards may be attained.

(e) Range — The range is much greater than visual range. It depends upon the earth's curvature, as in the case of the radius of visibility of lights, and upon the characteristics of the set. It is not unusual to detect a high mountain at a range of 150 miles. The calculated distance to the moon was checked by radar, considerably prior to the making of lunar flights.

(f) Use as an anticollision device — The radar supplies information about the movements of nearby ships. Conning of the ship may be accomplished by reference to the PPI scope.

(g) Storm tracking — Radar is useful in tracking violent storms.

(h) Remote indication — The PPI scope presentation may be automatically indicated at remote locations.

The limitations of radar are:

(a) Mechanical and electrical character — It is subject to mechanical and/or electrical failure.

(b) Minimum and maximum range limitations — There is a minimum range limitation resulting from the echo of signals from nearby wave crests. These echoes are called "sea return." The radius of the sea return is a few hundred yards depending upon the adjustment of the equipment. Nearby objects may be obscured by the sea return thus establishing a minimum range. As previously mentioned, the maximum range depends upon the earth's curvature and the characteristics of the set.

(c) Interpretation — This is often difficult. The operator should be able to provide navigational information through the recognition of electron patterns. There is not always enough information for definite scope interpretation.

(d) Bearing inaccuracy — The radio waves travel as fan-shaped beams which result in echoes greater in width by several degrees than the angle subtended by the reflecting surface. If the beam width in degrees is known, the operator should add half the width to left tangents and subtract half the width from right tangents.

(e) Susceptibility to interference — Both natural (atmospheric) and artificial (jamming) interference may restrict usefulness of equipment.

(f) Necessity for transmission from the ship — This reduces security by breaking radio silence.

(g) Land shadows and sea return — These may cause objects not to be detected. Land shadows result when the land contour prevents radio waves from striking the entire surface. (A small hill in the rear of a high hill would appear in land shadow.)

806. ACCURACY OF RADAR

The accuracy of a radar position may be affected by the following:

(a) Beam width (bearing accuracy) — If visual bearings are available they should be used in lieu of radar bearings.

(b) Pulse length (range accuracy) — Range accuracy is usually greater than bearing accuracy.

(c) Mechanical adjustment.

(d) Ability of the operator.

(e) False targets — An example of a false target is surf which may reflect echoes and appear as a shore line.

(f) Shadows — This result of contours makes identification difficult as shapes on the scope may not correspond to actual shapes on the chart.

807. RADAR FIXES

The following methods, which are used in piloting, may be employed to establish a radar fix:

(a) Range and bearing of an object — The accuracy may be improved by the substitution of a visual bearing.

(b) Two or more bearings — Because of bearing inaccuracy this is not a preferred method.

(c) Two bearings and a range — If the range arc does not pass through the point of intersection of the bearings, the fix should be established as the point on the distance (range) arc equidistant from each bearing line.

(d) Two or more range arcs — This provides the best fix. Three arcs are better than two. Two circles may intersect at two points and thus force the navigator to choose between two possible positions.

(e) Three-arm protractor method — One may measure bearings of three objects and set up 3-arm protractor as described in art. 310.

808. VIRTUAL PPI REFLECTOSCOPE (VPR)

The VPR is an attachment which may be used in conjunction with the PPI scope of a radar to fix the position of the ship continuously on a navigation chart. It consists of a chart board upon which a navigation chart is secured, and a set of reflecting mirrors which serve to reflect the chart upon the PPI scope. The center of the PPI scope represents the position of the ship; therefore, if the reflected chart image is matched with the scope, the center of the scope marks the ship's position on the chart. VPR charts must be drawn to a scale which is consistent with the range scale of the PPI scope. Sometimes the VPR chart is a grid chart thus enabling the operator to read at any time the grid position of the ship. The navigator may transfer this position to a navigation grid chart characterized by the same grid system but not necessarily having the same scale.

809. RADAR BEACONS

Two common radar beacons are "racon" and "ramark." RACON, used primarily in aircraft, consists of a transmitter and a receiver on board the aircraft and a transponder at some designated position. The aircraft transmits a signal, which upon being received by the transponder, triggers the transponder and sends a signal back to the aircraft; this returning signal is received upon a scope similar to a PPI scope. Direction can be determined since the signal appears as a radial line of dots and dashes extending from the center of the scope to the spot which represents the beacon. The periphery of the scope is graduated in degrees, so the bearings can be easily read. The length of the line determines range. The dots and dashes, identify the transponder.

RAMARK, designed primarily for marine use, is a beacon which transmits signals continuously. These signals when received, also appear as a radial line emanating from the center of a scope graduated to permit the reading of direction. The range can not be determined, and there is no coding system for identification.

810. TACAN

The word "TACAN" is an abbreviation for "tactical air navigation." It, like radar, is a range-bearing navigation system. Operating in the ultra high frequency portion of the spectrum, TACAN is designed to provide a continuous bearing and distance to a ground station. TACAN stations are identified by transmissions in International Morse Code at 35 second intervals. TACAN as a system is superior to earlier very high frequency omni-directional range and distance measuring equipment used in air navigation because it is more accurate and easier to operate.

TACAN is installed in military aircraft, and in some aircraft carriers as a homing device. It is operated simply by turning on a power switch, selecting a station, and reading the range and bearing. Maximum range is 195 nautical miles, and thus it is a short-range system. TACAN has been accepted as the primary navigation aid for the Air Route Traffic Control System.

811. SHORAN

"Shoran" is an abbreviation for "short range navigation" and makes use of the principle that radar ranges are more accurate than radar bearings. Signals from either a ship or aircraft trigger two fixed transmitters which send out signals simultaneously. The intersection of two circles of position on the receiving scope is representative of the ship's position. These circles may be drawn on the chart using the transmitters as centers. Shoran, a circular close range navigation system, may give an accuracy as great as 25 feet but can accommodate only one ship or aircraft at a time and is limited in range by the curvature of the earth.

812. SONAR

"Sonar," an abbreviation for "Sound navigation ranging," operates in principle as the fathometer or echo sounder as described in art. 306 except that it radiates a signal which is generally horizontal rather than vertical. Accurate ranges on underwater objects may be obtained, and inasmuch as the sonar transducer can be rotated, reasonably accurate bearings may also be obtained. Using such ranges and bearings, or ranges alone, piloting procedures as also applicable to radar are used. In fog or other reduced visibility, the sonar may provide the most accurate and useful information, particularly if rock ledges are present. The sonar is also most helpful in detecting and avoiding ice bergs.

813. LORAN

"Loran," an abbreviation for "long range navigation," is a hyperbolic navigation system, developed in the Radiation Laboratories at Massachusetts Institute of Technology during World War II. It makes use of a cathode ray tube and electronic circuits to measure the time difference between receipt of two signals traveling at the speed of light (about 186,281 miles per second). Loran-A is standard loran. Another type of loran,

loran-C, is described later in this chapter. In contrast with radar, loran is characterized by:

(a) Having on board a ship or aircraft a receiver but not a transmitter (radar both transmits and receives).

(b) Measuring the time difference in receipt of two signals instead of measuring the time required for an outgoing signal to travel to a reflecting surface and return.

(c) Utilizing low frequencies (1750-1950 kHz in loran-A and 90-110 kHz in loran-C) while radar utilizes high frequencies.

(d) Requiring ground stations to transmit signals as pulse emissions. Radar requires no other station; it is complete in itself.

814. THEORY OF LORAN-A OPERATION

Loran-A operating stations (transmitting stations) are organized in pairs called "station pairs." The station pair consists of a master or key station and a secondary station; the two stations, on the average, are located 200 to 400 miles apart. Each station sends out synchronized pulses at regular intervals and the receipt of signals from a station pair by a ship or an aircraft makes it possible to read the time difference. The ship's line of position, based upon one time difference reading, is a hyperbolic line since such a curve defines all points a constant difference in distance from two fixes points (in this case from two transmitting stations). Time difference readings are measured in microseconds; a microsecond equals one millionth of a second, and is abbreviated "ms."

The arc of a great circle which connects two stations of a station pair is the baseline. The perpendicular bisector of the baseline is the centerline. Extensions of the baseline are simply called baseline extensions.

Loran-A equipment aboard ship consists of a receiver-indicator (fig. 8-2). The receiver picks up and amplifies a signal while the indicator provides a video presentation. The indicator also contains a timer by which the navigator can measure the interval in microseconds between times of receipt of pulse emissions from a given pair of stations.

Station pairs are identified by frequency (channel), basic pulse recurrence rate, and specific pulse recurrence rate. There are four channels expressed in kilo Hertz (khz), with frequencies as follows:

Channel 1 1950 kHz.   Channel 3 1900 kHz.
Channel 2 1850 kHz.   Channel 4 1750 kHz.

There are three basic pulse recurrence rates associated with each channel:

S—Special—20 pulses per second with 50,000 ms intervals

L—Low—25 pulses per second with 40,000 ms intervals.

H—High—33 1/3 pulses per second with 30,000 ms intervals.

The interval is the quotient when one million is divided by the number of pulses per second. There are eight station pairs, numbered from 0 to 7, associated with each basic pulse recurrence rate, each station pair having a specific pulse recurrence rate. In the case of station pair 0, the specific pulse recurrence rate equals the basic pulse recurrence rate. Other station pairs have a specific pulse recurrence rate less than the basic pulse recurrence rate and differing by a value equivalent to 100 ms times the station pair number. Examples of specific pulse recurrence rates are as follows:

Station Pair	Special BPRR Interval	Low BPRR Interval	High BPRR Interval
0	50,000 ms	40,000 ms	30,000 ms
1	49,900 ms	39,900 ms	29,900 ms
2	49,800 ms	39,800 ms	29,800 ms
3	49,700 ms	39,700 ms	29,700 ms

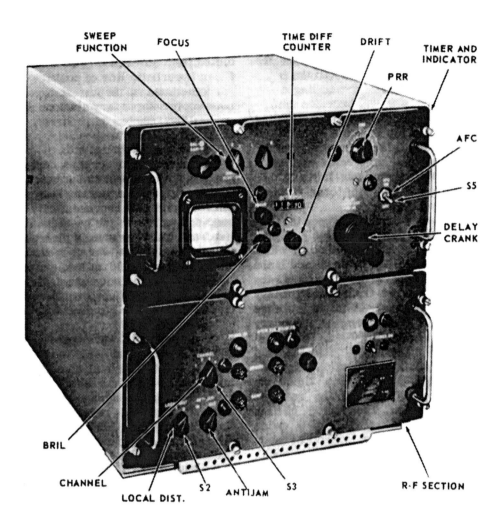

69.47

Figure 8-2. — Loran-A receiver-indicator.

Station pairs are identified by number, a letter, and a number such as "1H2" which signifies channel 1, high basic pulse recurrence rate, and station pair No. 2 (specific pulse recurrence rate: 29,800 ms intervals).

The simplest receiver would present electrons in a horizontal line with two pips a distance apart equal to the time difference. However, receiver scopes are designed having two traces, the upper or "A" trace and the lower or "B" trace. The B trace is actually the right hand half of a single trace presentation. By moving the pip on the lower trace, which is a signal from a secondary station, until it is directly beneath the signal from the master station on the A trace, we measure the time difference in microseconds.

In actual operation of the transmitting stations, three delays are introduced at the secondary station called (1) baseline delay, (2) half pulse recurrence rate delay, and (3) coding delay. The master station initiates a pulse which travels all directions (including along the baseline). This pulse, upon arrival at the secondary station, triggers the secondary transmitter. The delay thus introduced, the baseline delay, depends upon the speed of radio waves (speed of light) and the distance traveled, and is equal to the product of 6.18 ms and the length of the baseline in nautical miles; it insures that the master station signal will be received first. Upon receipt of a master signal by the secondary station, the half pulse recurrence rate delay is introduced, which is

71

the specific pulse recurrence rate interval in microseconds divided by two. This insures that one signal will appear on each trace, since the right half of the actual trace is underneath the left half and each half is equal to half the pulse recurrence rate. Last of all, the coding delay (950-1000 ms) is introduced; this provides a minimum reading and insures the operator of being able to determine which pip is to the right on the scope. The coding delay also provides security to the system in wartime, as it may be used to restrict the successful use of our loran-A stations.

To illustrate the relationship between the time difference reading and the observer's position, it may be helpful to examine the method by which a time difference reading can be predicted if the ship's position is known. In this example, the master station is 350 miles from the secondary station. The ship is located 400 miles from the master station and 200 miles from the secondary station. The coding delay is 1000 ms. The signal will travel from the master station to the ship in a time interval equal to 400 miles x 6.18 ms per mile or 2472 ms. At the same time, the same signal will travel along the baseline to the secondary station. The period of time which elapses during the travel of a pulse to the secondary station is dependent upon the length of the baseline and in this case is equal to 350 miles x 6.18 ms per mile or 2163 ms. Upon the arrival of the master station pulse at the secondary station, the secondary station is actuated, but before transmitting, it introduces first the half pulse recurrence rate delay and secondly the coding delay. It is not necessary that we know the value of the half pulse recurrence rate delay because our scope is so constructed that the half pulse recurrence rate delay does not enter into the measurement. Since the trace is divided into an A trace and a B trace, and since the lower pip is moved underneath the upper pip, the chief separation or half pulse recurrence rate delay cancels itself out. The lower pip is not moved as far as would be necessary if the scope contained a single trace, and this distance which it does not travel is the half pulse recurrence rate delay which ensures that one pip will appear on each trace. The coding delay is 1000 ms and this value will be measured by the loran receiver. At the end of coding delay, the secondary station will transmit, and the time required for the receipt of this transmission is 200 miles x 6.18 ms per mile or 1236 ms. Adding 2163 ms (baseline delay), 1000 ms (coding delay),

and 1236 ms (time of travel of signal from secondary station to ship), the sum is 4399 ms. Subtracting 2472 ms from 4399 ms we find the predicted time difference to be 1927 ms, which identifies a hyperbolic line of position.

Sometimes a master station will be located between two secondary stations and will transmit on two frequencies or recurrence rates in order to key (control) two secondary stations. This is called "double pulsing."

The accuracy of loran-A depends upon a ship's position with respect to the baseline. On the baseline, the greatest accuracy is experienced, as one microsecond may represent only 250 yards. Proceeding away from the baseline along the centerline, accuracy gradually decreases. Along the baseline extension, one microsecond may represent as much as 10 miles, and a fix obtained in this area may be inaccurate. If one microsecond represents more than 2 nautical miles, the loran can not be expected to give satisfactory results in navigation.

Two types of waves are used in loran-A, ground waves and sky waves. Ground waves are those which travel directly from the transmitting station to the ship and have a maximum range limitation under average conditions of 700 miles. Sky waves reflect from the ionosphere (ionized layers of atmosphere) and arrive after ground waves because of the greater distance traveled. For identification, the first sky wave reflected from the "E" layer of the ionosphere is known as the "one hop E," and the second as the "two hop E." The first sky wave to be reflected from the "F" layer accordingly is the "one hop F" and the second is the "two hop F." Sky waves have range limitations normally of 500 to 1400 miles. Five hundred and seven hundred miles mark the lower and upper boundaries of the critical range, inside of which wave identification is necessary. In matching pips, a ground wave from the secondary station is matched to the ground wave from the master station or a first sky wave is matched to a first sky wave. Only "one hop E" sky waves are used. Second sky waves are not dependable, and sky waves are not matched with ground waves. See fig. 8-3.

815. LORAN-A INTERFERENCE

Loran-A interference differs from most other interference in that it is visual, rather than audible as in the case of radio and sonar. Atmospheric interference makes the flow of electrons uneven on the scope; this interference is

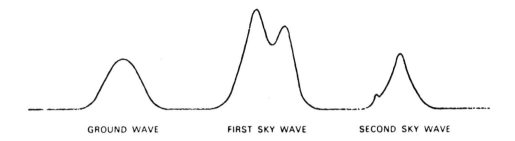

GROUND WAVE   FIRST SKY WAVE   SECOND SKY WAVE

190.13X

Figure 8-3. — Scope appearance of waves.

descriptively called "grass." Radar transmissions appear as evenly spaced pips on a loran trace; electrical influences and code sending also produce visual interference. Fortunately, most interference does not impair scope reading.

Additional signals known as spillover and ghost pulses may interfere. Spillover is the term used to describe signals received from adjacent frequencies; since some channels are only separated by 50 kHz it is as possible to receive signals from two stations on a loran receiver as on a radio receiver. If a signal is suspected to be spillover, the set should be tuned to an adjacent channel or frequency. If it is spillover, the signal will come in stronger; if not it will fade. Ghost pulses may be received from an adjacent basic recurrence rate. Ghost pulses are characterized by their instability.

When a loran-A station is out of synchronization the signals either appear and disappear or appear to shift to the right about 1000 ms then back, at intervals of approximately 1 second. Such blinking action warns the operator not to take readings. When the stations are again synchronized, which usually requires not more than a minute, blinking ceases.

816. ADVANTAGES AND LIMITATIONS OF LORAN-A

The advantages of loran-A include the following:

(a) Speedy fixes (1-5 minutes).
(b) Rapidly trained operators (4 days at fleet schools).
(c) Weather does not affect reliability of operation.
(d) 24 hour service.
(e) Long range (1400 miles).

(f) Land does not reduce accuracy (of particular interest to air navigators).
(g) Fix is independent of accurate time.
(h) Homing is convenient.
(i) Radio silence is maintained.
(j) Jamming is difficult.
(k) Possible wartime security.

Disadvantages or limitations include:

(a) Possible mechanical or electrical failure.
(b) Restricted coverage (lack of sites for transmitter stations, the expense of stations, and the need for agreements with foreign states).
(c) Identification of signals not always reliable.

817. LORAN-A CHARTS

Either loran-A charts (fig. 8-4), which are nautical charts over-printed with loran information, or loran-A tables (H.O. Pub. 221) may be used for converting loran-A readings into LOP's and fixes. Loran-A charts as normally available offer a rapid means, and have been made for those areas where loran-A signals are available.

Loran-A charts show hyperbolic lines of position usually for each 20 ms of time difference on large scale charts and for each 100 ms of time difference on small scale charts. The lines emanating from different station pairs are identified by their color as well as by a label of rate and ms time difference along each such hyperbolic line.

Charted hyperbolic lines are for ground wave time differences; if first sky waves are matched, then the time difference obtained must be corrected so as to be comparable to ground wave time differences. Corrections are found at the intersections of meridians and parallels and are

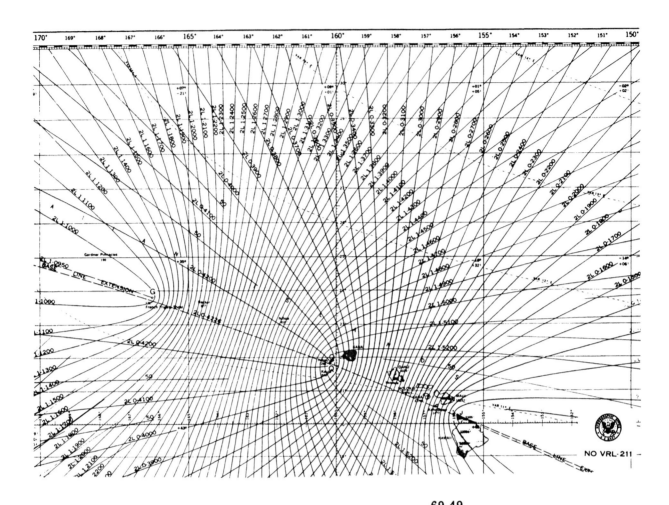

69.49
Figure 8-4.— A portion of a loran chart.

printed the same color as the rate to which they apply. Eye interpolation may be necessary to determine the sky wave correction, when the position of the ship is between tabulated values. When obtained, corrections are added or subtracted according to sign.

When plotting a loran-A fix, select two hyperbolic lines in the vicinity of the DR position between the values of which the actual time difference reading of a station pair lies. Using eye interpolation and a straight edge, draw a short line labeling it with the time above and the station pair number and ms time difference below. This is a loran-A line of position. By plotting two or more such LOP's (assuming they are obtained in rapid succession) a fix is obtained which is represented by a small circle and the time in four digits followed by the word "fix." If the LOP's are not obtained in rapid succession,

then they should be advanced or retarded to a common time using procedures described in the study of the running fix. If the charted hyperbolic lines are far apart, a self-explanatory linear interpolater appearing on loran charts may be used to increase the accuracy and lessen the difficulty of interpolation.

The accuracy of a loran-A fix depends upon the angle of intersection of LOP's, the position with respect to the transmitting stations, the synchronization of the station pair, and the operator's skill in identifying and matching signals.

818. LORAN-A OPERATION

The steps in taking and using a loran-A reading in the AN/UPN-12 and similar sets, are normally as follows:

(a) Determine from the approximate position of the ship, the transmitting station pairs which

74

serve the ship's position, and the type of signals expected from these transmitting station pairs.

(b) Turn on the receiving set by setting the power switch to the "standby" position.

(c) Allow a warm-up of at least one (1) minute before switching to "power-on." Turn the power switch to "power on" position.

(d) Refer to the Loran-A Charts of the approximate geographical location of the ship. Set the "pulse recurrence rate" (PRR) and "channel" to correspond to a loran-A transmitting station pair determined in Step 1. Set "sweep function" switch to one, the AFC switch to "off" and the "time difference" counter to approximately 11,000 with "delay" crank.

(e) Adjust the "gain" and "bal" controls to equalize signal heights. Set "Local-dist" switch to D, I, or L, dependent upon which position will obtain best operating conditions.

(f) Use "drift," "gain," "bal," and "L-R" controls to locate the desired signals, then turn the "drift" control to a point where the signals are locked in on the indicator screen. Readjust the "gain" and "bal" controls so that signals are of convenient operating amplitude.

(g) Determine ground and sky-wave components of the signals and decide whether ground or sky-wave matching is to be used.

(h) Use the "L-R" switch to position the upper (master) pulse selected for matching at the leading (left) edge of the upper pedestal.

(i) Set the "AFC" switch to the "on" position. Unless noise pulses cause pulse jitter, leave the "AFC" switch in this position for the remainder of the following procedures and leave the "antijam" switch in the "out" position. If heavy interference is encountered, leave the "AFC" switch off and set "antijam" switch to the "in" position.

(j) Use the "delay" crank in the "coarse" position to place the leading edge of the lower pedestal under the lower (secondary) pulse which corresponds to the selected master pulse.

(k) Set the "sweep function" switch to position 2.

(l) With the "delay" crank in the "fine" position, align the two selected pulses vertically.

(m) Set the "sweep function" switch to position 3.

(n) Match the two pulses, using the "delay" crank (in the "fine" position) "gain" and "bal" controls. (See fig. 8-5.)

(o) Record the "time difference" counter-reading.

(p) Repeat steps d through o, setting the "PRR" and "channel" switches to the pulse recurrence rate and channel corresponding to the others of the loran-A transmitting pairs.

(q) Apply necessary corrections to the "difference" readings, referring to Loran-A navigation tables or charts. Take into account the time of day at which readings were taken, whether received signals were strong or weak, and whether ground or sky waves were used to match signals. Plot lines of position.

(r) Obtain loran-A fix, considering the relative accuracy of the various lines of position which depend, among other things, on the spacing

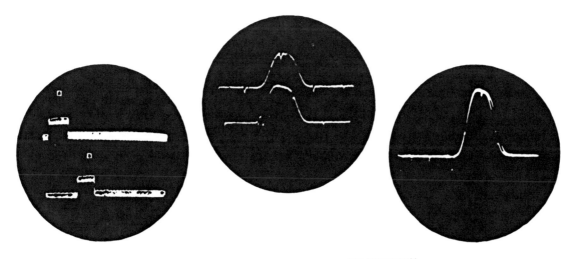

70.99(190)X

Figure 8-5. — Matching Loran-A signals.

of the lines of position in the geographical area of the ship.

(s) Compare the loran-A fix with other navigational information, and make the necessary record entries of the exact location of the ship.

(t) Turn the "power" switch to the "standby" or "off" position.

819. LORAN-C

Loran-C is a pulsed, hyperbolic, long-range navigation system, operating on a radio frequency of 90-110 kHz. It was developed for greater range and accuracy, and first became operational in 1957. Because of its lower frequency, and greater baseline distance (500 to 700 miles as compared to 200 to 400 miles in Loran-A), reasonable accuracy to 1200 nautical miles for ground waves and 3000 nautical miles for sky waves can be attained. Basic principles of operation are similar to those which apply to Loran-A, however, greater convenience of operation is provided.

A Loran-C network consists of one master and two or more secondary stations. As in Loran-A, the signal from the master activates each secondary station. Network arrangements include (a) the triad, with a master between two secondaries; (b) the star or "Y" formation with a master positioned between three secondaries; and (c) the square. It should also be noted that a master station may serve as a secondary station in another network. Loran-C uses a multi-pulsed transmission with eight pulses each 1000 ms, except for signals from the master station, which include a ninth pulse for identification. Pulses are phase-coded, which protects against interference from outside sources and reduces the contamination of ground waves by sky waves. Loran-C receivers are specially designed; however, the system is sufficiently compatible with Loran-A that receivers in the latter system can be modified for Loran-C use, except for 12 specific pulse recurrence rates, but with less accuracy. Phase measurement, which is helpful in station identification and in discrimination between ground waves and sky waves, as well as most other operations with Loran-C receivers, is automatic; read-outs are direct. The constant time difference obtained from the reading on one station pair, as in Loran-A, provides a hyperbolic line of position.

A major difference between systems is that in Loran-C, all stations share the same radio frequency (RF) channel. There are six basic pulse recurrence rates as follows:

H	33 1/2	pulses/second
L	25	pulses/second
S	20	pulses/second
SH	16 2/3	pulses/second
SL	12 1/2	pulses/second
SS	10	pulses/second

Associated with each basic pulse recurrence rate are eight specific pulse recurrence rates. As in Loran-A, specific pulse recurrence rates are separated from the basic pulse recurrence rate by multiples of 100 ms. Station type designators consist of one or more letters to indicate the basic pulse recurrence rate (H, L, S, SH, SL, or SS), a number (0-7) to indicate the specific pulse recurrence rate, and letters such as X or Y to indicate a particular secondary station.

Ground wave coverage is a function of propagation strength, and the strength of signal to noise ratio. Ground waves may extend as far as 2000 nautical miles and are normally reliable to 1200 nautical miles for 300 KW pulse power. First hop-E sky waves extend out to 2300 miles, and second hop-E sky waves may reach out to 3400 miles. To be sufficiently stable for use, complete darkness is usually necessary for receipt of second hop-E sky waves. Accuracy of Loran-C pulse transmissions, as made possible by phase comparison and longer baselines, depends upon atmospheric conditions, noise and interference. Ground waves are normally accurate to 0.1 percent of the distance traveled. Sky wave accuracy is usually to 3 to 5 miles.

Plotting procedures in Loran-A and Loran-C are similar. A single observation provides readings which establish lines of positions for all pairs within a network. For maximum accuracy, Loran-C tables (H.O. Pub. 221 series) may be used. In those circumstances in which modified Loran-A equipment is used, because of elapsed time between readings, it may be advisable to advance or retard certain LOPs using running fix procedures.

Loran-C provides for (a) electronic navigation; (b) systemized long-range time distribution; (c) time standardization between widely separated receiving locations; and (d) the study of electromagnetic wave propagation.

820. DECCA

Decca is a low frequency British hyperbolic radio navigation system first used in World

War II to guide allied forces to the Normandy beaches. It is highly accurate and reliable, and like other electronic systems, its operation, although slightly affected by atmospheric conditions, is not precluded by low visibility. In this system, chains are established, with each chain consisting of one master and three secondary stations. Preferably, the secondary stations are equally spaced on a circle with a radius of 70 to 80 miles and with the master station at the center. Decca operates in the 70 to 130 kHz band.

Secondary stations are identified by the colors purple, red, and green. These, and the master, transmit a continuous wave at different frequencies. A hyperbolic line of position is determined by the phase relationship of a secondary signal as compared with the signal of the master. Two secondaries and a master provide readings from which a fix can be obtained. The third secondary in a chain serves as a check. Fixes are plotted on Decca charts showing hyperbolic lines in color corresponding to that of the associated secondary station. The Decca receiver consists of four radio receivers, one for each frequency. By the reading of dials called Decometers, the necessary information for plotting a fix is obtained.

Decca coverage is available over most of Western Europe, in parts of the Indian Ocean including the Persian Gulf, along the coasts of Eastern Canada and the Northeastern United States, and along the coast of Southern California. Its reliable operational range, accurate to about 150 yards in daytime and 800 yards at night, is approximately 250 miles. Decca receivers may be carried in aircraft as well as ships.

United States and Canadian rights to the Decca system are held by the Pacific Division of Bendix Aviation Corporation, which also produces a long-range companion of Decca called Dectra. Useful to both ships and aircraft, Dectra primarily serves transatlantic aviation.

CHAPTER 9

ADVANCED ELECTRONIC NAVIGATION SYSTEMS

901. GENERAL

Electronic navigation, essentially an extension of piloting, has been characterized since 1950 by a proliferation of systems. Basic electronic navigation devices, as developed and earlier accepted for general use, were described in Chapter 8. This chapter, while not addressing all of the many new devices and systems in use today, provides basic descriptive data for the newer and more sophisticated systems in use.

One method of classification of electronic navigation systems, based upon the form of the line of position or fix obtained, includes five types or categories as follows:

(a) Hyperbolic — Loran and Decca, and as described in this chapter, Omega and some types of Raydist.

(b) Circular — Shoran, and Raydist.

(c) Azimuthal — Radio direction finder, and as described herein, Consol and Consolan.

(d) Range-bearing — Radar and Tacan. This includes "Ratan," a limited form of radar navigation described in this chapter.

(e) Motion sensing — As described herein, Satellite Navigation (NAVSAT), Inertial Navigation, and Acoustic Doppler.

A second and equally as valid a method of classification is based upon range, as follows:

(a) Short-range — Radar (including Ratan) and Shoran.

(b) Mid-range — Raydist.

(c) Long-range — Radio direction finder, Decca, and Loran, and as described in this chapter, Consol, Consolan, Omega, Satellite Navigation (NAVSAT), Inertial Navigation and Acoustic Doppler.

902. RATAN

Currently undergoing consideration and in limited use is the Radar Television Aid to Navigation, called RATAN. It is simply an extension or a refinement to radar navigation making use of shore stations, high-definition radar, and UHF television equipment, to transmit a radar image. The receiver, an inexpensive transistorized television receiver, provides a display of the shore line, channel buoys, lighthouses, other markers, and moving ship traffic. Whereas radar shows a ship as the focal point on a radar scope, RATAN presents a fixed background with the ship moving within the pattern. An added feature is a scan coverter which stores the radar image and identifies moving objects on the screen. Moving vessels are identified on the scope by their "fading tails," an indication of relative movement.

RATAN is important because it is an all-weather navigation device and inexpensive, but has the disadvantage of being dependent upon a transmitting station ashore. Furthermore, on board reception has been poor, and needed frequencies have not yet been allocated. Assuming that reception can be improved and frequencies allocated, it is being considered as a possible adjunct to Marine Traffic System Installations.

903. RAYDIST

Raydist, through precise tracking of CW transmitters, is useful in navigation, surveying, and other position plotting. It is used extensively by the National Ocean Survey, commercial organizations such as those engaged in offshore oil exploration, and foreign governments. An early form of Raydist, Type E was used for tracking the first U.S. satellites.

Raydist is considered here as a mid-range navigation system. It employs radio distance measuring to produce either circular or hyperbolic lines of position; however, types of Raydist earlier used to produce the latter are now gradually being replaced by circular distance measuring forms which are non-saturable and have greater potential for accuracy. An example of the newer forms is the Type N.

In operation, Raydist requires two CW transmitters on a baseline, with a separation of as much as 100 miles. Operating frequencies are in the 1.6 to 5 mHz range, permitting effective transmission beyond line of sight range. Depending upon power, ranges up to 200 miles may be reached. Stations differ by about 400 cycles per second, which permits phase comparison at other locations. An accuracy of one to three meters may be achieved.

Raydist equipment, including the transmitters, is generally small, compact, and light in weight. The equipment is fully automatic, providing a direct reading of phase comparison.

904. LORAN-D

This is a low-frequency, pulsed-type, semimobile, hyperbolic, navigation system. Being transportable, it can be moved to new areas and used as needed. The frequency range, as in Loran-C, is 90 to 110 kHz and signal characteristics are similar except that Loran-D uses groups of 16 pulses, repeated each 500 microseconds. The system is (a) highly accurate over a range of 500 miles using ground waves; (b) quite resistant to electronic jamming; (c) relatively mobile; and (d) equally useful in surface vessels and high speed aircraft.

905. CONSOL

Consol is a long-range, azimuthal, radio navigation aid. It was developed and used by the Germans (and known as SONNE) during World War II. It was later improved by the British. As a system, it can be considered as an improved version of the radio direction finder (RDF). An observer, using an ordinary receiver, interprets a pattern, and through either RDF or dead reckoning information, determines his sector of the pattern. Lines of position, with much greater accuracy than obtainable with RDF, are plotted on special charts. Maximum ranges reach 500 to 1400 nautical miles, generally with an LOP accuracy of a fraction of one degree. Minimum range is 25 to 50 nautical miles. It operates in a frequency range of 250 to 350 kHz.

Consol is highly reliable because of the simplicity of equipment. Consol transmitters, situated at consol shore stations, feed three antennas

with energy of the proper phase and amplitude, thus generating the field pattern. The receiver is equipped with an omnidirectional antenna. Consol stations are located in Western Europe, ranging from southern Spain to the Soviet Arctic.

906. CONSOLAN

Consolan is an American version of Consol, and accordingly is a long-range, azimuthal navigation system. In contrast with Consol, Consolan uses two transmitting antennas rather than three. Consolan increases coverage by using higher power levels and lower frequencies (190 to 194 kHz). The pattern generated is the same as that provided by Consol. Special charts and tables are provided for use with Consolan, by the U.S. Naval Oceanographic Office. U.S. Consolan stations are located in San Francisco and Nantucket.

907. OMEGA

A new electronic, hyperbolic, navigational system, similar to Loran, is Omega. It is a long range, pulsed, phase-difference, very low frequency (VLF) system, operating on a frequency of 10 to 14 kHz. It is a worldwide, all-weather system, of use to ships, aircraft, and submarines, including submarines submerged. Its accuracy is about one mile during the day and two miles during the night. Phase difference measurements are made on continuous wave (CW) radio transmissions. Like Loran, shore transmitting stations are used. Theoretically, six such stations are required for worldwide coverage; however, two additional stations are required to provide a degree of redundancy necessary to accommodate station repair.

In the Omega system, the phase-difference measurement of a 10.2 kHz signal transmitted from two stations provides a hyperbolic line of position. At least one additional phase-difference measurement is required to establish a fix, and two or more are desirable. Unlike other hyperbolic navigation systems, any two stations from which signals can be received may be paired to produce a line of position. Special charts are provided by the U.S. Naval Oceanographic Office for Omega plotting.

Since the wavelength of a 10.2 kHz signal is approximately 16 miles, and phase readings repeat themselves twice within this distance (see figure 9-1), lanes eight miles in width are established. Thus each lane or band is the equivalent in distance of one half of a wave length. The

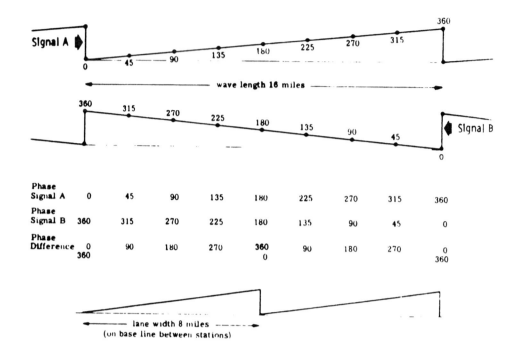

190.14X

Figure 9-1. — 1.2 kHz phase-difference measurement.

actual phase-difference reading establishes the line of position within the lane.

To avoid ambiguity in lane identification, Omega stations transmit also on 13.6 kHz, a frequency having a wave length exactly one third shorter than 10.2 kHz. Every fourth contour of this frequency coincides with every third contour on 10.2 kHz, and thus one broad lane matches three narrow lanes obtained on the 10.2 frequency.

All Omega stations transmit on the same dual frequencies, at different times. Eight stations share a ten second time interval. The receiver (see figure 9-2) identifies each station by its place in the sequence and by the precise time duration of its signal.

Long base lines of approximately 5000 nautical miles and sometimes as much as 6000 miles, are used. The system is serviceable to about 6000 miles. For greater accuracy of position, the navigator should consider the geometrical relationship and select station pairs yielding lines of position which will cross at angles of 60 to 90 degrees.

A technique known as differential Omega has been established to attain greater accuracy in a particular area. Two or more receivers are compared and the distance between them determined

from the difference in their readings. For example, one may be located at a known position ashore and its reading continuously broadcast, for comparison with readings obtained by vessels nearby. In this manner, long distance propagation errors can be generally eliminated.

Omega was developed in the early 1960's by the U.S. Navy for use throughout the Defense Establishment and commercially. It is simple for the user to operate, accurate, and provides worldwide coverage. At some future time it is possible that Omega will replace Loran.

908. SATELLITE NAVIGATION (NAVSAT)

As Project Transit, the U.S. Navy developed a Navy Navigation Satellite System at the Applied Physics Laboratory of the John Hopkins University. In use since 1964, the system now known as "NAVSAT" provides for accurate, all weather, world-wide navigation of surface ships, submarines, and aircraft. The accuracy is exceptional, the navigational error normally not exceeding 200 yards. Although NAVSAT was developed initially for naval use, it has been available to commercial shipping since 1968.

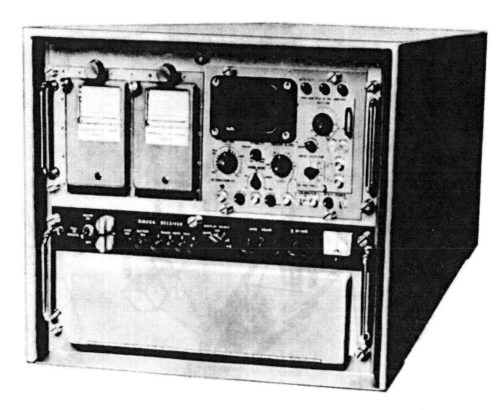

120.48
Figure 9-2. — AN/SRN-12 Omega Shipboard Navigation Receiver.

The operation of NAVSAT involves a phenomenon known as Doppler shift, which in radio waves is the apparent change in frequency when the distance between transmitter and receiver changes. Dependent upon relative motion, Doppler shift is proportional to the velocity of an approaching or receding NAVSAT satellite. With the approach, the frequency shifts upward; accordingly, with a satellite in recession, the frequency shifts downward. The Doppler shift actually experienced depends upon the position of the receiver with respect to the path of a transmitting satellite.

Components of the NAVSAT system include one or more satellites, ground tracking stations, a computing center, an injection station, accurate Greenwich mean or Universal time from the Naval Observatory, and the shipboard receiver and computer.

Each NAVSAT satellite travels in a polar orbit, at an altitude of approximately 600 nautical miles, circling the earth once each 105 minutes. The orbital planes of the satellites, while essentially fixed in space, intersect the earth's axis and make the satellites appear to be traversing the longitudinal meridians as the earth turns beneath

them. The orbital planes are separated by approximately 45° of longitude. Only one satellite need be used to establish a position. Each satellite continuously broadcasts data giving the fixed and variable parameters which describe its own orbit, together with a time reference. Periodically, approximately every 12 hours, a ground injection station broadcasts to each satellite, updating the data stored and enabling the satellite to broadcast current information. This updating information passed by an injection station is obtained from a computing center at Point Mugu, California which receives orbital inputs from a ground tracking station, and time from the Naval Observatory. See figure 9-3.

Because of the effect of the ionosphere upon radio waves, NAVSAT satellites use two ultra high broadcast frequencies, 150 and 400 mHz. As each frequency is differently affected by the ionosphere, Doppler signals received can be compared and the effect determined. Allowance is then made in position calculations for the ionospheric effect.

Unlike a planet in space, which travels in an elliptical orbit in accordance with Newton's laws

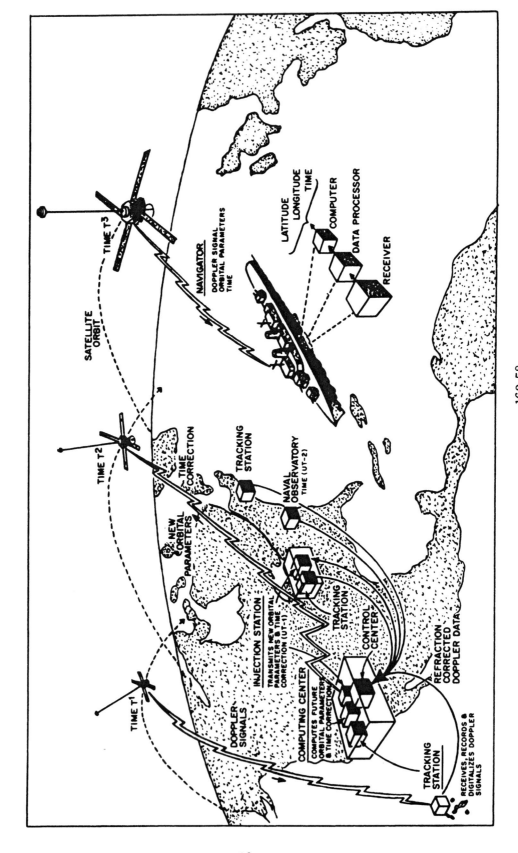

162.58

Figure 9-3. — NAVSAT.

of motion (see Appendix B), a NAVSAT satellite operating at an approximate altitude of 600 nautical miles is affected by the shape of the earth and its irregular gravitational field. Since it is not operating in a complete vacuum, the satellite experiences some atmospheric drag. It is also affected by the gravitational attraction of the sun and moon, charged particles in space, and the earth's magnetic field. These disturbances to the Keplerian orbit are predictable and can be computer programmed.

Four satellite tracking stations monitor the Doppler signal of the satellites as a function of time. The Naval Observatory monitors the satellite time signal. Comparison information is passed to the computing center. NAVSAT users receive operational information of the satellites or "birds" through messages from the U.S. Naval Astronautics Group, Point Mugu, California.

Shipboard equipment consists of a receiver, a computer, and a tape read-out unit. The ship's estimated position and speed are required as local inputs to the shipboard equipment. The estimated position need not be accurate; however, accuracy of the speed input is essential. An inaccuracy of one knot in ship's speed may cause an error of 0.25 miles in a NAVSAT fix. Speed errors with a mainly north-south component cause a greater position error than speed errors largely with an east-west component. The shipboard equipment is quite sophisticated and requires expert maintenance.

A NAVSAT fix can be obtained when a passing satellite's observed maximum altitude is between 10° and 70°. NAVSAT is most convenient to use inasmuch as the tape readout unit provides the latitude and longitude of the ship's position in typewritten form. In addition to being a convenient, all-weather system, NAVSAT has proved to be extremely accurate and reliable.

909. INERTIAL NAVIGATION

Inertial navigation is essentially an improved form of dead reckoning in which velocity and position are determined through relatively accurate sensing of acceleration and direction. Inertial systems, used for long range navigation, are completely self contained, require no shore support, and are independent of weather.

The first known application of inertial navigation was in the guidance system of German V-2 rockets. Following World War II, the United

States continued the development of inertial systems, with the first satisfactory system appearing in the early 1950's. U.S. models were first developed for use in aircraft, later were used in ballistic missiles and spacecraft, then widely used in Polaris submarines, and finally were accepted for general use in surface ships and attack submarines. The system used in the U.S. Navy is called the Ship's Inertial Navigation System (SINS), an early model of which was designed by the Massachusetts Institute of Technology and was installed by the Sperry Gyroscope Division of Sperry Rand Corporation in USS COMPASS ISLAND in 1956.

The inertial navigator through instrumentation measures the total acceleration vector of a vehicle in a gyroscope stabilized coordinate system. Integrating acceleration with time, and applying the computed components to initial velocities, makes it possible to determine actual velocity components and distances traveled. As in other forms of dead reckoning, any error, small though it may be, will with time contribute to a position error. Accordingly, using the systems approach, the position data is not only subjected to internal monitoring, but it is periodically corrected, based upon navigational information from external sources. For example, SINS can be associated with NAVSAT, sharing in some instances a SINS general purpose computer; the inertial position can be updated based upon satellite information.

The basic sensors used in inertial navigation are gyroscopes and accelerometers. Three gyroscopes are normally mounted on a platform as follows:

(a) Gyro "x" with its spin axis aligned in a North-South direction;

(b) Gyro "y" with its spin axis aligned in an East-West direction;

(c) Gyro "z" with its spin axis perpendicular to the "x" and "y" gyros.

The purposes of the "x" and "y" gyros are to sense roll and pitch of the ship, and through the use of torqueing motors, to keep the platform perpendicular to a line passing from the center of the platform to the center of the earth. The purpose of the "z" gyro is to supply heading. Thus the gyroscopes provide a stable platform and a direction reference.

Two accelerometers are used to establish acceleration in the North-South and the East-West directions. The accelerations and decelerations sensed by accelerometers are algebraically added to the speed stored in the computer, thereby continually updating the ship's speed. Such inputs in N-S and E-W components, are resolved by computor into actual or true speed. True speed and heading are continually used to update the ship's position, giving readouts in latitude and longitude.

Since the force of gravity can be interpreted as an acceleration by the accelerometers, it is vital that the accelerometer platform be kept in the proper plane and that unusual gravitational anomalies, such as unusually large vertical land masses, be noted and compensated.

Advances in computer technology have made it possible to make quite complicated mathematical calculations which are essential to inertial navigation. Sophisticated instrumentation measures the progress of a vessel in a spatial direction. By mechanization of Newtonian Laws of Motion, this complex system can provide position coordinates and other related information. For example, SINS provides a continuous read-out of latitude, longitude, and ship's heading. For stabilization purposes, it provides data on roll, pitch, and velocity. It provides information on ship's motion to NAVSAT; without SINS, inputs for course and speed must be given to the NAVSAT computer by the gyrocompass and log respectively. Currently, various inertial systems are coming into use to meet expanding navigational and other guidance requirements.

910. ACOUSTIC DOPPLER NAVIGATION

Acoustic Doppler, or Doppler sonar, is a relatively new development. It provides a new form of motion sensor, making it possible to measure (a) speed with respect to the bottom; (b) distance traveled; and (c) drift angle, which when added to true heading provides the true course made good over the bottom. In principle, it makes use of the phenomenon of "Doppler Shift" as in satellite navigation; it differs operationally from NAVSAT in that the Doppler shift measured is in a sea-water medium. Importantly, the Doppler shift phenomenon occurs throughout the frequency spectrum, and is equally applicable to visible light, electromagnetic waves, and acoustic or sound waves. Of prime consideration in Acoustic Doppler is the speed of sound, and signal attenuation and reverberation of sonic radiation in the sea-water medium.

Acoustic Doppler is in one respect similar to inertial navigation since both systems represent improvements to ordinary dead reckoning. Unlike inertial navigation, Acoustic Doppler is limited in depth. When the ocean bed is used for a reflecting surface, its use is limited by signal attenuation to depths under the keel of less than 100 fathoms. However, echoes from thermal gradients and marine life can be used in Doppler navigation, provided such reverberations produce a signal level greater than the noise level at the receiver.

A "Doppler Navigator" developed by the Raytheon Company and designated the AN/SQS-12, uses four beams of sonic energy, spaced 90° apart. Transducers, activated by a transmitter, send out the sound signal and receive the echo. Serving as hydrophones, the transducers convert the echoes into electrical energy. A receiver amplifies and compares the electrical input from the four transducers and develops the Doppler frequency. The receiver also, by comparison of frequency shifts, senses motion and direction. The transducer array is oriented geographically by an input from the ship's gyrocompass. It is also stabilized in the horizontal plane by the gyrocompass.

Acoustic Doppler Navigation with the AN/SQS-12, as in satellite and inertial systems, provides a highly accurate direct read-out of latitude and longitude, and automatic tracking. A smaller Doppler navigator developed for use in depths less than 250 feet by small craft, and designated the Janus SN-400, displays the results in digital form and requires manual plotting.

CHAPTER 10

NAUTICAL ASTRONOMY

1001. ASTRONOMY

Celestial navigation is dependent upon certain principles of astronomy, particularly as the latter relates to the positions, magnitudes, and motions of celestial bodies. Astronomy is considered to be the oldest of the sciences. The term "astronomy" is derived from the compounding of two Greek words, "astron" meaning a star or constellation, and "nomos" or law, and is translated literally as the "law of the stars." Ordinarily, it is defined as the science which treats of the heavenly bodies. It is indeed a science of great antiquity.

Three great systems of astronomy have evolved. The Ptolemaic system, now considered an hypothesis, was originated by the Alexandrian astronomer Ptolemy in the second century A.D. Ptolemy placed the earth at rest in the center of the universe, with the moon, Mercury, Venus, the sun, Mars, Jupiter and Saturn revolving about it. The second system, also an hypothesis, was originated by Tycho Brahe in the sixteenth century. Brahe had tried to reconcile astronomy with a literal translation of Scripture, and in so doing, developed a new concept of the solar system. In the Brahean system, the earth is at rest with the sun and the moon revolving about it; the other planets are considered to be revolving about the sun. The third system, which actually antedated that of Tycho Brahe, was conceived earlier in the sixteenth century by the mathematician and astronomer Nicolaus Copernicus. The Copernican theory, now universally adopted as the true solar system, places the sun at the center, with primary planets, including the earth, revolving about the sun from west to east. The earth is considered to be turning on its axis, and the moon is revolving about the earth. Other secondary planets revolve about their primaries. Beyond the solar system, fixed stars serve as centers to other systems. The Copernican concept is the basis of modern astronomy. Further refinements have been made by noted astronomers such as

Johann Kepler. Through his work, which followed that of Tycho Brahe, the true nature of planetary orbits was realized. (See Appendix B for Kepler's laws.)

With this brief introduction to astronomy, that portion with nautical significance is further considered. Predicted positions of celestial bodies will be compared with observed positions. Such comparisons provide the basis for celestial lines of position.

1002. UNIVERSE IN MOTION

Motion in the universe is viewed as actual and apparent. We will commence our study by considering the actual motion of (a) the earth, (b) the sun, (c) the planets, (d) the moon, and (e) the stars and galaxies.

a. The earth, the platform from which we observe the universe, engages in four principal motions as follows:

1. Rotation. The earth rotates once each day about its axis, from west to east. The period of rotation is the basis of the calendar day. We can prove the direction of rotation by observing the flow of water from an ordinary wash basin filled with water; when the stopper is removed and the water is allowed to run down the drain, the water will spiral clockwise in the southern hemisphere and counterclockwise in the northern hemisphere. The reason for this action by the water is that two forces are acting upon it. First, gravity acts to cause the water to flow down the drain. Secondly the rotation of the earth, a force that is considered to be concentrated at the earth's equator, acts upon the column of water causing spiral motion, the direction of the spiral depending upon which side of the concentrated force the water column happens to be located.

2. Revolution. The earth revolves about the sun once each year (365 1/4 days), from west to east. The period of revolution is the basis of the calendar year. The difference between rotation and revolution is that rotation is commonly used to refer to turning on an axis while revolution usually refers to travel in an orbit. The actual length of time required for the earth to complete one revolution is a little less than 365 1/4 days and therefore the establishment of an accurate calendar has been a problem. The Gregorian calendar, which replaced that of Julius Caesar, practically eliminated the discrepancy by the elimination of 3 leap years (3 days) per 400 years. This was accomplished by eliminating leap years on turns of the century not divisible by 400. For example, the years 1700, 1800, and 1900 were 365 days in length, while the year 2000 will be 366 days (leap year) in length. Although the calendar of Pope Gregory leaves something to be desired, its error is only 3 days in 10,000 years.

The earth's orbit is elliptical; during the winter months in the northern hemisphere, the earth travels nearer the sun, thus making the sun appear wider in diameter at that time. Also, due to the sun's proximity, the relative speed of the earth as compared to that of the sun is greater in winter than during the summer months in the northern hemisphere, resulting in northern winters being 7 days shorter than northern summers, and southern winters being 7 days longer than southern summers. The average speed of the earth in its orbit is 18 1/2 miles per second.

3. Precession. The earth precesses about an ecliptic axis (i.e., a line passing through the earth's center perpendicular to the plane of the earth's orbit) once each 25,800 years in a counterclockwise direction. This motion is analogous to the motion sometimes observed in a spinning top. When a top is spun, two forces act, (1) the spinning force which tends to keep the top upright and (2) the force of gravity which tends to pull the top from an upright position. The result of these two forces is precession, which is the conical motion of an axis around a perpendicular to the plane upon which it is spun. The earth has a spinning motion of rotation about its axis, which is not perpendicular to the plane of its orbit, and it is acted upon by the gravitational forces of attraction of the moon and the sun; these gravitational torques tend to align the earth's axis with the ecliptic axis. The result of the earth's precession is a difference in location of the stars in our heavens with respect to our north pole. At present, Polaris (north star) is almost directly

above the north pole of the earth. In years to come a vertical line through our north pole will point to other stars. It will point in the direction of Deneb in the year 10,000 and in the direction of Vega in 14,000. Again in the year 27,900 Polaris will be above our north pole.

4. Space Motion. The earth and the other members of our solar system are moving through space in the direction of the star Vega at a speed of about 12 miles per second.

b. The sun, the center of our solar system, rotates upon its axis, which is inclined 7 degrees to its path of travel, and travels through space as does the earth.

c. The planets of our solar system rotate upon their axes from west to east, revolve about the sun from west to east in ellipses of small eccentricity, and engage in space motion.

d. The moon, a secondary planet, rotates upon its axes from west to east, revolves about the earth from west to east once in 29 1/2 solar days, and joins other members of our solar system in space motion. The period of rotation of the moon upon its axis, the rotation of the earth, and the revolution of the moon about the earth, is so synchronized that from the earth we see but one side of the moon.

e. The stars engage in space motion and also rotation as does the sun. They are arranged in groups called galaxies. Our galaxy, the Milky Way, contains possibly 100 billion stars. The universe may contain 100 million galaxies, all of which have space motion independent of, and more significant than, the space motion of our solar system. The stars are considered to be an infinite distance from the earth.

A notable observation in the case of actual motion is that most bodies of the universe rotate from west to east, travel from west to east in their orbits, and according to some theories, behave in general as electrons in the structure of the atom.

The astronomer studies actual motion; the navigator concerns himself with apparent motion. The navigator stops the earth, so to speak, and observes the celestial bodies rise in the east, travel westward, and set in the west. The astronomer tabulates information which the navigator uses to fix his position.

1003. CELESTIAL SPHERE CONCEPT

Because of the necessity for location of celestial bodies in the heavens, we use a system of coordinates similar to latitude and longitude on the surface of the earth; the system established is known as the celestial sphere concept. The following terms constitute the concept:

CELESTIAL SPHERE. — A sphere of infinite radius with the earth as center. Whenever convenient we think of the earth as a point, and as a point it has no magnitude. We portray all of the heavenly bodies on the surface of the celestial sphere. We consider apparent rather than actual motion, and thus actual distances are immaterial.

CELESTIAL POLES. — Points on the surface of the celestial sphere which mark the point of intersection of the celestial sphere and the earth's axis extended. The north celestial pole is abbreviated Pn and the south celestial pole is abbreviated Ps.

ELEVATED POLE. — The celestial pole which corresponds in name to the observer's latitude.

EQUINOCTIAL. — A great circle on the surface of the celestial sphere everywhere 90 degrees from the celestial poles. Sometimes called the CELESTIAL EQUATOR, the equinoctial lies in a plane which is the plane of the equator extended to intersect the celestial sphere and which is perpendicular to the axis of the earth (and of the celestial sphere). The equinoctial, like the equator, supplies a reference for north-south measurement.

CELESTIAL MERIDIAN. — A great circle on the surface of the celestial sphere which passes through the celestial poles and over a given position on earth. There are an infinite number of celestial meridians. Each meridian has an upper branch (180 degrees of arc passing over a position and terminating at the celestial poles) and a lower branch (remaining 180 degrees of arc). In common usage, the term "celestial meridian" refers to the upper branch.

HOUR CIRCLE. — A half of a great circle on the surface of the celestial sphere which passes through a celestial body and terminates at the celestial poles. The hour circle, contrasted to the celestial meridian, moves with the celestial body progressively with time from east to west (since we consider apparent motion), while the position of the celestial meridian remains fixed. With knowledge of the earth's rotation (one turn upon its axis per 24 hours) we can realize that each celestial body crosses our meridian once each 24 hours. Dividing 360 degrees (number of degrees in a circle) by 24 hours, we find that an hour circle advances about 15 degrees per hour.

DECLINATION. — The angular distance of a body north or south of the equinoctial measured along the hour circle. Declination resembles latitude and like latitude must be labeled north or south. Declination is abbreviated "dec."

GREENWICH HOUR ANGLE (GHA). — The angle between the celestial meridian of Greenwich, England, and the hour circle of a body, measured westward along the arc of the equinoctial, and expressed in degrees from 0 to 360. Also equal to the angle at the celestial pole between the Greenwich celestial meridian and the hour circle, measured westward.

LOCAL HOUR ANGLE (LHA). — The angle between the celestial meridian of the observer and the hour circle of a body, measured westward along the arc of the equinoctial, and expressed in degrees from 0 to 360. Also equal to the angle at the celestial pole between the local celestial meridian and the hour circle, measured westward. In west longitude LHA is found by subtracting the longitude of the observer from the GHA. In east longitude LHA is found by adding the longitude of the observer to the GHA.

ECLIPTIC. — The apparent path of the sun among the stars over a period of a year; a great circle on the surface of the celestial sphere lying in a plane which intersects the plane of the equinoctial making an angle of approximately 23 1/2 degrees.

ZODIAC. — A belt extending 8 degrees to each side of the ecliptic. The apparent paths of all the planets within our solar system fall within this belt except for Venus which occasionally appears to travel outside the zodiac. The zodiac was divided into 12 sectors (signs) by the ancients to correspond to months, each sector being named for the constellation which the sun appeared to be passing through or near at that time. Each sector or sign extends 30 degrees in arc.

EQUINOXES. — Two great circles on a spherical surface share two points of intersection. The points of intersection of the equinoctial and the ecliptic are called the vernal equinox (March equinox) and the autumnal equinox. The sun normally arrives at the vernal equinox on March 21; at that time (the beginning of spring), the declination of the sun is 0 and the sun passes from south to north declination. The sun normally arrives at the autumnal equinox on September 23; at that time (the beginning of autumn), the declination is also 0 and the sun passes from north to south declination.

SOLSTICES. — When the sun reaches its maximum northern declination (23 1/2 N) on or about June 22, we speak of the time as the summer solstice (the beginning of summer). When the sun reaches its maximum southern declination (23 1/2 S) on or about December 22, we speak of the time as the winter solstice (the beginning of winter).

DIURNAL CIRCLE. — A small circle on the surface of the celestial sphere which describes the apparent daily path of a celestial body. The diurnal circle of the sun at the summer solstice projected to the earth is called the Tropic of Cancer; located 23 1/2 degrees north of the equator, and named for the sign of the zodiac containing the sun at that time, it marks the northern limit of the tropics. The diurnal circle of the sun at the winter solstice projected to the earth is called the Tropic of Capricorn; located 23 1/2 degrees south of the equator, and named for the sign of the zodiac containing the sun at that time, it marks the southern limit of the tropics. When the sun is over the Tropic of Cancer (summer solstice), its rays extend 90 degrees to either side causing continual daylight (midnight sun) in the region north of 66 1/2 degrees North Latitude, and continual darkness in the region south of 66 1/2 degrees South Latitude. When the sun is over the Tropic of Capricorn, the region north of 66 1/2 degrees North Latitude has continual darkness and the region south of 66 1/2 degrees South Latitude has continual daylight. This is the basis for our establishment of the Arctic and Antarctic Circles.

FIRST POINT OF ARIES. — Abbreviated by (the ram's horns or the Greek letter upsilon), the first point of Aries is a reference point on the ecliptic and is another name for the vernal or March equinox. Although it is an imaginary point,

we may establish an hour circle through it for measurement of sidereal hour angle and right ascension.

SIDEREAL HOUR ANGLE (SHA). — The angle between the hour circle of the first point of Aries and the hour circle of a body measured westward along the arc of the equinoctial, expressed in degrees from 0 to 360. The word "sidereal" normally means "of or pertaining to stars" and the SHA for navigational stars is tabulated in the Nautical Almanac. SHA, unlike the other hour angles, does not increase with time but remains relatively constant. The reason for this is that the hour circles between which the measurement is made are traveling at practically the same speed, and thus have a relative speed of nearly zero.

RIGHT ASCENSION. — The angle between the hour circle of the first point of Aries and the hour circle of a body, measured eastward along the arc of the equinoctial, and expressed in either degrees or in hours. Right ascension (in degrees) plus sidereal hour angle equals 360 degrees.

TRANSIT. — The passage of a body across a meridian. The crossing of the upper branch of the celestial meridian is the "upper transit"; the crossing of the lower branch is the "lower transit."

CULMINATION. — A synonym of "upper transit."

MERIDIAN ANGLE (t). — The angle between the celestial meridian of the observer and the hour circle of a body measured eastward or westward along the arc of the equinoctial from the celestial meridian, and expressed in degrees from 0 to 180. Meridian angle always carries a suffix "E" or "W" to indicate direction of measurement. When LHA is less than 180 degrees, t equals LHA, and is labeled west. When LHA is greater than 180 degrees, t equals 360-LHA, and is labeled east.

POLAR DISTANCE. — The angular distance of a body from the elevated pole measured along the hour circle. When declination and elevated pole are of the same name (both north or both south), polar distance is the complement of declination and may be referred to as co-dec. When elevated pole and declination are of different names (one north and one south), polar distance equals 90 degrees plus declination.

1004. TIME DIAGRAM

The relationship between various reference circles of the celestial sphere which measure angular quantities in an east-west direction may be best understood through the construction of a time diagram. This is a view of the celestial sphere, in the plane of the equinoctial, as seen from the south celestial pole. Easterly direction is clockwise and westerly direction is counterclockwise. A radial line is drawn from Ps in the center, in any direction, but generally in the vertical, to locate the celestial meridian of the observer. From the celestial meridian, using the observer's longitude, the celestial meridian of Greenwich is located and plotted. From the celestial meridian of Greenwich, using tabulated GHA's, the hour circles of the sun, the planets, the moon, and the first point of Aries may be plotted. From the hour circle of the first point of Aries, using SHA as tabulated, the hour circle of the stars may be located and plotted. This diagram makes possible the derivation of (1) LHA, and (2) t.

Typical time diagrams are illustrated in figure 10-1. Figure 10-2 illustrates certain additional relationships.

From the time diagram we may derive the following relationships:

$$LHA = GHA - W \lambda$$
$$LHA = GHA + E \lambda$$
$$GHA* = GHA\Upsilon + SHA*$$
$$LHA* = LHA\Upsilon + SHA*$$
$$RA = 360 - SHA$$
$$SHA = 360 - RA$$

t = LHA, if LHA is less than 180 degrees
t = 360 - LHA, if LHA is greater than 180 degrees.
    If t = LHA, t is west.
    If t = 360 - LHA, t is east.

1005. HORIZON SYSTEM OF COORDINATES

Location of points on the celestial sphere by declination and hour angle is not always practical for an observer, since the equinoctial is an imaginary circle. For the observer, the horizon offers a better reference. The horizon system employs the following terms.

ZENITH.— Point on the celestial sphere directly above the observer. Abbreviated "Z". A point on the surface of the earth having a star in its zenith is called the star's geographic position, sub-astral, or ground point.

NADIR.— Point on the celestial sphere directly below the observer. Abbreviated "Na."

CELESTIAL HORIZON.— A great circle on the surface of the celestial sphere everywhere 90 degrees from the zenith. The visual horizon is the line at which the earth appears to meet the sky. If a plane is passed through the observer's position and perpendicular to the zenith-nadir axis we have the sensible horizon. The visual horizon is corrected to the sensible horizon by application of a correction for height of observer's eye. If a plane is passed through the center of the earth perpendicular to the zenith-nadir axis, we have the rational horizon. When projected to the celestial sphere, both the sensible and the rational horizon meet at the celestial horizon. This occurs because the planes of the sensible and rational horizons are parallel and parallel lines meet at infinity (the radius of the celestial sphere).

VERTICAL CIRCLE.— A great circle on the surface of the celestial sphere passing through the zenith and nadir and through some celestial body. Although it is by definition a complete circle, in actual usage we speak of the 180 degrees through the body and terminating at the zenith and nadir respectively, as the vertical circle. In practice we make use of the 90 degree arc from the zenith to the horizon through the body; the remaining 90 degrees below the horizon is not visible and serves no purpose.

PRIME VERTICAL.— A vertical circle passing through the east and west points of the horizon. The prime vertical arc above the horizon terminates at the points of intersection of the equinoctial and the celestial horizon.

ALTITUDE (h).— The angular distance of a body above the horizon measured along the vertical circle.

ZENITH DISTANCE.— The angular distance of a body from the zenith measured along the vertical circle; it is the complement of the altitude and is abbreviated either "z" or "coalt."

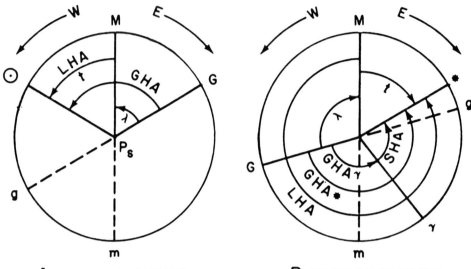

LEGEND:

M   – Upper branch of observer's meridian

m   – Lower branch of observer's meridian

G   – Upper branch of Greenwich meridian

g   – Lower branch of Greenwich meridian

⊙   – Hour circle of sun

♈   – Hour circle of First Point of Aries

✳   – Hour circle of star

Ps   – South Celestial pole

λ   – Longitude

GHA – Greenwich hour angle

LHA – Local hour angle

t   – Meridan angle

SHA – Sidereal hour angle

190.15

Figure 10-1.—Time diagrams. (a. West Longitude, b. East Longitude.)

AZIMUTH (Zn).— The true direction of a celestial body; the angle between the celestial meridian and the vertical circle measured right or clockwise from north to the vertical circle.

AZIMUTH ANGLE (Z).— The angle between the local celestial meridian and the vertical circle; the arc of the horizon measured from either the north or south points of the horizon (depending upon which pole is elevated) right or left to the vertical circle and expressed in degrees from 0 to 180. Azimuth angle must be prefixed by N or S to indicate which is the elevated pole, and suffixed by E or W to indicate the direction of measurement. If meridian angle is east, the suffix will be "E"; if meridian angle is west, the suffix will be "W."

We may establish certain relationships between azimuth and azimuth angle (see fig. 10-3) as follows:

(a) When azimuth angle is measured north to east (north pole elevated, east meridian angle), azimuth equals azimuth angle.

90

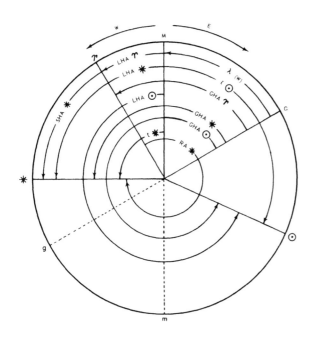

From the time diagram we may derive the following relationships:

LHA = GHA - W λ

LHA = GHA + E λ

GHA* = GHAϒ + SHA*

LHA* = LHAϒ + SHA*

RA = 360 - SHA

SHA = 360 - RA

t = LHA, if LHA is less than 180 degrees

t = 360 - LHA, if LHA is greater than 180 degrees

If t = LHA, t is west

If t = 360 - LHA, t is east.

190.16

Figure 10-2. — Time diagram.

(b) When azimuth angle is measured north to west (north pole elevated, west meridian angle), azimuth equals the explement of, or 360 minus, the azimuth angle.

(c) When azimuth angle is measured south to east (south pole elevated, east meridian angle), azimuth equals the supplement of azimuth angle.

(d) When azimuth angle is measured south to west (south pole elevated, west meridian angle), azimuth equals 180 degrees plus azimuth angle.

LATITUDE OF THE OBSERVER. — This value is projected on the celestial sphere as the angular distance between the equinoctial and the zenith, measured along the celestial meridian.

POLAR DISTANCE OF THE ZENITH. — The angular distance between the zenith and the elevated pole measured along the celestial meridian; the complement of the latitude and usually referred to as "co-lat."

1006. ASTRONOMICAL TRIANGLE

Combining the celestial sphere concept and the horizon system of coordinates (fig. 10-4A), we derive a triangle on the surface of the celestial sphere known as the astronomical triangle (fig. 10-4B). This triangle projected back to the earth's surface is the navigational triangle; in practice, the terms astronomical and navigational as applied to triangles are synonomous.

In the astronomical (or navigational) triangle as illustrated, two sides and the included angle are given (co-lat, t, co-dec) and the opposite side (co-alt) and one angle (Z) are solved for. Actually, latitude of the observer and co-lat are not known exactly, but are assumed, as is longitude in arriving at "t." The actual altitude is measured, and, by its comparison with the computed altitude, the discrepancy in the assumptions of latitude and longitude may be determined.

Solution of the astronomical triangle may be accomplished using the cosine-haversine law. However, practical navigators no longer resort to spherical trigonometry for the solution of the triangle. Instead they make use of such tables as H.O. 214 which actually are tabulations of the results of solutions of all possible triangles. In preparing these tables, it was customary to break the astronomical triangle into two right spherical triangles by dropping a perpendicular from one vertex to the opposite side. For convenience, these tables are so tabulated as to make unnecessary the computation of complements.

1007. SPECIAL CELESTIAL RELATIONSHIPS

The relationships below are worthy of note in any study of the celestial sphere:

(a) A body on the observer's celestial meridian has an azimuth of either 000 or 180 and is either at its greatest or least altitude depending upon whether it is transiting the upper or lower branch of the meridian.

(b) A body on the prime vertical has an azimuth of either 090 or 270.

91

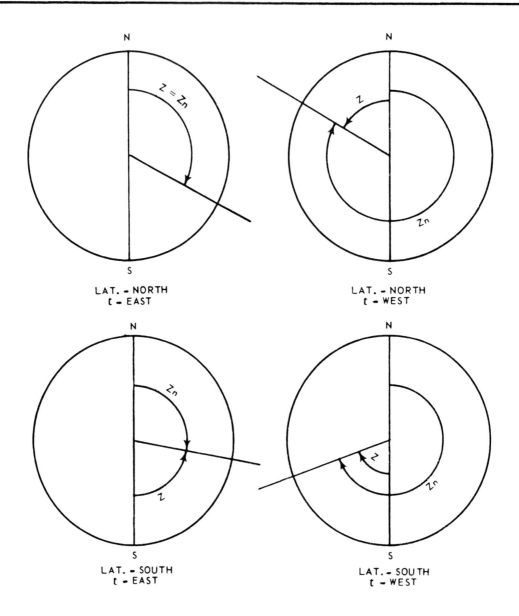

190.17

Figure 10-3. — Azimuth angles and azimuth.

(c) When a body is on the horizon it is either rising or setting.

(d) When the declination and latitude are of the same name, the body will be above the horizon more than half the time, and it will rise and set between the prime vertical and the elevated pole.

(e) If declination and latitude are of the same name and equal, the body will pass through the zenith. When in the zenith, it has no azimuth or azimuth angle.

(f) When the declination is of the same name as the latitude and numerically greater than the co-lat, the body is circumpolar (it never sets).

(g) When declination is 0 degrees, a body rises in the east and sets in the west.

(h) When the declination is of contrary name (as compared to latitude), and greater than the co-lat, the body never rises.

(i) At the equator, the celestial poles coincide with the celestial horizon. There are no

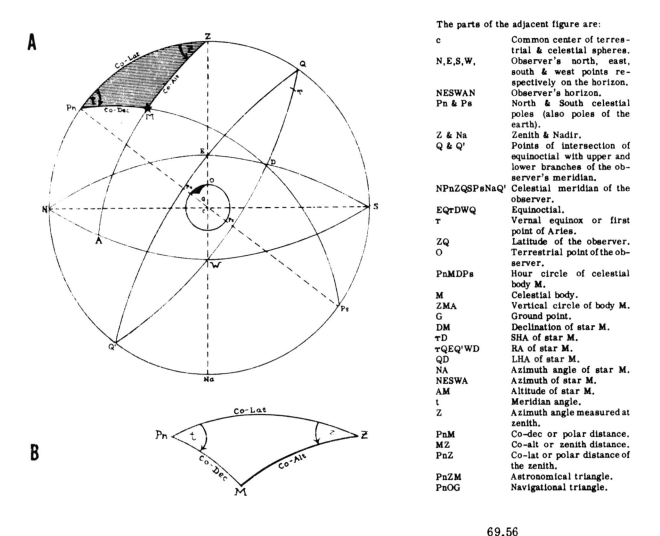

The parts of the adjacent figure are:

c	Common center of terrestrial & celestial spheres.
N,E,S,W,	Observer's north, east, south & west points respectively on the horizon.
NESWAN	Observer's horizon.
Pn & Ps	North & South celestial poles (also poles of the earth).
Z & Na	Zenith & Nadir.
Q & Q'	Points of intersection of equinoctial with upper and lower branches of the observer's meridian.
NPnZQSPsNaQ'	Celestial meridian of the observer.
EQᴛDWQ	Equinoctial.
ᴛ	Vernal equinox or first point of Aries.
ZQ	Latitude of the observer.
O	Terrestrial point of the observer.
PnMDPs	Hour circle of celestial body M.
M	Celestial body.
ZMA	Vertical circle of body M.
G	Ground point.
DM	Declination of star M.
ᴛD	SHA of star M.
ᴛQEQ'WD	RA of star M.
QD	LHA of star M.
NA	Azimuth angle of star M.
NESWA	Azimuth of star M.
AM	Altitude of star M.
t	Meridian angle.
Z	Azimuth angle measured at zenith.
PnM	Co-dec or polar distance.
MZ	Co-alt or zenith distance.
PnZ	Co-lat or polar distance of the zenith.
PnZM	Astronomical triangle.
PnOG	Navigational triangle.

69.56

Figure 10-4. — The celestial sphere. B. Astronomical triangle.

circumpolar stars nor stars that never rise. Stars rise and set in planes which are perpendicular to the plane of the horizon.

(j) At the poles, the equinoctial coincides with the celestial horizon, the only bodies visible are those with a declination of the same name as latitude, and all these are circumpolar. Altitude then equals declination, and azimuth is insignificant since all directions at the north pole are south and at the south pole all directions are north.

CHAPTER 11

TIME

1101. INTRODUCTION

With the nautical astronomy background gained through the study of Chapter 10 as a prerequisite, the practice of celestial navigation may now be approached, commencing with a brief study of time and timepieces.

During the Newtonian era, great advances in mathematics and in the physical sciences made available (a) a great deal of information concerning the positions of stars and planets; (b) greater knowledge of gravitation; and (c) more information in general concerning the celestial bodies beyond our solar system. The Post-Newtonian era was characterized by the practical application of the new knowledge of astronomy.

An early problem was that of determining longitude at sea. As we shall see in Chapter 13, latitude can be readily determined by a meridian sight without knowledge of exact time or resort to spherical trigonometry. However, longitude can not be so easily obtained. Accordingly, in 1714, British sea captains petitioned the House of Commons for a solution to the problem of determining longitude. By 1735, John Harrison had produced a marine chronometer which advanced considerably the practice of navigation, making it possible to more accurately compute longitude.

1102. TIME MEASUREMENT

With this brief historical introduction, time may now be defined as the sum of all the days in the past, today, and all the days of the future. However, we think of time, as a quantity which can be measured. Time may be expressed as a measured duration, such as three hours, and also as "clock time," for example, 0200. The instrument for making this measurement is a timepiece. The earth is our celestial timepiece. Each turn upon its axis provides a unit of time known as the day. Time is important to the navigator

because as we have seen, of its relationship to longitude.

Two general types of time measurement are solar time and sidereal time. Solar time is based upon the rotation of the earth with respect to the sun while sidereal time is based upon the rotation of the earth with respect to the stars.

1103. SOLAR TIME

We will at first restrict our discussion to solar time, commencing with a type called apparent time which is time measured upon the basis of the apparent motion of the real sun. By apparent time, when the sun transits the upper branch of the local celestial meridian, the time is spoken of as local apparent noon (LAN) or 1200 apparent time. When the sun transits the lower branch of the local celestial meridian, the time may be spoken of as local apparent midnight or 2400 (also 0000). Unfortunately, the length of the apparent day varies. This results because of two reasons:

(a) The ellipticity of the earth's orbit. The earth when relatively near the sun rotates once with respect to the sun in less time than when relatively far from the sun. This occurs because the earth is moving in its orbit while rotating.

(b) The sun's apparent movement with respect to the earth is faster at the solstices, when the sun is moving almost parallel to the equinoctial, than at the equinoxes when the direction of the sun's apparent motion has a larger north-south component.

Since apparent days are unequal in length it is impractical for man-made timepieces to keep apparent time, and as an expedient we have averaged the length of the 365 1/4 apparent days (1 solar year) and arrived at a measurement known as mean time. One mean day is 24 hours in length, each hour consisting of 60 minutes and each minute consisting of 60 seconds. We can say that mean time is based upon the motion of an imaginary sun moving westward in the equinoctial at a uniform speed. At the instant the imaginary sun transits the upper branch of the local celestial meridian, we witness local mean noon (1200 local mean time), and at the instant the imaginary sun transits the lower branch of the local celestial meridian, we observe local mean midnight (2400 or 0000 local mean time). The difference between mean time and apparent time is the "equation of time," a value which is tabulated in the Nautical Almanac.

Mean time changes with longitude, and since there are an infinite number of local celestial meridians the keeping of mean time is a system lacking in uniformity. To keep a timepiece set to mean time, we would have to reset it with each change in position. Since this would be just as impractical as using apparent time, we have established standard or zone time, (fig. 11-1) abbreviated ZT, which provides that a zone 15 degrees wide in longitude may keep the same time throughout the zone. THE ZONE TIME OF ANY ZONE IS THE MEAN TIME OF THE CENTRAL MERIDIAN. The geographic extent of the time zone is 7 1/2 degrees to either side of the central meridian. The local mean time for a meridian may be converted to zone time. This is accomplished by (1) converting the difference in longitude (between local and standard meridians) from arc to time, and (2) adding such correction to the local mean time if the local meridian is to the west and subtracting it if to the east. See articles 1303 and 1305 for examples of conversion of local mean time to zone time. Conversely, zone time may be converted to local mean time. The origin of time zones is the meridian of Greenwich which is the central meridian of time zone "0." Time zone 0 keeps standard or zone time which is exactly the same as the mean time of Greenwich, abbreviated GMT. In all time zones, except 0 zone, the longitude of the central meridian is divisible by 15. Each time zone is assigned a zone description (ZD). The zone description consists of a number from 0 to 12 commencing with 0 at Greenwich and counting both to the east and to the west. Time zones in the eastern hemisphere are distinquished from the time zones in the western hemisphere by a prefix; eastern time zones are prefixed by a minus sign while western time zones are prefixed by a plus sign. The zone description indicates the hours difference between the zone time of a zone and GMT; applying the ZD in accordance with sign to the ZT we arrive at

GMT. For example, longitude 175 West is in a time zone known by the zone description + 12 (175/15). If the zone time is 11-09-22 (conventional means of expressing hours, minutes, and seconds), then GMT is 11-09-22 plus 12-00-00 or 23-09-22. If our longitude is 36 East, our ZD must be -2, and if ZT is 08-16-32, GMT must be 08-16-32 minus 02-00-00 or 06-16-32. Since we can find GMT by applying the ZD according to sign to the ZT, conversely, we can find ZT by applying the ZD with the sign reversed to GMT.

The 180th meridian is the central meridian of time zone 12 which is common to both hemispheres. However the half in the eastern hemisphere has a ZD of -12, and the half in the western hemisphere has a ZD of +12. For this reason, and since the Greenwich time zone is known as 0, we have 24 time zones but 25 zone descriptions.

Sometimes, in order to make the best use of daylight hours, all clocks are advanced 1 hour; this system of keeping time is call daylight saving time. In time of war, clocks may be advanced 1 hour and the time referred to as war time. When either daylight saving or war time is being kept, in effect, the zone is keeping the standard time of the adjacent zone to eastward, and instead of observing the sun on the meridian between 1130 and 1230, upper transit of the central meridian will occur normally between 1230 and 1330.

The time zone system has been generally adopted except in Saudi Arabia, in the polar regions, and in a few remote islands. Saudi Arabia keeps "Arabic time" by which all timepieces are set to midnight at sundown. Through island groups and over land, the time zone boundaries may be somewhat irregular. For example, the eastern time zone in the U.S. (ZD + 5) is separated from the central time zone (ZD + 6) in the north by the west shore of Lake Michigan and in the extreme south by the Appalachicola River of Florida. Ordinarily at sea, as a ship proceeds from one time zone to another, ship's clocks are reset. When traveling in company with other vessels, the officer in tactical command may be expected to initiate the signal. When steaming independently, the zone time is changed at the discretion of the commanding officer. When traveling eastward, zone time

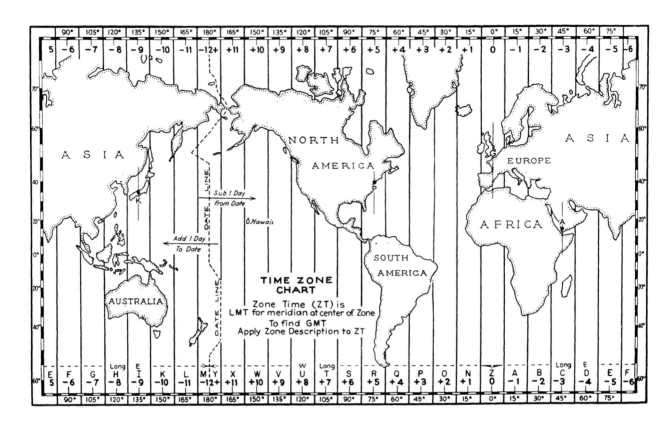

13.76(69)

Figure 11-1. — Standard time zones.

is changed by advancing the clocks 1 hour. When traveling westward, the clocks are retarded 1 hour upon entering a new time zone.

When the sun transits the celestial meridian of Greenwich, the date throughout the world is the same. At every other instant, there are two dates in the world simultaneously. The new local date at a given location on the earth begins with the sun's transit of the lower branch of the celestial meridian; the new Greenwich date begins with the sun's transit of the 180th meridian (which with occasional deviations for the benefit of island groups is the international date line). Within the 12th time zone all time is the same but the date in the western hemisphere section is always 1 day earlier than in the eastern hemisphere section. When traveling from the western hemisphere to the eastern we advance the calendar 1 day (for example, 2 Jan. to 3 Jan.); when traveling from the eastern hemisphere to the western hemisphere

we retard the calendar 1 day (for example, 2 Jan. to 1 Jan.).

In a time diagram if the hour circle of a celestial body plots between the lower branches of the local celestial meridian and the Greenwich celestial meridian, the local date differs from the Greenwich date. If the local meridian is in west longitude the Greenwich date is 1 day later than the local date; if the local meridian is in east longitude, the local date is one day later than the Greenwich date. When ZD is applied to ZT to obtain GMT, if the GMT is over 24 hours, then 24 hours must be subtracted; the remainder is the GMT and the Greenwich date is 1 day later than the local date. If, when ZD is applied to ZT to obtain GMT, the result is anticipated to be a minus value because of the necessity of subtracting ZD, the navigator adds 24 hours to the ZT before subtracting the ZD and notes that the Greenwich date is a day earlier than the local date. It is necessary to know the Greenwich mean time and Greenwich date because upon it all tabulated astronomical data used by the navigator is based.

EXAMPLE 1: Convert ZT 0800 15 Dec. in ZD + 4 to GMT.

SOLUTION:
ZT   0800 15 Dec.

ZD   +4
_____

GMT 1200 15 Dec.

EXAMPLE 2: Convert ZT 1500 28 Dec. in longitude 81°E to GMT.

SOLUTION:
ZD = 81/15 = -5

ZT   1500 28 Dec.

ZD   -5
_____

GMT 1000 28 Dec.

EXAMPLE 3: Convert ZT 0500 12 Jan. in longitude 167° -30'E to GMT.

SOLUTION:
ZD = 167 - 30/15 = -11

ZT 0500 12 Jan. or   2900 11 Jan.

ZD   -11
_____

GMT   1800 11 Jan.

EXAMPLE 4: Convert 0600 14 Feb. GMT to ZT in longitude 120°W.

SOLUTION:

ZD = 120/15 = +8

GMT 0600 14 Feb.   or   3000 13 Feb.

ZD +8 (with sign reversed) -8
_____

ZT   2200 13 Feb.

1104. TIME AND ARC

Since the equinoctial is a circle containing 360 degrees, and since there are 24 hours in a day, we may use these figures to establish a basis for the conversion of arc to time and time to arc. The conversion is as follows:

Time		Arc
24 hrs.	=	360°
1 hr.	=	15°
60 min.	=	15°
4 min.	=	1°
4 min.	=	60'
1 min.	=	15'
60 sec.	=	15'
4 sec.	=	1'
4 sec.	=	60''
1 sec.	=	15''

EXAMPLE 1: Convert 344° 16'33'' to time.

344° = 22 hrs. 56 min.

16' =   1 min.   4 sec.

33'' =   2.2 sec.
_____

Answer: 22 hrs. 57 min. 6.2 sec.

EXAMPLE 2: Convert 18 hrs. 37 min. 20 sec. to arc.

18 hrs. =   270°

37 min. =   9° 15'

20 sec. =   5'
_____

Answer: 279° 20'

An easier method of conversion is offered by a conversion table in the back of the Nautical Almanac. (See Appendix F-3)

1105. SIDEREAL TIME

Sidereal time, or star time, is based upon the earth's rotation with respect to the stars. Sidereal and solar time differ in the four following ways:

(a) Reference. The sun is the reference point for solar time; the first point of Aries is the reference point for sidereal time.

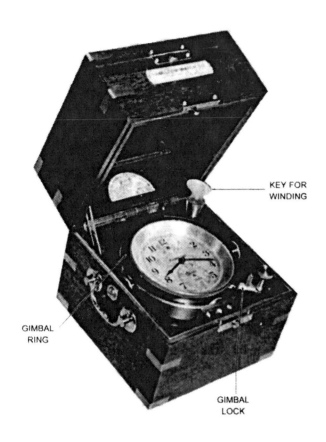

KEY FOR
WINDING

GIMBAL
RING

GIMBAL
LOCK

69.38
Figure 11-2. — Ships chronometer in its case.

(b) Commencement of Day. A solar day commences when the sun transits the lower branch of the local celestial meridian (midnight); a sidereal day commences when the first point of Aries transits the upper branch of the local celestial meridian (sidereal noon).

(c) Date. There is no sidereal date.

(d) Length of Day. A sidereal day is 3 minutes and 56 seconds shorter than a solar day which provides for 366 1/4 sidereal days in a solar year (365 1/4 solar days). The reason for a sidereal day being shorter is the fact that while the earth rotates with respect to the sun it also travels in its orbit. When the earth has rotated once with respect to the stars, its travel in its orbit has necessitated that it turn almost an additional degree in order to have rotated once with respect to the sun.

1106. TIMEPIECES

Timepieces, as previously introduced in art. 309, consist of chronometers, comparing watches, ship's clocks, and stop watches.

The chronometer (fig. 11-2) is the navigator's most accurate timepiece. There are two sizes. The larger, referred to as size 85, is a regular ship's chronometer, made by the Hamilton Watch Company. The smaller, size 35, is a high-grade watch, and is often referred to as a chronometer watch. It is usually stowed so as to be protected against shock, electrical influence, and extreme changes in temperature. Most vessels carry 3 chronometers for comparison purposes thus making it possible for the quartermaster to readily detect the error in any instrument which may develop an erratic rate. The chronometer is set to GMT and never reset until returned to a chronometer pool (source of chronometers used in Navy ships) for cleaning and adjustment which is necessary every 2 to 3 years. The chronometer is wound daily at 1130; this (and the fact that a comparison was made) is reported at 1155 to the commanding officer as part of the 12 o'clock report. Chapter 9240, Section I, Part 3, of the Naval Ships Technical Manual and the chronometer record book contain detailed instruction for chronometer care.

Time signals, for checking the current accuracy of chronometers, may be received from Radio Stations WWV and WWVH, of the National Bureau of Standards, Department of Commerce, transmitting from Colorado and Hawaii respectively, and from Naval Radio Station, NSS, Annapolis, Maryland. Upon receiving a radio time signal, the quartermaster checks the chronometer and establishes the chronometer error, labeling it fast or slow as appropriate. The average daily difference in error, called the daily rate and labeled "gaining" or "losing," is also computed and recorded. With the chronometer error for a given date in the past, and the daily rate, we can predict the chronometer error for either the present or a future date.

Quartz oscillator clocks are coming into use as marine chronometers. Currently, military specifications for such timepieces are being prepared. These clocks, which are electrically (usually battery) powered, are known to be exceptionally accurate. They are also quite resistant to shock and vibration and do not require gimbal mounting.

The comparing watch is a high grade pocket watch carried by the navigator or quartermaster when making celestial observations. It may be set exactly on GMT since by extending the stem the second hand may be stopped; to set the watch on GMT the quartermaster must mentally consider current chronometer error. Some navigators prefer setting the comparing watch to zone time which necessitates the application of ZD in order to find GMT. If the quartermaster is unsuccessful in setting the watch exactly to zone time or GMT, he should ascertain the watch error (WE on ZT or WE on GMT). Such correction must be applied to the watch time of each observation.

A stop watch may be started upon making a celestial observation; then upon subsequent observations the seconds elapsed may be recorded. At a given instant, upon completion of celestial observations, a comparison may be made with the chronometer and the chronometer time of observation (or observations) computed. By applying the current chronometer error to the chronometer time we arrive at correct GMT. The only advantage of a stop watch is that the second hand reading is easier to make. Whenever reading time for an observation, the hands should be read in the order of their speed — second hand, minute hand, hour hand.

Marine clocks, designated according to usage as boat, deck, or general purpose clocks, are normally of the eight day mechanical type. Some general purpose clocks have 24 hour dials; all others have 12 hour dials. Marine clocks are manufactured by the Chelsea Clock Company, and by Seth Thomas Clocks, Division of General Time Corporation. Clocks are normally wound weekly, and reset as necessary when wound. After winding and setting, the bezel or case must be closed to prevent dust from entering the case.

CHAPTER 12

SIGHT REDUCTION

1201. INTRODUCTION

In the advancement of the practice of celestial navigation, perhaps the milestone next following the appearance of Harrison's chronometer was the discovery in 1837 by an American shipmaster, Captain Thomas A. Sumner, of a solution for a celestial line of position. From the observation of an altitude of the sun, he made three computations for longitude using a different latitude in each, because of uncertainty as to his latitude. After a plot of three positions from these computations, he noted that the three could be connected by a straight line, which he correctly assumed to be a locus or line of position. Subsequently, a landfall gave further evidence of the correctness of his assumption. Since Sumner's discovery, solution for and use of such a line of position, has been the essence of celestial navigation.

Unfortunately, to obtain a "Sumner's line," multiple computations are required. However, in 1875, the computation was simplified by a procedure introduced by Commander Marcq de St. Hilaire, French Navy. By the St. Hilaire or "Altitude Intercept" method, the altitude and azimuth of a celestial body are computed for an approximate or assumed position of the ship at a given time of observation. By comparison of the observed altitude and the computed altitude, the difference, known as "intercept," is determined in minutes of arc. A line is drawn through the assumed position from which the computed altitude was obtained, in the direction of the azimuth. If the observed altitude is greater than the computed, the observer is nearer the body, and conversely, if the computed altitude is greater than the observed, the observer is farther away; accordingly, the intercept in minutes of arc is directly converted to nautical miles and is measured from the assumed position along the azimuth line, toward or away from the celestial body, as appropriate. At the point thus

established, a line of position is drawn, at right angles to the azimuth line. This celestial line of position, although a straight line, is representative of a short arc, taken from a circle of equal altitude drawn about the geographical position (GP) of the observed body. See figures 12-1 and 12-2. Mathematically, a Sumner's line is actually a chord of such a circle; the Marcq de St. Hilaire line is a tangent.

The altitude intercept method as introduced by Commander St. Hilaire was widely adopted. For solution of the astronomical or navigational triangle for computed altitude and azimuth, the use of a cosine-haversine formula was adopted, a haversine of an angle being equal to one half the quantity of one minus the cosine of such angle. Thus, the solution of the triangle, while somewhat easier, still required resort to spherical trigonometry. However, the solution was further simplified by Ogura of Japan, among others, and in the 1930's several new methods were introduced, making use of tables of solutions for spherical triangles of various dimensions.

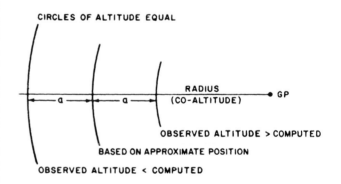

190.18

Figure 12-1.—Relationship of circles of equal altitude and intercept "a."

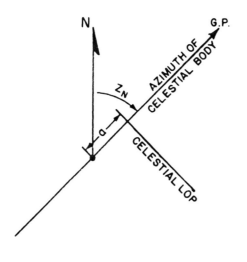 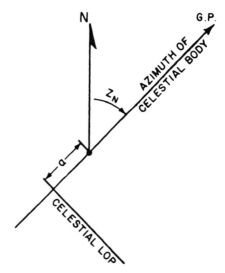

ALTITUDE INTERCEPT "A" IS
"TOWARD", AS ALTITUDE OBSERVED
IS GREATER THAN COMPUTED.

ALTITUDE INTERCEPT "A" IS
"AWAY", AS ALTITUDE OBSERVED
IS LESS THAN COMPUTED.

190.19
Figure 12-2.—Plot of LOP.

In this chapter, sight reduction by later and more modern methods will be described, together with the plotting of celestial lines of position and celestial fixes. Preliminary to actual sight reduction, the marine sextant and its use, corrections to sextant altitudes, the use of the Nautical Almanac for finding Greenwich hour angle and declination, and the computation of meridian angle from Greenwich hour angle, will be considered.

1202. MARINE SEXTANT

Previously introduced in Art. 308, the sextant (figure 12-3) is used to measure altitudes of celestial bodies above the visual horizon. Measurement is effected by bringing into coincidence the images, one direct and one reflected, of the visual horizon and the celestial body. The sextant was so named because its arc represents approximately one-sixth of a circle. Nevertheless, because of its optical principle of double reflection as briefly described herein, the sextant can usually measure twice as much arc, or something greater than a third of a circle. Its optical principle was first described by Sir Isaac Newton and later independently rediscovered in 1731 by Hadley in England and Godfrey in Philadelphia.

The marine sextant consists of the following parts:

A. Frame—Support for other parts.
B. Limb—An arc (approximately 1/6 of a circle) graduated in degrees.
C. Index arm—Arm pivoting from center of curvature; lower end indicates reading on limb and mounts the micrometer drum.
D. Micrometer—Provides a scale for reading minutes and tenths of minutes.
E. Index mirror—Mirror on upper end of index arm which is perpendicular to the plane of the limb.
F. Horizon glass—A glass window, the left half of which is clear glass and the right half a mirror, mounted on frame and parallel to the index mirror at an instrument setting of 0 degrees.
G. Telescope—Inserted in collar attached to frame to magnify field of vision.
H. Index and horizon filters (in some instruments, shades).

The optical principle upon which the sextant is based is that the angle between the first and last direction of a ray of light that has undergone two reflections in the same plane is twice the

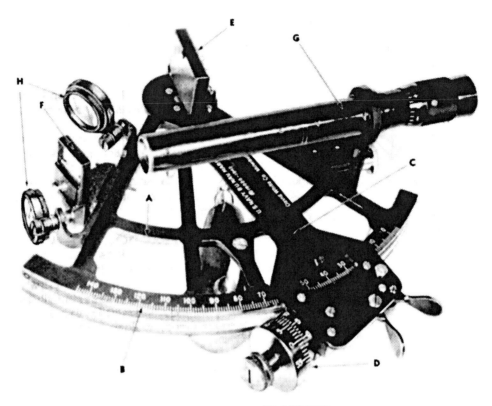

29.268(190)
Figure 12-3.— Marine sextant.

angle that the two reflecting surfaces make with each other.

To make a reading with the sextant, set the index arm to 0 degrees. Look through the mirror half of the horizon glass at the celestial body which also appears in the clear glass half. Move the index arm forward slowly, at the same time tilting the instrument forward, until the reflected image is in coincidence with the horizon. Fine adjustment may then be made using the microm-eter drum on the index arm. Read altitude in degrees on the limb, read minutes on the forward movable part of the drum at the 0 mark, and read tenths of a minute on the micrometer scale (which makes a 10:9 ratio with the minutes scale).

In observing a star or a planet, bring the center of the star or planet into coincidence with the horizon. In the case of the sun, normally the lower limb (lower edge) is brought into coincidence; however, if the upper limb is more clearly defined, an upper limb shot may be taken if so identified. Moon observations, like sun ob-servations, may be of either limb.

In observing stars, if difficulty is experienced in bringing stars to the horizon, the instrument may be inverted and the index arm moved to bring the horizon up to the celestial body without any tilt of the instrument or movement of the field of vision.

When the horizon is "fuzzy," or indefinite directly beneath a celestial body, the navigator may face the reciprocal of its azimuth and use the sextant to measure the supplement of the altitude. When this is done in the case of the sun or the moon, if a lower limb observation is desired the navigator makes what appears to him to be an upper limb observation, other-wise he must add the sun's (or moon's diameter to the sextant reading.

Before or after observing altitudes with the sextant, the navigator determines index correc-tion, a current error in his instrument. To do this, he sets the instrument on absolute zero and looks through the horizon glass at a distant horizon. If the horizon forms an unbroken line in both halves of the horizon glass, the index correction (abbreviated IC) is 0. If the line is broken, he should move the micrometer drum until it is straight and read the discrepancy between absolute 0 and the corrected reading. If the corrected drum setting moves the index arm to the right of 0 on the limb, the IC is additive. If the corrected drum setting moves the index arm to the left of 0 on the limb, the IC is subtractive.

If a sextant is in complete adjustment the following will be true:

(a) The index mirror will be perpendicular to the plane of the limb.

(b) The horizon glass will be perpendicular to the plane of the limb.

(c) The horizon glass will be parallel to the index mirror at absolute zero.

(d) The line of sight of the telescope (if used) will be parallel to the plane of the limb.

The index mirror is perpendicular to the plane of the instrument if the limb and its reflection appears in the index glass as an unbroken line. The horizon glass is perpendicular to the plane of the instrument if when tilted and set to 0, the horizon appears as an unbroken line in both halves of the glass. The horizon glass and the index mirror are parallel if at a 0 setting (untilted), the horizon appears as an unbroken line in both halves. To adjust, two set screws are associated with each mirror. Always slack off on one set screw before tightening its mate. In addition to the mirrors, the collar of the telescope should be adjusted if the extended line of sight (axis of the telescope) diverges from the extended plane of the instrument.

Sextants are equipped with colored filters or shades for sun observations; these lenses protect the navigator's eyes from the bright rays of the sun.

An excellent marine sextant used today is known generally as the endless tangent screw sextant.

1203. CORRECTING SEXTANT ALTITUDES

The altitude of a celestial body as observed by a navigator does not necessarily correspond to the altitude measured from the celestial horizon. To differentiate, we abbreviate sextant altitude as Hs and observed altitude as Ho. Sextant altitude (Hs) is corrected or converted to Ho by applying corrections for the following:

INDEX CORRECTION (IC).—A correction peculiar to an individual instrument and changeable in value. May be a plus or minus correction.

DIP (D).—The horizon from which measurement is referenced depends upon the altitude (height above sea level of the observer); at higher altitudes the horizon is at a greater distance and sextant altitude will read in excess of altitude based upon the true celestial horizon. Dip is always a minus correction and increases with the height from which the observation is made.

REFRACTION (R).—When the rays of light pass from a less dense medium (space) to a more dense medium (earth's atmosphere), they are bent toward the vertical, resulting in the celestial body appearing higher than its actual position. Refraction error is maximum at low altitudes, making observations of bodies having altitudes less than 10 degrees less reliable; the error decreases at higher altitudes, and is zero at an altitude of 90°. The correction for refraction is always a minus correction.

AIR TEMPERATURE—ATMOSPHERIC PRESSURE (TB).—An additional correction for refraction due to nonstandard atmospheric conditions. May be a positive or negative correction.

PARALLAX (P).—The center of the earth is considered to be the center of the celestial sphere. For all bodies beyond our solar system, the distance is so great as compared to the radius of the earth that the latter is of no consequence. In the case of bodies within our solar system, their distance is not so great when compared to the earth's radius and we must take into account the earth's radius to reduce the sight to the altitude as measured from the center of the earth. Parallax at altitude 0° is called horizontal parallax (HP). Parallax is always a plus correction, and is maximum at altitude 0°.

SEMIDIAMETER (SD).—Tabulated Astronomical data is normally based upon the center of celestial bodies. However, it is not practicable to measure the altitude to the center of either the sun or the moon as their diameters are wider and their centers do not afford a definite reference for measurement. Accordingly, all measurements are made to either the upper limb (upper edge) or lower limb (lower edge), abbreviated UL and LL respectively, and the semidiameter is subtracted or added as appropriate. Also, tables may be compiled so that semidiameter is always a plus correction. Whether the upper limb or the lower limb of the sun or moon is used depends upon which limb is most clearly defined.

AUGMENTATION (A).—An increase in the semidiameter of the moon which increases with altitude. Correction has the same sign as the semidiameter.

IRRADIATION (J).—Correction for the expansion of the upper limb of the sun and the contraction of the horizon because of optical illusion. Always a negative correction.

PHASE (F).—A correction for compensation for the difference between the apparent and actual

centers of the planets Venus and Mars. It may be positive or negative.

These corrections may be summarized as shown in Table 12-1, the letters "NA" signifying "Nautical Almanac." Corrections (1) and (2) for instrument error and height of eye (dip) are applied to the sextant altitude (Hs) to determine the apparent altitude (Ha), which in turn is used as the argument for entry in the other tables by which corrections (3) and (4) are computed. However, for simplification of computations, Ha is generally computed mentally and all corrections are totaled and applied to Hs to find Ho.

Note 1:

In tables A-2 and A-3 for the sun, separate corrections are given for "Oct. - Mar." and "Apr. - Sept."

Table 12-1.—Corrections to sextant altitudes

	Correction	Applies to	Found	Corrects	+ or -	Notes
(1)	Index	All sights	Sextant	IC	Either	
(2)	Height of eye	All sights	NA, Table A-2 and inside of back cover	D	Minus	
(3)	Altitude	Stars & Planets	NA, Tables A-2, A-3	R	Minus	
		Sun	NA, Tables A-2, A-3	R, P & S.D.	+(LL) −(UL)	See Note 1
		Moon	NA, Inside back cover	R, P A & S.D. (Standard values)	Plus	See Note 2
(4)	Additional	All sights	NA, Table A-4	TB	Either	
		Venus & Mars	NA, Table A-2	P, F	Plus	See Note 3
		Moon	NA, Inside back cover	P	Plus	See Note 2

190.21

Note 2:

The altitude and additional corrections for the moon are to be added regardless of which limb is observed, but 30' must be subtracted from the apparent altitude in an upper limb observation. Horizontal parallax (HP) is taken from the daily page of the NA for use as argument for entry in the table for the additional alt. corr.

Note 3:

The correction in table A-2 for Venus applies only when the sun is below the horizon. (For daylight observation of Venus, parallax and phase are computed directly using the formula $p \cos H - k \cos \emptyset$, where H is the altitude, $\emptyset$ is the angle of the planet between the vertical and the sun, and p and k are functions for parallax and phase related to dates, and recorded in the explanation pages in the back of the Nautical Almanac.) In actual practice, the additional computation for a daylight observation of Venus can be omitted.

EXAMPLE 1:

Given: Hs of the sun (lower limb) is 69-18.7' on 1 Jan 1970. Height of eye is 64 feet. IC is plus 1.5'. Standard atmospheric conditions.

Required: Ho.

Solution:

Corrections	Plus	Minus
IC	1.5	
HE		7.8
Alt.	15.8	
Sum	+17.3	-7.8
	-7.8	
	+9.5	
Hs	69-18.7'	
Ho	69-28.2	

Note: There is no additional correction for the sun from Table A-4 because the altitude exceeded 50°.

EXAMPLE 2:

Given: Hs of Venus is 17-10.5' on 2 Jan. 1970. Twilight observation. Height of eye is 37 feet. IC is -1.0'. Temp. 62°F, Bar. pressure 30.00 in.

Required: Ho.
Solution:

Corrections	Plus	Minus
IC		1.0
HE		5.9
Alt.		3.1
Add.	0.2*	
Sum	+0.2	-10.0
		+0.2
		-9.8
Hs		17-10.5
Ho		17-00.7

*0.1 From Table A-2,
0.1 From Table A-4.

EXAMPLE 3:

Given: Hs of the moon's lower limb is 26-19.5' at 1200 GMT on 3 Jan 1970. Height of eye is 49 feet. IC is plus 2.0'. Barometric pressure and temperature normal.

Required: Ho.

Solution:

Corrections	Plus	Minus
IC	2.0	
HE		6.8
Alt.	60.4	
Add.	5.6*	
Sum	+68.0	-6.8
	-6.8	
	+61.2	
Hs	26-19.5'	
Ho	27-20.7	

*H.P. From Daily Page is 58.2

Note: Had this been an observation of the upper limb, an additional -30' correction would have been applied.

EXAMPLE 4:

Given: Hs of Capella is 54-10.5'. Height of eye is 30 feet. IC is 0.0.
Required: Ho.
Solution:

Corrections	Plus	Minus
HE		5.3
Alt.		0.7
		-6.0
Hs		54-10.5'
Ho		54-04.5'

1204. FINDING GREENWICH HOUR ANGLE AND MERIDIAN ANGLE

The Nautical Almanac tabulates:

a. For each hour of GMT, the GHA of the first point of Aries, navigational planets, sun, and moon.

b. The SHA's by dates for all navigational stars.

c. Additional increments of GHA for minutes and seconds elapsed after the hour.

The first step in finding meridian angle "t" is the computation of GHA which is accomplished as follows:

SUN.—Using GMT, and Greenwich date of observation, enter Nautical Almanac and record tabulated hourly value of GHA. Turn to the yellow pages of the Nautical Almanac, and entering with the minutes and seconds after the hour, find the increase in the sun's GHA since the last tabulated (hourly) value. Add the tabulated value and the increase for elapsed minutes and seconds.

MOON AND PLANETS.— Proceed as with the sun, but record a code value identified as "v" together with sign which appears at the foot of the GHA sub-column for planets, and to the right of each tabulated GHA for the moon. Find the sum of the hourly value and the minute-second increment, as in the case of the sun, but using column headed "moon" or "sun-planets" as appropriate, then apply a code correction according to the sign of the code. This code correction is found in the yellow pages of the Nautical Almanac, entering with minutes elapsed since beginning of hour, and the code. The code correction is always plus for GHA except in the case of the inferior planet Venus, which has an orbit inside the earth's orbit. Its apparent motion westward, as compared with the sun's motion, shows that Venus has a numerically lesser, relative speed; when its correction should be subtracted, the code letter "v" will be prefixed by a minus sign. The purpose of the code correction is to simplify interpolation and to keep tabulated values at a minimum. For the planets, the code correction makes possible the use of the GHA value for minutes and seconds as tabulated for the sun.

STARS.—Determine the SHA from the daily page, entering with the star name and Greenwich date. Find the GHA of Υ in the same manner as used to find the GHA of the sun (except that in the yellow pages a separate column is provided for Υ). Adding the GHA of Υ and the SHA of the star we find the GHA of the star.

A code correction is never used in connection with the sun's GHA, the GHA of Υ, or the SHA of a star. To convert GHA to LHA, and LHA to meridian angle (t), the following relationships, as developed in art. 1004, are used:

LHA = GHA - Wλ
LHA = GHA + Eλ
GHA* = GHAΥ + SHA*
LHA > 180, t = 360 - LHA, and t is east.
LHA < 180, t = LHA, and t is west.

The following examples illustrate the complete problem of finding GHA and "t":

EXAMPLE 1:

Given: 1 Jan. 1970, ZT 11-18-45, Long. 71-30 W.

Required: GHA and t of sun.

Solution:

ZT	11-18-45	1 Jan.
ZD	+5	(71-30/15)
GMT	16-18-45	1 Jan.
GHA (16 hrs.)	59-06.0	
Min-sec (18-45)	4-41.3	
GHA of sun	63-47.3 or 423-47.3	
Long.		-71-30.0 W.
LHA		352-17.3
t = 360 - LHA or		7-42.7 E.

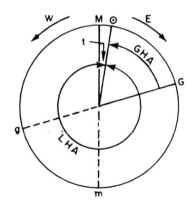

EXAMPLE 2:

Given: 2 Jan. 1970, ZT 09-19-55, Long. 169-15 E.

Required: GHA and t of moon.

Solution:

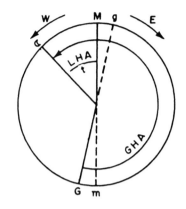

ZT	09-19-55	2 Jan.
ZD	-11	(169-15/15)
GMT	22-19-55	1 Jan.
GHA (22 hrs.)	231-39.4 (13.8)	
Min-sec (19-55)	4-45.1	
Code Corr.	4.5	
GHA of Moon	236-29.0	
Long.	+169-15.0 E.	
	405-44.0	
	-360-00.0	
LHA	45-44.0	
t = LHA or	45-44.0 W.	

EXAMPLE 3:

Given: 2 Jan. 1970, ZT 18-20-00, Long. 110-10 W.

Required: GHA and t of Venus.

Solution:

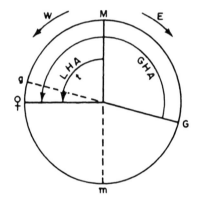

ZT	18-20-00	2 Jan.
ZD	+7	(104-10/15)
GMT	01-20-00	3 Jan.
GHA (01 hr.)	199-34.6 (1.0)	
Min-sec (20 min)	5-00.0	
Code Corr.	- 0.3	
GHA of Venus	204-34.3	
Long.	110-10.0 W.	
LHA	94-24.3	
t = LHA or	94-24.3 W.	

EXAMPLE 4:

Given: 3 Jan. 1970, ZT 06-00-00, Long. 92-00 E.

Required: GHA and t of Vega.

Solution: Using star name, enter SHA table on daily page; SHA is 81-01.6. Find GHA of Aries.

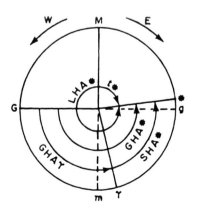

ZT	06-00-00	3 Jan.
ZD	-6	(92-00/15).
GMT	00-00-00	3 Jan.
GHAϒ (00 hrs.)	102-12.1	
SHA of Vega	81-01.6	
GHA of Vega	183-13.7	
Long.	+92-00.0 E.	
LHA	275-13.7	
t = 360 - LHA or	84-46.3 E.	

In the actual practice of sight reduction, an "assumed longitude" is used in lieu of the "actual longitude." This procedure simplifies subsequent computation as it permits the assumption of a longitude which, when combined with the GHA, results in a local hour angle, and a meridian angle, in even degrees. For example, in west longitude, the longitude assumed should include precisely the same number of minutes (and tenths of minutes) as the GHA; upon subtracting the assumed longitude the remaining local hour angle will result accordingly in even degrees. In east longitude, the longitude assumed should include the number of minutes (and tenths) which when added to the GHA will also result in a local hour angle, and "t," in even degrees. In using this procedure, a longitude should be assumed within 30' of the navigator's best estimate of his position.

1205. FINDING DECLINATION

The Nautical Almanac tabulates declination for the sun, moon, and navigational planets for each hour of GMT. At the foot of each declination sub-column which applies to the sun or planets, a code may be found which is useful for interpolation for any number of minutes. The code follows each tabulated declination of the moon, since the moon's declination changes rapidly as compared to the declination of the sun and planets. To find the change in declination for a part of an hour, enter the yellow pages with the number of minutes and the code. The tabulated declination is prefixed by either an N or S, indicating north or south declination, respectively; the sign of the code correction for elapsed minutes must be determined by inspection of the declination column, noting if declination is increasing or decreasing, between the two hours in question. Combine the tabulated declination and the code correction and label the result with "north" or "south" as appropriate.

To find the tabulated declination of a star, enter the daily page with the star name and Greenwich date. No code correction is necessary since the declination is relatively constant and can not be expected to change within any 3 day period.

EXAMPLE 1:

Given: GMT 11-18-45   2 Jan. 1970.

Required: Declination of the sun.

Solution: Declination (11 hrs.) S 22-56.1 (0.2)
             Code Correction   −0.1
             Declination   22-56.0 South

EXAMPLE 2:

Given: GMT 18-19-25   1 Jan. 1970.
Required: Declination of the moon.
Solution: Declination (18 hrs.) S 10-41.3 (14.3)
             Code Correction   +4.6
             Declination   10-45.9 South

EXAMPLE 3:

Given: GMT 05-18-26   3 Jan. 1970.
Required: Declination of Saturn.
Solution: Declination (5 hrs.) N 9-49.8 (0.0)
             Declination   9-49.8 North

EXAMPLE 4:

Given: 2 Jan. 1970.
Required: Declination of Dubhe.
Solution: Tabulated declination of Dubhe is 61-54.5 North on 2 Jan. 1970.

In most celestial computations, GHA and declination are determined concurrently rather than separately, thereby saving time in obtaining vital data from the almanac.

1206. GHA AND DECLINATION BY AIR ALMANAC

The Air Almanac, as introduced in Art. 412, may also be used for the determination of GHA and declination. Issued thrice annually, each volume tabulates data for a four month period. Based upon GMT, the daily pages tabulates the GHA and declination of the sun, moon, Venus, Mars, Jupiter, and Aries at ten minute intervals.

To determine GHA and declination of the sun, the planets, and the moon, enter the Air Almanac with the GMT, nearest and prior to, the actual GMT. The declination tabulated requires no incremental correction. The GHA, however, will normally require an incremental correction, tabulated for minutes and seconds on the inside front cover; one column provides the correction for the sun and the planets, (and for Aries), and a separate column provides for the moon. If a precision of 0.1' is desired for the GHA of the sun (or for Aries), special tables in the back of the Air Almanac should be used. The incremental corrections are always additive.

To find the GHA of a star, the GHA of Aries must be determined, and added to the SHA of that star. The GHA of Aries is found by using the same procedure as in the case of the sun. The SHA of a star, and its declination, is found in the inside front cover of the Almanac, tabulated to the nearest minute for a four month period. If greater precision is desired, separate tables provide such by month for SHA and declination to an accuracy of 0.1' in the back of the Air Almanac.

The Air Almanac, although less precise than the Nautical Almanac, may be used in the correction of sextant altitudes.

1207. SOLUTION OF THE ASTRONOMICAL TRIANGLE BY H.O. 214

There are several methods for solving the astronomical triangle, and each method has certain advantages over the others. However, for combined accuracy, completeness, convenience, and availability, the method that makes use of Tables of Computed Altitude and Azimuth (H.O. 214) has been generally preferred. H.O. 214 consists of nine volumes, one for each 10 degrees of latitude. Each volume is divided into sections, each section tabulating solutions for a single degree of latitude. Vertical columns within a section are headed by declination values, usually at intervals of 30'. On the left hand page, solutions are for cases in which latitude and declination are of the same name. On the right hand page, solutions are usually for cases in which latitude and declination are of contrary names; however, when it is possible for meridian angle to exceed 90 degrees with declination and latitude being of the same name, the left hand page tabulations may be continued on the right hand page and so identified. Horizontal lines are labeled with meridian angle, identified not as "t" but as H.A., with each line or entry being 1 degree apart. Against meridian angle, declination, and latitude, the tabulated altitude (Ht) and azimuth angle (Z), identified as "Alt" and "Az" respectively, are given. H.O. 214 then affords solutions for all possible astronomical triangles except those based upon certain circumpolar stars having declinations extremely high and not tabulated. Solutions by other methods, H.O. 249, H.O. 229, and H.O. 211, are briefly described in Articles 1209-1211.

A logical approach to the solution for a line of position would be to locate the GP (geographic position) by GHA and declination, and using the GP as center, draw a circle with a radius equal to the co-alt in degrees multiplied by 60 (co-alt in minutes or miles), thus arriving at our locus of position (called a circle of equal altitude). Since the distance of an observer from the GP is a function of the altitude of the star, the altitude would remain constant for a ship traveling in a circle having the GP as center; as the radius increased, the altitude would decrease,

and as the radius decreased, the altitude would increase. Since two circles may intersect at two points, two positions are possible as the result of two observations. However, the correct position could be chosen by considering the azimuth.

The plot of circles of equal altitude is impractical since the navigator for greater accuracy uses a large scale chart depicting an area too small to accommodate a plot containing both the GP's and the points of intersection of circles of equal altitude. For this reason, in our H.O. 214 solution, we plot an assumed position (AP), and for that position solve for the altitude and azimuth for a given time. The computed altitude (Hc) is the altitude which would be observed if the navigator had been at the assumed position at the given time, and the complement of the computed altitude, converted to nautical miles, is the distance to the GP from the assumed position, measured along the azimuth. The observed altitude thus locates the circle of equal altitude which is the observer's locus of position. The difference between the computed altitude (Hc) and the observed altitude (Ho) is the distance between the assumed and the actual circles of equal altitude and is called altitude difference or intercept, abbreviated "a."

If Hc is greater than Ho, intercept is labeled "away" because the actual position is at a greater distance from the GP than the assumed position. Conversely, if the Hc is less than the Ho, the intercept is labeled "toward" because the actual position is nearer the GP than the assumed position. A thumb rule is "Coast Guard Academy" meaning "computed greater away." See figure 12-1.

To plot a line of position, using the altitude intercept method as introduced in Art. 1201, locate and plot the AP; through the AP plot the azimuth line. Along the azimuth, measure a distance equal to the intercept. This is measured from the AP, along the azimuth in the direction of the GP if "toward," and the reciprocal of the azimuth (away from GP) if "away." At the point on the azimuth line established by the intercept, erect a perpendicular to the azimuth line; this perpendicular is a celestial line of position, and the intersection of two or more such lines of position will provide a celestial fix. The LOP is labeled with the time expressed in four digits above the line and the name or symbol of the celestial body below the line. See figure 12-2.

The Nautical Almanac is generally used in conjunction with the appropriate volume of H.O.

214 to compute intercept and azimuth. The steps in the solution are:

a. Correct Hs, and determine Ho.

b. Apply zone description to zone time of sight and local date to find the Greenwich mean time and Greenwich date.

c. With GMT, enter the Nautical Almanac and compute GHA.

d. With GMT, enter the Nautical Almanac and compute declination.

e. Assume a longitude which, when applied to the GHA (added if east longitude and subtracted if west longitude), results in a LHA in even degrees. This will later make it unnecessary to interpolate for t.

f. From LHA, compute t.

g. Assume a latitude in even degrees to make it unnecessary to interpolate for latitude. When assuming latitude and longitude, the assumed position should be within 30 minutes of the estimated or DR position.

h. Enter H.O. 214 with t, dec. (to the nearest tabulated value), and assumed latitude. Record the tabulated altitude (Ht), and the azimuth angle (Z). To interpolate altitude for declination difference, record the interpolation factor known as Δd which immediately follows the tabulated altitude. Note the value of Ht in the adjoining declination column having a declination value which is second nearest to the actual declination. If the previously recorded Ht is the least of the two values, the Δd is a plus value; if the previously recorded Ht is the greater of the two values, the Δd is a minus value. Multiply the Δd value, which is in hundredths, by the difference between the actual and the tabulated declination with which H.O. 214 was entered (in minutes and tenths of minutes) to find the correction to tabulated altitude (Ht). This may be expedited by using a self explanatory multiplication table in the inside back cover of each volume of H.O. 214. Apply the correction (according to the sign of Δd) to Ht. This will provide the computed altitude (Hc); numerically, the value of Hc will lie between the Ht's of the two declination columns which are nearest and "bracket" the actual declination. In sight reduction, it is not necessary to interpolate azimuth angle for declination difference.

i. Compare Hc and Ho. Compute intercept by subtracting the lesser from the greater. Label intercept as toward (T) or away (A).

j. Label azimuth angle making the prefix the sign of the elevated pole (latitude) and the suffix the sign of the meridian angle. From azimuth angle, compute and record azimuth (Zn).

Summarized, the solution for a line of position is as follows:

a. Enter Nautical Almanac with:
(1) Hs of celestial body.
(2) IC of sextant.
(3) Height of eye.
(4) DR or estimated position.
(5) Zone time, zone description, and date.

b. Compute, and enter H.O. 214 with:
(1) Meridian angle (t).
(2) Declination (dec).
(3) Assumed latitude.

c. Compute and use in conjunction with assumed position to plot LOP:
(1) True azimuth (Zn).
(2) Intercept (a).

d. Steps in plotting:
(1) Plot AP.
(2) Plot Zn through AP.
(3) Measure intercept from AP along Zn in proper direction.
(4) Erect a perpendicular to Zn at the altitude intercept distance from AP.
(5) Label perpendicular as a celestial line of position.

If it is apparent that an error has been made, Appendix H, which contains the mechanics of error finding, may be consulted.

EXAMPLES OF SOLUTIONS

EXAMPLE 1:
Sun (LL). Hs 24°-46.8, IC -1.0, HE 36 ft., Lat. 35-25 N. Long. 77-42 W. at ZT 14-18-10 1 Jan. 1970. Temp. 35°F, Bar. Press. 30.25".

EXAMPLE 2:
Venus. Hs 32°-48.2, IC +1.8, HE 35 ft., Lat. 32-40 N. Long. 51-15 W. at ZT 11-19-28 on 1 Jan. 1970. Temp. 50°F., Bar. Press. 29.80". Daylight observation.

EXAMPLE 3:
Moon (LL). Hs 66°-38.3', IC -2.0, HE 60 ft., Lat. 35-10 S. Long. 59-38 E. at ZT 06-18-30 2 Jan. 1970. Temp. and pressure normal.

EXAMPLE 4:
Peacock. Hs 42°-39.6', IC -1.5, HE 20 ft., Lat. 36-18 S. Long. 82-03 W. at ZT 18-18-05 3 Jan. 1970. Temp. and pressure normal.

For solutions to examples 1 to 3, see the following page, a typical, multiple sight form. Example 4 next following is a typical, single sight form. Appendix I contains an alternate sight form example.

SOLUTIONS FOR EXAMPLES 1, 2, AND 3.

DR POSIT	Lat. 35-25 N Long. 77-42 W 1 Jan		Lat. 32-40 N Long. 51-15 W 1 Jan		Lat. 35-10 S Long. 59-38 E 2 Jan	
TIME DIAGRAMS						
BODY	SUN (LL)		VENUS		MOON (LL)	
	Plus	Minus	Plus	Minus	Plus	Minus
I.C.		1.0	1.8			2.0
H.E.		5.8		5.7		7.5
Corr.	14.2			1.5	33.2	
Add'l		0.1			4.3	
Totals	14.2	6.9	1.8	7.2	37.5	9.5
Hs	24-46.8		32-48.2		66-38.3	
Corr.	+7.3		-5.4		+28.0	
Ho	24-54.1		32-42.8		67-06.3	
WT WE	This space may be used to convert watch time to zone time by the application of watch error					
ZT ZD	14-18-10 +5		11-19-28 +3		06-18-30 -4	
GMT Date	19-18-10 1 Jan 1970		14-19-28 1 Jan 1970		02-18-30 2 Jan 1970	
GHA(hours) min/sec Code Corr. SHA(Stars)	104-05.2 4-32.5		35-08.6 4-52.0 (-1.0)-0.3 360-00.0		289-50.0 4-24.9 (+13.4) 4.1	
Total GHA a Long.	108-37.7 77-37.7W		400-00.3 51-00.3W		294-19.0 59-41.0E	
LHA t	31 31W		349 11E		354 6E	
Dec. Tab. Code Corr.	(-0.2) 22-59.6S -0.1		(-0.1) 23-37.6S 0.0		(+14.0) 12-34.8S +4.3	
Dec.	22-59.5S		23-37.6S		12-39.1S	
Enter Dec. H.O. t 214 a Lat.	23-00.0S 31W 35N		23-30.0S 11E 33N		12-30.0S 6E 35S	
Ht Corr.	d diff 0.5 Δd +88 24-58.4 +0.4		d diff 7.6 Δd -99 32-32.1 -7.5		d diff 9.1 Δd +98 66-51.2 +8.9	
Hc Ho	24-58.8 24-54.1		32-24.6 32-42.8		67-00.1 67-06.3	
a Z Zn	4.7 A N 148.5 W 211.5(T)		18.2 T N 168.0 E 168.0(T)		6.2 T S 165 E 015 (T)	
Advance*						

* See Art. 1208

SOLUTION FOR EXAMPLE 4

BODY: __Peacock__

DATE: __3 Jan 1970__

DR POSIT: LAT. __36-18S__

LONG. __82-03W__

	+	−
I.C.		1.5
H.E.		4.3
CORR.		1.1
		−6.9
Hs	42 – 39.6	
Ho	42 – 32.7	
ZT	18-18-05	
ZD	+5	
GMT	23-18-05	3 JAN
GHA ♈	88 – 08.8	
M-S CORR	4 – 32.0	
SHA*	54 – 11.1	
GHA*	146 – 51.9	
a. Long.	81 – 51.9W	
LHA	65	

t	65W	
dec.	56-50.2S	
a. Lat.	36S	
Ht	42-46.7	(−05)
CORR	−0.5	
Hc	42-46.2	
Ho	42-32.7	
a	13.5A	
Z	S042.3W	
Zn	222.3	

1208. PLOTTING THE CELESTIAL FIX

In celestial navigation, lines of position are rarely obtained simultaneously; this is especially true during the day when the sun may be the only available celestial body. A celestial line of position may be advanced for 3 or 4 hours, if necessary to obtain a celestial running fix (fig. 12-4) in the same manner as described in chapter 7. It may also be advanced by advancing the AP in direction and distance an amount consistent with the ship's travel during the interval between two successive observations. In the latter procedure, the azimuth line is drawn through the advanced AP without any change in direction; the advanced LOP is drawn perpendicular to the azimuth, a distance from the AP equal to the intercept, and toward or away from the GP as appropriate.

At morning and evening twilight, the navigator may succeed in observing the altitudes of a number of celestial bodies in a few minutes and thus establish a celestial fix. If 2 or more minutes elapse between observations, the navigator must consider:

a. elapsed time;
b. speed of ship; and
c. scale of the chart or plotting sheet;

to determine whether or not a more accurate fix can be obtained by advancing AP's to a common time. It is possible during the day to obtain a celestial fix rather than a celestial running fix if two or more of the three following bodies are visible:

a. sun;
b. moon;
c. Venus.

EXAMPLE 1—Star plotting problem (fig. 12-5):

Given: The 0635 DR position of your ship is Lat. 36 N., Long. 120W. Between 0600 and 0700 your course is 000 (T), speed 20 knots. At morning twilight, you observe available stars and through computations obtain the following data:

Time	Body	a Lat	a Long	Advance*	Zn	a
0610	Vega	36N	120-36W	8.3	025	6.0T
0620	Peacock	36N	119-55W	5.0	100	24.0A
0635	Canopus	36N	120-20W	Base	330	10.3T

* Computation of advance is necessary because the stars were not observed simultaneously, and to fix our position, we must use a common time (preferable method is to choose as a common time the time of the last sight). To use a common time we adjust our AP's, except in the case of the AP of the star observed at the common time (in this problem, Canopus, which is considered the base star). Advance is computed as follows:

Body	Time	Speed	Distance of Advance
Vega	0635 - 0610 = 25 min.	20 kts.	8.3 mi.
Peacock	0635 - 0620 = 15 min.	20 kts.	5.0 mi.

Required: Plot the 0635 fix.

Solution:
a. Label plotting sheet with center meridian as 120 W.
b. Plot 0635 DR.
c. Plot AP's of Vega. Peacock, and Canopus, using assumed latitude and longitude. Label AP's.
d. Advance AP Vega in direction 000 a distance of 8.3 mi. Advance AP Peacock in direction 000 a distance of 5.0 mi. Erase old AP's of Vega and Peacock, if desired.
e. Plot azimuths, intercepts, and LOP's. Label LOP's and fix.

NOTE: If the reason for advancement of earlier AP's is not clear, then the following exercise should be completed:
a. Plot AP's of Vega, Peacock, and Canopus using assumed latitude and longitude. Label AP's.
b. Plot azimuths, intercepts, and LOP's. Label LOP's.
c. Advance LOP Vega and LOP Peacock in direction 000, in accordance with the procedure in plotting running fixes in piloting.
d. Check latitude and longitude of fix against coordinates obtained in previous method of solution.

ANSWER: Lat. 36-10.5 N; Long. 120-23.0 W.

1209. SIGHT REDUCTION BY H.O. 249

Designed for aerial use, Sight Reduction Tables for Air Navigation (H.O. 249) are useful in both air and surface navigation, when in the latter case, somewhat less precision is acceptable. See Appendix I. These tables, similar to H.O. 214, consist of three volumes. The first volume is used for seven stars, selected on the basis of azimuth, declination, hour angle, and magnitude, and to provide such distribution or continuity as to be generally useful worldwide.

Volume I differs from H.O. 214 in that the arguments for entry are the LHA♈ and the name of the star, rather than meridian angle, declination and assumed latitude; it also differs in that altitudes and azimuths are recorded to the nearest minute and nearest degree respectively. Additionally, and more conveniently, Volume I tabulates the true azimuth (Zn) rather than azimuth angle (Z).

Volumes II and III have greater similarity to H.O. 214 than to Volume I. Volume II provides altitude and azimuth solutions for latitudes

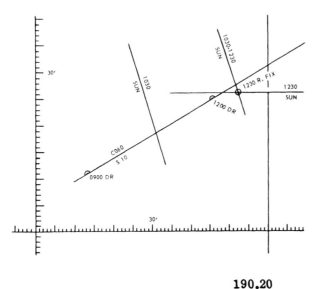

190.20
Figure 12-4.—Celestial running fix.

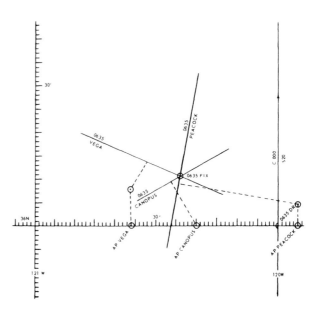

69.75
Figure 12-5.—Star fix.

0° to 39°; Volume III provides for latitudes 40° to 89°. These two volumes provide for bodies having declinations as great as 29°, and thus are useful in sight reduction of all bodies within the solar system and for stars having a declination of 29° or less. Entering arguments are latitude, declination of same or contrary name, and LHA, all to the nearest degree. Longitude is assumed so as to provide an even degree of LHA. Unlike Volume I, Volumes II and III record azimuth angle (Z) rather than true azimuth (Zn). Inasmuch as these tables are designed primarily for aviation use, LHAs are included for stars with a negative altitude as might be visible from an aircraft.

In all volumes of H.O. 249, whenever the declination is not an even degree, as is the usual case, the next lower declination column is used; to correct the tabulated altitude for the declination difference, a factor called "d," recorded after each tabulated altitude, must be multiplied by the declination difference, and applied according to sign to the tabulated altitude. Multiplication tables are conveniently located in the back of each volume for determining this correction.

1210. SIGHT REDUCTION BY H.O. 229

Sight Reduction Tables for Marine Navigation (H.O. 229) is the marine or surface counterpart of H.O. 249 and will eventually supersede H.O. 214. See Appendix J. It is issued in six volumes, with one volume for each 15° band of

latitude. Each volume is divided into two sections, based upon latitude, and contains tabulated altitudes and azimuths for 16° of latitude. For example, the two sections of Volume I are applicable to latitudes of 0° to 7° and 8° to 15° respectively; data pertaining to 15° latitude is also contained at the beginning of the first section of Volume II. An accuracy of 0.1' for altitude and 0.1° for azimuth angle may be attained in calculations through the use of applicable corrections to the tabulated data.

Entering arguments are latitude, declination, and local hour angle, all in whole degrees. Although H.O. 229 provides for entry with the exact DR latitude, the tables are intended to be entered with an assumed latitude of the nearest whole degree, and an assumed longitude which will result in a local hour angle of an integral degree. The local hour angle determines the page of entry, upon which altitude and azimuth data is tabulated in columns headed by latitude entries; vertical columns on the right and left margins of each page provides for the declination entry. For each entry of LHA, the left hand page provides tabulations for latitude and declination of the same name. The right-hand page, upper portion, provides for latitude and declination of contrary name; the lower portion of the right-hand page is a continuation of the page to the left, and contains tabulations for latitude and declination of the same name, as applicable to values of LHA in excess of 90° but less than 270°.

As in the use of H.O. 249, the declination entry is the nearest tabulated value which is equal to or numerically less than the actual declination. To the right of each tabulated altitude, under a column sub-headed as "d," is the incremental change in altitude based upon a declination increase of one degree, together with sign. An interpolation table is conveniently included, and is entered with the declination increase (difference between the actual declination and the declination integer used as an argument of entry) and the altitude difference (d). The interpolation table is entered in two steps. In the first, the declination increase, and even tens of minutes of altitude difference (d), are used; in the second, the declination increase, and the remaining altitude difference (d) in minutes and tenths of minutes, are used to find the correction to altitude. In this step, decimals (tenths) may be found as a vertical argument. Values found in these two steps are combined and applied to the tabulated altitude in accordance with the sign of altitude difference (d). This is the first of two procedures known as difference corrections.

For greater precision, a second difference correction is sometimes appropriate. When this is the case, the value of "d" is printed in H.O. 229 in italics and is followed by a dot. The second difference is found by comparing the altitude differences above and below the base value; for example, if the declination argument for entry is 20°, the altitude difference values for 19° and 21° are compared, and the difference between the two is the double second difference. Interpolation tables contain, on their right-hand edge, a double column which is identified as a double second difference and correction column; this a critical table and correction values are taken therefrom directly. The second difference correction is always additive. As appropriate, first and second difference corrections are thusly obtained, combined, and applied to the tabulated altitude to determine computed altitude.

H.O. 229 tabulates, following altitude difference (d), the azimuth angle (Z) to the nearest tenth of a degree. For greater accuracy, mental interpolation may be used, not only to correct the azimuth angle for the declination increase or difference, but also for differences in latitude and LHA. Rules are given on each page of H.O. 229 for conversion of azimuth angle (Z) to true azimuth (Zn).

The following sight reduction for the star Aldebaran illustrates the use of H.O. 229.

Local Date 2 JAN 1970 Course ___060°___ Speed ___15 kts___ Body ___Aldebaran___			
DR: Lat	34	15N	
Long	63	45W	
ZT	1740-19		
ZD	+4		
GMT Gr Date	2140-19 2 JAN		
GHA (hrs)	57	04.7	
GHA (m & s)	10	06.4	
v corr or SHA	291	26.7	
Total GHA	358	37.8	
a Long	63	37.8	E ⓦ
LHA	295		
Dec Tab	16	27.2	ⓝ S
d. corr (±)	( )		
Total Dec.	16	27.2	ⓝ S
Enter LHA	295		
H.O. Dec	16		ⓝ S
229 a Lat	34		ⓝ S
Dec Inc (±) d	27.2	30.1	
tens DS diff	30	13.6	
units DS corr	.1	+00	
Total corr (±)		13.6	
Hc (tab Alt)	29	24.1	
HC	29	37.7	
Sext. Corr.	+	−	
I. C.	0.8		
Dip (36 ft)		5.8	
Main Corr		1.7	
Add'l			
SUMS	0.8	7.5	
Corr		−6.7	
Hs	29	52.5	
Ho	29	45.8	
Hc	29	37.7	
a		8.1 A ⓣ	
Az (interpolate)	089.4		
Zn	089.4		
Advance			

1211. SIGHT REDUCTION BY H.O. 211

Based upon a concept developed by the late Rear Admiral Arthur A. Ageton, while serving as a Lieutenant at the Postgraduate School, U.S. Naval Academy, Annapolis, and published by him in 1931, Dead Reckoning Altitude and Azimuth Tables (H.O. 211) have, in usefulness, stood the test of time. This volume, appropriately and popularly known as "Ageton," includes formulas derived from Napier's rules, and in support of such formulas, tables of log secants and log cosecants for each 0.5' of arc. In a small, compact volume of 49 pages, these tables are useful worldwide, regardless of declination or altitude. A unique feature is that the concept is based upon a DR, rather than an assumed, position.

H.O. 211 advanced the practice of celestial navigation and was widely used until generally replaced by H.O. 214 during World War II. H.O. 211 is briefly described herein because of the economy it offers; a single volume for sight reduction is all that is required. However, the advantage of its economy is perhaps more than offset today by the greater convenience of H.O. 214, H.O. 249, or H.O. 229. For the navigator who wishes, nevertheless, to use H.O. 211, the Ageton method for sight solution or reduction is most adequately described therein.

CHAPTER 13

OTHER CELESTIAL COMPUTATIONS

1301. INTRODUCTION

As important as sight reduction is to celestial navigation, knowledge of such alone will not suffice. Essential supplementary celestial computations are described in this chapter, and include the determination of:

(a) Latitude by meridian sight;
(b) Time of transit, including local apparent noon (LAN);
(c) Latitude by Polaris;
(d) Time of phenomena such as sunrise, moonrise and twilight;
(e) Identification of navigational stars and planets;
(f) Compass error by azimuth of the sun;
(g) Compass error by azimuth of Polaris.

1302. LATITUDE BY MERIDIAN SIGHT

Since the latitude of a position may be determined by finding the distance between the equinoctial and the zenith, one needs to know only the declination and zenith distance (co-altitude) of a body to determine latitude. The procedure involved has been used by mariners for many centuries because of its simplicity. Before the discovery of the Sumner line, and particularly prior to the Harrison chronometer, longitude was most difficult to compute. Accordingly, early mariners seized upon the technique of "latitude or parallel sailing," by which they traveled north or south to the known latitude of their destination, then east or west as appropriate, often using the meridian sight as their only celestial computation. The meridian sight as described herein is applicable to all celestial bodies, although in practice it is primarily used with the sun. As described in Art. 1304, latitude by Polaris, a polar star, is a special case of the meridian sight, and is procedurally a different computation. With this brief introduction, the meridian sight is now considered.

When the altitude of a celestial body is measured as it transits the meridian, we speak of the observation, and the subsequent solution for a line of position, as a "meridian sight." This sight includes observations of bodies on the lower branch of the meridian (lower transit) as well as on the upper branch (upper transit); circumpolar stars may be observed on either branch of the celestial meridian. In practice, however, bodies are seldom observed on the lower branch, and the sun is normally the only body observed. In polar latitudes, when the declination of the sun corresponds in name to the latitude of the observer, the sun may be observed when in lower transit, but generally, meridian sights of the sun are made when it is in upper transit (LAN).

The meridian sight is important for the following reasons:

(a) It provides a celestial LOP without resort to trigonometry;
(b) The intersection of the LOP, obtained at LAN, and advanced morning sun lines, establishes a celestial running fix;
(c) It is practically independent of time;
(d) The knowledge of the approximate position is unnecessary; and
(e) The LOP is a latitude line, and is useful in latitude or parallel sailing.

To observe a body when on the meridian we must first determine the time of local transit. This may be accomplished by one of the three following methods:

(a) MAXIMUM ALTITUDE. — At upper transit the altitude of a celestial body is maximum for a particular 24 hour period. At lower transit the altitude is at a minimum.

(b) AZIMUTH METHOD. — When a celestial body transits the meridian, unless it is in the observer's zenith (GP corresponding to the observer's position), the azimuth will be either north (000) or south (180).

(c) COMPUTATION METHOD.—Should the approximate longitude be known, it is possible to compute the time of transit. This, the most common method, is described in article 1303.

When making the observation, stand by with a sextant 5 minutes prior to the expected time of transit. Continuously measure the altitude. When the altitude commences to decrease (on an upper branch observation), cease measurement, and record the highest attained value of altitude.

The theory of the meridian sight may be condensed as follows:

(a) It is a special case of the astronomical triangle. Since the local celestial meridian and the hour circle coincide, t equals 0 degrees and we are dealing with an arc rather than a triangle. Geometry, rather than spherical trigonometry, is necessary for solution.

(b) The vertical circle, the hour circle, and the local celestial meridian, coincide.

(c) The azimuth is either 000 or 180, except in the case of a body in the observer's zenith.

(d) The declination of a body is the latitude of the GP.

(e) The zenith distance of a body is the angular distance between the GP of the body and the observer, measured along the meridian.

(f) To find the latitude, it is only necessary to compute declination and zenith distance (co-alt), which may be combined after the derivation of the correct formula.

To derive the correct formula, draw the half of the celestial sphere which extends above the horizon, as viewed by an observer beyond the west point of the horizon (fig. 13-1). The circumference of this half circle represents the observer's celestial meridian which, as we have already noted, coincides with the hour circle and the vertical circle of the body. The zenith-nadir line, the equinoctial, and the polar axis, are all represented as radial lines extending outward from the observer's position at the center of the base line of the diagram. Label the north and south points of the horizon and the zenith. Depending upon the azimuth (north or south), using the observed altitude, measure from the north or south point of the horizon along the vertical circle and locate the position of the celestial body; label the position. Using the declination, locate and label the equinoctial

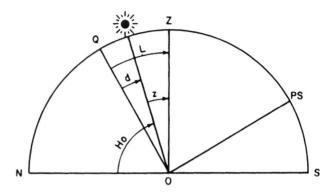

190.27
Figure 13-1.—Sun on meridian.

(Q). If the declination is north, the body will be between N and Q; if the declination is south, the body will be between S and Q. Arc ZQ then equals the latitude of the observer. We can readily see the relationship between declination and zenith distance, and derive formulae for the three possible cases, as follows:

(a) Latitude and declination of different names:

$$L = z - d$$

(b) Latitude and declination of same name with L < d:

$$L = d - z$$

(c) Latitude and declination of same name with L > d:

$$L = z + d$$

The following special cases are worthy of note:

(a) If Ho + d = 90°, then latitude is 0

(b) When latitude is nearly 0, and name of latitude unknown:

(1) If (Ho + d) > 90, latitude is of the same name as the direction of the body.

(2) If (Ho + d) < 90, latitude is of contrary name to the direction of the body.

(c) Ho plus polar distance equals the latitude at lower transit.

EXAMPLE 1:

Given: DR Lat. 47-26 S, Long. 130-26 W. ZT 11-45-41 on 2 Jan.
           1970. Hs of sun (LL) 65-18.3. Zn 000. IC + 2.0. Height
           of eye 44 feet.
Required: Latitude of the observer.
Solution:

				Plus	Minus
ZT	11-45-41 2 Jan.				
ZD	+9	(130-26/15)	IC	2.0	
GMT	20-45-41 2 Jan.		HE		6.4
Dec.	S 22-54.1 Code -2		Corr.	15.8	
Code Corr. -0.2*					
Dec.	22-53.9 S		Sum	+17.8	-6.4 = +11.4

*Dec. code -2 indicates that
declination changes 0.2' northward per hour and therefore the
change to the nearest tenth for
45 min. is also 0.2'.

Hs	65-18.3	90 = 89-60.0
Corr.	+11.4	Ho 65-29.7
Ho	65-29.7	z 24-30.3

(1) Plot sun using Ho and Zn (Draw diagram)
(2) Plot Q using declination and position of sun.
(3) Plot Ps using Q.
(4) ZQ equals latitude. Label angles or arcs in diagram which repre-
    sent dec, z, and latitude.
(5) Formula is L = z + d

          z 24-30.3
          d 22-53.9
    Lat.   47-24.2-South

1303. COMPUTING ZONE TIME OF LOCAL APPARENT NOON (LAN)

The navigator, using the Nautical Almanac, computes zone time of the sun's upper transit to an accuracy which permits his being on the bridge with sextant in hand just prior to LAN. Of a number of methods available for determining time of LAN, the GHA method is generally used, and for that reason is described herein.

In west longitude, when the sun is on the meridian the GHA equals the longitude. In east longitude, when the sun is on the meridian the GHA is the explement of the longitude. These relationships are illustrated in figure 13-2.

For the purpose of establishing a dead reckoning position to use as an initial estimate, we may assume that the sun will transit our meridian at zone time 1200; we accordingly use the longitude of the 1200 DR position for computing the GHA of the sun at LAN, as LAN will occur

between 1130 and 1230, plus or minus the equation of time (unless the observer is keeping a zone time other than standard time for his longitude). Enter the Nautical Almanac with GHA on the correct day, and determine GMT (the reverse of entering with GMT and finding GHA). In conversion of GHA to GMT, first select a value in the GHA column nearest, but less than, the sun's GHA. Record the GMT hours and subtract the GHA at the tabulated hour from the sun's predetermined GHA at LAN. Enter the yellow pages, and in the column headed by Sun—Planets, locate the remainder (minutes and seconds correction to GHA), and record the minutes and seconds. Time—arc conversion tables are also sufficiently accurate for this computation. Combine hours, minutes, and seconds to obtain the GMT of LAN. Apply the zone description, reversing the sign, to obtain zone time of transit.

The time of transit as computed above is the zone time the sun would transit the meridian of

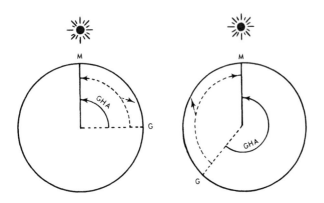

190.28

Figure 13-2. — GHA of sun at LAN.

the 1200 DR position. If this time differs from 1200, and you are the navigator of a moving vessel, then obviously the sun will not transit your meridian exactly at the time computed because of the difference in longitude between your position at 1200 and your position at your first estimated time of LAN. Ship's speeds are relatively slow, and a second estimate is generally not considered necessary. However, if a second estimate is desired, plot the DR corresponding to the time of the first estimate. With dividers, determine the difference in longitude (in minutes of arc) between the 1200 DR and the DR position corresponding to the first estimate of time of LAN. Convert the difference in longitude (in arc) to time, and apply as a correction to the zone time of the first estimate. Keeping in mind that the sun appears to travel from east to west, add the correction if the last plotted DR position is west of the 1200 DR, and subtract the correction if the last plotted DR position is to the eastward.

EXAMPLE 1:

Given: 1200 DR Lat. 36-18 N; Long. 71-19 W. 2 Jan 1970.

Required: ZT of LAN.

Solution:

ZT 1200 Long.	71-19 W.	
GHA at LAN	71-19.0	
16 hrs.	58-59.0	
49 min. 20 sec.	12-20.0	
GMT equals	16-49-20	
ZD	+5	(rev)
ZT	11-49-20	

EXAMPLE 2:

Given: 1200 DR Lat. 31-10S; Long.163-10E. 1 Jan 1970

Required: ZT of LAN.

Solution:

ZT 1200 Long.	163-10.0 E	
GHA at LAN	196-50.0	(360-163-10')
01 hours	194-10.5	
10 min. 38 sec.	2-39.5	
GMT	01-10-38	
ZD	-11	(rev)
ZT	12-10-38	

If the time of LAN is required only to the nearest minute, which is often the case, it can be more quickly determined. One need only to apply a difference in longitude correction to the time of meridian passage of the sun over the Greenwich meridian, as recorded on the daily pages of the Nautical Almanac. See Appendix F. The time of meridian passage, as recorded, is both the Greenwich mean time (GMT), and the local mean time (LMT) of local apparent noon. As mean time, it differs from apparent time (1200) by the equation of time, which is also recorded. As local mean time, it is also the zone time on the central meridian of each time zone. Thus, to find the zone time of local apparent noon on meridians other than the central meridian, the local mean time is corrected to zone time by converting the difference in longitude between the central and the observer's meridians from arc to time, and applying the result to the mean time of meridian passage. The correction is subtracted when east of the central meridian, and added when west.

1304. LATITUDE BY POLARIS

In the diagram used in the derivation of formulae for the solution of meridian sights, we found that arc ZQ equals the latitude of the observer. We can prove geometrically, using the same diagram, that the altitude of the elevated pole equals the declination of the zenith (arc ZQ), and also the latitude.

Although Pn and Ps are not well defined positions which make measurement feasible, a second magnitude star called Polaris (north star) provides a reference for measurement in the northern hemisphere; Polaris has no counterpart in the southern hemisphere. Polaris may be located in the northern sky between the constellations Ursa Major (big dipper) and Cassiopeia. The two stars in the bowl of the dipper at the greatest distance from the handle, point toward the north star.

Polaris travels in a diurnal circle of small radius around Pn as shown in the diagram in figure 13-3. The polar distance, or radius of the diurnal circle, is "p." The meridian angle is "t." Point 0 is the intersection of the observer's celestial meridian and the celestial horizon. Ho equals the observed altitude. PnH equals p cos t, and is the correction which must be added or subtracted, depending upon whether Polaris is below or above Pn.

It can readily be seen that the value of the correction will depend upon the meridian angle (t), or the position of the observer's meridian with respect to the hour circle of Polaris. Since the SHA is relatively constant, the correction is also a function of the LHAΥ. For Polaris, the Nautical Almanac tabulates corrections based upon the LHAΥ, the observer's latitude, and the

month of the year. In table a_0, the correction is based upon a mean value of SHA and declination of Polaris, and a mean value of 50° north latitude as the position of the observer. Table a_1, entered with LHAΥ and latitude, corrects for the difference between actual latitude and the mean. Table a_2, entered with LHAΥ and the month of the year, corrects for variation in the position of Polaris from its selected mean position. All corrections from these tables contain constants, which make the corrections positive, and which when added together, equal 1 degree. Thus, the correction is added to the Ho, and 1 degree is subtracted to determine latitude.

In summary, latitude may be ascertained in the northern hemisphere by observing the Hs of Polaris, at a known time. From the time, and the DR or estimated longitude, compute the LHA of Aries. Correct Hs to Ho, and using the LHAΥ, approximate latitude, and date, determine corrections from Polaris tables a_0, a_1 and a_2. Add total correction to Ho, and subtract 1 degree to obtain latitude.

EXAMPLE 1:

Given: Date 2 Jan. 1970. DR Lat. 67-25.0 N; Long. 116-35.0 W.
            WT 18-18-45, WE on ZT is 10 seconds fast. Hs 68-21.3.
            IC + 1.5. HE 42 feet.
Required: Latitude of the observer.
Solution:

			Plus	Minus
WT	18-18-45 2 Jan	IC	1.5	
WE	-10 fast	HE		6.3
ZT	18-18-35	Corr.		0.4
ZD	+8	Sum	+ 1.5	-6.7
GMTΥ	02-18-35 3 Jan			+1.5
GHA	132-17.0	Corr.		-5.2
M-S	4-39.5	Hs		68-21.3
GHA Υ	136-56.5	Ho		68-16.1
Long.	116-35.0 W	Table	+	
LHA Υ	20-21.5	a_0	7.6	
Ho	68-16.1	a_1	0.6	
Corr.	-51.1	a_2	0.7	
Lat.	67-25.0 North	Sum	+8.9	
			-60.0	
		Corr.	-51.1	

The reason the Polaris sight cannot be worked by HO 214 is that its declination is about 89 degrees North, and HO 214 does not contain solutions for astronomical triangles based upon any celestial body with such an extreme declination.

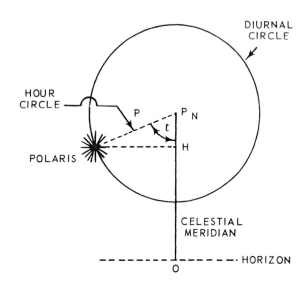

190.29
Figure 13-3. — Polaris.

1305. SUNRISE, MOONRISE, AND TWILIGHT

We associate the following phenomena with the apparent motion of the sun and the moon:

SUNRISE — The instant the upper limb of the sun appears on the visible horizon;

MOONRISE — The instant the upper limb of the moon appears on the visible horizon;

SUNSET — The instant the upper limb of the sun disappears beyond the visible horizon;

MOONSET — The instant the upper limb of the moon disappears beyond the visible horizon;

TWILIGHT — The period of semi-darkness occurring just before sunrise (morning twilight), or just after sunset (evening twilight).

The navigator utilizes morning and evening twilight for star observations because during twilight the darkness makes the stars visible, yet permits sufficient light to define the horizon. Both conditions are necessary if an accurate Hs is to be obtained. There are four stages of twilight, based upon the position of the sun with respect to the horizon. They are:

ASTRONOMICAL TWILIGHT. — The sun is 18 degrees below the horizon. Too dark for observations.

NAUTICAL TWILIGHT. — The sun is 12 degrees below the horizon. Favorable for observations. Recorded in Nautical Almanac.

OBSERVATIONAL TWILIGHT. — The sun is 10 degrees below the horizon. Best for observations.

CIVIL TWILIGHT. — The sun is 6 degrees below the horizon. Too light for observations. Also recorded in Nautical Almanac.

In practice, the navigator should be ready to commence his morning observations about 40 minutes before sunrise. For evening observations, he should be ready not later than 15 minutes after sunset.

In the Nautical Almanac the times of sunrise, morning nautical and civil twilight, sunset, and evening nautical and civil twilight, are tabulated against latitude on each daily page for a 3 day period. The time tabulated is Greenwich mean time on the Greenwich meridian but may be regarded as local mean time (LMT) of the phenomena (also the zone time at the central meridian of each time zone). To find the time of sunrise, for example, we turn to the page of the Nautical Almanac for the given date; interpolating for latitude, we find the local mean time of sunrise (zone time on central meridian). If desired, interpolation for latitude can be simplified by the use of a self explanatory table in the back of the Nautical Almanac (see appendix F). Next, we consider the difference in longitude between our meridian and the central meridian. Keeping in mind that 1 degree of arc equals 4 minutes of time, we convert the difference in longitude to time, and apply this correction to the LMT, to find zone time. If the local celestial meridian is to the east of the central meridian of the time zone, subtract the correction; conversely, if the local celestial meridian is to the west, add the correction. Round off answers to the nearest minute.

On a moving ship the problem is slightly more involved. The latitude and longitude chosen for solution should be found by entering the Nautical Almanac with an approximate latitude for sunrise (or sunset, or twilight) and noting the LMT. Plot the DR for the LMT, and using the coordinates of the DR, work the problem in the usual manner, first interpolating for latitude, and secondly applying the correction for longitude. A second estimate is seldom necessary because the required accuracy of 1 minute would not be exceeded unless the vessel traversed more than 15 minutes of longitude between the position of the first estimate and the position reached at the actual time of the phenomenon.

EXAMPLE 1:

Given: Position Lat. 22 N; Long 18 W, 3 Jan. 1970

Required: **ZT** of sunrise, beginning of morning nautical twilight, sunset, and end of evening civil twilight.

Solution:

	Sunrise	Morning Nautical Twilight	Sunset	Evening Civil Twilight
LMT 30 N	0656	0600	1712	1738
LMT 20 N	0635	0544	1732	1756
diff. for 10	21.0	16.0	20.0	18.0
diff. for 1	2.1	1.6	2.0	1.8
diff. for 2	4.2	3.2	4.0	3.6
LMT 22 N	0639	0547	1728	1752
d Long.*	+12.0	+12.0	+12.0	+12.0
'ZT	0651	0559	1740	1804

*(18 - 15) x 4

The Nautical Almanac also tabulates the GMT of moonrise and moonset, which closely approximates values of LMT. The time of moonrise (or moonset) on two successive dates differs a great amount, which makes interpolation for longitude as necessary as interpolation for latitude. To find the precise time of either moonrise or moonset, first find the GMT of moonrise (or moonset) for your latitude; this may necessitate interpolation between given values in the Nautical Almanac, or use of table I. Determine the GMT of moonrise or moonset for the desired date and the preceding date when in east longitude, and for the desired date and the succeeding date, when in west longitude. Compute the time difference between the two GMTs and enter table II with this difference and your longitude. Apply the resulting corection to the GMT of moonrise or moonset on the desired day, generally adding in west or subtracting in east longitude as necessary to arrive at an IMT which in sequence lies between the two previously computed GMTs. Apply a time correction for longitude to the LMT; the result is zone time of moonrise (or moonset).

EXAMPLE 1:

Given: 1 Jan 1970 at Lat. 37-30 N; Long. 63 W.

Required: **ZT** of moonrise.

Solution:

Jan. 1 GMT Lat. 37-30 N	0016	
Jan. 2 GMT Lat. 37-30 N	0119	
Difference	63	min.
Correction (from table II)	+10	
LMT (0016 + 10)	0026	
Corr. for longitude: (63-60) x 4	+12	
ZT of moonrise	0038	

1306. STAR IDENTIFICATION

It is just as necessary for the navigator to correctly identify an observed star as it is for him to identify a navigational landmark in piloting. There are two general systems available,

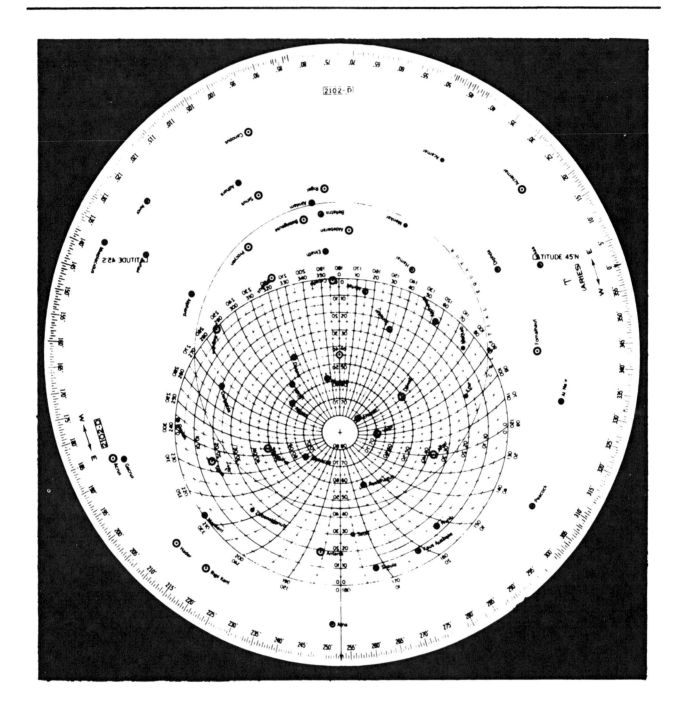

69.67
Figure 13-4.— Star finder with template.

identification by constellation, and identification by azimuth and altitude. The latter method is most practical, since it permits identification of single stars at twilight when the constellations are not clearly outlined, and of stars visible through breaks in a cloudy sky when constellations are partially or completely obscured.

The navigator's aid to star identification is the Star Identifier (HO 2102D) (fig. 13-4). It consists of a star disc, and a circular transparent template for each 10 degrees of latitude (5, 15, 25, 35, 45, 55, 65, 75, and 85); it also includes a meridian angle template. The star disc is so constructed that the stars normally seen in north latitudes are shown on the north side located so as to indicate their proper Right Ascension (RA) and declination; similarly, those stars normally seen in south latitudes are shown on the south side of the disc. The center of the north side of the disc represents the north celestial pole, and the center of the south side represents the south celestial pole. The edge of the star disc is graduated in degrees (0 to 360) for measurement of both SHA and RA.

To identify stars by their location, using altitude and azimuth, first compute the LHA of Aries for the desired time of observation. Using the side of the star base which corresponds to latitude (north or south), select and mount the transparent template which most nearly corresponds to DR latitude. Since the templates are printed upon both sides, in order to serve for both north and south latitudes, it is necessary to place the template with the side up which corresponds in name (north or south) to your latitude. The template is rotated until a north-south line on the template coincides with the LHA of Aries on the star disc. The printing on the template, which now covers the star base, consists of a network of concentric ellipses and radial lines. The stars which appear within the network are visible at the time of observation (or at least are above the horizon), and have altitudes greater than 10 degrees. The stars outside the network either are below the horizon or will have altitudes less than 10 degrees, and therefore are poor for observation because of inaccuracies in predicted refraction errors. The center of the network represents the observer's zenith. The radial lines represent azimuth, and are 5 degrees apart; at their extremities, the value of the azimuth of any star on that line may be read directly. The concentric ellipses represent circles of equal altitude from 10 to 90 degrees, and are 5 degrees apart; these ellipses

are appropriately labeled. Eye interpolation is normally used, and azimuths and altitudes are noted to the nearest degree.

The planets of our solar system do not appear upon the star base because of their constantly changing SHA. To locate or identify planets, the navigator computes the right ascension and declination using the Nautical Almanac. The right ascension of a planet equals the GHA of Aries minus the GHA of the planet. RA may be computed using the GHA's tabulated against a given hour. Once computed and plotted, the navigator will find it unnecessary to replot the planet more often than once every two weeks because the daily change in RA is relatively small.

To plot the planets on the star base, use the red-lined meridian angle template, which can be quickly identified as it contains a rectangular slot. Mount the template according to latitude on the appropriate side of the star base. Set the red pointer, which is adjacent to the slot, so that it indicates the RA of the planet, as read on the periphery of the star base. The planet may then be temporarily plotted through the rectangular slot, using a declination scale on the template adjacent to the slot, to locate its position.

The celestial bodies commonly referred to as morning and evening stars are actually planets, having GHAs which approximate the GHA of the sun. If the GHA of the planet is less than the GHA of the sun, the planet may be called an evening star. If the GHA of the planet is greater than the GHA of the sun, it may be called a morning star.

Consideration in selecting stars for observation are:

(a) Altitude—Between 15 and 70 degrees is preferable. Bodies below 15 degrees have refraction corrections which are predicted with slightly less accuracy. Altitudes above 70 degrees are difficult to measure.

(b) Azimuth—The stars selected should have azimuths which will provide a spread essential to establishing an accurate fix.

(c) Magnitude —Solutions are available for approximately sixty of the brightest stars. Stars of the first magnitude (brightest), are generally used in preference to second magnitude stars because the measurement of the Hs of a bright star is easier than the measurement of the Hs of a dim star.

EXAMPLE 1:

Given: Ho 2102D, North latitude, 1 Jan. 1970.

Required: Plotting of planets.

Solution: RA of a planet equals GHA of Aries minus GHA of planet.

	Venus	Mars	Jupiter	Saturn
GHA of Aries	460-13.8	460-13.8	460-13.8	100-13.8
GHA of Planets	185-22.2	116-17.9	249-40.2	69-27.8
RA of Planets	274-51.6	343-55.9	210-33.6	30-46.0
Dec. of Planets	23-37.9S	7-43.3S	11-08.9S	9-49.3N

The GHA♈ is actually 100-13.8, as indicated above under Saturn; however, it is appropriate to add 360° to the GHA♈ in the above cases for Venus, Mars, and Jupiter, to facilitate subtraction of the GHAs of those bodies. For simplification, the GHAs have all been recorded for 0 hours on 1 Jan., the given date. This is feasible because the hourly change in GHA♈ is practically the same as the hourly change in the GHA of the planets. The difference, or RA, does not differ appreciably during a given day. In fact, the change is so small that once plotted, planets can be used without re-computation and replotting for a fortnight. Planets are plotted using the red-lined, meridian angle template in accordance with their computed right ascensions and declinations. The moon may be plotted, if desired, using its right ascension and declination.

EXAMPLE 2:

Given: ZT 18-20-00 1 Jan. 1970 at Lat. 34-00N, Long. 77-45W, HO 2102D.

Required: List of first magnitude stars and planets visible with altitudes between 15 and 70 degrees.

Solution:

ZT	18-20 1 Jan.	Star finder set-up:
ZD	+5	Disc — north side up.
GMT	23-20 1 Jan.	Template — 35 North.
GHA♈	86-10.5	LHA♈ -13-26.3 Planets should
M/S	5-00.8	already be plotted as required by
GHA	91-11.3	example (1) above.
Long.	77-45.0 W	
LHA	13-26.3	

Body	Zn	H
Capella	056	40
Betelgeux	093	17
Aldebaran	096	38
Rigel	112	15
Fomalhaut	207	20
Deneb	302	41
Vega	305	18
Mars	220	40
Saturn	126	55

1307. AZIMUTH OF THE SUN

Computation of compass error at sea depends upon the observation of the azimuth of celestial bodies; the sun is most commonly used for this purpose. Upon observation, the observed azimuth, which is abbreviated Zo, is recorded. The time (to the nearest second), and the DR position, are also noted. With DR position and time, the navigator computes Zn. The difference between Zo (compass direction) and Zn (true direction) is compass error (C.E.). It should be appropriately labeled. The fact must be kept in mind that accuracy depends upon the navigator's knowledge of his position and the correct time.

To compute Zn by HO 214, use the Nautical Almanac to solve for t and dec. Using t, dec, and Lat. (all to the nearest tabulated value) enter HO 214, and record the base azimuth angle (Z tab). Next, make an interpolation for difference in t, dec, and Lat.; add algebraically the changes in azimuth angle for the difference between actual and tabulated values. Apply the total interpolative correction to Z tab to obtain Z. Convert Z to Zn. Compare Zn with Zo to determine compass error.

EXAMPLE 1:

Given: Zo 054.6 at Lat. 33-48 S, Long. 161-51 E at WT 11-19-16, 3 Jan. 1970. WE on ZT is 1 min. 6 sec. fast.

Required: Compass error.

Solution:

WT	11-19-16	GHA	178-56.7	
WE	1-06 fast	M/S	4-32.5	
ZT	11-18-10	Long.	161-51.0E	
ZD	-11	LHA	345-20.2	
GMT	00-18-10 3 Jan.	t	14-39.8E	
		dec	S22-53.2 Code -2	
		code corr.	- 0.1	
		dec	22-53.1S	

						Plus	Minus
t	14-39.8E	t diff + 2.2	t corr.	0.7		
d	22-53.2	d diff + 1.2	d corr.	0.3		
L	33-48.0S	L diff - 2.7	L corr.		0.5
Z tab	126.0		Sum	+1.0	-0.5
Corr.	+0.5		Corr.	+0.5	
Z	S126.5E				
Zn	053.5				
Zo	054.6				
C.E.	1.1 West				

EXAMPLE 2: (By H.O. 229)

DATE 2 JAN 1970	GB 227.5
** DR LAT 33°12'N	DR LONG 21°22'W
ZT	1554 12
ZD (+W) (–E)	+1
GMT	1654 12
GR DATE	2 JAN 1970
GHA (hrs)	58 59.0
GHA (m & s)	13 33.0
TOTAL GHA	72 32.0
DR LONG (+E) (–W)	21 22.0
** LHA	51 10.0
TAB DEC	22 55.0
d CORR (.2) +	.2
TOTAL DEC	22 54.8

(CORR = FACTOR x AZ DIFF)

	EXACT	LOWEST TAB	FACTOR	AZ TAB	AZ INTER'P	AZ DIFF	CORR +	CORR –
DEC	22 54.8	22	$\frac{54.8}{60}$ = .7	131.3	1 32.0	+.7	.64	
DR LAT	33 12.0	33	$\frac{12}{60}$ = .2	131.3	131.5	+.2	.04	
LHA	51 10.0	51	$\frac{10}{60}$ = .8	131.3	130.5	–.8		.13

AZ TAB	131.3
CORR	+.6
** AZ	N 131.9 W
	360.0
	– 131.9
ZN	228.1
GB	227.5
GE	.6 E

TOTAL CORR +.55 or .6

** CONVERT AZ TO ZN

NORTH LAT LHA GREATER THAN 180°.. ZN = AZ
LHA LESS THAN 180°....... ZN = 360° – AZ

SOUTH LAT LHA GREATER THAN 180°... ZN = 180° – AZ
LHA LESS THAN 180° .... ZN = 180° + AZ

COMPASS BEST ERROR WEST
COMPASS LEAST ERROR EAST

1308. AZIMUTH BY POLARIS

To determine compass error at night in north latitudes, find Zo of Polaris by observation. Compute the LHA of Aries. Enter the Nautical Almanac in the Polaris table entitled "Azimuth" with the arguments (1) LHA of Aries and (2) latitude of the observer. Zn is read directly from this table. Compare Zn and Zo, in the manner described for the sun in the preceding article, and determine compass error.

CHAPTER 14

DUTIES OF THE NAVIGATOR

1401. INTRODUCTION

The duties of the navigator are basically the same regardless of the type or the employment of the vessel; differences arise in methods employed because of available equipment. The duties of the navigator of a Navy vessel stem from, and are found in, Navy Regulations as revised in 1948 and since amended.

1402. DETAILED DUTIES

Extracts from Navy Regulations governing navigation are quoted herewith:

"0929. General Duties

The head of the navigation department of a ship shall be designated the navigator. The navigator normally shall be senior to all watch and division officers. The Chief of Naval Personnel will order an officer as navigator aboard large combatant ships. Aboard other ships the commanding officer shall assign such duties to any qualified officer serving under his command. In addition to those duties prescribed elsewhere in the regulations for the head of department, he shall be responsible, under the commanding officer, for the safe navigation and piloting of the ship. He shall receive all orders relating to navigational duties directly from the commanding officer, and shall make all reports in connection therewith directly to the commanding officer.

0930. Specific Duties

The duties of the navigator shall include:

1. Advising the commanding officer and officer of the deck as to the ship's movements and, if the ship is running into danger, as to a safe course to be steered. To this end he shall:

(a) Maintain an accurate plot of the ship's position by astronomical, visual, electronic or other appropriate means.

(b) Prior to entering pilot waters, study all available sources of information concerning the navigation of the ship therein.

(c) Give careful attention to the course of the ship and depth of water when approaching land or shoals.

(d) Maintain record books of all observations and computations made for the purpose of navigating the ship, with results and dates involved. Such books shall form a part of the ship's official records.

(e) Report in writing to the commanding officer, when under way the ship's position (fig. 14-1) at 0800, 1200, and 2000 each day, and at such other times as the commanding officer may require.

(f) Procure and maintain all hydrographic and navigational charts, sailing directions, light lists, and other publications and devices for navigation as may be required. Maintain records of corrections affecting such charts and publications. Correct navigational charts and publications as directed by the commanding officer and in any event prior to any use for navigational purposes from such records and in accordance with such reliable information as may be supplied to the ship or the navigator is able to obtain.

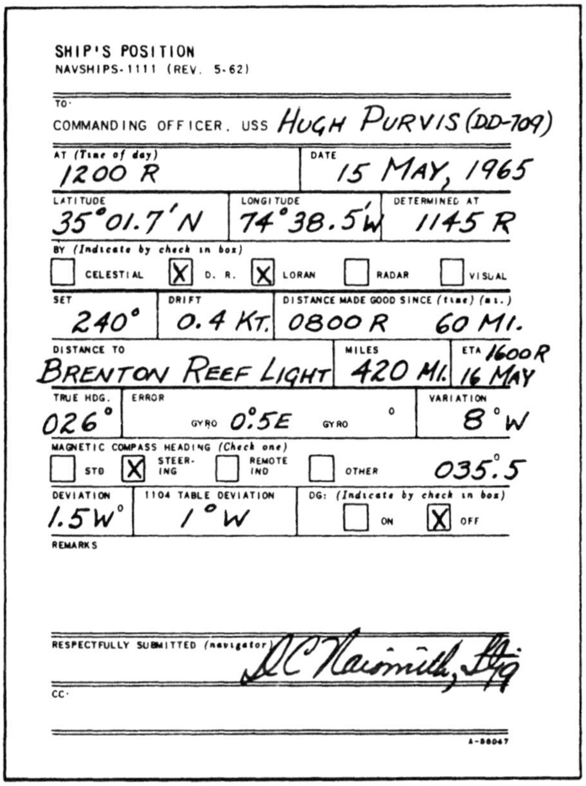

SHIP'S POSITION
NAVSHIPS-1111 (REV. 5-62)

TO·
COMMANDING OFFICER, USS *Hugh Purvis (DD-709)*

AT (Time of day) *1200 R*   DATE *15 May, 1965*

LATITUDE *35°01.7'N*   LONGITUDE *74°38.5'W*   DETERMINED AT *1145 R*

BY (Indicate by check in box)
☐ CELESTIAL ☒ D. R. ☒ LORAN ☐ RADAR ☐ VISUAL

SET *240°*   DRIFT *0.4 Kt.*   DISTANCE MADE GOOD SINCE (time) (mi.) *0800 R   60 Mi.*

DISTANCE TO *Brenton Reef Light*   MILES *420 Mi.*   ETA *1600R 16 May*

TRUE HDG. *026°*   ERROR GYRO *0.5E* GYRO *0°*   VARIATION *8°W*

MAGNETIC COMPASS HEADING (Check one)
☐ STD ☒ STEER- ING ☐ REMOTE IND ☐ OTHER   *035.5°*

DEVIATION *1.5W°*   1104 TABLE DEVIATION *1°W*   DG: (Indicate by check in box) ☐ ON ☒ OFF

REMARKS

RESPECTFULLY SUBMITTED (navigator)

CC·

A-58047

112.97
Figure 14-1.—Ships position report.

2. The operation, care, and maintenance of the ship's navigational equipment. To this end he shall:

(a) When the ship is under way and weather permits, determine daily the error of the master gyro and standard magnetic compasses, and report the result to the commanding officer in writing. He shall cause frequent comparisons of the gyro and magnetic compasses to be made and recorded. He shall adjust and compensate the magnetic compasses when necessary, subject to the approval of the commanding officer. He shall prepare tables of deviations, and shall keep correct copies posted at the appropriate compass stations.

(b) Insure that the chronometers are wound daily, that comparisons are made to determine their rates and error, and

that the ship's clocks are properly set in accordance with the standard zone time of the locality or in accordance with the orders of the senior officer present.

(c) Insure that the electronic navigational equipment assigned to him is kept in proper adjustment and, if appropriate, that calibration curves or tables are maintained and checked at prescribed intervals.

3. The care and proper operation of the steering gear in general, except the steering engine and steering motors.

4. The preparation and care of the deck log. He shall daily, and more often when necessary, inspect the deck log and the quartermaster's notebook and shall take such corrective action as may be necessary, and within his authority, to insure that they are properly kept.

5. The preparation of such reports and records as are required in connection with his navigational duties, including those pertaining to the compasses, hydrography, oceanography, and meteorology.

6. The relieving of the officer of the deck as authorized or directed by the commanding officer.

0931. Duties When Pilot is on Board
The duties prescribed for a navigator in these regulations shall be performed by him whether or not a pilot is on board.

1403. LEAVING AND ENTERING PORT

The navigator may expect to employ all methods of navigation except celestial, when leaving or entering port. Between a ship's berth and the open sea, the diversified tasks which the navigator must perform may be organized with the use of a check-off list.

The following check-off lists are, with slight modification, appropriate for ships of any type:

(a) Navigation Check-Off List for Getting Under-way—

24 hours before—

1. Make a pre-voyage check of instruments.

2. Check chronometer; determine error and daily rate.
3. Check adjustment of electronic equipment.
4. Read coast pilot or sailing directions which apply to harbor.
5. Determine estimated time of departure.
6. Consult Chief Quartermaster; locate and study desired charts and insure that applicable corrections have been made.
7. Plot courses and distances on harbor and sailing charts. Include route points and times of arrival at route points.
8. Plot danger bearings and danger angles.
9. Determine state of tide upon departure.
10. Determine state of current upon departure.
11. Study light list; plot visibility arcs for lights.
12. Study harbor chart of destination, particularly noting peculiarities which will affect navigation.
13. Check proposed track against dangers to navigation such as wrecks and shoals.
14. Determine total distance and required average speed for the ETA if established.
15. Note available electronic aids.
16. Instruct the navigation detail as to individual piloting tasks while leaving port.
17. Study pilot charts for information relative to the voyage (current and weather).
18. Check markings on the lead line.
19. Determine boundary between inland and international waters.
20. Confer with commanding officer.

4 hours before —

1. If not in operation, start master gyro-compass.

30 minutes before —

1. Station navigation detail.
2. Test fathometer, DRT, electronic equipment, and communication system.
3. Check gyro and repeaters against magnetic compass to determine gyro error.
4. Check vicinity of magnetic compass binnacle to insure that all gear is in place and that no stray magnetic material will influence compass.
5. Record the draft of the ship.
6. Check availability of bearing book, binoculars, stop watch, drafting machine, parallel rulers, navigator's case, charts, maneuvering boards, nautical slide rule (for computations involving time, speed, and distance), sharp pencils, art gum eraser, and

thumb tacks. Drafting machine should be oriented to chart.
7. Check readiness of navigation publications (including information concerning local navigational aids).
8. Insure that hand lead is on deck.
9. If anchored, take frequent rounds of bearings during weighing of anchor to detect drift.

Upon getting underway —

1. Keep running plot of ship's position using available landmarks.
2. Advise conning officer of desired courses and speeds and upon ship control.
3. Man chains.
4. Man searchlights at night.
5. CIC commence radar navigation regardless of weather. If fog is encountered, make a decision either to proceed by radar navigation or to anchor.
6. Note dangers to navigation and deficiencies in navigational aids for reporting to Oceanographic Office.
7. Check state of tide and current, and compare with predictions.

Upon leaving channel and passing sea buoy —

1. Lower pit sword (if so equipped); commence operation of log.
2. Secure chains. Continue operation of fathometer.
3. Set latitude and longitude dials, and start DRT.

Before losing sight of land —

1. Obtain departure fix.
2. Secure fathometer, unless desired.
3. Secure piloting instruments.

(b) Navigation Check-Off List for Entering Port —

Before sighting land —

1. Read coast pilots or sailing directions and note comments.
2. Determine estimated time of arrival.
3. Consult Chief Quartermaster; locate and study desired charts and insure their correction (check for late changes in local navigational aids).
4. Determine state of tide upon arrival.
5. Determine expected currents.

6. Start fathometer; record sounding periodically and check approach.

7. Determine expected landmarks and their characteristics.

8. Locate ranges and study buoyage.

9. Plot courses to be used while entering port.

10. Plot danger bearings and danger angles.

11. Study anchorage chart and determine assigned berth.

12. Ascertain pilot regulations and requirements.

13. Check local harbor regulations and/or applicable operation order or plan (garbage, landings, customs, quarantine, forbidden anchorage, cable locations, dredges, survey stations, survey boats, speeds, and special orders).

14. Locate electronic aids to navigation (radio direction finder, radio beacon, coast radar stations, loran stations, etc.).

15. Determine whether or not a degaussing range is available and if a degaussing check is necessary or desirable.

16. Determine boundary between inland and international waters. Log time of crossing; notify captain and conning officer.

17. If at night, determine characteristics of expected lights and check chart data with light list; record the expected time of sighting of major lights. Give a list to the OOD.

18. Check markings on lead line.

19. Exercise watch on both surface search and air search radar to determine distance and shape of coast.

Upon sighting land –

1. Locate position of ship by landmarks as soon as practicable. Correct latitude and longitude dials on DRT.

2. Take soundings continuously.

3. Check compass error on available ranges. Insure proper speed setting on master gyrocompass.

4. Note dangers to navigation and deficiencies in navigational aids for reporting to Oceanographic Office.

5. Station navigation detail. Prepare bearing book.

6. Keep running plot of ship's position using available landmarks.

7. CIC commence radar navigation regardless of weather. If fog is encountered, make a decision either to proceed by radar navigation or to anchor.

8. Check state of tide and current, and compare with predictions.

9. Set watch on lookout sound-powered phone circuit (JL).

10. Man searchlight at night.

Upon entering channel or harbor –

1. Continue above as practicable.

2. House pit sword and sound dome, if required.

3. Determine anchorage bearings; note adjacent ships and other possible dangers.

4. Plot anchorage approach course (against current if possible).

5. Clear sides if mooring alongside ship or dock.

6. Man the chains.

7. Advise conning officer of desired courses and speeds.

8. When approaching berth, advise upon ship control (including the letting go of anchor).

After anchoring or mooring –

1. If anchored, get actual anchorage bearings, plot and enter them in the log. Use sextant and 3-arm protractor if necessary.

2. Determine draft of ship and enter in the log.

3. Advise as to desired scope of anchor chain if anchored. Plot scope of chain (radius of swing).

4. Determine and log the actual depth of water and type of bottom.

5. Check distances to adjacent ships and landmarks. Compare with radar ranges.

6. If in unsurveyed anchorage, determine soundings and character of bottom in circular area having a radius equal to 1 1/2 times the swinging circle, with the anchor at center.

7. Check expected currents and if anchored, put over drift lead.

8. Locate landings if anchored. Notify OOD of boat compass course to and from landings.

9. Recheck ship's position if anchored as soon as ship is steadied against current. Advise captain whether anchor is holding.

10. If anchored, station the anchor watch. Take bearings to detect dragging.

1404. COASTAL PILOTING

Coastal piloting makes use of the same principles as harbor piloting. Although the period practiced may be so extended as to work a physical hardship on the navigator, safety requires that the navigator identify all aids and be on deck to witness all course changes. This requirement is necessary because of the proximity of danger. The navigator should constantly be governed by the thought "a mariner's first consideration is the safety of his vessel."

1405. NAVIGATION AT SEA

The navigator's sea routine is as follows:

Morning twilight—Observe stars and compute star fix.

Sunrise (or after)—Compute compass error.

0800—Make position report.

Forenoon—Obtain morning sun line. Compute time of LAN.

LAN—Observe sun on meridian and compute latitude. Advance morning sun line and obtain running fix.

1200—Make position report.

Afternoon—Obtain afternoon sun line. Advance latitude line obtained at LAN and plot afternoon running fix. Compute time of sunset and prepare list of evening stars.

Evening twilight—Observe stars and compute star fix.

2000—Make position report.

Night—Compute time of sunrise and prepare a list of morning stars. Plot DR for night, making allowance for expected changes in course, speed, and zone time. Observe Polaris, if a compass error check is desired, and if in northern latitudes. Provide navigational data for captain's night orders.

1406. PREPARATION OF THE POSITION REPORT

The following condensed instructions should enable the navigator to properly fill in and submit written reports of the ship's position:

(a) OBJECTIVE—To inform the commanding officer and flag officer (if embarked) of the ship's position, together with recommendations that may be appropriate.

(b) INSTRUCTIONS FOR PREPARATION—

(1) Heading: Record name of ship, time and date on first and second blank lines. Time will be 0800, 1200, 2000, or such time as the CO desires.

(2) Position: In line three, record latitude and longitude (for 0800, 1200 or 2000) and time of observations upon which position is based. In line four, indicate type of fix (celestial, D.R., loran, radar or visual). Label latitude and longitude. Label time, indicating zone.

(3) Set and drift: Compute and record on line five as follows: The set is the direction of the fix from the DR position of the same time. The drift in knots is the distance in nautical miles between the fix and the DR position divided by the number of hours between the times of the last two fixes. Drift is speed.

(4) Distance: Also on line five, record distance made good since last report, giving the time first and the distance second. After "Distance to," on line six, write in either the name of the destination, or a designated route point, and record the distance in nautical miles. Note the time and date of ETA.

(5) Compass data: Record true heading and gyro error. Two blanks are available for gyro error since heavy ships may carry two gyrocompasses. Record variation. Check "STD," "Steering," or "remote IND" to identify the magnetic compass. Record the compass heading which differs from true course by compass error. Record actual and table deviation. Remember that the algebraic sum of variation and deviation is compass error. Use degrees and tenths of degrees and label all values except heading as "east" or "west." Check degaussing as either "on" or "off."

(6) Remarks: Make recommendations as to changes in course, speed, and zone time. Inform the captain of navigational aids expected to be sighted, using back of report if necessary. This report ordinarily should be sufficiently complete to provide the captain with all information necessary to write the night orders.
Example: "Recommend c/c to 050 (T) at 2200 with Frying Pan Shoals Lt. Ship abeam to port, distance 4 miles. Sight Diamond Shoals Lt. Ship bearing 045(T) at 0623, distance 16 miles. Characteristics—GpFl W ev 26 sec (3 flashes). At 0700 with Diamond Shoals Lt. Ship abeam to port, distance 7 miles, recommend c/c to 000(T); c/s to 17 kts." If you are unable to obtain necessary data, leave appropriate spaces blank and explain under remarks.

(7) Signature: Sign name and indicate rank.

(8) Addressees: The report always goes to the commanding officer. If any flag officers are embarked, insert their titles under "commanding officer" and prepare copies for them. Retain one copy for your file.

1407. LIFE BOAT NAVIGATION

Should an emergency arise which restricts the navigator's tools to the equipage of his life boat, then he must modify the procedures described in this compendium to fit the situation. Success in life boat navigation may be a measure of the navigator's foresight and resourcefulness.

The forehanded navigator accepts the possibility of shipwreck and prepares one or more navigation kits to supplement the equipage regularly carried by his ship's life boats. The navigation kit should contain the following:

(a) An OILCLOTH CHART of sufficient area to show the ship's position if abandoned.

(b) SEXTANT. An inexpensive instrument may be substituted for the commonly used endless tangent screw sextant since accuracy is not paramount.

(c) COMPASS. A pocket compass is small and inexpensive and may be the only direction reference if the boat compass carried by your life boat becomes lost or damaged.

(d) ALMANAC. The convenience of using the Nautical Almanac and especially the star diagrams which it contains makes this publication worth its space. An oilcloth copy of the star diagrams, such as may be found in the Air Almanac, should be carried if available.

(e) TABLES. The appropriate volume of H.O. 214, or other navigational table.

(f) PLOTTING EQUIPMENT. A Hoey position plotter, pencils, and erasers are essential. The Hoey plotter is especially important since it provides both a protractor and a straight-edge; it is also a crude substitute for a sextant.

(g) NOTEBOOK. This book should contain space for computations and a section devoted to a compilation of useful formulae; if an Almanac is not available within the navigation kit, then extracts may be recorded in the notebook. In addition to this notebook, position plotting sheets or other suitable plotting paper should be included in the kit. If a chart is not available, then the coordinates of several ports should be recorded in the notebook. It is advisable to include data on prevailing winds and currents.

(h) AMERICAN PRACTICAL NAVIGATOR. This volume can be most valuable. It contains much information on weather and currents, tables for sight reduction, a long-term almanac, traverse tables for mathematical dead reckoning, and tabulated coordinates of world ports. If including the entire volume is not desirable because of

size, appropriate information should be extracted and retained.

(i) PORTABLE RADIO. To obtain time signals, a portable radio is useful.

(j) SLIDE RULE. A slide rule with a sine scale can be used in sight reduction.

(k) DRAMAMINE. Since a sea sickness preventative may act in the interest of the navigator's personal efficiency, dramamine tablets have a place in the kit.

When the ship is abandoned the navigator should accomplish the following if possible:

(a) Wind the watch and determine the watch error.

(b) Record (or at least remember) the date.

(c) Record the ship's position. A recent fix or a fairly accurate EP is most essential when abandoning ship and also on the occasion of "man overboard."

(d) Record magnetic bearing of nearest land and the magnetic variation.

(e) Insure presence of the navigation kit.

After the ship is abandoned, make an estimate of the situation. Consider every possibility, then (1) mentally list and compare the advantages and disadvantages of each, (2) compare the possible outcomes of each, and (3) formulate an alternate plan to be followed in the event of failure of each major plan. Make a decision as to your course of action. Generally, the choice will be between remaining in the immediate vicinity and proceeding toward some land or haven. Record the decision in your notebook and start a log. Make a comparison of watches, if more than one is present, as insurance of correct time. Check speed by the chip log method (art. 303) and insure that the compass is free from magnetic influence other than the earth's. Establish your daily routine.

Start a dead reckoning track upon your chart, or commence dead reckoning mathematically, in order to carry out your course of action. If dead reckoning is to be accomplished by mathematical rather than graphic means, the navigator may use the traverse tables which provide a simplified method of solving any right triangle; if desired, extracts from these tables (which appear as Table 3 in the American Practical Navigator) may be recorded in the notebook during the preparation of the navigation kit. Check the accuracy of your compass in the northern hemisphere by observing Polaris, assuming that its Zn is 000. Magnetic variation should constitute the entire compass error in a life boat. In either north or south latitude, any body will reach its highest altitude when in upper transit (azimuth 000 or 180) and will thereby provide a compass check. At night, not only Polaris, but any star near the prime vertical, if visible, can be used for a direction reference.

To measure the altitude of celestial bodies in the absence of a sextant, attach a weight to

the end of the drafting arm of the Hoey plotter. Sight along the straightedge of the protractor (diameter) and allow the weighted drafting arm to seek alignment with the direction of the force of gravity. Record the angle on the protractor scale between the 0 mark opposite the body and the center of the drafting arm. This angle is the altitude. To correct a measured altitude when the Nautical Almanac is not available, the following information should be tabulated in the notebook:

Refraction Correction for Altitude				Semidiameter
Alt.	Corr.	Alt.	Corr.	Sun (upper limb) − 16'
5–6°	−9'	13–15°	−4'	Sun (lower limb) +16'
7°	−8'	16–21°	−3'	
8°	−7'	22–33°	−2'	
9–10°	−6'	34–63°	−1'	
11–12°	−5'	64–90°	−0	

To find the approximate declination of the sun, draw a circle with horizontal and vertical diameters. Label the points of termination of the diameters as follows, commencing at the top and moving clockwise: June 22, Sept. 23, Dec. 22, and Mar. 21. Locate a given date on the circle with respect to the equinoxes and solstices using proportional parts of any quadrant. Divide the upper vertical radius into 23.45 equal parts to indicate north declination, and divide the lower vertical radius into 23.45 equal parts to indicate south declination. Draw a line from any given date on the circle perpendicular to the vertical to determine the declination on the given date.

The LATITUDE may be determined as follows:

(a) In the northern hemisphere, by an observation of Polaris.

(b) By a meridian sight of any body.

(c) Note bodies at or near the zenith. The latitude of an observer equals the declination of a body in his zenith.

(d) If the Nautical Almanac is available and the date is known, note the duration of daylight which is a function of latitude.

The LONGITUDE may be found by observing and noting time of meridian transit.

A LINE OF POSITION may be obtained by noting the time of sunrise or sunset, or the instant any celestial body coincides with the visual horizon.

To obtain a line of position by a horizon sight, no sextant is needed. For a horizon sight in the case of the sun or the moon, either limb may be used. The Hs, which is 0°, is corrected for height of eye (dip), refraction and semidiameter. Sight reduction may be accomplished using H.O. 211 or H.O. 229; H.O. 214, however, is not applicable for sights of less than 5° altitude. It should be noted that when both H_0 and H_C are negative, the intercept is "away" if H_0 is the greater, and conversely, the intercept is "toward" if H_C is the greater.

Horizon sights may be reduced through the use of a slide rule with a sine scale. The following formula applies:

$$\sin H_C = \sin L \sin d \underset{\sim}{+} \cos L \cos d \cos t$$

In the formula above, if $t < 90°$, and latitude and declination are of the same name, the sign is positive; when latitude and declination are of contrary name and $t < 90°$, the lesser quantity is subtracted from the greater. If $t > 90°$, and latitude and declination are of the same name, the lesser quantity is also subtracted from the greater; if latitude and declination are of contrary name and $t > 90°$, the sign is positive. If the sine of H is negative, H_C is negative. Azimuth angle may be found using the formula:

$$\sin Z = \frac{\cos d \sin t}{\cos H_C}$$

136

Since the cosine of H_c in a low altitude sight approaches one, or unity, division by cos H_c is generally unnecessary.

In horizon sights, the azimuth should also be checked to determine compass error. To compute Zn, one needs to know only the declination. With north declination, the body will rise and set at points on the horizon north of the prime vertical an angular distance equal to the declination. With south declination, the body will rise and set at points on the horizon south of the prime vertical an angular distance equal to the declination.

Should the watch or other timepiece stop, it can be reset by an observation of the stars and a reference to a star chart. The navigator remembers that sidereal time and solar time are equal at the autumnal equinox; at the vernal equinox, sidereal time is 12 hours fast on solar time. For any date in between the equinoxes, we can compute the difference between sidereal time and solar time as we know that sidereal time gains 3 minutes and 56 seconds daily. If we see on the star chart that the RA of Diphda (for example) is 10°-30' or 42 minutes of time,

then when Diphda is in upper transit, the local sidereal time is 0042 because Aries transits our local meridian (LST 0000) earlier than any given star by an amount of time equal to the RA. From sidereal time we subtract the difference between it and solar time (which depends upon date as explained above) and we arrive at solar mean time.

It is generally best to practice latitude or parallel sailing, since latitude computations are apt to be more accurate than longitude computations. In parallel sailing, the navigator sails in a general direction of either north or south until he reaches the latitude of his destination. Then he changes course to east or west and makes adjustments as necessary enroute in order that his track will adhere to the parallel of latitude of the destination. The navigator should try to compute his daily advance, which among other uses, acts as a check against the longitude when traveling east or west, and as a check against the latitude when traveling north or south.

When landfall is finally made, identify available landmarks and approach with caution until able to select a safe landing site.

APPENDICES

Appendix A

GENERAL REMARKS

Chart No. 1 contains the standard symbols and abbreviations which have been approved for use on nautical charts published by the United States of America.

Symbols and abbreviations shown on Chart No. 1 apply to the regular nautical charts and may differ from those shown on certain reproductions and special charts. Symbols and abbreviations on certain reproductions and on foreign charts may be interpreted by reference to the Symbol Sheet or Chart No. 1 of the originating country.

Terms, symbols and abbreviations are numbered in accordance with a standard form approved by a Resolution of the Sixth International Hydrographic Conference, 1952.

Vertical figures indicate those items where the symbol and abbreviation are in accordance with the Resolutions of the International Hydrographic Conferences.

Slanting figures indicate no International Hydrographic Bureau symbol adopted.

Slanting figures underscored indicate U.S.A. and I.H.B. symbols do not agree.

Slanting figures asterisked indicate no U.S.A. symbol adopted.

An up-to-date compilation of symbols and abbreviations approved by resolutions of the International Hydrographic Conference is not currently available. Use of I.H.B. approved symbols and abbreviations by member nations is not mandatory.

Slanting letters in parentheses indicate that the items are in addition to those shown on the approved standard form.

Colors are optional for characterizing various features and areas on the charts.

Lettering styles and capitalization as used on Chart No. 1 are not always rigidly adhered to on the charts.

Longitudes are referred to the Meridian of Greenwich.

Scales are computed on the middle latitude of each chart, or on the middle latitude of a series of charts.

Buildings - A conspicuous feature on a building may be shown by a landmark symbol with descriptive note (See I-n & L-63). Prominent buildings that are of assistance to the mariner are crosshatched (See I-3a,5,47 & 66).

Shoreline is the line of Mean High Water, except in marsh or mangrove areas, where the outer edge of vegetation (berm line) is used. A heavy line (A-9) is used to represent a firm shoreline. A light line (A-7) represents a berm line.

Heights of land and conspicuous objects are given in feet above Mean High Water, unless otherwise stated in the title of the chart.

Depth Contours and Soundings may be shown in meters on charts of foreign waters.

Visibility of a light is in nautical miles for an observer's eye 15 feet above water level.

Buoys and Beacons - On entering a channel from seaward, buoys on starboard side are red with even numbers, on port side black with odd numbers. Lights on buoys on starboard side of channel are red or white, on port side white or green. Mid-channel buoys have black-and-white vertical stripes. Junction or obstruction buoys, which may be passed on either side, have red-and-black horizontal bands. This system does not always apply to foreign waters. The dot of the buoy symbol, the small circle of the light vessel and mooring buoy symbols, and the center of the beacon symbol indicate their positions.

Improved channels are shown by limiting dashed lines, the depth, month, and the year of latest examination being placed adjacent to the channel, except when tabulated.

U. S. Coast Pilots, Sailing Directions, Light Lists, Radio Aids, and related publications furnish information required by the navigator that cannot be shown conveniently on the nautical chart.

U. S. Nautical Chart Catalogs and Indexes list nautical charts, auxiliary maps, and related publications, and include general information (marginal notes, etc.) relative to the charts.

A glossary of foreign terms and abbreviations is generally given on the charts on which they are used, as well as in the Sailing Directions.

Charts already on issue will be brought into conformity as soon as opportunity affords.

All changes since the September 1963 edition of this publication are indicated by the symbol † in the margin immediately adjacent to the item affected.

Published at Washington, D.C.

U.S. DEPARTMENT OF COMMERCE
ENVIRONMENTAL SCIENCE SERVICES ADMINISTRATION
COAST AND GEODETIC SURVEY

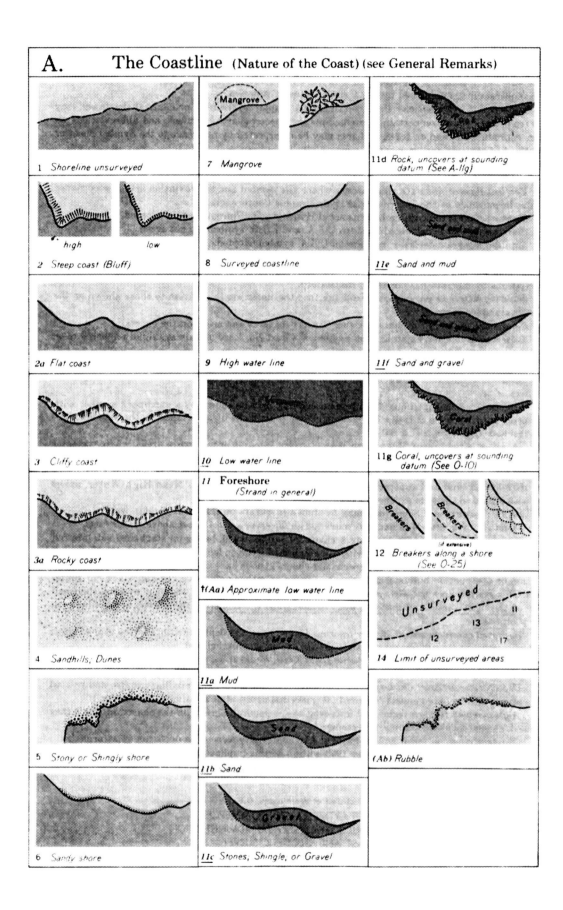

A. The Coastline (Nature of the Coast) (see General Remarks)

1   Shoreline unsurveyed

2   Steep coast (Bluff)

    high   low

2a   Flat coast

3   Cliffy coast

3a   Rocky coast

4   Sandhills; Dunes

5   Stony or Shingly shore

6   Sandy shore

7   Mangrove

8   Surveyed coastline

9   High water line

10   Low water line

11   Foreshore (Strand in general)

†(Aa)   Approximate low water line

11a   Mud

11b   Sand

11c   Stones, Shingle, or Gravel

11d   Rock, uncovers at sounding datum (See A-11g)

11e   Sand and mud

11f   Sand and gravel

11g   Coral, uncovers at sounding datum (See O-10)

12   Breakers along a shore (See O-25)

14   Limit of unsurveyed areas

(Ab)   Rubble

140

B. Coast Features		
1	G	Gulf
2	B	Bay
(Ba)	B	Bayou
3	Fd	Fjord
4	L	Loch; Lough; Lake
5	Cr	Creek
5a	C	Cove
6	In	Inlet
7	Str	Strait
8	Sd	Sound
9	Pass	Passage; Pass
	Thoro	Thorofare
10	Chan	Channel
10a		Narrows
11	Entr	Entrance
12	Est	Estuary
12a		Delta
13	Mth	Mouth
14	Rd	Road; Roadstead
15	Anch	Anchorage
16	Hbr	Harbor
16a	Hn	Haven
17	P	Port
(Bb)	P	Pond
18	I	Island
19	It	Islet
20	Arch	Archipelago
21	Pen	Peninsula
22	C	Cape
23	Prom	Promontory
24	Hd	Head; Headland
25	Pt	Point
26	Mt	Mountain; Mount
27	Rge	Range
27a		Valley
28		Summit
29	Pk	Peak
30	Vol	Volcano
31		Hill
32	Bld	Boulder
33	Ldg	Landing
34		Table-land (Plateau)
35	Rk	Rock
36		Isolated rock
(Bc)	Str	Stream
(Bd)	R	River
(Be)	Slu	Slough
(Bf)	Lag	Lagoon
(Bg)	Apprs	Approaches
(Bh)	Rky	Rocky

C. The Land (Natural Features)

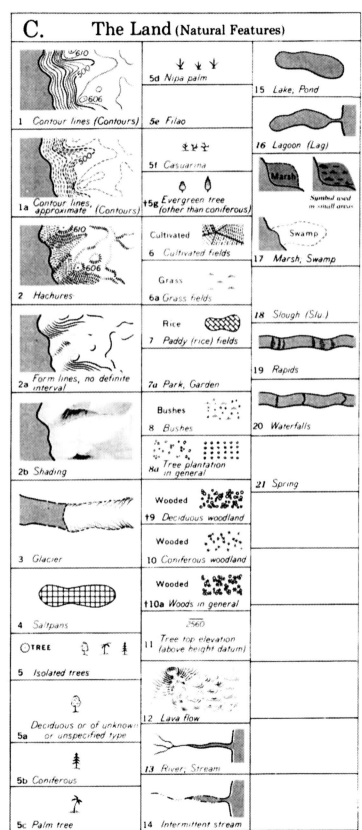

1 Contour lines (Contours)

1a Contour lines, approximate (Contours)

2 Hachures

2a Form lines, no definite interval

2b Shading

3 Glacier

4 Saltpans

5 Isolated trees

5a Deciduous or of unknown or unspecified type

5b Coniferous

5c Palm tree

5d Nipa palm

5e Filao

5f Casuarina

†5g Evergreen tree (other than coniferous)

6 Cultivated fields

6a Grass fields

7 Paddy (rice) fields

7a Park, Garden

8 Bushes

8a Tree plantation in general

†9 Deciduous woodland

10 Coniferous woodland

†10a Woods in general

11 Tree top elevation (above height datum)

12 Lava flow

13 River; Stream

14 Intermittent stream

15 Lake, Pond

16 Lagoon (Lag)

17 Marsh; Swamp

18 Slough (Slu.)

19 Rapids

20 Waterfalls

21 Spring

141

D. Control Points

1	△		Triangulation point (station)
†1a			Astronomic Station
2	⊙		Fixed point (landmark) (See L-63)
†(Da)	o		Fixed point (landmark, position approx.)
3	· 256		Summit of height (Peak) (when not a landmark)
(Db)	◎ 256		Peak, accentuated by contours
(Dc)	☼ 256		Peak, accentuated by hachures
(Dd)	☼		Peak, elevation not determined
(De)	⊙ 256		Peak, when a landmark
4	⊕	Obs Spot	Observation spot
*5		BM	Bench mark
†6	View X		View point
7			Datum point for grid of a plan
8			Graphical triangulation point
9		Astro	Astronomical
10		Tri	Triangulation
(Df)		C of E	Corps of Engineers
12			Great trigonometrical survey station
13			Traverse station
14		Bdy Mon	Boundary monument
(Dg)	◇		International boundary monument

E. Units

1	hr	Hour	†14a		Greenwich	
2	m. min	Minute (of time)	15	pub	Publication	
3	sec	Second (of time)	16	Ed	Edition	
4	m	Meter	17	corr	Correction	
4a	dm	Decimeter	18	alt	Altitude	
4b	cm	Centimeter	19	ht. elev	Height; Elevation	
4c	mm	Millimeter	20	°	Degree	
4d	m²	Square meter	21	'	Minute (of arc)	
4e	m³	Cubic meter	22	"	Second (of arc)	
5	km	Kilometer	23	No	Number	
6	in	Inch	(Ea)	St M	Statute mile	
7	ft	Foot	(Eb)	msec	Microsecond	
8	yd	Yard	†(Ec)	Hz	Hertz (cps)	
9	fm	Fathom	†(Ed)	kHz	Kilohertz (kc)	
10	cbl	Cable length	†(Ee)	MHz	Megahertz (Mc)	
11	M	Nautical mile	†(Ef)	cps	Cycles/second(Hz)	
12	kn	Knot	†(Eg)	kc	Kilocycle (kHz)	
12a	t	Ton	†(Eh)	Mc	Megacycle (MHz)	
12b	cd	Candela (new candle)				
13	lat	Latitude				
14	long	Longitude				

F. Adjectives, Adverbs and other abbreviations

1	gt	Great
2	lit	Little
3	lrg	Large
4	sml	Small
5		Outer
6		Inner
7	mid	Middle
8		Old
9	anc	Ancient
10		New
11	St	Saint
12	conspic	Conspicuous
13		Remarkable
14	D. Destr	Destroyed
15		Projected
16	dist	Distant
17	abt	About
18		See chart
18a		See plan
19		Lighted; Luminous
20	sub	Submarine
21		Eventual
22	AERO	Aeronautical
23		Higher
†23a		Lower
24	exper	Experimental
25	discontd	Discontinued
26	prohib	Prohibited
27	explos	Explosive
28	estab	Established
29	elec	Electric
30	priv	Private, Privately
31	prom	Prominent
32	std	Standard
33	subm	Submerged
34	approx	Approximate
†35		Maritime
†36	maintd	Maintained
†37	aband	Abandoned
†38	temp	Temporary
†39	occas	Occasional
†40	extr	Extreme
†41		Navigable
†42	N M	Notice to Mariners
†(Fa)	L N M	Local Notice to Mariners
†43		Sailing Directions
†44		List of Lights
(Fb)	unverd	Unverified
(Fc)	AUTH	Authorized
(Fd)	CL	Clearance
(Fe)	cor	Corner
(Ff)	concr	Concrete
(Fg)	fl	Flood
(Fh)	mod	Moderate
(Fi)	bet	Between
(Fj)	1st	First
(Fk)	2nd	Second
(Fl)	3rd	Third
(Fm)	4th	Fourth

1		Anch	Anchorage (large vessels)
†2		Anch	Anchorage (small vessels)
3		Hbr	Harbor
4		Hn	Haven
5		P	Port
6		Bkw	Breakwater
6a			Dike
7			Mole
8			Jetty (partly below MHW)
8a			Submerged jetty
(Ga)			Jetty (small scale)
9		Pier	Pier
10			Spit
11			Groin (partly below MHW)
12		ANCH PROHIB	Anchorage prohibited (See P-25)
†12a			Anchorage reserved
†12b		QUAR ANCH	Quarantine anchorage
13			Spoil ground
(Gb)			Dumping ground
(Gc)			Disposal area
14		Fish Stks	Fisheries; Fishing stakes
14a			Fish trap; Fish weirs (actual shape charted)
14b			Duck blind
15			Tunny nets (See G-14a)
15a		Oys	Oyster bed
16		Ldg	Landing place
17			Watering place
18		Whf	Wharf
19			Quay
20			Berth
20a			Anchoring berth
20b	3		Berth number
21		Dol	Dolphin
22			Bollard
23			Mooring ring
24			Crane
25			Landing stage
25a			Landing stairs
26		Quar	Quarantine
27			Lazaret
*28		Harbor Master	Harbor master's office
29		Cus Ho	Customhouse
30			Fishing harbor
31			Winter harbor
32			Refuge harbor
33		B Hbr	Boat harbor
34			Stranding harbor (uncovers at LW)
35			Dock
36			Dry dock (actual shape on large-scale charts)
37			Floating dock (actual shape on large-scale charts)
38			Gridiron; Careening grid
39			Patent slip; Slipway, Marine railway
39a		Ramp	Ramp
†40		Lock	Lock (point upstream) (See H-13)
41			Wet dock
42			Shipyard
43			Lumber yard
44		Health Office	Health officer's office
45		Hk	Hulk (actual shape on lrg scale charts)(See O-11)
46		PROHIBITED AREA	Prohibited area
†46a			Calling-in point for vessel traffic control
47			Anchorage for seaplanes
48			Seaplane landing area
49		Under construction	Work in progress
50			Under construction
†51			Work projected
(Gd)		Subm ruins	Submerged ruins

H.   Topography   (Artificial Features)

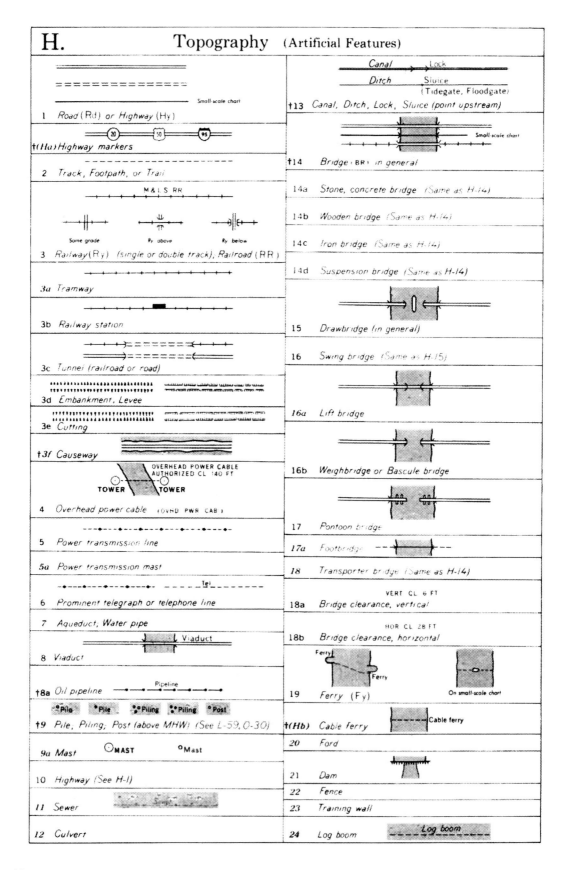

1 Road (Rd) or Highway (Hy)	†13 Canal, Ditch, Lock, Sluice (point upstream)
†(Ha) Highway markers	†14 Bridge (BR) in general
2 Track, Footpath, or Trail	14a Stone, concrete bridge (Same as H-14)
3 Railway (Ry) (single or double track), Railroad (RR)	14b Wooden bridge (Same as H-14)
3a Tramway	14c Iron bridge (Same as H-14)
3b Railway station	14d Suspension bridge (Same as H-14)
3c Tunnel (railroad or road)	15 Drawbridge (in general)
3d Embankment, Levee	16 Swing bridge (Same as H-15)
3e Cutting	16a Lift bridge
†3f Causeway	16b Weighbridge or Bascule bridge
4 Overhead power cable (OVHD PWR CAB)	17 Pontoon bridge
5 Power transmission line	17a Footbridge
5a Power transmission mast	18 Transporter bridge (Same as H-14)
6 Prominent telegraph or telephone line	18a Bridge clearance, vertical
7 Aqueduct; Water pipe	18b Bridge clearance, horizontal
8 Viaduct	19 Ferry (Fy)
†8a Oil pipeline	†(Hb) Cable ferry
†9 Pile; Piling; Post (above MHW) (See L-59, O-30)	20 Ford
9a Mast	21 Dam
10 Highway (See H-1)	22 Fence
11 Sewer	23 Training wall
12 Culvert	24 Log boom

I. Buildings and Structures (see General Remarks)

1			City or Town (large scale)	26a	Locust Ave	Ave	Avenue
(1a)			City or Town (small scale)	†26b	Grand Blvd	Blvd	Boulevard
2			Suburb	27		Tel	Telegraph
3		Vil	Village	28		Tel Off	Telegraph office
3a			Buildings in general	29		P O	Post office
4		Cas	Castle	30		Govt Ho	Government house
5			House	31			Town hall
6			Villa	32		Hosp	Hospital
7			Farm	33			Slaughterhouse
8		Ch	Church	34		Magz	Magazine
8a		Cath	Cathedral	34a			Warehouse; Storehouse
8b	SPIRE	Spire	Spire; Steeple	35	MON	Mon	Monument
9			Roman Catholic Church	36	CUP	Cup	Cupola
†10			Temple	37	ELEV	Elev	Elevator; Lift
11			Chapel	(1e)		Elev	Elevation; Elevated
†12			Mosque	38			Shed
†12a			Minaret	39			Zinc roof
(1b)			Moslem Shrine	40	Ruins	Ru	Ruins
†13			Marabout	41	TR	Tr	Tower
†14		Pag	Pagoda	†(1f)	ABAND LT HO		Abandoned lighthouse
†15			Buddhist Temple; Joss-House	42	WINDMILL		Windmill
†15a			Shinto Shrine	†43			Watermill
16			Monastery; Convent	43a	WINDMOTOR		Windmotor
17			Calvary; Cross	44	CHY	Chy	Chimney; Stack
17a			Cemetery, Non-Christian	45	S'PIPE	S'pipe	Water tower; Standpipe
18	Cem		Cemetery, Christian	46			Oil tank
18a			Tomb	47		Facty	Factory
19			Fort (actual shape charted)	48			Saw mill
†20			Battery	49			Brick kiln
21			Barracks	50			Mine; Quarry
22			Powder magazine	51	Well		Well
23	Airport		Airplane landing field	52			Cistern
24			Airport, large scale (See P-13)	53	TANK	Tk	Tank
(1c)			Airport, military (small scale)	54			Noria
†(1d)			Airport, civil (small scale)	55			Fountain
25			Mooring mast				
26	King St	St	Street				

145

I.			Buildings and Structures (continued)					
61		Inst	Institute	72	⊙GAB	°Gab	Gable
62			Establishment	73			Wall
63			Bathing establishment	†74			Pyramid
64		Ct Ho	Courthouse	†75			Pillar
65		Sch	School	†76			Oil derrick
(Ig)		H S	High school	(Ii)		Ltd	Limited
(Ih)		Univ	University	(Ij)		Apt	Apartment
66	▪ ▨ □	Bldg	Building	(Ik)		Cap	Capitol
67		Pav	Pavilion	(Il)		Co	Company
68			Hut	(Im)		Corp	Corporation
69			Stadium	(In)	⊙		Landmark (conspicuous object)
70		T	Telephone	(Io)	o		Landmark (position approx.)
71	⊕ ●		Gas tank; Gasometer				

J.			Miscellaneous Stations					
1		Sta	Any kind of station	13			Tide signal station
2		Sta	Station	14			Stream signal station
3	C G		Coast Guard station (Similar to Lifesaving Sta.)	15			Ice signal station
				16			Time signal station
(Ja)	⊙C G WALLIS SANDS		Coast Guard station (when landmark)	†16a			Manned oceanographic station
				†16b			Unmanned oceanographic station
†4	⊙LOOK TR		Lookout station; Watch tower	17			Time ball
5			Lifeboat station	18			Signal mast
6	LS S		Lifesaving station (See J-3)	19	⊙FS °FS	°FP °FP	Flagstaff; Flagpole
7		Rkt Sta	Rocket station	†19a	⊙F TR	°F Tr	Flag tower
8	◉ ⊙PIL STA		Pilot station	20			Signal
9		Sig Sta	Signal station	21		Obsy	Observatory
10		Sem	Semaphore	22		Off	Office
11		S Sig Sta	Storm signal station	(Jc)	°BELL		Bell (on land)
12			Weather signal station	(Jd)	°HECP		Harbor entrance control post
(Jb)	⊙W B SIG STA		Weather Bureau signal station				

K. (✦ new optional symbol) Lights

No.	Abbr.	Description		No.	Abbr.	Description
†1		Position of light		29	F Fl	Fixed and flashing light
2	Lt	Light		30	F Gp Fl	Fixed and group flashing light
†(Ka)		Riprap surrounding light		†30a	Mo	Morse code light
3	Lt Ho	Lighthouse		31	Rot	Revolving or Rotating light
4	AERO ●AERO	Aeronautical light (See F-22)		41		Period
4a		Marine and air navigation light		42		Every
5	Bn ● ● Bn	Light beacon		43		With
6		Light vessel; Lightship		44		Visible (range)
8		Lantern		(Kb)	M	Nautical mile (See E-11)
9		Street lamp		(Kc)	m; min	Minutes (See E-2)
10	REF	Reflector		(Kd)	sec	Seconds (See E-3)
11	Ldg Lt	Leading light		45	Fl	Flash
12	Sector light			46	Occ	Occultation
13	Directional light			46a		Eclipse
14		Harbor light		47	Gp	Group
15		Fishing light		48	Occ	Intermittent light
16		Tidal light		49	SEC	Sector
17	Prv maintd	Private light (maintained by private interests; to be used with caution)		50		Color of sector
21	F	Fixed light		51	Aux	Auxiliary light
22	Occ	Occulting light		52		Varied
23	Fl	Flashing light		61	Vi	Violet
†23a	E Int	Isophase light (equal interval)		62		Purple
24	Qk Fl	Quick flashing (scintillating) light		63	Bu	Blue
25	Int Qk Fl / I Qk Fl	Interrupted quick flashing light		64	G	Green
25a	S Fl	Short flashing light		65	Or	Orange
26	Alt	Alternating light		66	R	Red
27	Gp Occ	Group occulting light		67	W	White
28	Gp Fl	Group flashing light		67a	Am	Amber
28a	S-L Fl	Short-long flashing light		68	OBSC	Obscured light
28b		Group short flashing light		†68a	Fog Det Lt	Fog detector light (See N-Nb)

147

K.			Lights (continued)				
_69_			Unwatched light	_79_			Front light
_70_	Occas		Occasional light	_80_	Vert		Vertical lights
_71_	Irreg		Irregular light	_81_	Hor		Horizontal lights
_72_	Prov		Provisional light	(Kf)		VB	Vertical beam
_73_	Temp		Temporary light	(Kg)		RGE	Range
(Ke)	D. Destr		Destroyed	(Kh)		Exper	Experimental light
_74_	Exting		Extinguished light	(Ki)		TRLB	Temporarily replaced by lighted buoy showing the same characteristics
_75_			Faint light	(Kj)		TRUB	Temporarily replaced by unlighted buoy
_76_			Upper light				
_77_			Lower light	(Kk)		TLB	Temporary lighted buoy
_78_			Rear light	(Kl)		TUB	Temporary unlighted buoy

L.		Buoys and Beacons (see General Remarks)			
_1_	Position of buoy		_17_	Bifurcation buoy (RBHB)
_2_	Light buoy		_18_	Junction buoy (RBHB)
_3_	Bell buoy		_19_	Isolated danger buoy (RBHB)
_3a_	Gong buoy		_20_	Wreck buoy (RBHB or G)
_4_	Whistle buoy		_20a_	Obstruction buoy (RBHB or G)
_5_	Can or Cylindrical buoy		_21_	Telegraph-cable buoy
_6_	Nun or Conical buoy		_22_	Mooring buoy (colors of mooring buoys never carried)
_7_	Spherical buoy		_22a_	Mooring
_8_	Spar buoy		_22b_	Mooring buoy with telegraphic communications
†_8a_	Pillar or Spindle buoy		_22c_	Mooring buoy with telephonic communications
_9_	Buoy with topmark (ball) (see L-70)		_23_	Warping buoy
_10_	Barrel or Ton buoy		_24_	Quarantine buoy
(La)	Color unknown		†_24a_	Practice area buoy
(Lb)	Float		_25_	Explosive anchorage buoy
_12_	Lightfloat		_25a_	Aeronautical anchorage buoy
_13_	Outer or Landfall buoy		_26_	Compass adjustment buoy
_14_	Fairway buoy (BWVS)		_27_	Fish trap (area) buoy (BWHB)
_14a_	Mid-channel buoy (BWVS)		_27a_	Spoil ground buoy
†_15_	Starboard-hand buoy (entering from seaward)		†_28_	Anchorage buoy (marks limits)
_16_	Port-hand buoy (entering from seaward)		†_29_	Private aid to navigation (buoy) (maintained by private interests, use with caution)

_30_			Temporary buoy (See K1,j,k,l)
_30a_			Winter buoy
_31_	♪	HB	Horizontal stripes or bands
_32_	∅	VS	Vertical stripes
_33_	∅	Chec	Checkered
†_33a_	∅	Diag	Diagonal bands
41	☐	W	White
42	■	B	Black
43	▨	R	Red
44	⬚	Y	Yellow
45	▨	G	Green
46		Br	Brown
47		Gy	Gray
48	▤	Bu	Blue
†_48a_		Am	Amber
†_48b_		Or	Orange
_51_	∅		Floating beacon
_52_	△RW Bn △W Bn ▲R Bn		Fixed beacon (unlighted or daybeacon)
	▲ Bn		Black beacon
	△ Bn		Color unknown
†(Lc)	⊙MARKER °Marker		Private aid to navigation
_53_		Bn	Beacon, in general (See L-52)
_54_			Tower beacon

_55_			Cardinal marking system
_56_	△ Deviation Bn		Compass adjustment beacon
_57_			Topmarks (See L-9, 70)
_58_			Telegraph-cable (landing) beacon
†_59_	°Piles •Piles		Piles (See O-30, H-9)
	⊥⊥		Stakes
	°Stumps		Stumps (See O-30)
	⊥⊥		Perches
61	⊙CAIRN °Cairn		Cairn
62			Painted patches
63	⊙		Landmark (conspicuous object) (See D-2)
(Ld)	°		Landmark (position approximate)
64		REF	Reflector
65	⊙MARKER		Range targets, markers
(Le)	∅W Or ∅W Or		Special-purpose buoys
†66			Oil installation buoy
†67			Drilling platform (See O-0b, O-0c)
_70_	Note:		TOPMARKS on buoys and beacons may be shown on charts of foreign waters. The abbreviation for black is not shown adjacent to buoys or beacons.
(Lf)	⌣ [Ra Ref]		Radar reflector (See M-13)

149

M.   Radio and Radar Stations

1	°R Sta	Radio telegraph station	12	Racon	Radar responder beacon
2	°R T	Radio telephone station	13	Ra Ref	Radar reflector (See L-Lf)
3	R Bn	Radiobeacon	14	Ra (conspic)	Radar conspicuous object
4	R Bn	Circular radiobeacon	14a		Ramark
5	R D	Directional radiobeacon; Radio range	15	D F S	Distance finding station (synchronized signals)
6		Rotating loop radiobeacon	†16	AERO R Bn 302 ▄▄▄	Aeronautical radiobeacon
7	R D F	Radio direction finding station	†17	°Decca Sta	Decca station
(Ma)	TELEM ANT	Telemetry antenna	†18	o Loran Sta Venice	Loran station (name)
†(Mb)	R RELAY MAST	Radio relay mast	†19	CONSOL Bn 190 Kc MMF ▄▄.	Consol (Consolan) station
†(Mc)	MICRO TR	Microwave tower	(Md)	AERO R Rge 342 ▄▄▄	Aeronautical radio range
9	R MAST	Radio mast	(Me)	Ra Ref Calibration Bn	Radar calibration beacon
	R TR	Radio tower	(Mf)	LORAN TR SPRING ISLAND	Loran tower (name)
†9a	TV TR	Television mast; Television tower	†(Mg)	R TR F R Lt	Obstruction light
10	R TR (WBAL) 1090 Kc	Radio broadcasting station (commercial)			
10a	°R Sta	Q.T.G. Radio station			
11	Ra	Radar station			

N.   Fog Signals

1	Fog Sig	Fog-signal station	13	HORN	Fog horn
2		Radio fog-signal station	†13a	HORN	Electric fog horn
3	GUN	Explosive fog signal	14	BELL	Fog bell
4		Submarine fog signal	15	WHIS	Fog whistle
5	SUB-BELL	Submarine fog bell (action of waves)	16	HORN	Reed horn
6	SUB-BELL	Submarine fog bell (mechanical)	17	GONG	Fog gong
7	SUB-OSC	Submarine oscillator	†18		Submarine sound signal not connected to the shore (See N-5,6,7)
8	NAUTO	Nautophone	†18a		Submarine sound signal connected to the shore (See N-5,6,7)
9	DIA	Diaphone			
10	GUN	Fog gun	(Na)	HORN	Typhon
11	SIREN	Fog siren	(Nb)	Fog Det Lt	Fog detector light (See K 68a)
12	HORN	Fog trumpet			

O.   Dangers

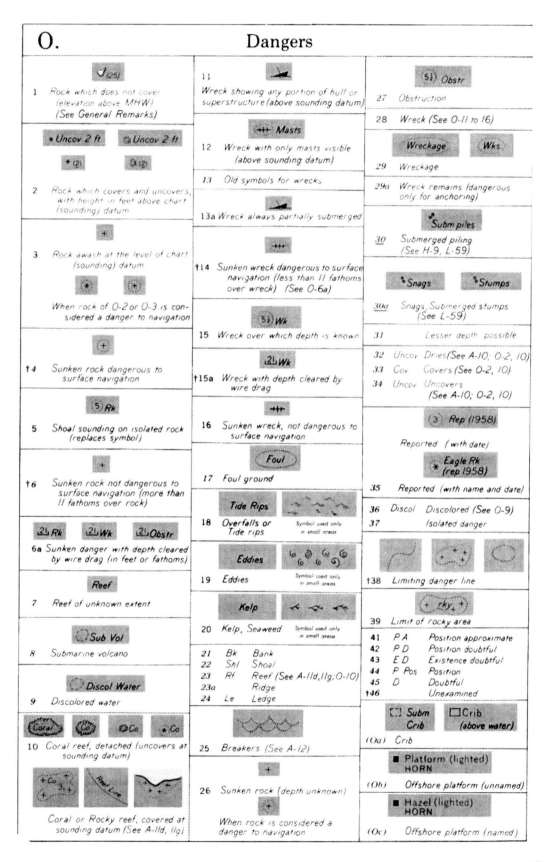

1 Rock which does not cover (elevation above MHW) (See General Remarks)

2 Rock which covers and uncovers, with height in feet above chart (sounding) datum

3 Rock awash at the level of chart (sounding) datum

When rock of O-2 or O-3 is considered a danger to navigation

†4 Sunken rock dangerous to surface navigation

5 Shoal sounding on isolated rock (replaces symbol)

†6 Sunken rock not dangerous to surface navigation (more than 11 fathoms over rock)

6a Sunken danger with depth cleared by wire drag (in feet or fathoms)

7 Reef of unknown extent

8 Submarine volcano

9 Discolored water

10 Coral reef, detached (uncovers at sounding datum)

Coral or Rocky reef, covered at sounding datum (See A-11d, 11g)

11 Wreck showing any portion of hull or superstructure (above sounding datum)

12 Wreck with only masts visible (above sounding datum)

13 Old symbols for wrecks

13a Wreck always partially submerged

†14 Sunken wreck dangerous to surface navigation (less than 11 fathoms over wreck) (See O-6a)

15 Wreck over which depth is known

†15a Wreck with depth cleared by wire drag

16 Sunken wreck, not dangerous to surface navigation

17 Foul ground

18 Overfalls or Tide rips — Symbol used only in small areas

19 Eddies — Symbol used only in small areas

20 Kelp, Seaweed — Symbol used only in small areas

21 Bk   Bank
22 Shl   Shoal
23 Rf   Reef (See A-11d,11g; O-10)
23a   Ridge
24 Le   Ledge

25 Breakers (See A-12)

26 Sunken rock (depth unknown)

When rock is considered a danger to navigation

27 Obstruction

28 Wreck (See O-11 to 16)

29 Wreckage

29a Wreck remains (dangerous only for anchoring)

30 Submerged piling (See H-9, L-59)

30a Snags, Submerged stumps (See L-59)

31 Lesser depth possible

32 Uncov   Dries (See A-10; O-2, 10)
33 Cov   Covers (See O-2, 10)
34 Uncov   Uncovers (See A-10; O-2, 10)

Reported (with date)

35 Reported (with name and date)

36 Discol   Discolored (See O-9)
37   Isolated danger

†38 Limiting danger line

39 Limit of rocky area

41 P A   Position approximate
42 P D   Position doubtful
43 E D   Existence doubtful
44 P Pos Position
45 D   Doubtful
†46   Unexamined

(Oa) Crib

(Ob) Offshore platform (unnamed)

(Oc) Offshore platform (named)

P. Various Limits, etc.

1		Leading line, Range line
2		Transit
3		In line with
4		Limit of sector
5		Channel, Course, Track recommended (marked by buoys or beacons) (See P-21)
(Pa)		Alternate course
†6		Radar guided track
7		Submarine cable (power, telegraph, telephone, etc.)
7a		Submarine cable area
†7b		Abandoned submarine cable (includes disused cable)
†8		Submarine pipeline
8a		Submarine pipeline area
9		Maritime limit in general
†(Pb)		Limit of restricted area
10		Limit of fishing zone (fish trap areas)
†(Pc)		U.S. Harbor Line
11		Limit of dumping ground, spoil ground (See P-9, G-13)
12		Anchorage limit
13		Limit of airport (See I-23, 24)
†13a		Limit of military practice areas
14		Limit of sovereignty (Territorial waters)
15		Customs boundary
16		International boundary (also State boundary)
17		Stream limit
18		Ice limit
19		Limit of tide
20		Limit of navigation
†21		Course recommended (not marked by buoys or beacons) (See P-5)
22		District or province limit
23		Reservation line
24	COURSE 053°00' TRUE MARKERS MARKERS	Measured distance
25	PROHIBITED AREA	Prohibited area (See G-12, 46)
†(Pd)	SAFETY FAIRWAY	Shipping safety fairway
†(Pe)		Directed traffic lanes
†(Pf)	Obstruction (fish haven)	Fish haven (fishing reef)

Q. Soundings

1	SD	Doubtful sounding
2	65	No bottom found
3		Out of position
4		Least depth in narrow channels
5	30 FEET APR 1968	Dredged channel (with controlling depth indicated)
6	24 FEET MAY 1968	Dredged area
7		Swept channel (See Q-9)
8	6	Drying (or uncovering) heights; in feet above chart (sounding) datum
9	17 119	Swept area, not adequately sounded (shown by green tint)
9a	29 23 3 30 8 21 4	Swept area adequately sounded (swept by wire drag to depth indicated)
†10		Hair-line depth figures
10a	8₂ 19	Figures for ordinary soundings
11	8₂ 19	Soundings taken from foreign charts
12	8₂ 19	Soundings taken from older surveys (or smaller scale chts)
13	8₂ 19	Echo soundings
14	8₂ 19	Sloping figures (See Q-12)
15	8₂ 19	Upright figures (See Q-10a)
†16	(25) (2)	Bracketed figures (See O-1, 2)
17	6	Underlined sounding figures (See Q-8)
18	3₂ 6₁	Soundings expressed in fathoms and feet
†22		Unsounded area
(Qa)	6 5 2ft	Stream

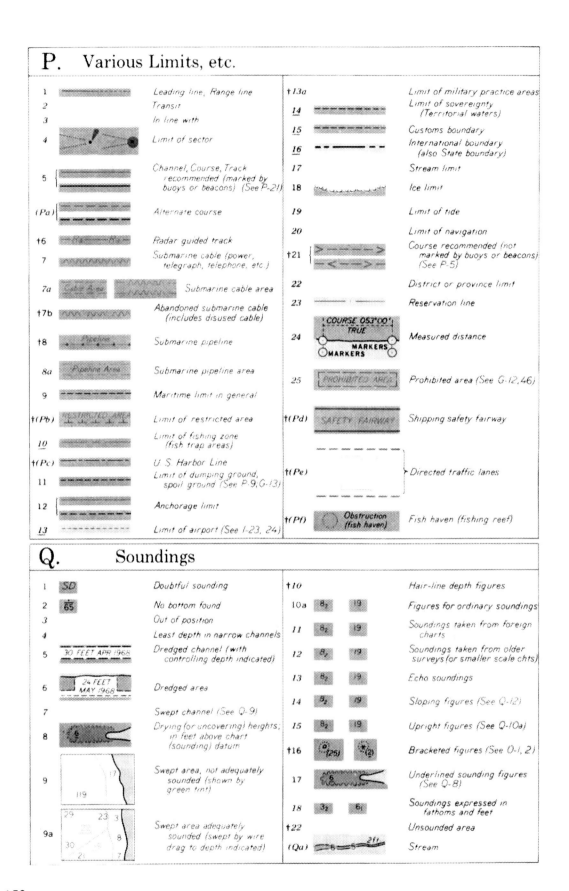

R. Depth Contours and Tints (see General Remarks)

Feet	Fathoms		Feet	Fathoms	
0	0		300	50	
6	1		600	100	
12	2		1,200	200	
18	3		1,800	300	
24	4		2,400	400	
30	5		3,000	500	
36	6		6,000	1,000	
60	10		12,000	2,000	
120	20		18,000	3,000	
180	30		Or continuous lines, with values		
240	40				

—— 5 —— (blue or black) —— 100 ——

S. Quality of the Bottom

†1	Grd	Ground	24	Oys	Oysters	50	spk	Speckled
2	S	Sand	25	Ms	Mussels	51	gty	Gritty
3	M	Mud; Muddy	26	Spg	Sponge	†52	dec	Decayed
4	Oz	Ooze	†27	K	Kelp	53	fly	Flinty
5	Ml	Marl	28	Wd	Sea-weed	54	glac	Glacial
6	Cl	Clay	28	Grs	Grass	†55	ten	Tenacious
7	G	Gravel	†29	Stg	Sea-tangle	56	wh	White
8	Sn	Shingle	†31	Spi	Spicules	57	bk	Black
9	P	Pebbles	32	Fr	Foraminifera	58	vi	Violet
10	St	Stones	33	Gl	Globigerina	59	bu	Blue
11	Rk; rky	Rock; Rocky	34	Di	Diatoms	60	gn	Green
11a	Blds	Boulders	35	Rd	Radiolaria	61	yl	Yellow
12	Ck	Chalk	36	Pt	Pteropods	62	or	Orange
12a	Ca	Calcareous	37	Po	Polyzoa	63	rd	Red
13	Qz	Quartz	†38	Cir	Cirripeda	64	br	Brown
†13a	Sch	Schist	†38a	Fu	Fucus	65	ch	Chocolate
14	Co	Coral	†38b	Ma	Mattes	66	gy	Gray
(Sa)	Co Hd	Coral head	39	fne	Fine	67	lt	Light
15	Mds	Madrepores	40	crs	Coarse	68	dk	Dark
16	Vol	Volcanic	41	sft	Soft			
(Sb)	Vol Ash	Volcanic ash	42	hrd	Hard	†70	vard	Varied
17	La	Lava	43	stf	Stiff	†71	unev	Uneven
18	Pm	Pumice	44	sml	Small	†(Sc)	S/M	Surface layer and Under layer
19	T	Tufa	45	lrg	Large			
20	Sc	Scoriae	46	stk	Sticky			
21	Cn	Cinders	47	brk	Broken			
†21a		Ash	47a	grd	Ground (Shells)	76		Fresh water springs in sea-bed
22	Mn	Manganese	†48	rt	Rotten			
23	Sh	Shells	†49	str	Streaky			

T.		**Tides and Currents**

1	HW	High water
1a	HHW	Higher high water
2	LW	Low water
(Ta)	LWD	Low water datum
2a	LLW	Lower low water
3	MTL	Mean tide level
4	MSL	Mean sea level
4a		Elevation of mean sea level above chart (sounding) datum
5		Chart datum (datum for sounding reduction)
6	Sp	Spring tide
7	Np	Neap tide
†7a	MHW	Mean high water
8	MHWS	Mean high water springs
8a	MHWN	Mean high water neaps
8b	MHHW	Mean higher high water
†8c	MLW	Mean low water
9	MLWS	Mean low water springs
9a	MLWN	Mean low water neaps
9b	MLLW	Mean lower low water
10	ISLW	Indian spring low water
11		High water full and change (vulgar establishment of the port)
12		Low water full and change
13		Mean establishment of the port
13a		Establishment of the port
14		Unit of height
15		Equinoctial
16		Quarter; Quadrature
17	Str	Stream
18	➤➤➤➤ 2 kn ➤	Current, general, with rate
19	➤➤ 2 kn ➤	Flood stream (current) with rate
20	2 kn ➤	Ebb stream (current) with rate
21	○ Tide gauge	Tide gauge, Tidepole, Automatic tide gauge
23	vel	Velocity; Rate
24	kn	Knots
25	ht	Height
26		Tide
27		New moon
28		Full moon
29		Ordinary
30		Syzygy
31	fl	Flood
32		Ebb
33		Tidal stream diagram
34	Ⓐ Ⓑ	Place for which tabulated tidal stream data are given
35		Range (of tide)
36		Phase lag
(Tb)		Current diagram, with explanatory note

U.		**Compass**

Compass Rose

The outer circle is in degrees with zero at true north. The inner circles are in points and degrees with the arrow indicating magnetic north.

1	N	North
2	E	East
3	S	South
4	W	West
5	NE	Northeast
6	SE	Southeast
7	SW	Southwest
8	NW	Northwest
9	N	Northern
10	E	Eastern
11	S	Southern
12	W	Western
21	brg	Bearing
†22	T	True
23	mag	Magnetic
24	var	Variation
25		Annual change
25a		Annual change nil
26		Abnormal variation; Magnetic attraction
27	deg	Degrees (See E-20)
28	dev	Deviation

AIDS TO NAVIGATION ON NAVIGABLE WATERWAYS
except Western Rivers and Intracoastal Waterway

LATERAL SYSTEM AS SEEN ENTERING FROM SEAWARD

PORT SIDE
ODD NUMBERED BUOYS OR STRUCTURES
WITH WHITE OR ☐ GREEN LIGHTS

FIXED
FLASHING
OCCULTING
QUICK FLASHING

LIGHTED BUOY "9"

BELL OR WHISTLE

CAN
C "7"

"1" ▲ DAYMARKS ▲ "3"

POINTER ▲ "5"

MID CHANNEL
NO NUMBERS MAY BE LETTERED
☐ WHITE LIGHT ONLY

MORSE CODE

BW "MoA"

CAN
BW C "T"

LIGHTED

NUN
BW N "B"

A BW

MID CHANNEL DAYMARK

JUNCTION
MARKS JUNCTION AND OBSTRUCTIONS. NO NUMBERS
PASS ON EITHER SIDE. MAY BE LETTERED
INTERRUPTED QUICK FLASHING

☐ WHITE OR ▨ GREEN   ☐ WHITE OR ■ RED

RB

LIGHTED

PREFERRED CHANNEL STARBOARD
TOPMOST BAND BLACK

PREFERRED CHANNEL PORT
TOPMOST BAND RED

CAN
RB C "N"

NUN
RB N "L"

L RB

J RB

STARBOARD SIDE
EVEN NUMBERED BUOYS OR STRUCTURES
WITH WHITE OR ■ RED LIGHTS

FIXED
FLASHING
OCCULTING
QUICK FLASHING

LIGHTED BUOY "8"

BELL OR WHISTLE

NUN
N "6"

DAYMARK ▲ "4"

POINTER ▲ "6"

BUOYS HAVING NO LATERAL SIGNIFICANCE—ALL WATERS

NO SPECIAL SHAPES, NO NUMBERS
(MAY BE LETTERED)
☐ WHITE LIGHTS ONLY

FIXED
FLASHING
OCCULTING

SPECIAL PURPOSE
WOr C

QUARANTINE ANCHORAGE
Y C

ANCHORAGE
W C "N"

FISH NET
BW C

DREDGING
GW C

RANGE DAYMARKS

DANGER

SUBMERGED DANGER JETTY

DAYMARKS NON-LATERAL SIGNIFICANCE

Appendix B
USEFUL PHYSICAL LAWS AND TRIGONOMETRIC FUNCTIONS.

A. Kepler's Laws

  1. The orbits of the planets are ellipses with the sun at a common focus.
  2. The straight line joining the sun and a planet sweeps over equal areas in equal intervals of time.
  3. The squares of the orbital (sidereal) periods of any two planets are proportional to the cubes of their mean distances from the sun.

B. Newton's Laws of Motion

  1. A body at rest or in uniform motion will remain at rest or in uniform motion unless some external force is applied to it.
  2. When a body is acted upon by a constant force, its resulting acceleration is proportional to the force, and inversely proportional to the mass.
  3. To every force there is an equal and opposite reaction force.

C. Newton's Law of Gravitation

(Universal Law of Gravitation)

Every particle of matter attracts every other particle with a force that varies directly as the product of their masses and inversely as the square of the distance between them.

D. Foucault's Law

A spinning body tends to swing around so as to place its axis parallel to the axis of an impressed force, such that its direction of rotation is the same as that of the impressed force.

E. Trigonometric functions

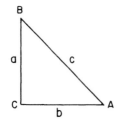

1. Sine A = a/c = $\dfrac{\text{side opposite}}{\text{hypotenuse}}$

156

Consine $A = b/c = \dfrac{\text{side adjacent}}{\text{hypotenuse}}$

Tangent $A = a/b = \dfrac{\text{side opposite}}{\text{side adjacent}}$

Cotangent $A = b/a = \dfrac{\text{side adjacent}}{\text{side opposite}}$

Secant $A = c/b = \dfrac{\text{hypotenuse}}{\text{side adjacent}}$

Cosecant $A = c/a = \dfrac{\text{hypotenuse}}{\text{side opposite}}$

2. Versed sine $A = 1 - \text{cosine } A$
   Co-versed sine $A = 1 - \text{sine } A$
   Haversine $A = 1/2 \ (1 - \text{cosine } A)$

3. The cosecant is the reciprocal of the sine.
   The secant is the reciprocal of the cosine.
   The cotangent is the reciprocal of the tangent.
   The tangent equals the sine divided by the cosine.

4. The complement of an angle equals 90° – that angle.
   The supplement of an angle equals 180° – that angle.
   The explement of an angle equals 360° – that angle.

5. The sine of an angle is the cosine of its complement.
   The tangent of an angle is the cotangent of its complement.
   The secant of an angle is the cosecant of its complement.

Appendix C-1

MAYPORT, FLA., 1970

TIMES AND HEIGHTS OF HIGH AND LOW WATERS

JULY

DAY	TIME H.M.	HT. FT.	DAY	TIME H.M.	HT. FT.
1 W	0024	0.0	16 TH	0536	3.7
	0630	3.7		1136	-0.4
	1218	-0.3		1818	5.0
	1900	4.9			
2 TH	0112	0.0	17 F	0030	-0.1
	0718	3.7		0636	3.9
	1300	-0.2		1230	-0.6
	1942	4.9		1912	5.3
3 F	0154	0.0	18 SA	0124	-0.4
	0806	3.7		0730	4.2
	1342	-0.2		1324	-0.8
	2024	4.8		2006	5.4
4 SA	0236	0.0	19 SU	0212	-0.6
	0848	3.7		0824	4.4
	1424	-0.1		1418	-0.9
	2106	4.7		2054	5.5
5 SU	0312	0.0	20 M	0300	-0.7
	0924	3.7		0918	4.7
	1506	0.0		1512	-0.8
	2142	4.6		2148	5.4
6 M	0348	0.0	21 TU	0354	-0.8
	1006	3.7		1012	4.8
	1542	0.1		1606	-0.7
	2218	4.4		2236	5.3
7 TU	0424	0.1	22 W	0442	-0.7
	1042	3.7		1106	4.9
	1624	0.3		1706	-0.5
	2254	4.3		2330	5.0
8 W	0500	0.1	23 TH	0536	-0.6
	1124	3.8		1200	4.9
	1706	0.4		1806	-0.3
	2330	4.1			
9 TH	0536	0.1	24 F	0024	4.7
	1206	3.8		0630	-0.4
	1754	0.5		1300	4.8
				1906	0.0
10 F	0012	3.9	25 SA	0118	4.3
	0618	0.2		0724	-0.3
	1240	3.9		1354	4.7
	1842	0.6		2012	0.2
11 SA	0054	3.7	26 SU	0218	4.0
	0700	0.2		0824	-0.1
	1336	3.9		1500	4.7
	1936	0.7		2118	0.4
12 SU	0142	3.6	27 M	0318	3.8
	0754	0.1		0924	0.0
	1424	4.1		1600	4.7
	2036	0.7		2224	0.4
13 M	0230	3.5	28 TU	0418	3.6
	0842	0.1		1018	0.0
	1524	4.3		17C0	4.7
	2142	0.6		2318	0.4
14 TU	0330	3.4	29 W	0518	3.6
	0942	-0.1		1112	0.1
	1618	4.5		1754	4.8
	2242	0.4			
15 W	0436	3.5	30 TH	0012	0.3
	1036	-0.2		0612	3.7
	1718	4.7		1200	0.1
	2336	0.1		1842	4.8
			31 F	0054	0.2
				0700	3.8
				1242	0.0
				1924	4.9

AUGUST

DAY	TIME H.M.	HT. FT.	DAY	TIME H.M.	HT. FT.
1 SA	0136	0.2	16 SU	0100	-0.3
	0748	3.9		0712	4.8
	1324	0.0		1312	-0.7
	2006	4.9		1942	5.7
2 SU	0212	0.1	17 M	0148	-0.5
	0824	4.0		0806	5.1
	1406	0.1		1406	-0.8
	2042	4.8		2036	5.7
3 M	0242	0.1	18 TU	0236	-0.7
	0900	4.1		0900	5.3
	1442	0.1		1454	-0.7
	2118	4.7		2124	5.6
4 TU	0318	0.1	19 W	0324	-0.7
	0936	4.2		0948	5.5
	1518	0.2		1548	-0.6
	2148	4.6		2212	5.4
5 W	0348	0.1	20 TH	0412	-0.6
	1012	4.2		1042	5.4
	1554	0.3		1642	-0.3
	2224	4.4		2306	5.1
6 TH	0424	0.1	21 F	0506	-0.4
	1048	4.2		1136	5.3
	1636	0.4		1742	0.0
	2254	4.2		2354	4.7
7 F	0454	0.2	22 SA	0554	-0.1
	1124	4.3		1230	5.2
	1718	0.6		1842	0.4
	2330	4.1			
8 SA	0530	0.2	23 SU	0048	4.4
	1206	4.3		0654	0.2
	1806	0.7		1330	5.0
				1948	0.7
9 SU	0012	3.9	24 M	0148	4.0
	0612	0.3		0754	0.4
	1254	4.3		1430	4.8
	1900	0.8		2054	0.8
10 M	0100	3.7	25 TU	0254	3.8
	0706	0.3		0854	0.6
	1348	4.4		1536	4.7
	2000	0.9		2200	0.9
11 TU	0154	3.6	26 W	0400	3.8
	0806	0.3		0954	0.6
	1448	4.5		1636	4.7
	2106	0.8		2300	0.8
12 W	0254	3.6	27 TH	0500	3.8
	0906	0.2		1054	0.6
	1548	4.7		1730	4.8
	2212	0.6		2348	0.7
13 TH	0406	3.7	28 F	0554	4.0
	1012	0.0		1142	0.5
	1654	4.9		1818	4.9
	2312	0.4			
14 F	0512	4.0	29 SA	0030	0.6
	1118	-0.2		0642	4.2
	1754	5.2		1224	0.4
				1900	5.0
15 SA	0006	0.3	30 SU	0106	0.4
	0618	4.4		0718	4.4
	1212	-0.5		1306	0.4
	1854	5.5		1936	5.0
			31 M	0142	0.3
				0800	4.6
				1342	0.3
				2012	5.0

SEPTEMBER

DAY	TIME H.M.	HT. FT.	DAY	TIME H.M.	HT. FT.
1 TU	0212	0.3	16 W	0212	-0.5
	0836	4.7		0836	6.0
	1418	0.3		1436	-0.4
	2048	4.9		2100	5.7
2 W	0242	0.3	17 TH	0300	-0.4
	0906	4.8		0924	6.0
	1454	0.4		1530	-0.2
	2118	4.8		2148	5.5
3 TH	0312	0.3	18 F	0342	-0.3
	0942	4.8		1018	5.9
	1530	0.5		1618	0.1
	2154	4.6		2236	5.2
4 F	0342	0.3	19 SA	0430	0.0
	1018	4.8		1106	5.7
	1606	0.6		1712	0.5
	2224	4.5		2324	4.8
5 SA	0418	0.4	20 SU	0524	0.3
	1054	4.8		1200	5.4
	1648	0.8		1812	0.8
	2300	4.3			
6 SU	0454	0.5	21 M	0018	4.4
	1136	4.8		0618	0.7
	1736	0.9		1300	5.1
	2342	4.1		1918	1.1
7 M	0536	0.5	22 TU	0118	4.1
	1218	4.8		0718	1.0
	1830	1.1		1400	4.9
				2024	1.3
8 TU	0030	4.0	23 W	0224	4.0
	0630	0.6		0824	1.1
	1318	4.8		1500	4.8
	1930	1.2		2130	1.3
9 W	0130	3.9	24 TH	0330	4.0
	0736	0.7		0930	1.2
	1418	4.8		1600	4.8
	2042	1.1		2224	1.2
10 TH	0242	4.0	25 F	0430	4.1
	0848	0.6		1030	1.1
	1530	5.0		1700	4.8
	2149	0.9		2312	1.0
11 F	0348	4.2	26 SA	0524	4.4
	1000	0.4		1118	0.9
	1636	5.2		1748	4.9
	2248	0.6		2354	0.8
12 SA	0500	4.6	27 SU	0612	4.6
	1100	0.1		1200	0.7
	1736	5.5		1830	5.0
	2348	0.2			
13 SU	0600	5.0	28 M	0030	0.7
	1200	-0.2		0648	4.9
	1830	5.7		1242	0.7
				1906	5.1
14 M	0036	-0.1	29 TU	0100	0.5
	0654	5.4		0724	5.1
	1254	-0.4		1318	0.6
	1924	5.8		1942	5.1
15 TU	0124	-0.3	30 W	0136	0.5
	0748	5.8		0800	5.2
	1348	-0.5		1354	0.5
	2012	5.8		2018	5.0

TIME MERIDIAN 75° W. 0000 IS MIDNIGHT. 1200 IS NOON.
HEIGHTS ARE RECKONED FROM THE DATUM OF SOUNDINGS ON CHARTS OF THE LOCALITY WHICH IS MEAN LOW WATER.

Appendix C-2

TIDAL DIFFERENCES AND OTHER CONSTANTS

No.	PLACE	POSITION		DIFFERENCES				RANGES		Mean Tide Level
				Time		Height				
		Lat.	Long.	High water	Low water	High water	Low water	Mean	Spring	
		° ′ N.	° ′ W.	h. m.	h. m.	feet	feet	feet	feet	feet
	GEORGIA and FLORIDA Cumberland Sound			on SAVANNAH RIVER ENT., p.106 Time meridian, 75°W.						
2821	St. Marys Entrance, north Jetty-----	30 43	81 26	+0 15	+0 15	-1.1	0.0	5.8	6.8	2.9
2823	Crooked River entrance--------------	30 51	81 29	+1 23	+1 12	-0.1	0.0	6.8	8.0	3.4
2825	Harrietts Bluff, Crooked River------	30 52	81 35	+2 09	+2 12	-0.5	0.0	6.4	7.5	3.2
2827	St. Marys, St. Marys River----------	30 43	81 33	+1 21	+1 13	-0.9	0.0	6.0	7.0	3.0
2829	Crandall, St. Marys River----------	30 43	81 37	+2 10	+1 59	-1.8	0.0	5.1	6.0	2.5
				on MAYPORT, p.114						
2831	Fernandina Beach (outer coast)------	30 38	81 26	-0 18	-0 01	+1.2	0.0	5.7	6.7	2.8
2833	Fernandina Beach, Amelia River------	30 40	81 28	+0 32	+0 16	+1.5	0.0	6.0	7.0	3.0
2835	Chester, Bells River---------------	30 41	81 32	+0 49	+0 41	+1.9	0.0	6.4	7.5	3.2
2837	S. A. L. RR. bridge, Kingsley Creek-	30 38	81 29	+0 59	+0 43	+1.5	0.0	6.0	7.0	3.0
	FLORIDA Nassau Sound and Fort George River									
2839	Nassau Sound-----------------------	30 31	81 27	-0 03	+0 06	+0.9	0.0	5.4	6.3	2.7
2841	Amelia City, South Amelia River-----	30 35	81 28	+0 54	+1 03	+1.1	0.0	5.6	6.6	2.8
2843	Nassauville, Nassau River-----------	30 34	81 31	+1 04	+1 37	+0.3	0.0	4.8	5.6	2.4
2845	Mink Creek entrance, Nassau River---	30 32	81 34	+1 58	+2 32	-0.6	0.0	3.9	4.6	1.9
2847	Halfmoon Island, highway bridge-----	30 34	81 36	+3 00	+3 21	-1.0	0.0	3.5	4.1	1.7
2849	Sawpit Creek entrance--------------	30 31	81 27	-0 02	+0 30	+0.5	0.0	5.0	5.8	2.5
2851	Fort George Island, Fort George R---	30 26	81 26	+0 29	+0 39	+0.3	0.0	4.8	5.6	2.4
	St. Johns River									
2853	South Jetty-----------------------	30 24	81 23	-0 23	-0 17	+0.4	0.0	4.9	5.7	2.4
2855	MAYPORT---------------------------	30 24	81 26	Daily predictions				4.5	5.3	2.3
2857	Pablo Creek bascule bridge---------	30 19	81 26	+1 39	+1 15	*0.64	*0.64	2.9	3.4	1.4
2859	Fulton----------------------------	30 23	81 30	+0 29	+0 42	-1.1	0.0	3.4	4.0	1.7
2861	Dame Point------------------------	30 23	81 33	+0 46	+0 55	*0.67	*0.67	3.0	3.5	1.5
2863	Phoenix Park (Cummers Mill)--------	30 23	81 38	+0 58	+1 25	*0.44	*0.44	2.0	2.3	1.0
2865	Jacksonville (Dredge Depot)--------	30 21	81 37	+1 24	+1 50	*0.44	*0.44	2.0	2.3	1.0
2867	Jacksonville (RR. bridge)----------	30 19	81 40	+2 06	+2 13	*0.27	*0.27	1.2	1.4	0.6
2869	Ortega River entrance-------------	30 17	81 42	+2 27	+2 50	*0.20	*0.20	0.9	1.1	0.5
2871	Orange Park-----------------------	30 10	81 42	+3 49	+4 14	*0.16	*0.16	0.7	0.8	0.3
2873	Green Cove Springs----------------	30 00	81 40	+5 26	+6 13	*0.18	*0.18	0.8	0.9	0.4
2875	East Tocoi------------------------	29 51	81 34	+6 47	+7 18	*0.22	*0.22	1.0	1.2	0.5
2877	Bridgeport------------------------	29 45	81 34	+6 58	+7 32	*0.24	*0.24	1.1	1.3	0.5
2879	Palatka---------------------------	29 39	81 38	+7 26	+8 21	*0.27	*0.27	1.2	1.4	0.6
2881	Welaka----------------------------	29 29	81 40	+7 46	+8 25	*0.11	*0.11	0.5	0.6	0.2
	FLORIDA, East Coast									
2883	Atlantic Beach--------------------	30 20	81 24	-0 25	-0 18	+0.7	0.0	5.2	6.0	2.6
2885	St. Augustine Inlet---------------	29 53	81 17	-0 21	-0 01	0.0	0.0	4.5	5.3	2.2
2887	St. Augustine--------------------	29 54	81 18	+0 14	+0 43	-0.3	0.0	4.2	5.0	2.1
2889	Daytona Beach (ocean)-------------	29 14	81 00	-0 33	-0 32	-0.4	0.0	4.1	4.9	2.0
				on MIAMI HBR. ENT., p.118						
2891	Ponce de Leon Inlet---------------	29 04	80 55	+0 06	+0 20	-0.2	0.0	2.3	2.7	1.2
2893	Cape Canaveral--------------------	28 26	80 34	-0 41	-0 41	+1.0	0.0	3.5	4.1	1.8
2894	Sebastian Inlet-------------------	27 52	80 27	-0 23	-0 31	-0.3	0.0	2.2	2.6	1.1
2895	Fort Pierce Inlet (breakwater)------	27 28	80 17	-0 14	-0 18	+0.1	0.0	2.6	3.0	1.3
2897	Fort Pierce (City Dock)-----------	27 27	80 19	+1 51	+2 11	*0.28	*0.28	0.7	0.8	0.3
2899	St. Lucie Inlet (jetty)-----------	27 10	80 09	-0 20	-0 21	+0.1	0.0	2.6	3.0	1.3
2901	Sewall Point, St. Lucie River------	27 11	80 12	+1 34	+2 33	*0.40	*0.40	1.0	1.2	0.5
2903	Jupiter Inlet (near lighthouse)-----	26 57	80 05	+1 04	+1 38	*0.52	*0.52	1.3	1.5	0.6
2905	Port of Palm Beach, Lake Worth-----	26 46	80 03	0 00	+0 12	+0.1	0.0	2.6	3.1	1.3
2907	Palm Beach (ocean)----------------	26 43	80 02	-0 21	-0 18	+0.3	0.0	2.8	3.3	1.4
2909	Hillsboro Inlet-------------------	26 15	80 05	+0 13	+0 36	-0.2	0.0	2.3	2.7	1.2
	Fort Lauderdale									
2911	Bahia Mar Yacht Club-----------	26 07	80 06	+0 28	+0 32	-0.2	0.0	2.3	2.8	1.1
2913	Andrews Ave. bridge, New River-	26 07	80 09	+1 06	+1 28	-0.7	0.0	1.8	2.2	0.9

*Ratio.

Appendix C-3

TABLE 3.—HEIGHT OF TIDE AT ANY TIME

						Time from the nearest high water or low water									
h. m.	h. m.	h. m.	h. m.	h. m.	h. m	h. m.	h. m	h. m	h. m	h. m.	h. m.	h. m.	h. m.	h. m.	h. m
4 00	0 08	0 16	0 24	0 32	0 40	0 48	0 56	1 04	1 12	1 20	1 28	1 36	1 44	1 52	2 00
4 20	0 09	0 17	0 26	0 35	0 43	0 52	1 01	1 09	1 18	1 27	1 35	1 44	1 53	2 01	2 10
4 40	0 09	0 19	0 28	0 37	0 47	0 56	1 05	1 15	1 24	1 33	1 43	1 52	2 01	2 11	2 20
5 00	0 10	0 20	0 30	0 40	0 50	1 00	1 10	1 20	1 30	1 40	1 50	2 00	2 10	2 20	2 30
5 20	0 11	0 21	0 32	0 43	0 53	1 04	1 15	1 25	1 36	1 47	1 57	2 08	2 19	2 29	2 40
5 40	0 11	0 23	0 34	0 45	0 57	1 08	1 19	1 31	1 42	1 53	2 05	2 16	2 27	2 39	2 50
6 00	0 12	0 24	0 36	0 48	1 00	1 12	1 24	1 36	1 48	2 00	2 12	2 24	2 36	2 48	3 00
6 20	0 13	0 25	0 38	0 51	1 03	1 16	1 29	1 41	1 54	2 07	2 19	2 32	2 45	2 57	3 10
6 40	0 13	0 27	0 40	0 53	1 07	1 20	1 33	1 47	2 00	2 13	2 27	2 40	2 53	3 07	3 20
7 00	0 14	0 28	0 42	0 56	1 10	1 24	1 38	1 52	2 06	2 20	2 34	2 48	3 02	3 16	3 30
7 20	0 15	0 29	0 44	0 59	1 13	1 28	1 43	1 57	2 12	2 27	2 41	2 56	3 11	3 25	3 40
7 40	0 15	0 31	0 46	1 01	1 17	1 32	1 47	2 03	2 18	2 33	2 49	3 04	3 19	3 35	3 50
8 00	0 16	0 32	0 48	1 04	1 20	1 36	1 52	2 08	2 24	2 40	2 56	3 12	3 28	3 44	4 00
8 20	0 17	0 33	0 50	1 07	1 23	1 40	1 57	2 13	2 30	2 47	3 03	3 20	3 37	3 53	4 10
8 40	0 17	0 35	0 52	1 09	1 27	1 44	2 01	2 19	2 36	2 53	3 11	3 28	3 45	4 03	4 20
9 00	0 18	0 36	0 54	1 12	1 30	1 48	2 06	2 24	2 42	3 00	3 18	3 36	3 54	4 12	4 30
9 20	0 19	0 37	0 56	1 15	1 33	1 52	2 11	2 29	2 48	3 07	3 25	3 44	4 03	4 21	4 40
9 40	0 19	0 39	0 58	1 17	1 37	1 56	2 15	2 35	2 54	3 13	3 33	3 52	4 11	4 31	4 50
10 00	0 20	0 40	1 00	1 20	1 40	2 00	2 20	2 40	3 00	3 20	3 40	4 00	4 20	4 40	5 00
10 20	0 21	0 41	1 02	1 23	1 43	2 04	2 25	2 45	3 06	3 27	3 47	4 08	4 29	4 49	5 10
10 40	0 21	0 43	1 04	1 25	1 47	2 08	2 29	2 51	3 12	3 33	3 55	4 16	4 37	4 59	5 20

						Correction to height									
Ft.	Ft.	Ft.	Ft.	Ft.	Ft.	Ft.	Ft.	Ft.	Ft.	Ft.	Ft.	Ft.	Ft.	Ft.	Ft.
0.5	0.0	0.0	0.0	0.0	0.0	0.0	0.1	0.1	0.1	0.1	0.1	0.2	0.2	0.2	0.2
1.0	0.0	0.0	0.0	0.0	0.1	0.1	0.1	0.2	0.2	0.2	0.3	0.3	0.4	0.4	0.5
1.5	0.0	0.0	0.0	0.1	0.1	0.1	0.2	0.2	0.3	0.4	0.4	0.5	0.6	0.7	0.8
2.0	0 0	0.0	0.0	0.1	0.1	0.2	0.3	0.3	0.4	0.5	0.6	0.7	0.8	0.9	1.0
2.5	0.0	0.0	0.1	0.1	0.2	0.2	0.3	0.4	0.5	0.6	0.7	0.9	1.0	1.1	1.2
3.0	0 0	0.0	0.1	0.1	0 2	0.3	0.4	0.5	0.6	0.8	0.9	1.0	1.2	1.3	1.5
3.5	0 0	0.0	0.1	0.2	0.2	0.3	0.4	0.6	0.7	0.9	1.0	1.2	1.4	1.6	1.8
4.0	0.0	0.0	0.1	0.2	0.3	0.4	0.5	0.7	0.8	1.0	1.2	1.4	1.6	1.8	2.0
4.5	0.0	0.0	0.1	0.2	0.3	0.4	0.6	0.7	0.9	1.1	1.3	1.6	1.8	2.0	2.2
5.0	0.0	0.1	0.1	0.2	0.3	0.5	0.6	0.8	1.0	1.2	1.5	1.7	2.0	2.2	2.5
5.5	0 0	0.1	0.1	0.2	0.4	0.5	0.7	0.9	1.1	1.4	1.6	1.9	2.2	2.5	2.8
6.0	0 0	0.1	0.1	0.3	0.4	0.6	0.8	1.0	1.2	1.5	1.8	2.1	2.4	2.7	3.0
6.5	0.0	0.1	0.2	0.3	0.4	0.6	0.8	1.1	1.3	1.6	1.9	2.2	2.6	2.9	3.2
7.0	0.0	0.1	0.2	0.3	0.5	0.7	0.9	1.2	1.4	1.8	2.1	2.4	2.8	3.1	3.5
7.5	0.0	0.1	0.2	0.3	0.5	0.7	1.0	1.2	1.5	1.9	2.2	2.6	3.0	3.4	3.8
8.0	0.0	0.1	0.2	0.3	0.5	0.8	1.0	1.3	1.6	2.0	2.4	2.8	3.2	3.6	4.0
8.5	0.0	0.1	0.2	0.4	0.6	0.8	1.1	1.4	1.8	2.1	2.5	2.9	3.4	3.8	4.2
9.0	0.0	0.1	0.2	0.4	0.6	0.9	1.2	1.5	1.9	2.2	2.7	3.1	3.6	4.0	4.5
9.5	0.0	0.1	0.2	0.4	0.6	0.9	1.2	1.6	2.0	2.4	2.8	3.3	3.8	4.3	4.8
10.0	0.0	0.1	0.2	0.4	0.7	1.0	1.3	1.7	2.1	2.5	3.0	3.5	4.0	4.5	5.0
10.5	0.0	0.1	0.3	0.5	0.7	1.0	1.3	1.7	2.2	2.6	3.1	3.6	4.2	4.7	5.2
11.0	0.0	0.1	0.3	0.5	0.7	1.1	1.4	1.8	2.3	2.8	3.3	3.8	4.4	4.9	5.5
11.5	0.0	0.1	0.3	0.5	0.8	1.1	1.5	1.9	2.4	2.9	3.4	4.0	4.6	5.1	5.8
12.0	0.0	0.1	0.3	0.5	0.8	1.1	1.5	2.0	2.5	3.0	3.6	4.1	4.8	5.4	6.0
12.5	0.0	0.1	0.3	0.5	0.8	1.2	1.6	2.1	2.6	3.1	3.7	4.3	5.0	5.6	6.2
13.0	0.0	0.1	0.3	0.6	0.9	1.2	1.7	2.2	2.7	3.2	3.9	4.5	5.1	5.8	6.5
13.5	0.0	0 1	0.3	0.6	0.9	1.3	1.7	2.2	2.8	3.4	4.0	4.7	5.3	6.0	6.8
14.0	0.0	0.2	0.3	0.6	0.9	1.3	1.8	2.3	2.9	3.5	4.2	4.8	5.5	6.3	7.0
14.5	0.0	0.2	0.4	0 6	1.0	1.4	1.9	2.4	3.0	3.6	4.3	5.0	5.7	6.5	7.2
15.0	0.0	0.2	0.4	0.6	1.0	1.4	1.9	2.5	3.1	3.8	4.4	5.2	5.9	6.7	7.5
15.5	0.0	0 2	0.4	0 7	1.0	1.5	2.0	2.6	3.2	3.9	4.6	5.4	6.1	6.9	7.8
16.0	0.0	0 2	0.4	0 7	1.1	1.5	2.1	2.6	3.3	4.0	4.7	5.5	6.3	7.2	8.0
16.5	0.0	0 2	0.4	0.7	1.1	1.6	2.1	2.7	3.4	4.1	4.9	5.7	6.5	7.4	8.2
17.0	0.0	0 2	0.4	0.7	1.1	1.6	2.2	2.8	3.5	4.2	5.0	5.9	6.7	7.6	8.5
17.5	0.0	0.2	0.4	0.8	1.2	1.7	2.2	2.9	3.6	4.4	5.2	6.0	6.9	7.8	8.8
18.0	0.0	0.2	0.4	0.8	1.2	1.7	2.3	3.0	3.7	4.5	5.3	6.2	7.1	8.1	9.0
18.5	0.1	0.2	0.5	0.8	1.2	1.8	2.4	3.1	3.8	4.6	5.5	6.4	7.3	8.3	9.2
19.0	0.1	0.2	0.5	0.8	1.3	1.8	2.4	3.1	3.9	4.8	5.6	6.6	7.5	8.5	9.5
19.5	0 1	0 2	0.5	0.8	1.3	1.9	2.5	3.2	4.0	4.9	5.8	6.7	7.7	8.7	9.8
20.0	0.1	0.2	0.5	0.9	1.3	1.9	2.6	3.3	4.1	5.0	5.9	6.9	7.9	9.0	10.0

Duration of rise or fall, see footnote (left margin, upper section)

Range of tide, see footnote (left margin, lower section)

Obtain from the predictions the high water and low water, one of which is before and the other after the time for which the height is required. The difference between the times of occurrence of these tides is the duration of rise or fall, and the difference between their heights is the range of tide for the above table. Find the difference between the nearest high or low water and the time for which the height is required.

Enter the table with the duration of rise or fall, printed in heavy-faced type, which most nearly agrees with the actual value, and on that horizontal line find the time from the nearest high or low water which agrees most nearly with the corresponding actual difference. The correction sought is in the column directly below, on the line with the range of tide.

When the nearest tide is high water, subtract the correction.

When the nearest tide is low water, add the correction.

160

Appendix D-1

ST. JOHNS RIVER ENTRANCE, FLA., 1970

F-FLOOD, DIR. 275° TRUE   E-EBB, DIR. 100° TRUE

MARCH

Days 1–15

DAY	SLACK WATER TIME (H.M.)	MAX. CURRENT TIME (H.M.)	VEL. (KNOTS)
1 SU		0136	1.9F
	0430	0706	1.9E
	1212	1406	1.1F
	1612	1918	2.2E
	2342		
2 M		0236	1.9F
	0536	0818	1.9E
	1312	1506	1.2F
	1724	2024	2.2E
3 TU	0054	0336	2.1F
	0636	0930	2.0E
	1406	1606	1.4F
	1836	2136	2.3E
4 W	0200	0436	2.3F
	0736	1036	2.2E
	1454	1706	1.8F
	1942	2248	2.5E
5 TH	0300	0536	2.5F
	0830	1142	2.5E
	1542	1800	2.1F
	2042	2354	2.7E
6 F	0354	0624	2.6F
	0924	1230	2.7E
	1624	1854	2.4F
	2142		
7 SA		0048	2.9E
	0448	0718	2.7F
	1012	1318	2.8E
	1712	1942	2.6F
	2230		
8 SU		0136	2.9E
	0536	0806	2.6F
	1054	1400	2.9E
	1754	2030	2.8F
	2324		
9 M		0224	2.9E
	0624	0854	2.5F
	1136	1442	2.9E
	1842	2118	2.7F
10 TU	0012	0312	2.8E
	0718	0936	2.2F
	1224	1518	2.8E
	1924	2206	2.6F
11 W	0100	0400	2.5E
	0812	1024	1.9F
	1306	1600	2.6E
	2018	2254	2.4F
12 TH	0148	0442	2.2E
	0906	1112	1.6F
	1348	1642	2.3E
	2112	2342	2.1F
13 F	0242	0530	1.9E
	1012	1206	1.3F
	1436	1730	2.0E
	2206		
14 SA		0036	1.9F
	0336	0624	1.7E
	1112	1300	1.1F
	1524	1818	1.8E
	2312		
15 SU		0130	1.7F
	0430	0730	1.5E
	1218	1400	0.9F
	1624	1918	1.6E

Days 16–31

DAY	SLACK WATER TIME (H.M.)	MAX. CURRENT TIME (H.M.)	VEL. (KNOTS)
16 M	0012	0230	1.5F
	0530	0900	1.4E
	1312	1500	0.9F
	1730	2030	1.5E
17 TU	0112	0330	1.5F
	0630	1036	1.5E
	1406	1600	1.0F
	1830	2148	1.5E
18 W	0206	0430	1.6F
	0718	1118	1.6E
	1454	1654	1.2F
	1924	2248	1.7E
19 TH	0254	0518	1.7F
	0806	1142	1.8E
	1530	1742	1.4F
	2018	2336	1.8E
20 F	0342	0600	1.9F
	0848	1206	1.9E
	1606	1818	1.7F
	2106		
21 SA		0012	2.0E
	0424	0642	1.8F
	0930	1230	2.1E
	1642	1900	1.9F
	2148		
22 SU		0048	2.2E
	0506	0718	1.9F
	1006	1300	2.2E
	1712	1942	2.0F
	2224		
23 M		0118	2.3E
	0542	0800	1.8F
	1042	1330	2.3E
	1742	2018	2.1F
	2306		
24 TU		0200	2.4E
	0624	0842	1.8F
	1112	1406	2.4E
	1812	2100	2.2F
	2348		
25 W		0236	2.5E
	0706	0924	1.6F
	1148	1442	2.5E
	1836	2148	2.2F
26 TH	0030	0318	2.5E
	0748	1006	1.5F
	1224	1524	2.5E
	1912	2230	2.2F
27 F	0118	0400	2.4E
	0836	1054	1.3F
	1306	1612	2.4E
	2000	2324	2.1F
28 SA	0206	0454	2.3E
	0936	1148	1.2F
	1354	1700	2.3E
	2054		
29 SU		0018	2.0F
	0306	0548	2.1E
	1042	1242	1.2F
	1454	1800	2.2E
	2212		
30 M		0112	1.9F
	0406	0648	2.0E
	1142	1342	1.2F
	1600	1900	2.1E
	2336		
31 TU		0218	1.9F
	0512	0754	2.0E
	1242	1448	1.4F
	1718	2012	2.1E

APRIL

Days 1–15

DAY	SLACK WATER TIME (H.M.)	MAX. CURRENT TIME (H.M.)	VEL. (KNOTS)
1 W	0048	0318	2.0F
	0612	0912	2.1E
	1336	1548	1.7F
	1924	2130	2.2E
2 TH	0148	0418	2.1F
	0712	1018	2.2E
	1424	1648	2.0F
	1930	2242	2.4E
3 F	0248	0512	2.2F
	0806	1112	2.5E
	1512	1742	2.3F
	2030	2342	2.6E
4 SA	0342	0606	2.3F
	0854	1206	2.6E
	1600	1830	2.6F
	2124		
5 SU		0036	2.8E
	0430	0654	2.3F
	0942	1248	2.7E
	1642	1918	2.7F
	2218		
6 M		0124	2.8E
	0524	0742	2.3F
	1024	1330	2.8E
	1724	2006	2.8F
	2306		
7 TU		0212	2.7E
	0612	0830	2.1F
	1106	1412	2.7E
	1812	2048	2.7F
	2348		
8 W		0254	2.6E
	0700	0912	1.9F
	1148	1448	2.6E
	1900	2136	2.5F
9 TH	0036	0336	2.4E
	0754	1000	1.7F
	1230	1530	2.4E
	1948	2224	2.3F
10 F	0124	0418	2.2E
	0848	1048	1.4F
	1318	1612	2.2E
	2036	2312	2.0F
11 SA	0212	0500	1.9E
	0942	1136	1.2F
	1406	1654	1.9E
	2136		
12 SU		0006	1.8F
	0300	0548	1.7E
	1042	1230	1.1F
	1500	1748	1.7E
	2236		
13 M		0100	1.6F
	0354	0642	1.6E
	1142	1330	1.0F
	1554	1842	1.5E
	2342		
14 TU		0154	1.4F
	0448	0748	1.5E
	1236	1430	1.0F
	1700	1948	1.5E
15 W	0042	0254	1.4F
	0542	0854	1.6E
	1324	1524	1.2F
	1800	2100	1.5E

Days 16–30

DAY	SLACK WATER TIME (H.M.)	MAX. CURRENT TIME (H.M.)	VEL. (KNOTS)
16 TH	0136	0348	1.4F
	0636	0948	1.7E
	1412	1618	1.4F
	1854	2206	1.7E
17 F	0230	0436	1.5F
	0724	1030	1.8E
	1448	1700	1.6F
	1948	2300	1.9E
18 SA	0312	0524	1.6F
	0806	1106	1.9E
	1524	1748	1.8F
	2036	2336	2.1E
19 SU	0400	0606	1.7F
	0848	1142	2.1E
	1600	1830	2.1F
	2118		
20 M		0018	2.2E
	0442	0648	1.7F
	0924	1218	2.2E
	1630	1912	2.2F
	2200		
21 TU		0054	2.4E
	0524	0730	1.7F
	1006	1254	2.4E
	1700	1948	2.4F
	2242		
22 W		0136	2.5E
	0606	0818	1.6F
	1042	1336	2.5E
	1730	2036	2.4F
	2324		
23 TH		0218	2.5E
	0648	0900	1.6F
	1118	1418	2.5E
	1806	2118	2.4F
24 F	0012	0300	2.5E
	0736	0948	1.5F
	1200	1500	2.5E
	1854	2206	2.3F
25 SA	0100	0348	2.5E
	0824	1036	1.4F
	1248	1554	2.4E
	1942	2300	2.2F
26 SU	0148	0436	2.4E
	0918	1130	1.4F
	1348	1648	2.3E
	2048	2354	2.1F
27 M	0248	0530	2.2E
	1018	1224	1.4F
	1448	1742	2.2E
	2206		
28 TU		0054	2.0F
	0342	0636	2.1E
	1118	1324	1.5F
	1600	1854	2.1E
	2324		
29 W		0154	1.9F
	0442	0742	2.1E
	1212	1424	1.7F
	1706	2006	2.1E
30 TH	0030	0254	1.9F
	0542	0848	2.2E
	1306	1524	1.9F
	1818	2124	2.2E

TIME MERIDIAN 75° W. 0000 IS MIDNIGHT. 1200 IS NOON.

Appendix D-2

CURRENT DIFFERENCES AND OTHER CONSTANTS

No.	PLACE	POSITION Lat.	POSITION Long.	TIME DIFFERENCES Slack water	TIME DIFFERENCES Maximum current	VELOCITY RATIOS Maximum flood	VELOCITY RATIOS Maximum ebb	MAXIMUM CURRENTS Flood Direction (true)	MAXIMUM CURRENTS Flood Average velocity	MAXIMUM CURRENTS Ebb Direction (true)	MAXIMUM CURRENTS Ebb Average velocity
		° ′	° ′	h. m.	h. m.			deg.	knots	deg.	knots
	ST. JOHNS RIVER—Continued	N.	W.	on ST. JOHNS RIVER ENTRANCE, p.94 Time meridian, 75°W.							
5380	St. Johns Bluff	30 23	81 30	+0 05	+0 50	0.8	1.0	245	1.6	60	2.2
5385	Drummond Point, channel south of	30 25	81 36	+2 00	+2 30	0.7	0.7	230	1.3	60	1.6
5390	Phoenix Park	30 23	81 38	+2 40	+3 10	0.6	0.4	190	1.1	350	1.0
5395	Chaseville, channel near	30 23	81 37	+2 35	+3 20	0.6	0.7	150	1.1	335	1.6
5400	Quarantine Station, Long Branch	30 21	81 37	+2 30	+3 05	0.6	0.5	185	1.1	0	1.2
5405	Commodore Point, terminal channel	30 19	81 38	+2 35	+3 10	0.5	0.4	210	1.0	60	1.0
5410	Jacksonville, off Washington St	30 19	81 39	+2 20	+2 50	0.9	0.8	280	1.8	120	1.9
5415	Jacksonville, F. E. C. RR. bridge	30 19	81 40	+2 20	+3 00	0.8	0.7	240	1.6	60	1.7
5420	Winter Point	30 18	81 40	+2 55	+3 10	0.6	0.5	200	1.1	15	1.1
5425	Mandarin Point	30 09	81 41	+3 00	+3 20	0.3	0.3	180	0.6	15	0.7
5430	Red Bay Point, bridge draw	29 59	81 38	(¹)	(¹)	0.5	0.3	115	0.9	300	0.6
5435	Tocoi to Lake George	-----	-----	*Current too weak and variable to be predicted.*							
	FLORIDA COAST			on MIAMI HARBOR ENTRANCE, p.100							
5440	Ft. Pierce Inlet	27 28	80 18	+0 50	+0 25	1.4	1.5	250	2.6	70	3.1
5445	Lake Worth Inlet, (between jetties)	26 46	80 02	-0 10	-0 15	1.3	1.7	275	2.4	95	3.6
5450	Fort Lauderdale, New River	26 07	80 07	-0 40	-0 40	0.4	0.2	5	0.8	130	0.5
	PORT EVERGLADES										
5455	Pier 2, 1.3 miles east of	26 06	80 06	-----	-----	----	----	(²)	0.2	(²)	0.4
5460	Entrance, between jetties	26 06	80 06	-0 40	-0 55	0.3	0.3	275	0.6	95	0.7
5465	Entrance from southward (canal)	26 05	80 07	+0 20	-0 15	0.7	0.8	165	1.3	0	1.7
5470	Turning Basin	26 06	80 07	-1 15	-1 20	0.1	0.2	320	0.2	155	0.5
5475	Turning Basin, 300 yards north of	26 06	80 07	-0 40	-0 55	0.5	0.9	350	0.9	160	1.8
5480	17th Street Bridge	26 06	80 07	-0 50	-1 05	1.0	0.9	350	1.9	170	1.9
	MIAMI HARBOR										
5485	Bakers Haulover Cut	25 54	80 07	-0 10	-0 15	1.5	1.2	270	2.9	90	2.5
5490	North Jetty (east end)	25 46	80 07	-0 40	-0 35	0.4	0.6	250	0.8	105	1.3
5495	Miami Outer Bay Cut entrance	25 46	80 06	See table 5.							
5500	MIAMI HARBOR ENT. (between jetties)	25 46	80 08	Daily predictions				290	1.9	125	2.1
5503	Fowey Rocks Light, 1.5 miles SW. of	25 35	80 07	*Current too weak and variable to be predicted.*							
	FLORIDA REEFS to MIDNIGHT PASS			on KEY WEST, p.106							
5505	Caesar Creek, Biscayne Bay	25 23	80 14	-0 05	-0 05	1.2	1.0	315	1.2	125	1.8
5510	Long Key, drawbridge east of	24 50	80 46	+1 40	+1 30	1.1	0.7	0	1.1	200	1.2
5515	Long Key Viaduct	24 48	80 52	+1 50	+1 40	0.9	0.7	350	0.9	170	1.2
5520	Moser Channel, drawbridge	24 42	81 10	+1 30	+1 40	1.4	1.0	340	1.4	165	1.8
5525	Bahia Honda Harbor, bridge	24 39	81 17	+1 25	+0 50	1.4	1.2	5	1.4	180	2.1
5530	No Name Key, NE. of	24 42	81 19	+1 10	+1 10	0.7	0.5	310	0.7	140	0.9
	Key West										
5535	Main Ship Channel entrance	24 28	81 48	-0 15	0 00	0.2	0.3	40	0.2	180	0.4
5540	Main Ship Channel	24 30	81 48	(³)	³+0 30	(³)	0.2	65	(³)	135	0.4
5545	KEY WEST, 0.3 mi. W. of Ft. Taylor	24 33	81 49	Daily predictions				20	1.0	195	1.7
5550	0.6 mile N. of Ft. Taylor	24 34	81 49	+0 05	+0 15	0.6	0.7	40	0.6	200	1.2
5555	Turning Basin	24 34	81 48	+0 35	+0 55	0.8	0.6	50	0.8	215	1.1
5560	Northwest Channel	24 35	81 51	-0 10	-0 05	1.2	0.8	355	1.2	160	1.4
5565	Northwest Channel	24 37	81 53	-0 25	-0 20	0.6	0.4	345	0.6	170	0.6
5570	Boca Grande Channel	24 34	82 04	-0 20	-0 25	1.1	0.7	355	1.1	195	1.2
5575	New Ground†	24 39	82 25	+1 30	+1 35	0.7	0.4	70	0.7	245	0.7

¹ Flood begins, +2ʰ 35ᵐ; maximum flood, +3ʰ 25ᵐ; ebb begins, +5ʰ 00ᵐ; maximum ebb, +4ʰ 00ᵐ.
² Flood usually occurs in a southerly direction and the ebb in a northeastwardly direction.
³ Times of slack are indefinite. Flood is weak and variable. Time difference is for maximum ebb.
† Current tends to rotate clockwise. At times for slack flood begins there may be a weak current flowing northward while at times for slack ebb begins there may be a weak current flowing southeastward.

Appendix D-3

TABLE 3.—VELOCITY OF CURRENT AT ANY TIME

TABLE A

Interval between slack and maximum current

Interval between slack and desired time (h. m.)	1 20	1 40	2 00	2 20	2 40	3 00	3 20	3 40	4 00	4 20	4 40	5 00	5 20	5 40
	f.	f.	f.	f.	f.	f.	f.	f.	f.	f.	f.	f.	f.	f.
0 20	0.4	0.3	0.3	0.2	0.2	0.2	0.2	0.1	0.1	0.1	0.1	0.1	0.1	0.1
0 40	0.7	0.6	0.5	0.4	0.4	0.3	0.3	0.3	0.3	0.2	0.2	0.2	0.2	0.2
1 00	0.9	0.8	0.7	0.6	0.6	0.5	0.5	0.4	0.4	0.4	0.3	0.3	0.3	0.3
1 20	1.0	1.0	0.9	C.8	0.7	0.6	0.6	0.5	0.5	0.5	0.4	0.4	0.4	0.4
1 40	---	1.0	1.0	0.9	0.8	0.8	0.7	0.7	0.6	0.6	0.5	0.5	0.5	0.4
2 00	---	---	1.0	1.0	0.9	0.9	0.9	0.8	0.7	0.7	0.6	0.6	0.6	0.5
2 20	---	---	---	1.0	1.0	1.0	0.9	0.9	0.8	0.8	0.7	0.7	0.6	0.6
2 40	---	---	---	---	1.0	1.0	1.0	0.9	0.9	0.8	0.8	0.7	0.7	0.7
3 00	---	---	---	---	---	1.0	1.0	1.0	0.9	0.9	0.8	0.8	0.8	0.7
3 20	---	---	---	---	---	---	1.0	1.0	1.0	0.9	0.9	0.9	0.8	0.8
3 40	---	---	---	---	---	---	---	1.0	1.0	1.0	0.9	0.9	0.9	0.9
4 00	---	---	---	---	---	---	---	---	1.0	1.0	1.0	1.0	0.9	0.9
4 20	---	---	---	---	---	---	---	---	---	1.0	1.0	1.0	1.0	0.9
4 40	---	---	---	---	---	---	---	---	---	---	1.0	1.0	1.0	1.0
5 00	---	---	---	---	---	---	---	---	---	---	---	1.0	1.0	1.0
5 20	---	---	---	---	---	---	---	---	---	---	---	---	1.0	1.0
5 40	---	---	---	---	---	---	---	---	---	---	---	---	---	1.0

TABLE B

Interval between slack and maximum current

Interval between slack and desired time (h. m.)	1 20	1 40	2 00	2 20	2 40	3 00	3 20	3 40	4 00	4 20	4 40	5 00	5 20	5 40
	f.	f.	f.	f.	f.	f.	f.	f.	f.	f.	f.	f.	f.	f.
0 20	0.5	0.4	0.4	0.3	0.3	0.3	0.3	0.3	0.2	0.2	0.2	0.2	0.2	0.2
0 40	0.8	0.7	0.6	0.5	0.5	0.5	0.4	0.4	0.4	0.4	0.3	0.3	0.3	0.3
1 00	0.9	0.8	0.8	0.7	0.7	0.6	0.6	0.5	0.5	0.5	0.4	0.4	0.4	0.4
1 20	1.0	1.0	0.9	0.8	0.8	0.7	0.7	0.6	0.6	0.6	0.5	0.5	0.5	0.5
1 40	---	1.0	1.0	0.9	0.9	0.8	0.8	0.7	0.7	0.7	0.6	0.6	0.6	0.6
2 00	---	---	1.0	1.0	0.9	0.9	0.9	0.8	0.8	0.7	0.7	0.7	0.7	0.6
2 20	---	---	---	1.0	1.0	1.0	0.9	0.9	0.8	0.8	0.8	0.7	0.7	0.7
2 40	---	---	---	---	1.0	1.0	1.0	0.9	0.9	0.9	0.8	0.8	0.8	0.7
3 00	---	---	---	---	---	1.0	1.0	1.0	0.9	0.9	0.9	0.9	0.8	0.8
3 20	---	---	---	---	---	---	1.0	1.0	1.0	1.0	0.9	0.9	0.9	0.8
3 40	---	---	---	---	---	---	---	1.0	1.0	1.0	1.0	0.9	0.9	0.9
4 00	---	---	---	---	---	---	---	---	1.0	1.0	1.0	1.0	0.9	0.9
4 20	---	---	---	---	---	---	---	---	---	1.0	1.0	1.0	1.0	0.9
4 40	---	---	---	---	---	---	---	---	---	---	1.0	1.0	1.0	1.0
5 00	---	---	---	---	---	---	---	---	---	---	---	1.0	1.0	1.0
5 20	---	---	---	---	---	---	---	---	---	---	---	---	1.0	1.0
5 40	---	---	---	---	---	---	---	---	---	---	---	---	---	1.0

Use Table A for all places except those listed below for Table B.
Use Table B for Cape Cod Canal, Hell Gate, Chesapeake and Delaware Canal and all stations in Table 2 which are referred to them.

1. From predictions find the time of slack water and the time and velocity of maximum current (flood or ebb), one of which is immediately before and the other after the time for which the velocity is desired.
2. Find the interval of time between the above slack and maximum current, and enter the top of Table A or B with the interval which most nearly agrees with this value.
3. Find the interval of time between the above slack and the time desired, and enter the side of Table A or B with the interval which most nearly agrees with this value.
4. Find, in the table, the factor corresponding to the above two intervals, and multiply the maximum velocity by this factor. The result will be the approximate velocity at the time desired.

163

Appendix E-1

LUMINOUS RANGE DIAGRAM

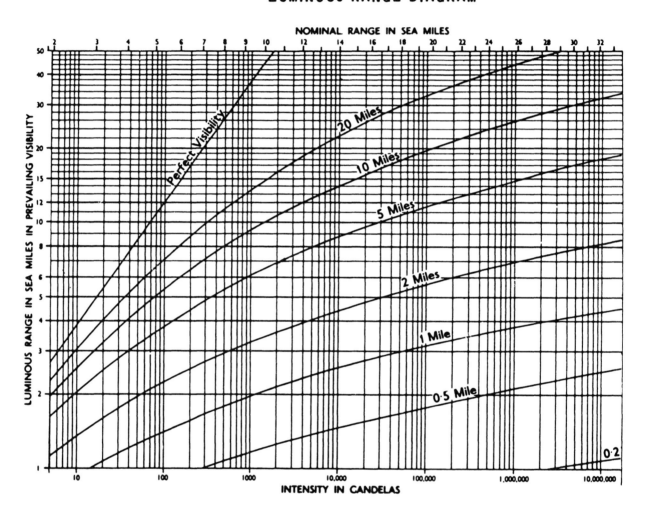

Appendix E-2

Distance of visibility of objects at sea:

Ht. in ft.	Naut. Mi.	Ht. in ft.	Naut. Mi.
1	1.1	55	8.5
2	1.7	60	8.9
3	2.0	65	9.2
4	2.3	70	9.6
5	2.5	75	9.9
6	2.8	80	10.3
7	2.9	85	10.6
8	3.1	90	10.9
9	3.5	95	11.2
10	3.6	100	11.5
11	3.8	105	11.7
12	4.0	110	12.0
13	4.2	115	12.3
14	4.3	120	12.6
15	4.4	125	12.9
16	4.6	130	13.1
17	4.7	135	13.3
18	4.9	140	13.6
19	5.0	145	13.8
20	5.1	150	14.1
21	5.3	160	14.5
22	5.4	170	14.9
23	5.5	180	15.4
24	5.6	190	15.8
25	5.7	200	16.2
26	5.8	210	16.6
27	6.0	220	17.0
28	6.1	230	17.4
29	6.2	240	17.7
30	6.3	250	18.2
31	6.4	260	18.5
32	6.5	270	18.9
33	6.6	280	19.2
34	6.7	290	19.6
35	6.8	300	19.9
36	6.9	310	20.1
37	6.9	320	20.5
38	7.0	330	20.8
39	7.1	340	21.1
40	7.2	350	21.5
41	7.3	360	21.7
42	7.4	370	22.1
43	7.5	380	22.3
44	7.6	390	22.7
45	7.7	400	22.9
50	8.1		

Appendix F-1

1970 JANUARY 1, 2, 3 (THURS., FRI., SAT.)

G.M.T.	ARIES G.H.A.	VENUS −3.5 G.H.A.	Dec.	MARS +1.0 G.H.A.	Dec.	JUPITER −1.5 G.H.A.	Dec.	SATURN +0.5 G.H.A.	Dec.	STARS Name	S.H.A.	Dec.
1 00	100 13·8	185 22·2 S 23 37·9		116 17·9 S 7 43·3		249 40·2 S 11 08·9		69 27·8 N 9 49·3		Acamar	315 42·8	S 40 25·5
01	115 16·3	200 21·2 37·9		131 18·6 42·6		264 42·3 09·0		84 30·2 49·3		Achernar	335 50·6	S 57 23·5
02	130 18·8	215 20·2 37·8		146 19·3 41·8		279 44·5 09·1		99 32·7 49·3		Acrux	173 46·3	S 62 55·7
03	145 21·2	230 19·3 ·· 37·8		161 20·1 ·· 41·0		294 46·6 ·· 09·2		114 35·2 ·· 49·4		Adhara	255 37·9	S 28 55·7
04	160 23·7	245 18·3 37·8		176 20·8 40·3		309 48·7 09·3		129 37·7 49·4		Aldebaran	291 26·7	N 16 27·2
05	175 26·2	260 17·3 37·8		191 21·6 39·5		324 50·9 09·4		144 40·2 49·4				
06	190 28·6	275 16·4 S 23 37·8		206 22·3 S 7 38·8		339 53·0 S 11 09·5		159 42·6 N 9 49·4		Alioth	166 49·1	N 56 07·0
07	205 31·1	290 15·4 37·8		221 23·1 38·0		354 55·1 09·7		174 45·1 49·4		Alkaid	153 24·6	N 49 27·4
T 08	220 33·5	305 14·4 37·8		236 23·8 37·3		9 57·3 09·8		189 47·6 49·4		Al Na'ir	28 24·8	S 47 06·7
H 09	235 36·0	320 13·4 ·· 37·7		251 24·6 ·· 36·5		24 59·4 ·· 09·9		204 50·1 ·· 49·4		Alnilam	276 19·3	S 1 13·1
U 10	250 38·5	335 12·5 37·7		266 25·3 35·8		40 01·5 10·0		219 52·6 49·4		Alphard	218 28·0	S 8 31·6
R 11	265 40·9	350 11·5 37·7		281 26·0 35·0		55 03·7 10·1		234 55·0 49·4				
S 12	280 43·4	5 10·5 S 23 37·7		296 26·8 S 7 34·2		70 05·8 S 11 10·2		249 57·5 N 9 49·4		Alphecca	126 38·9	N 26 48·6
D 13	295 45·9	20 09·6 37·7		311 27·5 33·5		85 07·9 10·3		265 00·0 49·4		Alpheratz	358 17·6	N 28 55·7
A 14	310 48·3	35 08·6 37·6		326 28·3 32·7		100 10·1 10·4		280 02·5 49·4		Altair	62 40·5	N 8 47·2
Y 15	325 50·8	50 07·6 ·· 37·6		341 29·0 ·· 32·0		115 12·2 ·· 10·5		295 05·0 ·· 49·4		Ankaa	353 47·8	S 42 28·3
16	340 53·3	65 06·6 37·6		356 29·8 31·2		130 14·4 10·6		310 07·4 49·4		Antares	113 06·8	S 26 22·1
17	355 55·7	80 05·7 37·5		11 30·5 30·5		145 16·5 10·7		325 09·9 49·5				
18	10 58·2	95 04·7 S 23 37·5		26 31·3 S 7 29·7		160 18·6 S 11 10·9		340 12·4 N 9 49·5		Arcturus	146 25·7	N 19 20·0
19	26 00·7	110 03·7 37·5		41 32·0 28·9		175 20·8 11·0		355 14·9 49·5		Atria	108 38·7	S 68 58·5
20	41 03·1	125 02·8 37·5		56 32·7 28·2		190 22·9 11·1		10 17·3 49·5		Avior	234 31·0	S 59 24·5
21	56 05·6	140 01·8 ·· 37·4		71 33·5 ·· 27·4		205 25·0 ·· 11·2		25 19·8 ·· 49·5		Bellatrix	279 06·8	N 6 19·6
22	71 08·0	155 00·8 37·4		86 34·2 26·7		220 27·2 11·3		40 22·3 49·5		Betelgeuse	271 36·4	N 7 24·3
23	86 10·5	169 59·8 37·3		101 35·0 25·9		235 29·3 11·4		55 24·8 49·5				
2 00	101 13·0	184 58·8 S 23 37·3		116 35·7 S 7 25·2		250 31·5 S 11 11·5		70 27·3 N 9 49·5		Canopus	264 10·1	S 52 40·6
01	116 15·4	199 57·9 37·3		131 36·5 24·4		265 33·6 11·6		85 29·7 49·5		Capella	281 22·4	N 45 58·4
02	131 17·9	214 56·9 37·2		146 37·2 23·6		280 35·7 11·7		100 32·2 49·5		Deneb	49 54·4	N 45 10·4
03	146 20·4	229 55·9 ·· 37·2		161 38·0 ·· 22·9		295 37·9 ·· 11·8		115 34·7 ·· 49·5		Denebola	183 06·9	N 14 44·3
04	161 22·8	244 55·0 37·1		176 38·7 22·1		310 40·0 11·9		130 37·2 49·6		Diphda	349 28·6	S 18 09·1
05	176 25·3	259 54·0 37·1		191 39·4 21·4		325 42·2 12·0		145 39·6 49·6				
06	191 27·8	274 53·0 S 23 37·1		206 40·2 S 7 20·6		340 44·3 S 11 12·2		160 42·1 N 9 49·6		Dubhe	194 31·0	N 61 54·5
07	206 30·2	289 52·0 37·0		221 40·9 19·8		355 46·4 12·3		175 44·6 49·6		Elnath	278 53·7	N 28 35·2
08	221 32·7	304 51·1 37·0		236 41·7 19·1		10 48·6 12·4		190 47·1 49·6		Eltanin	91 01·9	N 51 29·3
F 09	236 35·1	319 50·1 ·· 36·9		251 42·4 ·· 18·3		25 50·7 ·· 12·5		205 49·5 ·· 49·6		Enif	34 19·5	N 9 44·2
R 10	251 37·6	334 49·1 36·9		266 43·2 17·6		40 52·9 12·6		220 52·0 49·6		Fomalhaut	16 00·1	S 29 47·1
I 11	266 40·1	349 48·2 36·8		281 43·9 16·8		55 55·0 12·7		235 54·5 49·6				
D 12	281 42·5	4 47·2 S 23 36·8		296 44·7 S 7 16·1		70 57·1 S 11 12·8		250 57·0 N 9 49·6		Gacrux	172 37·7	S 56 56·5
A 13	296 45·0	19 46·2 36·7		311 45·4 15·3		85 59·3 12·9		265 59·4 49·6		Gienah	176 26·0	S 17 22·5
Y 14	311 47·5	34 45·2 36·7		326 46·2 14·5		101 01·4 13·0		281 01·9 49·6		Hadar	149 35·0	S 60 13·6
15	326 49·9	49 44·3 ·· 36·6		341 46·9 ·· 13·8		116 03·6 ·· 13·1		296 04·4 ·· 49·6		Hamal	328 37·7	N 23 19·5
16	341 52·4	64 43·3 36·5		356 47·7 13·0		131 05·7 13·2		311 06·9 49·7		Kaus Aust.	84 27·6	S 34 24·2
17	356 54·9	79 42·3 36·5		11 48·4 12·3		146 07·9 13·3		326 09·3 49·7				
18	11 57·3	94 41·4 S 23 36·4		26 49·2 S 7 11·5		161 10·0 S 11 13·4		341 11·8 N 9 49·7		Kochab	137 18·7	N 74 16·3
19	26 59·8	109 40·4 36·4		41 49·9 10·7		176 12·1 13·6		356 14·3 49·7		Markab	14 11·2	N 15 02·7
20	42 02·3	124 39·4 36·3		56 50·7 10·0		191 14·3 13·7		11 16·8 49·7		Menkar	314 49·1	N 3 58·5
21	57 04·7	139 38·5 ·· 36·2		71 51·4 ·· 09·2		206 16·4 ·· 13·8		26 19·2 ·· 49·7		Menkent	148 46·5	S 36 13·3
22	72 07·2	154 37·5 36·2		86 52·1 08·5		221 18·6 13·9		41 21·7 49·7		Miaplacidus	221 46·3	S 69 35·4
23	87 09·6	169 36·5 36·1		101 52·9 07·7		236 20·7 14·0		56 24·2 49·7				
3 00	102 12·1	184 35·5 S 23 36·0		116 53·6 S 7 06·9		251 22·9 S 11 14·1		71 26·6 N 9 49·7		Mirfak	309 27·1	N 49 45·7
01	117 14·6	199 34·6 36·0		131 54·4 06·2		266 25·0 14·2		86 29·1 49·7		Nunki	76 39·2	S 26 20·3
02	132 17·0	214 33·6 ·35·9		146 55·1 05·4		281 27·2 14·3		101 31·6 49·8		Peacock	54 11·1	S 56 50·2
03	147 19·5	229 32·6 ·· 35·9		161 55·9 ·· 04·7		296 29·3 ·· 14·4		116 34·1 ·· 49·8		Pollux	244 07·3	N 28 06·0
04	162 22·0	244 31·7 35·7		176 56·6 03·9		311 31·4 14·5		131 36·5 49·8		Procyon	245 33·6	N 5 18·3
05	177 24·4	259 30·7 35·7		191 57·4 03·2		326 33·6 14·6		146 39·0 49·8				
06	192 26·9	274 29·7 S 23 35·6		206 58·1 S 7 02·4		341 35·7 S 11 14·7		161 41·5 N 9 49·8		Rasalhague	96 37·2	N 12 34·6
07	207 29·4	289 28·8 35·5		221 58·9 01·6		356 37·9 14·8		176 43·9 49·8		Regulus	208 18·0	N 12 06·8
S 08	222 31·8	304 27·8 35·4		236 59·6 00·9		11 40·0 14·9		191 46·4 49·8		Rigel	281 43·2	S 8 14·0
A 09	237 34·3	319 26·8 ·· 35·4		252 00·4 7 00·1		26 42·2 ·· 15·0		206 48·9 ·· 49·8		Rigil Kent.	140 37·1	S 60 42·6
T 10	252 36·8	334 25·9 35·3		267 01·1 6 59·4		41 44·3 15·1		221 51·4 49·8		Sabik	102 50·4	S 15 41·5
U 11	267 39·2	349 24·9 35·2		282 01·9 58·6		56 46·5 15·3		236 53·8 49·9				
R 12	282 41·7	4 23·9 S 23 35·1		297 02·6 S 6 57·8		71 48·6 S 11 15·4		251 56·3 N 9 49·9		Schedar	350 18·2	N 56 22·7
D 13	297 44·1	19 22·9 35·0		312 03·4 57·1		86 50·8 15·5		266 58·8 49·9		Shaula	97 06·8	S 37 05·1
A 14	312 46·6	34 22·0 34·9		327 04·1 56·3		101 52·9 15·6		282 01·2 49·9		Sirius	259 02·2	S 16 40·3
Y 15	327 49·1	49 21·0 ·· 34·9		342 04·9 ·· 55·5		116 55·1 ·· 15·7		297 03·7 ·· 49·9		Spica	159 05·9	S 11 00·4
16	342 51·5	64 20·0 34·8		357 05·6 54·8		131 57·2 15·8		312 06·2 49·9		Suhail	223 16·3	S 43 18·5
17	357 54·0	79 19·1 34·7		12 06·4 54·0		146 59·3 15·9		327 08·6 49·9				
18	12 56·5	94 18·1 S 23 34·6		27 07·1 S 6 53·3		162 01·5 S 11 16·0		342 11·1 N 9 49·9		Vega	81 01·6	N 38 45·1
19	27 58·9	109 17·1 34·5		42 07·9 52·5		177 03·6 16·1		357 13·6 49·9		Zuben'ubi	137 41·9	S 15 55·1
20	43 01·4	124 16·2 34·4		57 08·6 51·7		192 05·8 16·2		12 16·1 50·0			S.H.A.	Mer. Pass.
21	58 03·9	139 15·2 ·· 34·3		72 09·4 ·· 51·0		207 07·9 ·· 16·3		27 18·5 ·· 50·0		Venus	83 45·9	11 41
22	73 06·3	154 14·2 34·2		87 10·1 50·2		222 10·1 16·4		42 21·0 50·0		Mars	15 22·7	16 13
23	88 08·8	169 13·3 34·1		102 10·9 49·5		237 12·2 16·5		57 23·5 50·0		Jupiter	149 18·5	7 17
Mer. Pass.	17 12·3	v −1·0 d 0·1		v 0·7 d 0·8		v 2·1 d 0·1		v 2·5 d 0·0		Saturn	329 14·3	19 15

166

1970 JANUARY 1, 2, 3 (THURS., FRI., SAT.) 11

G.M.T.	SUN G.H.A.	Dec.	MOON G.H.A.	v	Dec.	d	H.P.
d h	° '	° '	° '	'	° '	'	'
1 00	179 10·8	S 23 03·4	271 18·0	15·4	S 6 20·4	14·6	55·9
01	194 10·5	03·2	285 52·4	15·4	6 35·0	14·6	56·0
02	209 10·2	03·0	300 26·8	15·3	6 49·6	14·6	56·0
03	224 09·9 ··	02·8	315 01·1	15·2	7 04·2	14·6	56·0
04	239 09·6	02·6	329 35·3	15·2	7 18·8	14·6	56·1
05	254 09·3	02·4	344 09·5	15·1	7 33·4	14·5	56·1
06	269 09·0	S 23 02·2	358 43·6	15·1	S 7 47·9	14·6	56·1
T 07	284 08·7	02·0	13 17·7	14·9	8 02·5	14·5	56·2
H 08	299 08·4	01·8	27 51·6	14·9	8 17·0	14·5	56·2
U 09	314 08·1 ··	01·6	42 25·5	14·9	8 31·5	14·5	56·2
R 10	329 07·8	01·4	56 59·4	14·8	8 46·0	14·5	56·3
11	344 07·5	01·2	71 33·2	14·6	9 00·5	14·5	56·3
S 12	359 07·2	S 23 01·0	86 06·8	14·7	S 9 15·0	14·4	56·3
D 13	14 06·9	00·8	100 40·5	14·5	9 29·4	14·4	56·4
A 14	29 06·6	00·6	115 14·0	14·5	9 43·8	14·4	56·4
Y 15	44 06·3 ··	00·4	129 47·5	14·4	9 58·2	14·4	56·4
16	59 06·0	00·2	144 20·9	14·3	10 12·6	14·4	56·5
17	74 05·7	23 00·0	158 54·2	14·2	10 27·0	14·3	56·5
18	89 05·5	S 22 59·8	173 27·4	14·1	S 10 41·3	14·3	56·6
19	104 05·2	59·6	188 00·5	14·1	10 55·6	14·3	56·6
20	119 04·9	59·4	202 33·6	13·9	11 09·9	14·2	56·6
21	134 04·6 ··	59·2	217 06·5	13·9	11 24·1	14·2	56·6
22	149 04·3	58·9	231 39·4	13·8	11 38·3	14·2	56·7
23	164 04·0	58·7	246 12·2	13·7	11 52·5	14·1	56·7
2 00	179 03·7	S 22 58·5	260 44·9	13·6	S 12 06·6	14·1	56·8
01	194 03·4	58·3	275 17·5	13·5	12 20·7	14·1	56·8
02	209 03·1	58·1	289 50·0	13·4	12 34·8	14·0	56·8
03	224 02·8 ··	57·9	304 22·4	13·3	12 48·8	14·0	56·9
04	239 02·5	57·7	318 54·7	13·3	13 02·8	14·0	56·9
05	254 02·2	57·4	333 27·0	13·1	13 16·8	13·9	56·9
06	269 01·9	S 22 57·2	347 59·1	13·0	S 13 30·7	13·9	57·0
07	284 01·6	57·0	2 31·1	12·9	13 44·6	13·8	57·0
F 08	299 01·3	56·8	17 03·0	12·8	13 58·4	13·8	57·1
R 09	314 01·0 ··	56·6	31 34·8	12·7	14 12·2	13·8	57·1
I 10	329 00·8	56·3	46 06·5	12·6	14 26·0	13·7	57·1
11	344 00·5	56·1	60 38·1	12·5	14 39·6	13·7	57·2
D 12	359 00·2	S 22 55·9	75 09·6	12·4	S 14 53·3	13·6	57·2
A 13	13 59·9	55·7	89 41·0	12·3	15 06·9	13·5	57·3
Y 14	28 59·6	55·4	104 12·3	12·2	15 20·4	13·5	57·3
15	43 59·3 ··	55·2	118 43·5	12·0	15 33·9	13·5	57·3
16	58 59·0	55·0	133 14·5	11·9	15 47·4	13·5	57·4
17	73 58·7	54·8	147 45·4	11·9	16 00·7	13·5	57·4
18	88 58·4	S 22 54·5	162 16·3	11·7	S 16 14·0	13·3	57·5
19	103 58·1	54·3	176 47·0	11·6	16 27·3	13·2	57·5
20	118 57·8	54·1	191 17·6	11·4	16 40·5	13·1	57·5
21	133 57·5 ··	53·9	205 48·0	11·4	16 53·6	13·1	57·6
22	148 57·3	53·6	220 18·4	11·2	17 06·7	13·0	57·6
23	163 57·0	53·4	234 48·6	11·1	17 19·7	13·0	57·6
3 00	178 56·7	S 22 53·2	249 18·7	11·0	S 17 32·7	12·8	57·7
01	193 56·4	52·9	263 48·7	10·8	17 45·5	12·8	57·7
02	208 56·1	52·7	278 18·5	10·7	17 58·3	12·8	57·8
03	223 55·8 ··	52·5	292 48·2	10·6	18 11·1	12·6	57·8
04	238 55·5	52·2	307 17·8	10·5	18 23·7	12·6	57·9
05	253 55·2	52·0	321 47·3	10·3	18 36·3	12·5	57·9
06	268 54·9	S 22 51·8	336 16·6	10·2	S 18 48·8	12·4	57·9
S 07	283 54·6	51·5	350 45·8	10·1	19 01·2	12·3	58·0
A 08	298 54·3	51·3	5 14·9	10·0	19 13·5	12·3	58·0
T 09	313 54·1 ··	51·0	19 43·9	9·8	19 25·8	12·1	58·1
U 10	328 53·8	50·8	34 12·7	9·7	19 37·9	12·1	58·1
R 11	343 53·5	50·6	48 41·4	9·5	19 50·0	12·0	58·1
D 12	358 53·2	S 22 50·3	63 09·9	9·4	S 20 02·0	11·9	58·2
A 13	13 52·9	50·1	77 38·3	9·3	20 13·9	11·8	58·2
Y 14	28 52·6	49·8	92 06·6	9·1	20 25·7	11·7	58·3
15	43 52·3 ··	49·6	106 34·7	9·0	20 37·4	11·7	58·3
16	58 52·0	49·3	121 02·7	8·8	20 49·1	11·5	58·4
17	73 51·7	49·1	135 30·5	8·7	21 00·6	11·4	58·4
18	88 51·5	S 22 48·9	149 58·2	8·6	S 21 12·0	11·3	58·4
19	103 51·2	48·6	164 25·8	8·4	21 23·3	11·2	58·5
20	118 50·9	48·4	178 53·2	8·3	21 34·5	11·1	58·5
21	133 50·6 ··	48·1	193 20·5	8·2	21 45·6	11·0	58·5
22	148 50·3	47·9	207 47·7	8·0	21 56·6	10·9	58·6
23	163 50·0	47·6	222 14·7	7·8	22 07·5	10·8	58·6
	S.D. 16·3	d 0·2	S.D. 15·3		15·6		15·9

Lat.	Twilight Naut.	Civil	Sun-rise	Moonrise 1	2	3	4
°	h m	h m	h m	h m	h m	h m	h m
N 72	08 23	10 40	■■	01 23	03 47	■■	■■
N 70	08 04	09 48	■■	01 13	03 21	06 21	■■
68	07 49	09 16	■■	01 04	03 01	05 24	■■
66	07 37	08 52	10 26	00 58	02 46	04 51	08 02
64	07 26	08 33	09 49	00 52	02 33	04 27	06 43
62	07 17	08 18	09 22	00 47	02 23	04 08	06 07
60	07 09	08 05	09 02	00 43	02 14	03 52	05 41
N 58	07 02	07 54	08 45	00 39	02 06	03 39	05 20
56	06 55	07 44	08 31	00 35	01 59	03 28	05 04
54	06 49	07 35	08 19	00 32	01 53	03 18	04 50
52	06 44	07 28	08 08	00 30	01 47	03 10	04 37
50	06 39	07 20	07 58	00 27	01 42	03 02	04 26
45	06 28	07 05	07 38	00 22	01 32	02 46	04 04
N 40	06 18	06 52	07 22	00 18	01 23	02 32	03 46
35	06 09	06 40	07 08	00 14	01 15	02 21	03 31
30	06 00	06 30	06 56	00 10	01 09	02 11	03 18
20	05 44	06 11	06 35	00 05	00 58	01 54	02 56
N 10	05 28	05 54	06 17	00 00	00 48	01 40	02 37
0	05 12	05 38	06 00	24 39	00 39	01 26	02 19
S 10	04 53	05 20	05 43	24 30	00 30	01 13	02 01
20	04 31	05 00	05 24	24 20	00 20	00 59	01 43
30	04 02	04 35	05 03	24 09	00 09	00 42	01 22
35	03 44	04 21	04 50	24 03	00 03	00 33	01 09
40	03 22	04 03	04 35	23 56	24 22	00 22	00 55
45	02 52	03 41	04 18	23 48	24 10	00 10	00 38
S 50	02 08	03 12	03 56	23 38	23 55	24 18	00 18
52	01 42	02 57	03 45	23 34	23 48	24 08	00 08
54	01 02	02 40	03 33	23 29	23 40	23 57	24 23
56	////	02 19	03 20	23 24	23 32	23 45	24 06
58	////	01 51	03 04	23 18	23 22	23 30	23 46
S 60	////	01 08	02 44	23 11	23 11	23 14	23 21

Lat.	Sun-set	Twilight Civil	Naut.	Moonset 1	2	3	4
°	h m	h m	h m	h m	h m	h m	h m
N 72	■■	13 27	15 45	10 16	09 25	■■	■■
N 70	■■	14 19	16 03	10 30	09 54	08 35	■■
68	■■	14 52	16 18	10 40	10 15	09 33	■■
66	13 41	15 15	16 31	10 49	10 32	10 08	08 49
64	14 19	15 34	16 41	10 57	10 46	10 33	10 09
62	14 45	15 49	16 51	11 03	10 58	10 53	10 46
60	15 06	16 02	16 59	11 09	11 08	11 09	11 12
N 58	15 23	16 14	17 06	11 14	11 17	11 23	11 33
56	15 37	16 24	17 12	11 19	11 25	11 35	11 51
54	15 49	16 33	17 18	11 23	11 32	11 46	12 05
52	16 00	16 41	17 24	11 26	11 39	11 55	12 18
50	16 09	16 48	17 29	11 30	11 44	12 03	12 30
45	16 30	17 03	17 40	11 37	11 57	12 21	12 53
N 40	16 46	17 17	17 50	11 43	12 07	12 36	13 13
35	17 00	17 28	17 59	11 49	12 16	12 49	13 29
30	17 12	17 38	18 08	11 53	12 24	13 00	13 43
20	17 32	17 56	18 24	12 01	12 38	13 19	14 06
N 10	17 51	18 13	18 40	12 09	12 50	13 35	14 27
0	18 08	18 30	18 56	12 16	13 01	13 51	14 46
S 10	18 25	18 48	19 15	12 22	13 12	14 06	15 06
20	18 43	19 08	19 37	12 30	13 24	14 23	15 27
30	19 05	19 32	20 05	12 38	13 38	14 42	15 51
35	19 17	19 47	20 23	12 43	13 46	14 54	16 05
40	19 32	20 05	20 46	12 48	13 55	15 07	16 22
45	19 50	20 27	21 16	12 55	14 06	15 22	16 42
S 50	20 12	20 55	21 59	13 03	14 20	15 42	17 07
52	20 22	21 10	22 24	13 06	14 26	15 51	17 19
54	20 34	21 27	23 03	13 10	14 33	16 01	17 33
56	20 48	21 48	////	13 15	14 40	16 13	17 49
58	21 04	22 16	////	13 20	14 49	16 26	18 08
S 60	21 23	22 58	////	13 25	14 59	16 42	18 33

Day	SUN Eqn. of Time 00ʰ	12ʰ	Mer. Pass.	MOON Mer. Pass. Upper	Lower	Age	Phase
	m s	m s	h m	h m	h m	d	
1	03 16	03 30	12 04	06 05	18 27	23	
2	03 45	03 59	12 04	06 50	19 13	24	🌙
3	04 13	04 27	12 04	07 38	20 05	25	

Appendix F-3

CONVERSION OF ARC TO TIME

0°–59°		60°–119°		120°–179°		180°–239°		240°–299°		300°–359°			0′.00	0′.25	0′.50	0′.75
°	h m	°	h m	°	h m	°	h m	°	h m	°	h m	°	m s	m s	m s	m s
0	0 00	60	4 00	120	8 00	180	12 00	240	16 00	300	20 00	0	0 00	0 01	0 02	0 03
1	0 04	61	4 04	121	8 04	181	12 04	241	16 04	301	20 04	1	0 04	0 05	0 06	0 07
2	0 08	62	4 08	122	8 08	182	12 08	242	16 08	302	20 08	2	0 08	0 09	0 10	0 11
3	0 12	63	4 12	123	8 12	183	12 12	243	16 12	303	20 12	3	0 12	0 13	0 14	0 15
4	0 16	64	4 16	124	8 16	184	12 16	244	16 16	304	20 16	4	0 16	0 17	0 18	0 19
5	0 20	65	4 20	125	8 20	185	12 20	245	16 20	305	20 20	5	0 20	0 21	0 22	0 23
6	0 24	66	4 24	126	8 24	186	12 24	246	16 24	306	20 24	6	0 24	0 25	0 26	0 27
7	0 28	67	4 28	127	8 28	187	12 28	247	16 28	307	20 28	7	0 28	0 29	0 30	0 31
8	0 32	68	4 32	128	8 32	188	12 32	248	16 32	308	20 32	8	0 32	0 33	0 34	0 35
9	0 36	69	4 36	129	8 36	189	12 36	249	16 36	309	20 36	9	0 36	0 37	0 38	0 39
10	0 40	70	4 40	130	8 40	190	12 40	250	16 40	310	20 40	10	0 40	0 41	0 42	0 43
11	0 44	71	4 44	131	8 44	191	12 44	251	16 44	311	20 44	11	0 44	0 45	0 46	0 47
12	0 48	72	4 48	132	8 48	192	12 48	252	16 48	312	20 48	12	0 48	0 49	0 50	0 51
13	0 52	73	4 52	133	8 52	193	12 52	253	16 52	313	20 52	13	0 52	0 53	0 54	0 55
14	0 56	74	4 56	134	8 56	194	12 56	254	16 56	314	20 56	14	0 56	0 57	0 58	0 59
15	1 00	75	5 00	135	9 00	195	13 00	255	17 00	315	21 00	15	1 00	1 01	1 02	1 03
16	1 04	76	5 04	136	9 04	196	13 04	256	17 04	316	21 04	16	1 04	1 05	1 06	1 07
17	1 08	77	5 08	137	9 08	197	13 08	257	17 08	317	21 08	17	1 08	1 09	1 10	1 11
18	1 12	78	5 12	138	9 12	198	13 12	258	17 12	318	21 12	18	1 12	1 13	1 14	1 15
19	1 16	79	5 16	139	9 16	199	13 16	259	17 16	319	21 16	19	1 16	1 17	1 18	1 19
20	1 20	80	5 20	140	9 20	200	13 20	260	17 20	320	21 20	20	1 20	1 21	1 22	1 23
21	1 24	81	5 24	141	9 24	201	13 24	261	17 24	321	21 24	21	1 24	1 25	1 26	1 27
22	1 28	82	5 28	142	9 28	202	13 28	262	17 28	322	21 28	22	1 28	1 29	1 30	1 31
23	1 32	83	5 32	143	9 32	203	13 32	263	17 32	323	21 32	23	1 32	1 33	1 34	1 35
24	1 36	84	5 36	144	9 36	204	13 36	264	17 36	324	21 36	24	1 36	1 37	1 38	1 39
25	1 40	85	5 40	145	9 40	205	13 40	265	17 40	325	21 40	25	1 40	1 41	1 42	1 43
26	1 44	86	5 44	146	9 44	206	13 44	266	17 44	326	21 44	26	1 44	1 45	1 46	1 47
27	1 48	87	5 48	147	9 48	207	13 48	267	17 48	327	21 48	27	1 48	1 49	1 50	1 51
28	1 52	88	5 52	148	9 52	208	13 52	268	17 52	328	21 52	28	1 52	1 53	1 54	1 55
29	1 56	89	5 56	149	9 56	209	13 56	269	17 56	329	21 56	29	1 56	1 57	1 58	1 59
30	2 00	90	6 00	150	10 00	210	14 00	270	18 00	330	22 00	30	2 00	2 01	2 02	2 03
31	2 04	91	6 04	151	10 04	211	14 04	271	18 04	331	22 04	31	2 04	2 05	2 06	2 07
32	2 08	92	6 08	152	10 08	212	14 08	272	18 08	332	22 08	32	2 08	2 09	2 10	2 11
33	2 12	93	6 12	153	10 12	213	14 12	273	18 12	333	22 12	33	2 12	2 13	2 14	2 15
34	2 16	94	6 16	154	10 16	214	14 16	274	18 16	334	22 16	34	2 16	2 17	2 18	2 19
35	2 20	95	6 20	155	10 20	215	14 20	275	18 20	335	22 20	35	2 20	2 21	2 22	2 23
36	2 24	96	6 24	156	10 24	216	14 24	276	18 24	336	22 24	36	2 24	2 25	2 26	2 27
37	2 28	97	6 28	157	10 28	217	14 28	277	18 28	337	22 28	37	2 28	2 29	2 30	2 31
38	2 32	98	6 32	158	10 32	218	14 32	278	18 32	338	22 32	38	2 32	2 33	2 34	2 35
39	2 36	99	6 36	159	10 36	219	14 36	279	18 36	339	22 36	39	2 36	2 37	2 38	2 39
40	2 40	100	6 40	160	10 40	220	14 40	280	18 40	340	22 40	40	2 40	2 41	2 42	2 43
41	2 44	101	6 44	161	10 44	221	14 44	281	18 44	341	22 44	41	2 44	2 45	2 46	2 47
42	2 48	102	6 48	162	10 48	222	14 48	282	18 48	342	22 48	42	2 48	2 49	2 50	2 51
43	2 52	103	6 52	163	10 52	223	14 52	283	18 52	343	22 52	43	2 52	2 53	2 54	2 55
44	2 56	104	6 56	164	10 56	224	14 56	284	18 56	344	22 56	44	2 56	2 57	2 58	2 59
45	3 00	105	7 00	165	11 00	225	15 00	285	19 00	345	23 00	45	3 00	3 01	3 02	3 03
46	3 04	106	7 04	166	11 04	226	15 04	286	19 04	346	23 04	46	3 04	3 05	3 06	3 07
47	3 08	107	7 08	167	11 08	227	15 08	287	19 08	347	23 08	47	3 08	3 09	3 10	3 11
48	3 12	108	7 12	168	11 12	228	15 12	288	19 12	348	23 12	48	3 12	3 13	3 14	3 15
49	3 16	109	7 16	169	11 16	229	15 16	289	19 16	349	23 16	49	3 16	3 17	3 18	3 19
50	3 20	110	7 20	170	11 20	230	15 20	290	19 20	350	23 20	50	3 20	3 21	3 22	3 23
51	3 24	111	7 24	171	11 24	231	15 24	291	19 24	351	23 24	51	3 24	3 25	3 26	3 27
52	3 28	112	7 28	172	11 28	232	15 28	292	19 28	352	23 28	52	3 28	3 29	3 30	3 31
53	3 32	113	7 32	173	11 32	233	15 32	293	19 32	353	23 32	53	3 32	3 33	3 34	3 35
54	3 36	114	7 36	174	11 36	234	15 36	294	19 36	354	23 36	54	3 36	3 37	3 38	3 39
55	3 40	115	7 40	175	11 40	235	15 40	295	19 40	355	23 40	55	3 40	3 41	3 42	3 43
56	3 44	116	7 44	176	11 44	236	15 44	296	19 44	356	23 44	56	3 44	3 45	3 46	3 47
57	3 48	117	7 48	177	11 48	237	15 48	297	19 48	357	23 48	57	3 48	3 49	3 50	3 51
58	3 52	118	7 52	178	11 52	238	15 52	298	19 52	358	23 52	58	3 52	3 53	3 54	3 55
59	3 56	119	7 56	179	11 56	239	15 56	299	19 56	359	23 56	59	3 56	3 57	3 58	3 59

The above table is for converting expressions in arc to their equivalent in time ; its main use in this **Almanac** is for the conversion of longitude for application to L.M.T. (*added* if *west*, *subtracted* if *east*) to give G.M.T. or vice versa, particularly in the case of sunrise, sunset, etc.

Appendix F-4

ALTITUDE CORRECTION TABLES 10°–90°—SUN, STARS, PLANETS

OCT.–MAR. SUN APR.–SEPT.						STARS AND PLANETS			DIP			
App. Alt.	Lower Limb	Upper Limb	App. Alt.	Lower Limb	Upper Limb	App. Alt.	Corrn	App. Alt. Additional Corrn	Ht. of Eye	Corrn	Ht. of Eye	Corrn
9 34	+10·8	−21·5	9 39	+10·6	−21·2	9 56	−5·3	**1970**	ft. 1·1	−1·1	ft. 44	−6·5
9 45	+10·9	−21·4	9 51	+10·7	−21·1	10 08	−5·2	**VENUS**	1·4	−1·2	45	−6·6
9 56	+11·0	−21·3	10 03	+10·8	−21·0	10 20	−5·1	Jan. 1–July 22	1·6	−1·3	47	−6·7
10 08	+11·1	−21·2	10 15	+10·9	−20·9	10 33	−5·0	0 +0·1	1·9	−1·4	48	−6·8
10 21	+11·2	−21·1	10 27	+11·0	−20·8	10 46	−4·9	42	2·2	−1·5	49	−6·9
10 34	+11·3	−21·0	10 40	+11·1	−20·7	11 00	−4·8	July 23–Sept. 5	2·5	−1·6	51	−7·0
10 47	+11·4	−20·9	10 54	+11·2	−20·6	11 14	−4·7	0 +0·2	2·8	−1·7	52	−7·1
11 01	+11·5	−20·8	11 08	+11·3	−20·5	11 29	−4·6	47	3·2	−1·8	54	−7·2
11 15	+11·6	−20·7	11 23	+11·4	−20·4	11 45	−4·5	Sept. 6–Oct. 1	3·6	−1·9	55	−7·3
11 30	+11·7	−20·6	11 38	+11·5	−20·3	12 01	−4·4	0 +0·3	4·0	−2·0	57	−7·4
11 46	+11·8	−20·5	11 54	+11·6	−20·2	12 18	−4·3	46	4·4	−2·1	58	−7·5
12 02	+11·9	−20·4	12 10	+11·7	−20·1	12 35	−4·2		4·9	−2·2	60	−7·6
12 19	+12·0	−20·3	12 28	+11·8	−20·0	12 54	−4·1	Oct. 2–Oct. 16	5·3	−2·3	62	−7·7
12 37	+12·1	−20·2	12 46	+11·9	−19·9	13 13	−4·0	0 +0·4	5·8	−2·4	63	−7·8
12 55	+12·2	−20·1	13 05	+12·0	−19·8	13 33	−3·9	11	6·3	−2·5	65	−7·9
13 14	+12·3	−20·0	13 24	+12·1	−19·7	13 54	−3·8	41 +0·5	6·9	−2·6	67	−8·0
13 35	+12·4	−19·9	13 45	+12·2	−19·6	14 16	−3·7		7·4	−2·7	68	−8·1
13 56	+12·5	−19·8	14 07	+12·3	−19·5	14 40	−3·6	Oct. 17–Oct. 24	8·0	−2·8	70	−8·2
14 18	+12·6	−19·7	14 30	+12·4	−19·4	15 04	−3·5	0 +0·5	8·6	−2·9	72	−8·3
14 42	+12·7	−19·6	14 54	+12·5	−19·3	15 30	−3·4	6 +0·6	9·2	−3·0	74	−8·4
15 06	+12·8	−19·5	15 19	+12·6	−19·2	15 57	−3·3	20 +0·7	9·8	−3·1	75	−8·5
15 32	+12·9	−19·4	15 46	+12·7	−19·1	16 26	−3·2	31	10·5	−3·2	77	−8·6
15 59	+13·0	−19·3	16 14	+12·8	−19·0	16 56	−3·1	Oct. 25–Nov. 28	11·2	−3·3	79	−8·7
16 28	+13·1	−19·2	16 44	+12·9	−18·9	17 28	−3·0	0 +0·6	11·9	−3·4	81	−8·8
16 59	+13·2	−19·1	17 15	+13·0	−18·8	18 02	−2·9	4 +0·7	12·6	−3·5	83	−8·9
17 32	+13·3	−19·0	17 48	+13·1	−18·7	18 38	−2·8	12 +0·8	13·3	−3·6	85	−9·0
18 06	+13·4	−18·9	18 24	+13·2	−18·6	19 17	−2·7	22	14·1	−3·7	87	−9·1
18 42	+13·5	−18·8	19 01	+13·3	−18·5	19 58	−2·6		14·9	−3·8	88	−9·2
19 21	+13·6	−18·7	19 42	+13·4	−18·4	20 42	−2·5	Nov. 29–Dec. 6	15·7	−3·9	90	−9·3
20 03	+13·7	−18·6	20 25	+13·5	−18·3	21 28	−2·4	0 +0·5	16·5	−4·0	92	−9·4
20 48	+13·8	−18·5	21 11	+13·6	−18·2	22 19	−2·3	6 +0·6	17·4	−4·1	94	−9·5
21 35	+13·9	−18·4	22 00	+13·7	−18·1	23 13	−2·2	20 +0·7	18·3	−4·2	96	−9·6
22 26	+14·0	−18·3	22 54	+13·8	−18·0	24 11	−2·1	31	19·1	−4·3	98	−9·7
23 22	+14·1	−18·2	23 51	+13·9	−17·9	25 14	−2·0	Dec. 7–Dec. 21	20·1	−4·4	101	−9·8
24 21	+14·2	−18·1	24 53	+14·0	−17·8	26 22	−1·9	0 +0·4	21·0	−4·5	103	−9·9
25 26	+14·3	−18·0	26 00	+14·1	−17·7	27 36	−1·8	11 +0·5	22·0	−4·6	105	−10·0
26 36	+14·4	−17·9	27 13	+14·2	−17·6	28 56	−1·7	41	22·9	−4·7	107	−10·1
27 52	+14·5	−17·8	28 33	+14·3	−17·5	30 24	−1·6	Dec. 22–Dec. 31	23·9	−4·8	109	−10·2
29 15	+14·6	−17·7	30 00	+14·4	−17·4	32 00	−1·5	0 +0·3	24·9	−4·9	111	−10·3
30 46	+14·7	−17·6	31 35	+14·5	−17·3	33 45	−1·4	46	26·0	−5·0	113	−10·4
32 26	+14·8	−17·5	33 20	+14·6	−17·2	35 40	−1·3		27·1	−5·1	116	−10·5
34 17	+14·9	−17·4	35 17	+14·7	−17·1	37 48	−1·2		28·1	−5·2	118	−10·6
36 20	+15·0	−17·3	37 26	+14·8	−17·0	40 08	−1·1		29·2	−5·3	120	−10·7
38 36	+15·1	−17·2	39 50	+14·9	−16·9	42 44	−1·0		30·4	−5·4	122	−10·8
41 08	+15·2	−17·1	42 31	+15·0	−16·8	45 36	−0·9	**MARS**	31·5	−5·5	125	−10·9
43 59	+15·3	−17·0	45 31	+15·1	−16·7	48 47	−0·8	Jan. 1–Dec. 31	32·7	−5·6	127	−11·0
47 10	+15·4	−16·9	48 55	+15·2	−16·6	52 18	−0·7	0 +0·1	33·9	−5·7	129	−11·1
50 46	+15·5	−16·8	52 44	+15·3	−16·5	56 11	−0·6	60	35·1	−5·8	132	−11·2
54 49	+15·6	−16·7	57 02	+15·4	−16·4	60 28	−0·5		36·3	−5·9	134	−11·3
59 23	+15·7	−16·6	61 51	+15·5	−16·3	65 08	−0·4		37·6	−6·0	136	−11·4
64 30	+15·8	−16·5	67 17	+15·6	−16·2	70 11	−0·3		38·9	−6·1	139	−11·5
70 12	+15·9	−16·4	73 16	+15·7	−16·1	75 34	−0·2		40·1	−6·2	141	−11·6
76 26	+16·0	−16·3	79 43	+15·8	−16·0	81 13	−0·1		41·5	−6·3	144	−11·7
83 05	+16·1	−16·2	86 32	+15·9	−15·9	87 03	−0·1		42·8	−6·4	146	−11·8
90 00			90 00			90 00	0·0		44·2		149	

App. Alt. = Apparent altitude = Sextant altitude corrected for index error and dip.

For daylight observations of Venus, see page 260.

Appendix F-5

ALTITUDE CORRECTION TABLES 0°–10°—SUN, STARS, PLANETS A3

App. Alt.	OCT.–MAR. SUN Lower Limb	Upper Limb	APR.–SEPT. SUN Lower Limb	Upper Limb	STARS PLANETS
° ′	′	′	′	′	′
0 00	−18·2	−50·5	−18·4	−50·2	−34·5
03	17·5	49·8	17·8	49·6	33·8
06	16·9	49·2	17·1	48·9	33·2
09	16·3	48·6	16·5	48·3	32·6
12	15·7	48·0	15·9	47·7	32·0
15	15·1	47·4	15·3	47·1	31·4
0 18	−14·5	−46·8	−14·8	−46·6	−30·8
21	14·0	46·3	14·2	46·0	30·3
24	13·5	45·8	13·7	45·5	29·8
27	12·9	45·2	13·2	45·0	29·2
30	12·4	44·7	12·7	44·5	28·7
33	11·9	44·2	12·2	44·0	28·2
0 36	−11·5	−43·8	−11·7	−43·5	−27·8
39	11·0	43·3	11·2	43·0	27·3
42	10·5	42·8	10·8	42·6	26·8
45	10·1	42·4	10·3	42·1	26·4
48	9·6	41·9	9·9	41·7	25·9
51	9·2	41·5	9·5	41·3	25·5
0 54	−8·8	−41·1	−9·1	−40·9	−25·1
0 57	8·4	40·7	8·7	40·5	24·7
1 00	8·0	40·3	8·3	40·1	24·3
03	7·7	40·0	7·9	39·7	24·0
06	7·3	39·6	7·5	39·3	23·6
09	6·9	39·2	7·2	39·0	23·2
1 12	−6·6	−38·9	−6·8	−38·6	−22·9
15	6·2	38·5	6·5	38·3	22·5
18	5·9	38·2	6·2	38·0	22·2
21	5·6	37·9	5·8	37·6	21·9
24	5·3	37·6	5·5	37·3	21·6
27	4·9	37·2	5·2	37·0	21·2
1 30	−4·6	−36·9	−4·9	−36·7	−20·9
35	4·2	36·5	4·4	36·2	20·5
40	3·7	36·0	4·0	35·8	20·0
45	3·2	35·5	3·5	35·3	19·5
50	2·8	35·1	3·1	34·9	19·1
1 55	2·4	34·7	2·6	34·4	18·7
2 00	−2·0	−34·3	−2·2	−34·0	−18·3
05	1·6	33·9	1·8	33·6	17·9
10	1·2	33·5	1·5	33·3	17·5
15	0·9	33·2	1·1	32·9	17·2
20	0·5	32·8	0·8	32·6	16·8
25	−0·2	32·5	0·4	32·2	16·5
2 30	+0·2	−32·1	−0·1	−31·9	−16·1
35	0·5	31·8	+0·2	31·6	15·8
40	0·8	31·5	0·5	31·3	15·5
45	1·1	31·2	0·8	31·0	15·2
50	1·4	30·9	1·1	30·7	14·9
2 55	1·6	30·7	1·4	30·4	14·7
3 00	+1·9	−30·4	+1·7	−30·1	−14·4
05	2·2	30·1	1·9	29·9	14·1
10	2·4	29·9	2·1	29·7	13·9
15	2·6	29·7	2·4	29·4	13·7
20	2·9	29·4	2·6	29·2	13·4
25	3·1	29·2	2·9	28·9	13·2
3 30	3·3	29·0	3·1	28·7	13·0
3 30	+3·3	−29·0	+3·1	−28·7	−13·0
35	3·6	28·7	3·3	28·5	12·7
40	3·8	28·5	3·5	28·3	12·5
45	4·0	28·3	3·7	28·1	12·3
50	4·2	28·1	3·9	27·9	12·1
3 55	4·4	27·9	4·1	27·7	11·9
4 00	+4·5	−27·8	+4·3	−27·5	−11·8
05	4·7	27·6	4·5	27·3	11·6
10	4·9	27·4	4·6	27·2	11·4
15	5·1	27·2	4·8	27·0	11·2
20	5·2	27·1	5·0	26·8	11·1
25	5·4	26·9	5·1	26·7	10·9
4 30	+5·6	−26·7	+5·3	−26·5	−10·7
35	5·7	26·6	5·5	26·3	10·6
40	5·9	26·4	5·6	26·2	10·4
45	6·0	26·3	5·8	26·0	10·3
50	6·2	26·1	5·9	25·9	10·1
4 55	6·3	26·0	6·0	25·8	10·0
5 00	+6·4	−25·9	+6·2	−25·6	−9·9
05	6·6	25·7	6·3	25·5	9·7
10	6·7	25·6	6·4	25·4	9·6
15	6·8	25·5	6·6	25·2	9·5
20	6·9	25·4	6·7	25·1	9·4
25	7·1	25·2	6·8	25·0	9·2
5 30	+7·2	−25·1	+6·9	−24·9	−9·1
35	7·3	25·0	7·0	24·8	9·0
40	7·4	24·9	7·2	24·6	8·9
45	7·5	24·8	7·3	24·5	8·8
50	7·6	24·7	7·4	24·4	8·7
5 55	7·7	24·6	7·5	24·3	8·6
6 00	+7·8	−24·5	+7·6	−24·2	−8·5
10	8·0	24·3	7·8	24·0	8·3
20	8·2	24·1	8·0	23·8	8·1
30	8·4	23·9	8·1	23·7	7·9
40	8·6	23·7	8·3	23·5	7·7
6 50	8·7	23·6	8·5	23·3	7·6
7 00	+8·9	−23·4	+8·6	−23·2	−7·4
10	9·1	23·2	8·8	23·0	7·2
20	9·2	23·1	9·0	22·8	7·1
30	9·3	23·0	9·1	22·7	7·0
40	9·5	22·8	9·2	22·6	6·8
7 50	9·6	22·7	9·4	22·4	6·7
8 00	+9·7	−22·6	+9·5	−22·3	−6·6
10	9·9	22·4	9·6	22·2	6·4
20	10·0	22·3	9·7	22·1	6·3
30	10·1	22·2	9·8	22·0	6·2
40	10·2	22·1	10·0	21·8	6·1
8 50	10·3	22·0	10·1	21·7	6·0
9 00	+10·4	−21·9	+10·2	−21·6	−5·9
10	10·5	21·8	10·3	21·5	5·8
20	10·6	21·7	10·4	21·4	5·7
30	10·7	21·6	10·5	21·3	5·6
40	10·8	21·5	10·6	21·2	5·5
9 50	10·9	21·4	10·6	21·2	5·4
10 00	+11·0	−21·3	+10·7	−21·1	−5·3

Additional corrections for temperature and pressure are given on the following page.
For bubble sextant observations ignore dip and use the star corrections for Sun, planets, and stars.

ALTITUDE CORRECTION TABLES—ADDITIONAL CORRECTIONS
ADDITIONAL REFRACTION CORRECTIONS FOR NON-STANDARD CONDITIONS

App. Alt.	A	B	C	D	E	F	G	H	J	K	L	M	N	App. Alt.
0 00	−6·9	−5·7	−4·6	−3·4	−2·3	−1·1	0·0	+1·1	+2·3	+3·4	+4·6	+5·7	+6·9	0 00
0 30	5·2	4·4	3·5	2·6	1·7	0·9	0·0	0·9	1·7	2·6	3·5	4·4	5·2	0 30
1 00	4·3	3·5	2·8	2·1	1·4	0·7	0·0	0·7	1·4	2·1	2·8	3·5	4·3	1 00
1 30	3·5	2·9	2·4	1·8	1·2	0·6	0·0	0·6	1·2	1·8	2·4	2·9	3·5	1 30
2 00	3·0	2·5	2·0	1·5	1·0	0·5	0·0	0·5	1·0	1·5	2·0	2·5	3·0	2 00
2 30	−2·5	−2·1	−1·6	−1·2	−0·8	−0·4	0·0	+0·4	+0·8	+1·2	+1·6	+2·1	+2·5	2 30
3 00	2·2	1·8	1·5	1·1	0·7	0·4	0·0	0·4	0·7	1·1	1·5	1·8	2·2	3 00
3 30	2·0	1·6	1·3	1·0	0·7	0·3	0·0	0·3	0·7	1·0	1·3	1·6	2·0	3 30
4 00	1·8	1·5	1·2	0·9	0·6	0·3	0·0	0·3	0·6	0·9	1·2	1·5	1·8	4 00
4 30	1·6	1·4	1·1	0·8	0·5	0·3	0·0	0·3	0·5	0·8	1·1	1·4	1·6	4 30
5 00	−1·5	−1·3	−1·0	−0·8	−0·5	−0·2	0·0	+0·2	+0·5	+0·8	+1·0	+1·3	+1·5	5 00
6	1·3	1·1	0·9	0·6	0·4	0·2	0·0	0·2	0·4	0·6	0·9	1·1	1·3	6
7	1·1	0·9	0·7	0·6	0·4	0·2	0·0	0·2	0·4	0·6	0·7	0·9	1·1	7
8	1·0	0·8	0·7	0·5	0·3	0·2	0·0	0·2	0·3	0·5	0·7	0·8	1·0	8
9	0·9	0·7	0·6	0·4	0·3	0·1	0·0	0·1	0·3	0·4	0·6	0·7	0·9	9
10 00	−0·8	−0·7	−0·5	−0·4	−0·3	−0·1	0·0	+0·1	+0·3	+0·4	+0·5	+0·7	+0·8	10 00
12	0·7	0·6	0·5	0·3	0·2	0·1	0·0	0·1	0·2	0·3	0·5	0·6	0·7	12
14	0·6	0·5	0·4	0·3	0·2	0·1	0·0	0·1	0·2	0·3	0·4	0·5	0·6	14
16	0·5	0·4	0·3	0·3	0·2	0·1	0·0	0·1	0·2	0·3	0·3	0·4	0·5	16
18	0·4	0·4	0·3	0·2	0·2	0·1	0·0	0·1	0·2	0·2	0·3	0·4	0·4	18
20 00	−0·4	−0·3	−0·3	−0·2	−0·1	−0·1	0·0	+0·1	+0·1	+0·2	+0·3	+0·3	+0·4	20 00
25	0·3	0·3	0·2	0·2	0·1	−0·1	0·0	+0·1	0·1	0·2	0·2	0·3	0·3	25
30	0·3	0·2	0·2	0·1	0·1	0·0	0·0	0·0	0·1	0·1	0·2	0·2	0·3	30
35	0·2	0·2	0·1	0·1	0·1	0·0	0·0	0·0	0·1	0·1	0·1	0·2	0·2	35
40	0·2	0·1	0·1	0·1	−0·1	0·0	0·0	0·0	+0·1	0·1	0·1	0·1	0·2	40
50 00	−0·1	−0·1	−0·1	−0·1	0·0	0·0	0·0	0·0	0·0	+0·1	+0·1	+0·1	+0·1	50 00

The graph is entered with arguments temperature and pressure to find a zone letter; using as arguments this zone letter and apparent altitude (sextant altitude corrected for dip), a correction is taken from the table. This correction is to be applied to the sextant altitude in addition to the corrections for standard conditions (for the Sun, planets and stars from the inside front cover and for the Moon from the inside back cover).

Appendix F-7

ALTITUDE CORRECTION TABLES 0°–35°—MOON

App. Alt.	0°–4° Corrⁿ	5°–9° Corrⁿ	10°–14° Corrⁿ	15°–19° Corrⁿ	20°–24° Corrⁿ	25°–29° Corrⁿ	30°–34° Corrⁿ	App. Alt.
00	0° 33·8	5° 58·2	10° 62·1	15° 62·8	20° 62·2	25° 60·8	30° 58·9	00
10	35·9	58·5	62·2	62·8	62·1	60·8	58·8	10
20	37·8	58·7	62·2	62·8	62·1	60·7	58·8	20
30	39·6	58·9	62·3	62·8	62·1	60·7	58·7	30
40	41·2	59·1	62·3	62·8	62·0	60·6	58·6	40
50	42·6	59·3	62·4	62·7	62·0	60·6	58·5	50
00	1° 44·0	6° 59·5	11° 62·4	16° 62·7	21° 62·0	26° 60·5	31° 58·5	00
10	45·2	59·7	62·4	62·7	61·9	60·4	58·4	10
20	46·3	59·9	62·5	62·7	61·9	60·4	58·3	20
30	47·3	60·0	62·5	62·7	61·9	60·3	58·2	30
40	48·3	60·2	62·5	62·7	61·8	60·3	58·2	40
50	49·2	60·3	62·6	62·7	61·8	60·2	58·1	50
00	2° 50·0	7° 60·5	12° 62·6	17° 62·7	22° 61·7	27° 60·1	32° 58·0	00
10	50·8	60·6	62·6	62·6	61·7	60·1	57·9	10
20	51·4	60·7	62·6	62·6	61·6	60·0	57·8	20
30	52·1	60·9	62·7	62·6	61·6	59·9	57·8	30
40	52·7	61·0	62·7	62·6	61·5	59·9	57·7	40
50	53·3	61·1	62·7	62·6	61·5	59·8	57·6	50
00	3° 53·8	8° 61·2	13° 62·7	18° 62·5	23° 61·5	28° 59·7	33° 57·5	00
10	54·3	61·3	62·7	62·5	61·4	59·7	57·4	10
20	54·8	61·4	62·7	62·5	61·4	59·6	57·4	20
30	55·2	61·5	62·8	62·5	61·3	59·6	57·3	30
40	55·6	61·6	62·8	62·4	61·3	59·5	57·2	40
50	56·0	61·6	62·8	62·4	61·2	59·4	57·1	50
00	4° 56·4	9° 61·7	14° 62·8	19° 62·4	24° 61·2	29° 59·3	34° 57·0	00
10	56·7	61·8	62·8	62·3	61·1	59·3	56·9	10
20	57·1	61·9	62·8	62·3	61·1	59·2	56·9	20
30	57·4	61·9	62·8	62·3	61·0	59·1	56·8	30
40	57·7	62·0	62·8	62·2	60·9	59·1	56·7	40
50	57·9	62·1	62·8	62·2	60·9	59·0	56·6	50

H.P.	L U	L U	L U	L U	L U	L U	L U	H.P.
54·0	0·3 0·9	0·3 0·9	0·4 1·0	0·5 1·1	0·6 1·2	0·7 1·3	0·9 1·5	54·0
54·3	0·7 1·1	0·7 1·2	0·7 1·2	0·8 1·3	0·9 1·4	1·1 1·5	1·2 1·7	54·3
54·6	1·1 1·4	1·1 1·4	1·1 1·4	1·2 1·5	1·3 1·6	1·4 1·7	1·5 1·8	54·6
54·9	1·4 1·6	1·5 1·6	1·5 1·6	1·6 1·7	1·6 1·8	1·8 1·9	1·9 2·0	54·9
55·2	1·8 1·8	1·8 1·8	1·9 1·9	1·9 1·9	2·0 2·0	2·1 2·1	2·2 2·2	55·2
55·5	2·2 2·0	2·2 2·0	2·3 2·1	2·3 2·1	2·4 2·2	2·4 2·3	2·5 2·4	55·5
55·8	2·6 2·2	2·6 2·2	2·6 2·3	2·7 2·3	2·7 2·4	2·8 2·4	2·9 2·5	55·8
56·1	3·0 2·4	3·0 2·5	3·0 2·5	3·0 2·5	3·1 2·6	3·1 2·6	3·2 2·7	56·1
56·4	3·4 2·7	3·4 2·7	3·4 2·7	3·4 2·7	3·4 2·8	3·5 2·8	3·5 2·9	56·4
56·7	3·7 2·9	3·7 2·9	3·8 2·9	3·8 2·9	3·8 3·0	3·8 3·0	3·9 3·0	56·7
57·0	4·1 3·1	4·1 3·1	4·1 3·1	4·1 3·1	4·2 3·1	4·2 3·2	4·2 3·2	57·0
57·3	4·5 3·3	4·5 3·3	4·5 3·3	4·5 3·3	4·5 3·3	4·5 3·4	4·6 3·4	57·3
57·6	4·9 3·5	4·9 3·5	4·9 3·5	4·9 3·5	4·9 3·5	4·9 3·6	4·9 3·6	57·6
57·9	5·3 3·8	5·3 3·8	5·2 3·8	5·2 3·7	5·2 3·7	5·2 3·7	5·2 3·7	57·9
58·2	5·6 4·0	5·6 4·0	5·6 4·0	5·6 4·0	5·6 3·9	5·6 3·9	5·6 3·9	58·2
58·5	6·0 4·2	6·0 4·2	6·0 4·2	6·0 4·2	6·0 4·1	5·9 4·1	5·9 4·1	58·5
58·8	6·4 4·4	6·4 4·4	6·4 4·4	6·3 4·4	6·3 4·3	6·3 4·3	6·2 4·2	58·8
59·1	6·8 4·6	6·8 4·6	6·7 4·6	6·7 4·6	6·7 4·5	6·6 4·5	6·6 4·4	59·1
59·4	7·2 4·8	7·1 4·8	7·1 4·8	7·1 4·8	7·0 4·7	7·0 4·7	6·9 4·6	59·4
59·7	7·5 5·1	7·5 5·0	7·5 5·0	7·5 5·0	7·4 4·9	7·3 4·8	7·2 4·7	59·7
60·0	7·9 5·3	7·9 5·3	7·9 5·2	7·8 5·2	7·8 5·1	7·7 5·0	7·6 4·9	60·0
60·3	8·3 5·5	8·3 5·5	8·2 5·4	8·2 5·4	8·1 5·3	8·0 5·2	7·9 5·1	60·3
60·6	8·7 5·7	8·7 5·7	8·6 5·7	8·6 5·6	8·5 5·5	8·4 5·4	8·2 5·3	60·6
60·9	9·1 5·9	9·0 5·9	9·0 5·9	8·9 5·8	8·8 5·7	8·7 5·6	8·6 5·4	60·9
61·2	9·5 6·2	9·4 6·1	9·4 6·1	9·3 6·0	9·2 5·9	9·1 5·8	8·9 5·6	61·2
61·5	9·8 6·4	9·8 6·3	9·7 6·3	9·7 6·2	9·5 6·1	9·4 5·9	9·2 5·8	61·5

DIP

Ht. of Eye (ft.)	Corrⁿ	Ht. of Eye (ft.)	Corrⁿ	Ht. of Eye (ft.)	Corrⁿ
4·0		24		63	
4·4	−2·0	26	−4·9	65	−7·8
4·9	−2·1	27	−5·0	67	−7·9
5·3	−2·2	28	−5·1	68	−8·0
5·8	−2·3	29	−5·2	70	−8·1
6·3	−2·4	30	−5·3	72	−8·2
6·9	−2·5	31	−5·4	74	−8·3
7·4	−2·6	32	−5·5	75	−8·4
8·0	−2·7	33	−5·6	77	−8·5
8·6	−2·8	35	−5·7	79	−8·6
9·2	−2·9	36	−5·8	81	−8·7
9·8	−3·0	37	−5·9	83	−8·8
10·5	−3·1	38	−6·0	85	−8·9
11·2	−3·2	40	−6·1	87	−9·0
11·9	−3·3	41	−6·2	88	−9·1
12·6	−3·4	42	−6·3	90	−9·2
13·3	−3·5	44	−6·4	92	−9·3
14·1	−3·6	45	−6·5	94	−9·4
14·9	−3·7	47	−6·6	96	−9·5
15·7	−3·8	48	−6·7	98	−9·6
16·5	−3·9	49	−6·8	101	−9·7
17·4	−4·0	51	−6·9	103	−9·8
18·3	−4·1	52	−7·0	105	−9·9
19·1	−4·2	54	−7·1	107	−10·0
20·1	−4·3	55	−7·2	109	−10·1
21·0	−4·4	57	−7·3	111	−10·2
22·0	−4·5	58	−7·4	113	−10·3
22·9	−4·6	60	−7·5	116	−10·4
23·9	−4·7	62	−7·6	118	−10·5
24·9	−4·8	63	−7·7	120	−10·6

MOON CORRECTION TABLE

The correction is in two parts; the first correction is taken from the upper part of the table with argument apparent altitude, and the second from the lower part, with argument H.P., in the same column as that from which the first correction was taken. Separate corrections are given in the lower part for lower (L) and upper (U) limbs. All corrections are to be **added** to apparent altitude, *but 30' is to be subtracted from the altitude of the upper limb.*

For corrections for pressure and temperature see page A4.

For bubble sextant observations ignore dip, take the mean of upper and lower limb corrections and subtract 15' from the altitude.

App. Alt. = Apparent altitude = Sextant altitude corrected for index error and dip.

ALTITUDE CORRECTION TABLES 35°-90°—MOON

App. Alt.	35°-39° Corrⁿ	40°-44° Corrⁿ	45°-49° Corrⁿ	50°-54° Corrⁿ	55°-59° Corrⁿ	60°-64° Corrⁿ	65°-69° Corrⁿ	70°-74° Corrⁿ	75°-79° Corrⁿ	80°-84° Corrⁿ	85°-89° Corrⁿ	App. Alt.
00	35 56.5	40 53.7	45 50.5	50 46.9	55 43.1	60 38.9	65 34.6	70 30.1	75 25.3	80 20.5	85 15.6	00
10	56.4	53.6	50.4	46.8	42.9	38.8	34.4	29.9	25.2	20.4	15.5	10
20	56.3	53.5	50.2	46.7	42.8	38.7	34.3	29.7	25.0	20.2	15.3	20
30	56.2	53.4	50.1	46.5	42.7	38.5	34.1	29.6	24.9	20.0	15.1	30
40	56.2	53.3	50.0	46.4	42.5	38.4	34.0	29.4	24.7	19.9	15.0	40
50	56.1	53.2	49.9	46.3	42.4	38.2	33.8	29.3	24.5	19.7	14.8	50
00	36 56.0	41 53.1	46 49.8	51 46.2	56 42.3	61 38.1	66 33.7	71 29.1	76 24.4	81 19.6	86 14.6	00
10	55.9	53.0	49.7	46.0	42.1	37.9	33.5	29.0	24.2	19.4	14.5	10
20	55.8	52.8	49.5	45.9	42.0	37.8	33.4	28.8	24.1	19.2	14.3	20
30	55.7	52.7	49.4	45.8	41.8	37.7	33.2	28.7	23.9	19.1	14.1	30
40	55.6	52.6	49.3	45.7	41.7	37.5	33.1	28.5	23.8	18.9	14.0	40
50	55.5	52.5	49.2	45.5	41.6	37.4	32.9	28.3	23.6	18.7	13.8	50
00	37 55.4	42 52.4	47 49.1	52 45.4	57 41.4	62 37.2	67 32.8	72 28.2	77 23.4	82 18.6	87 13.7	00
10	55.3	52.3	49.0	45.3	41.3	37.1	32.6	28.0	23.3	18.4	13.5	10
20	55.2	52.2	48.8	45.2	41.2	36.9	32.5	27.9	23.1	18.2	13.3	20
30	55.1	52.1	48.7	45.0	41.0	36.8	32.3	27.7	22.9	18.1	13.2	30
40	55.0	52.0	48.6	44.9	40.9	36.6	32.2	27.6	22.8	17.9	13.0	40
50	55.0	51.9	48.5	44.8	40.8	36.5	32.0	27.4	22.6	17.8	12.8	50
00	38 54.9	43 51.8	48 48.4	53 44.6	58 40.6	63 36.4	68 31.9	73 27.2	78 22.5	83 17.6	88 12.7	00
10	54.8	51.7	48.2	44.5	40.5	36.2	31.7	27.1	22.3	17.4	12.5	10
20	54.7	51.6	48.1	44.4	40.3	36.1	31.6	26.9	22.1	17.3	12.3	20
30	54.6	51.5	48.0	44.2	40.2	35.9	31.4	26.8	22.0	17.1	12.2	30
40	54.5	51.4	47.9	44.1	40.1	35.8	31.3	26.6	21.8	16.9	12.0	40
50	54.4	51.2	47.8	44.0	39.9	35.6	31.1	26.5	21.7	16.8	11.8	50
00	39 54.3	44 51.1	49 47.6	54 43.9	59 39.8	64 35.5	69 31.0	74 26.3	79 21.5	84 16.6	89 11.7	00
10	54.2	51.0	47.5	43.7	39.6	35.3	30.8	26.1	21.3	16.5	11.5	10
20	54.1	50.9	47.4	43.6	39.5	35.2	30.7	26.0	21.2	16.3	11.4	20
30	54.0	50.8	47.3	43.5	39.4	35.0	30.5	25.8	21.0	16.1	11.2	30
40	53.9	50.7	47.2	43.3	39.2	34.9	30.4	25.7	20.9	16.0	11.0	40
50	53.8	50.6	47.0	43.2	39.1	34.7	30.2	25.5	20.7	15.8	10.9	50

H.P.	L U	L U	L U	L U	L U	L U	L U	L U	L U	L U	L U	H.P.
54.0	1.1 1.7	1.3 1.9	1.5 2.1	1.7 2.4	2.0 2.6	2.3 2.9	2.6 3.2	2.9 3.5	3.2 3.8	3.5 4.1	3.8 4.5	54.0
54.3	1.4 1.8	1.6 2.0	1.8 2.2	2.0 2.5	2.3 2.7	2.5 3.0	2.8 3.2	3.0 3.5	3.3 3.8	3.6 4.1	3.9 4.4	54.3
54.6	1.7 2.0	1.9 2.2	2.1 2.4	2.3 2.6	2.5 2.8	2.7 3.0	3.0 3.3	3.2 3.5	3.5 3.8	3.7 4.1	4.0 4.3	54.6
54.9	2.0 2.2	2.2 2.3	2.3 2.5	2.5 2.7	2.7 2.9	2.9 3.1	3.2 3.3	3.4 3.5	3.6 3.8	3.9 4.0	4.1 4.3	54.9
55.2	2.3 2.3	2.5 2.4	2.6 2.6	2.8 2.8	3.0 2.9	3.2 3.1	3.4 3.3	3.6 3.5	3.8 3.7	4.0 4.0	4.2 4.2	55.2
55.5	2.7 2.5	2.8 2.6	2.9 2.7	3.1 2.9	3.2 3.0	3.4 3.2	3.6 3.4	3.7 3.5	3.9 3.7	4.1 3.9	4.3 4.1	55.5
55.8	3.0 2.6	3.1 2.7	3.2 2.8	3.3 3.0	3.5 3.1	3.6 3.3	3.8 3.4	3.9 3.6	4.1 3.7	4.2 3.9	4.4 4.0	55.8
56.1	3.3 2.8	3.4 2.9	3.5 3.0	3.6 3.1	3.7 3.2	3.8 3.3	4.0 3.4	4.1 3.6	4.2 3.7	4.3 3.8	4.5 4.0	56.1
56.4	3.6 2.9	3.7 3.0	3.8 3.1	3.9 3.2	3.9 3.3	4.0 3.4	4.1 3.5	4.3 3.6	4.4 3.7	4.5 3.8	4.6 3.9	56.4
56.7	3.9 3.1	4.0 3.1	4.1 3.2	4.1 3.3	4.2 3.3	4.3 3.4	4.3 3.5	4.4 3.6	4.5 3.7	4.6 3.8	4.7 3.8	56.7
57.0	4.3 3.2	4.3 3.3	4.3 3.3	4.4 3.4	4.4 3.4	4.5 3.5	4.5 3.5	4.6 3.6	4.7 3.7	4.7 3.7	4.8 3.8	57.0
57.3	4.6 3.4	4.6 3.4	4.6 3.4	4.6 3.5	4.7 3.5	4.7 3.5	4.7 3.6	4.8 3.6	4.8 3.6	4.8 3.7	4.9 3.7	57.3
57.6	4.9 3.6	4.9 3.6	4.9 3.6	4.9 3.6	4.9 3.6	4.9 3.6	4.9 3.6	4.9 3.6	5.0 3.6	5.0 3.6	5.0 3.6	57.6
57.9	5.2 3.7	5.2 3.7	5.2 3.7	5.2 3.7	5.2 3.7	5.1 3.6	5.1 3.6	5.1 3.6	5.1 3.6	5.1 3.6	5.1 3.6	57.9
58.2	5.5 3.9	5.5 3.8	5.5 3.8	5.4 3.8	5.4 3.7	5.4 3.7	5.3 3.7	5.3 3.6	5.2 3.6	5.2 3.5	5.2 3.5	58.2
58.5	5.9 4.0	5.8 4.0	5.8 3.9	5.7 3.9	5.6 3.8	5.6 3.8	5.5 3.7	5.5 3.6	5.4 3.6	5.3 3.5	5.3 3.4	58.5
58.8	6.2 4.2	6.1 4.1	6.0 4.1	6.0 4.0	5.9 3.9	5.8 3.8	5.7 3.7	5.6 3.6	5.5 3.5	5.4 3.5	5.3 3.4	58.8
59.1	6.5 4.3	6.4 4.3	6.3 4.2	6.2 4.1	6.1 4.0	6.0 3.9	5.9 3.8	5.8 3.6	5.7 3.5	5.6 3.4	5.4 3.3	59.1
59.4	6.8 4.5	6.7 4.4	6.6 4.3	6.5 4.2	6.4 4.1	6.2 3.9	6.1 3.8	6.0 3.7	5.8 3.5	5.7 3.4	5.5 3.2	59.4
59.7	7.1 4.6	7.0 4.5	6.9 4.4	6.8 4.3	6.6 4.1	6.5 4.0	6.3 3.8	6.2 3.7	6.0 3.5	5.8 3.3	5.6 3.2	59.7
60.0	7.5 4.8	7.3 4.7	7.2 4.5	7.0 4.4	6.9 4.2	6.7 4.0	6.5 3.9	6.3 3.7	6.1 3.5	5.9 3.3	5.7 3.1	60.0
60.3	7.8 5.0	7.6 4.8	7.5 4.7	7.3 4.5	7.1 4.3	6.9 4.1	6.7 3.9	6.5 3.7	6.3 3.5	6.0 3.2	5.8 3.0	60.3
60.6	8.1 5.1	7.9 5.0	7.7 4.8	7.6 4.6	7.3 4.4	7.1 4.2	6.9 3.9	6.7 3.7	6.4 3.4	6.2 3.2	5.9 2.9	60.6
60.9	8.4 5.3	8.2 5.1	8.0 4.9	7.8 4.7	7.6 4.5	7.3 4.2	7.1 4.0	6.8 3.7	6.6 3.4	6.3 3.2	6.0 2.9	60.9
61.2	8.7 5.4	8.5 5.2	8.3 5.0	8.1 4.8	7.8 4.5	7.6 4.3	7.3 4.0	7.0 3.7	6.7 3.4	6.4 3.1	6.1 2.8	61.2
61.5	9.1 5.6	8.8 5.4	8.6 5.1	8.3 4.9	8.1 4.6	7.8 4.3	7.5 4.0	7.2 3.7	6.9 3.4	6.5 3.1	6.2 2.7	61.5

Appendix F-9

INCREMENTS AND CORRECTIONS

18ᵐ	SUN PLANETS	ARIES	MOON	v or d	Corrⁿ	v or d	Corrⁿ	v or d	Corrⁿ	19ᵐ	SUN PLANETS	ARIES	MOON	v or d	Corrⁿ	v or d	Corrⁿ	v or d	Corrⁿ
s	° ′	° ′	° ′	′	′	′	′	′	′	s	° ′	° ′	° ′	′	′	′	′	′	′
00	4 30·0	4 30·7	4 17·7	0·0	0·0	6·0	1·9	12·0	3·7	00	4 45·0	4 45·8	4 32·0	0·0	0·0	6·0	2·0	12·0	3·9
01	4 30·3	4 31·0	4 17·9	0·1	0·0	6·1	1·9	12·1	3·7	01	4 45·3	4 46·0	4 32·3	0·1	0·0	6·1	2·0	12·1	3·9
02	4 30·5	4 31·2	4 18·2	0·2	0·1	6·2	1·9	12·2	3·8	02	4 45·5	4 46·3	4 32·5	0·2	0·1	6·2	2·0	12·2	4·0
03	4 30·8	4 31·5	4 18·4	0·3	0·1	6·3	1·9	12·3	3·8	03	4 45·8	4 46·5	4 32·7	0·3	0·1	6·3	2·0	12·3	4·0
04	4 31·0	4 31·7	4 18·7	0·4	0·1	6·4	2·0	12·4	3·8	04	4 46·0	4 46·8	4 33·0	0·4	0·1	6·4	2·1	12·4	4·0
05	4 31·3	4 32·0	4 18·9	0·5	0·2	6·5	2·0	12·5	3·9	05	4 46·3	4 47·0	4 33·2	0·5	0·2	6·5	2·1	12·5	4·1
06	4 31·5	4 32·2	4 19·1	0·6	0·2	6·6	2·0	12·6	3·9	06	4 46·5	4 47·3	4 33·4	0·6	0·2	6·6	2·1	12·6	4·1
07	4 31·8	4 32·5	4 19·4	0·7	0·2	6·7	2·1	12·7	3·9	07	4 46·8	4 47·5	4 33·7	0·7	0·2	6·7	2·2	12·7	4·1
08	4 32·0	4 32·7	4 19·6	0·8	0·2	6·8	2·1	12·8	3·9	08	4 47·0	4 47·8	4 33·9	0·8	0·3	6·8	2·2	12·8	4·2
09	4 32·3	4 33·0	4 19·8	0·9	0·3	6·9	2·1	12·9	4·0	09	4 47·3	4 48·0	4 34·2	0·9	0·3	6·9	2·2	12·9	4·2
10	4 32·5	4 33·2	4 20·1	1·0	0·3	7·0	2·2	13·0	4·0	10	4 47·5	4 48·3	4 34·4	1·0	0·3	7·0	2·3	13·0	4·2
11	4 32·8	4 33·5	4 20·3	1·1	0·3	7·1	2·2	13·1	4·0	11	4 47·8	4 48·5	4 34·6	1·1	0·4	7·1	2·3	13·1	4·3
12	4 33·0	4 33·7	4 20·6	1·2	0·4	7·2	2·2	13·2	4·1	12	4 48·0	4 48·8	4 34·9	1·2	0·4	7·2	2·3	13·2	4·3
13	4 33·3	4 34·0	4 20·8	1·3	0·4	7·3	2·3	13·3	4·1	13	4 48·3	4 49·0	4 35·1	1·3	0·4	7·3	2·4	13·3	4·3
14	4 33·5	4 34·2	4 21·0	1·4	0·4	7·4	2·3	13·4	4·1	14	4 48·5	4 49·3	4 35·4	1·4	0·5	7·4	2·4	13·4	4·4
15	4 33·8	4 34·5	4 21·3	1·5	0·5	7·5	2·3	13·5	4·2	15	4 48·8	4 49·5	4 35·6	1·5	0·5	7·5	2·4	13·5	4·4
16	4 34·0	4 34·8	4 21·5	1·6	0·5	7·6	2·3	13·6	4·2	16	4 49·0	4 49·8	4 35·8	1·6	0·5	7·6	2·5	13·6	4·4
17	4 34·3	4 35·0	4 21·8	1·7	0·5	7·7	2·4	13·7	4·2	17	4 49·3	4 50·0	4 36·1	1·7	0·6	7·7	2·5	13·7	4·5
18	4 34·5	4 35·3	4 22·0	1·8	0·6	7·8	2·4	13·8	4·3	18	4 49·5	4 50·3	4 36·3	1·8	0·6	7·8	2·5	13·8	4·5
19	4 34·8	4 35·5	4 22·2	1·9	0·6	7·9	2·4	13·9	4·3	19	4 49·8	4 50·5	4 36·6	1·9	0·6	7·9	2·6	13·9	4·5
20	4 35·0	4 35·8	4 22·5	2·0	0·6	8·0	2·5	14·0	4·3	20	4 50·0	4 50·8	4 36·8	2·0	0·7	8·0	2·6	14·0	4·6
21	4 35·3	4 36·0	4 22·7	2·1	0·6	8·1	2·5	14·1	4·3	21	4 50·3	4 51·0	4 37·0	2·1	0·7	8·1	2·6	14·1	4·6
22	4 35·5	4 36·3	4 22·9	2·2	0·7	8·2	2·5	14·2	4·4	22	4 50·5	4 51·3	4 37·3	2·2	0·7	8·2	2·7	14·2	4·6
23	4 35·8	4 36·5	4 23·2	2·3	0·7	8·3	2·6	14·3	4·4	23	4 50·8	4 51·5	4 37·5	2·3	0·7	8·3	2·7	14·3	4·6
24	4 36·0	4 36·8	4 23·4	2·4	0·7	8·4	2·6	14·4	4·4	24	4 51·0	4 51·8	4 37·7	2·4	0·8	8·4	2·7	14·4	4·7
25	4 36·3	4 37·0	4 23·7	2·5	0·8	8·5	2·6	14·5	4·5	25	4 51·3	4 52·0	4 38·0	2·5	0·8	8·5	2·8	14·5	4·7
26	4 36·5	4 37·3	4 23·9	2·6	0·8	8·6	2·7	14·6	4·5	26	4 51·5	4 52·3	4 38·2	2·6	0·8	8·6	2·8	14·6	4·7
27	4 36·8	4 37·5	4 24·1	2·7	0·8	8·7	2·7	14·7	4·5	27	4 51·8	4 52·5	4 38·5	2·7	0·9	8·7	2·8	14·7	4·8
28	4 37·0	4 37·8	4 24·4	2·8	0·9	8·8	2·7	14·8	4·6	28	4 52·0	4 52·8	4 38·7	2·8	0·9	8·8	2·9	14·8	4·8
29	4 37·3	4 38·0	4 24·6	2·9	0·9	8·9	2·7	14·9	4·6	29	4 52·3	4 53·1	4 38·9	2·9	0·9	8·9	2·9	14·9	4·8
30	4 37·5	4 38·3	4 24·9	3·0	0·9	9·0	2·8	15·0	4·6	30	4 52·5	4 53·3	4 39·2	3·0	1·0	9·0	2·9	15·0	4·9
31	4 37·8	4 38·5	4 25·1	3·1	1·0	9·1	2·8	15·1	4·7	31	4 52·8	4 53·6	4 39·4	3·1	1·0	9·1	3·0	15·1	4·9
32	4 38·0	4 38·8	4 25·3	3·2	1·0	9·2	2·8	15·2	4·7	32	4 53·0	4 53·8	4 39·7	3·2	1·0	9·2	3·0	15·2	4·9
33	4 38·3	4 39·0	4 25·6	3·3	1·0	9·3	2·9	15·3	4·7	33	4 53·3	4 54·1	4 39·9	3·3	1·1	9·3	3·0	15·3	5·0
34	4 38·5	4 39·3	4 25·8	3·4	1·0	9·4	2·9	15·4	4·7	34	4 53·5	4 54·3	4 40·1	3·4	1·1	9·4	3·1	15·4	5·0
35	4 38·8	4 39·5	4 26·1	3·5	1·1	9·5	2·9	15·5	4·8	35	4 53·8	4 54·6	4 40·4	3·5	1·1	9·5	3·1	15·5	5·0
36	4 39·0	4 39·8	4 26·3	3·6	1·1	9·6	3·0	15·6	4·8	36	4 54·0	4 54·8	4 40·6	3·6	1·2	9·6	3·1	15·6	5·1
37	4 39·3	4 40·0	4 26·5	3·7	1·1	9·7	3·0	15·7	4·8	37	4 54·3	4 55·1	4 40·8	3·7	1·2	9·7	3·2	15·7	5·1
38	4 39·5	4 40·3	4 26·8	3·8	1·2	9·8	3·0	15·8	4·9	38	4 54·5	4 55·3	4 41·1	3·8	1·2	9·8	3·2	15·8	5·1
39	4 39·8	4 40·5	4 27·0	3·9	1·2	9·9	3·1	15·9	4·9	39	4 54·8	4 55·6	4 41·3	3·9	1·3	9·9	3·2	15·9	5·2
40	4 40·0	4 40·8	4 27·2	4·0	1·2	10·0	3·1	16·0	4·9	40	4 55·0	4 55·8	4 41·6	4·0	1·3	10·0	3·3	16·0	5·2
41	4 40·3	4 41·0	4 27·5	4·1	1·3	10·1	3·1	16·1	5·0	41	4 55·3	4 56·1	4 41·8	4·1	1·3	10·1	3·3	16·1	5·2
42	4 40·5	4 41·3	4 27·7	4·2	1·3	10·2	3·1	16·2	5·0	42	4 55·5	4 56·3	4 42·0	4·2	1·4	10·2	3·3	16·2	5·3
43	4 40·8	4 41·5	4 28·0	4·3	1·3	10·3	3·2	16·3	5·0	43	4 55·8	4 56·6	4 42·3	4·3	1·4	10·3	3·3	16·3	5·3
44	4 41·0	4 41·8	4 28·2	4·4	1·4	10·4	3·2	16·4	5·1	44	4 56·0	4 56·8	4 42·5	4·4	1·4	10·4	3·4	16·4	5·3
45	4 41·3	4 42·0	4 28·4	4·5	1·4	10·5	3·2	16·5	5·1	45	4 56·3	4 57·1	4 42·8	4·5	1·5	10·5	3·4	16·5	5·4
46	4 41·5	4 42·3	4 28·7	4·6	1·4	10·6	3·3	16·6	5·1	46	4 56·5	4 57·3	4 43·0	4·6	1·5	10·6	3·4	16·6	5·4
47	4 41·8	4 42·5	4 28·9	4·7	1·4	10·7	3·3	16·7	5·1	47	4 56·8	4 57·6	4 43·2	4·7	1·5	10·7	3·5	16·7	5·4
48	4 42·0	4 42·8	4 29·2	4·8	1·5	10·8	3·3	16·8	5·2	48	4 57·0	4 57·8	4 43·5	4·8	1·6	10·8	3·5	16·8	5·5
49	4 42·3	4 43·0	4 29·4	4·9	1·5	10·9	3·4	16·9	5·2	49	4 57·3	4 58·1	4 43·7	4·9	1·6	10·9	3·5	16·9	5·5
50	4 42·5	4 43·3	4 29·6	5·0	1·5	11·0	3·4	17·0	5·2	50	4 57·5	4 58·3	4 43·9	5·0	1·6	11·0	3·6	17·0	5·5
51	4 42·8	4 43·5	4 29·9	5·1	1·6	11·1	3·4	17·1	5·3	51	4 57·8	4 58·6	4 44·2	5·1	1·7	11·1	3·6	17·1	5·6
52	4 43·0	4 43·8	4 30·1	5·2	1·6	11·2	3·5	17·2	5·3	52	4 58·0	4 58·8	4 44·4	5·2	1·7	11·2	3·6	17·2	5·6
53	4 43·3	4 44·0	4 30·3	5·3	1·6	11·3	3·5	17·3	5·3	53	4 58·3	4 59·1	4 44·7	5·3	1·7	11·3	3·7	17·3	5·6
54	4 43·5	4 44·3	4 30·6	5·4	1·7	11·4	3·5	17·4	5·4	54	4 58·5	4 59·3	4 44·9	5·4	1·8	11·4	3·7	17·4	5·7
55	4 43·8	4 44·5	4 30·8	5·5	1·7	11·5	3·5	17·5	5·4	55	4 58·8	4 59·6	4 45·1	5·5	1·8	11·5	3·7	17·5	5·7
56	4 44·0	4 44·8	4 31·1	5·6	1·7	11·6	3·6	17·6	5·4	56	4 59·0	4 59·8	4 45·4	5·6	1·8	11·6	3·8	17·6	5·7
57	4 44·3	4 45·0	4 31·3	5·7	1·8	11·7	3·6	17·7	5·5	57	4 59·3	5 00·1	4 45·6	5·7	1·9	11·7	3·8	17·7	5·8
58	4 44·5	4 45·3	4 31·5	5·8	1·8	11·8	3·6	17·8	5·5	58	4 59·5	5 00·3	4 45·9	5·8	1·9	11·8	3·8	17·8	5·8
59	4 44·8	4 45·5	4 31·8	5·9	1·8	11·9	3·7	17·9	5·5	59	4 59·8	5 00·6	4 46·1	5·9	1·9	11·9	3·9	17·9	5·8
60	4 45·0	4 45·8	4 32·0	6·0	1·9	12·0	3·7	18·0	5·6	60	5 00·0	5 00·8	4 46·3	6·0	2·0	12·0	3·9	18·0	5·9

20ᵐ   INCREMENTS AND CORRECTIONS   **21ᵐ**

20	SUN PLANETS	ARIES	MOON	v or d	Corrⁿ	v or d	Corrⁿ	v or d	Corrⁿ
00	5 00·0	5 00·8	4 46·3	0·0	0·0	6·0	2·1	12·0	4·1
01	5 00·3	5 01·1	4 46·6	0·1	0·0	6·1	2·1	12·1	4·1
02	5 00·5	5 01·3	4 46·8	0·2	0·1	6·2	2·1	12·2	4·2
03	5 00·8	5 01·6	4 47·0	0·3	0·1	6·3	2·2	12·3	4·2
04	5 01·0	5 01·8	4 47·3	0·4	0·1	6·4	2·2	12·4	4·2
05	5 01·3	5 02·1	4 47·5	0·5	0·2	6·5	2·2	12·5	4·3
06	5 01·5	5 02·3	4 47·8	0·6	0·2	6·6	2·3	12·6	4·3
07	5 01·8	5 02·6	4 48·0	0·7	0·2	6·7	2·3	12·7	4·3
08	5 02·0	5 02·8	4 48·2	0·8	0·3	6·8	2·3	12·8	4·4
09	5 02·3	5 03·1	4 48·5	0·9	0·3	6·9	2·4	12·9	4·4
10	5 02·5	5 03·3	4 48·7	1·0	0·3	7·0	2·4	13·0	4·4
11	5 02·8	5 03·6	4 49·0	1·1	0·4	7·1	2·4	13·1	4·5
12	5 03·0	5 03·8	4 49·2	1·2	0·4	7·2	2·5	13·2	4·5
13	5 03·3	5 04·1	4 49·4	1·3	0·4	7·3	2·5	13·3	4·5
14	5 03·5	5 04·3	4 49·7	1·4	0·5	7·4	2·5	13·4	4·6
15	5 03·8	5 04·6	4 49·9	1·5	0·5	7·5	2·6	13·5	4·6
16	5 04·0	5 04·8	4 50·2	1·6	0·5	7·6	2·6	13·6	4·6
17	5 04·3	5 05·1	4 50·4	1·7	0·6	7·7	2·6	13·7	4·7
18	5 04·5	5 05·3	4 50·6	1·8	0·6	7·8	2·7	13·8	4·7
19	5 04·8	5 05·6	4 50·9	1·9	0·6	7·9	2·7	13·9	4·7
20	5 05·0	5 05·8	4 51·1	2·0	0·7	8·0	2·7	14·0	4·8
21	5 05·3	5 06·1	4 51·3	2·1	0·7	8·1	2·8	14·1	4·8
22	5 05·5	5 06·3	4 51·6	2·2	0·8	8·2	2·8	14·2	4·9
23	5 05·8	5 06·6	4 51·8	2·3	0·8	8·3	2·8	14·3	4·9
24	5 06·0	5 06·8	4 52·1	2·4	0·8	8·4	2·9	14·4	4·9
25	5 06·3	5 07·1	4 52·3	2·5	0·9	8·5	2·9	14·5	5·0
26	5 06·5	5 07·3	4 52·5	2·6	0·9	8·6	2·9	14·6	5·0
27	5 06·8	5 07·6	4 52·8	2·7	0·9	8·7	3·0	14·7	5·0
28	5 07·0	5 07·8	4 53·0	2·8	1·0	8·8	3·0	14·8	5·1
29	5 07·3	5 08·1	4 53·3	2·9	1·0	8·9	3·0	14·9	5·1
30	5 07·5	5 08·3	4 53·5	3·0	1·0	9·0	3·1	15·0	5·1
31	5 07·8	5 08·6	4 53·7	3·1	1·1	9·1	3·1	15·1	5·2
32	5 08·0	5 08·8	4 54·0	3·2	1·1	9·2	3·1	15·2	5·2
33	5 08·3	5 09·1	4 54·2	3·3	1·1	9·3	3·2	15·3	5·2
34	5 08·5	5 09·3	4 54·4	3·4	1·2	9·4	3·2	15·4	5·3
35	5 08·8	5 09·6	4 54·7	3·5	1·2	9·5	3·2	15·5	5·3
36	5 09·0	5 09·8	4 54·9	3·6	1·2	9·6	3·3	15·6	5·3
37	5 09·3	5 10·1	4 55·2	3·7	1·3	9·7	3·3	15·7	5·4
38	5 09·5	5 10·3	4 55·4	3·8	1·3	9·8	3·3	15·8	5·4
39	5 09·8	5 10·6	4 55·6	3·9	1·3	9·9	3·4	15·9	5·4
40	5 10·0	5 10·8	4 55·9	4·0	1·4	10·0	3·4	16·0	5·5
41	5 10·3	5 11·1	4 56·1	4·1	1·4	10·1	3·5	16·1	5·5
42	5 10·5	5 11·4	4 56·4	4·2	1·4	10·2	3·5	16·2	5·5
43	5 10·8	5 11·6	4 56·6	4·3	1·5	10·3	3·5	16·3	5·6
44	5 11·0	5 11·9	4 56·8	4·4	1·5	10·4	3·6	16·4	5·6
45	5 11·3	5 12·1	4 57·1	4·5	1·5	10·5	3·6	16·5	5·6
46	5 11·5	5 12·4	4 57·3	4·6	1·6	10·6	3·6	16·6	5·7
47	5 11·8	5 12·6	4 57·5	4·7	1·6	10·7	3·7	16·7	5·7
48	5 12·0	5 12·9	4 57·8	4·8	1·6	10·8	3·7	16·8	5·7
49	5 12·3	5 13·1	4 58·0	4·9	1·7	10·9	3·7	16·9	5·8
50	5 12·5	5 13·4	4 58·3	5·0	1·7	11·0	3·8	17·0	5·8
51	5 12·8	5 13·6	4 58·5	5·1	1·7	11·1	3·8	17·1	5·8
52	5 13·0	5 13·9	4 58·7	5·2	1·8	11·2	3·8	17·2	5·9
53	5 13·3	5 14·1	4 59·0	5·3	1·8	11·3	3·9	17·3	5·9
54	5 13·5	5 14·4	4 59·2	5·4	1·8	11·4	3·9	17·4	5·9
55	5 13·8	5 14·6	4 59·5	5·5	1·9	11·5	3·9	17·5	6·0
56	5 14·0	5 14·9	4 59·7	5·6	1·9	11·6	4·0	17·6	6·0
57	5 14·3	5 15·1	4 59·9	5·7	1·9	11·7	4·0	17·7	6·0
58	5 14·5	5 15·4	5 00·2	5·8	2·0	11·8	4·0	17·8	6·1
59	5 14·8	5 15·6	5 00·4	5·9	2·0	11·9	4·1	17·9	6·1
60	5 15·0	5 15·9	5 00·7	6·0	2·1	12·0	4·1	18·0	6·2

21	SUN PLANETS	ARIES	MOON	v or d	Corrⁿ	v or d	Corrⁿ	v or d	Corrⁿ
00	5 15·0	5 15·9	5 00·7	0·0	0·0	6·0	2·2	12·0	4·3
01	5 15·3	5 16·1	5 00·9	0·1	0·0	6·1	2·2	12·1	4·3
02	5 15·5	5 16·4	5 01·1	0·2	0·1	6·2	2·2	12·2	4·4
03	5 15·8	5 16·6	5 01·4	0·3	0·1	6·3	2·3	12·3	4·4
04	5 16·0	5 16·9	5 01·6	0·4	0·1	6·4	2·3	12·4	4·4
05	5 16·3	5 17·1	5 01·8	0·5	0·2	6·5	2·3	12·5	4·5
06	5 16·5	5 17·4	5 02·1	0·6	0·2	6·6	2·4	12·6	4·5
07	5 16·8	5 17·6	5 02·3	0·7	0·3	6·7	2·4	12·7	4·6
08	5 17·0	5 17·9	5 02·6	0·8	0·3	6·8	2·4	12·8	4·6
09	5 17·3	5 18·1	5 02·8	0·9	0·3	6·9	2·5	12·9	4·6
10	5 17·5	5 18·4	5 03·0	1·0	0·4	7·0	2·5	13·0	4·7
11	5 17·8	5 18·6	5 03·3	1·1	0·4	7·1	2·5	13·1	4·7
12	5 18·0	5 18·9	5 03·5	1·2	0·4	7·2	2·6	13·2	4·7
13	5 18·3	5 19·1	5 03·8	1·3	0·5	7·3	2·6	13·3	4·8
14	5 18·5	5 19·4	5 04·0	1·4	0·5	7·4	2·7	13·4	4·8
15	5 18·8	5 19·6	5 04·2	1·5	0·5	7·5	2·7	13·5	4·8
16	5 19·0	5 19·9	5 04·5	1·6	0·6	7·6	2·7	13·6	4·9
17	5 19·3	5 20·1	5 04·7	1·7	0·6	7·7	2·8	13·7	4·9
18	5 19·5	5 20·4	5 04·9	1·8	0·6	7·8	2·8	13·8	4·9
19	5 19·8	5 20·6	5 05·2	1·9	0·7	7·9	2·8	13·9	5·0
20	5 20·0	5 20·9	5 05·4	2·0	0·7	8·0	2·9	14·0	5·0
21	5 20·3	5 21·1	5 05·7	2·1	0·8	8·1	2·9	14·1	5·1
22	5 20·5	5 21·4	5 05·9	2·2	0·8	8·2	2·9	14·2	5·1
23	5 20·8	5 21·6	5 06·1	2·3	0·8	8·3	3·0	14·3	5·1
24	5 21·0	5 21·9	5 06·4	2·4	0·9	8·4	3·0	14·4	5·2
25	5 21·3	5 22·1	5 06·6	2·5	0·9	8·5	3·0	14·5	5·2
26	5 21·5	5 22·4	5 06·9	2·6	0·9	8·6	3·1	14·6	5·2
27	5 21·8	5 22·6	5 07·1	2·7	1·0	8·7	3·1	14·7	5·3
28	5 22·0	5 22·9	5 07·3	2·8	1·0	8·8	3·2	14·8	5·3
29	5 22·3	5 23·1	5 07·6	2·9	1·0	8·9	3·2	14·9	5·3
30	5 22·5	5 23·4	5 07·8	3·0	1·1	9·0	3·2	15·0	5·4
31	5 22·8	5 23·6	5 08·0	3·1	1·1	9·1	3·3	15·1	5·4
32	5 23·0	5 23·9	5 08·3	3·2	1·1	9·2	3·3	15·2	5·4
33	5 23·3	5 24·1	5 08·5	3·3	1·2	9·3	3·3	15·3	5·5
34	5 23·5	5 24·4	5 08·8	3·4	1·2	9·4	3·4	15·4	5·5
35	5 23·8	5 24·6	5 09·0	3·5	1·3	9·5	3·4	15·5	5·6
36	5 24·0	5 24·9	5 09·2	3·6	1·3	9·6	3·4	15·6	5·6
37	5 24·3	5 25·1	5 09·5	3·7	1·3	9·7	3·5	15·7	5·6
38	5 24·5	5 25·4	5 09·7	3·8	1·4	9·8	3·5	15·8	5·7
39	5 24·8	5 25·6	5 10·0	3·9	1·4	9·9	3·5	15·9	5·7
40	5 25·0	5 25·9	5 10·2	4·0	1·4	10·0	3·6	16·0	5·7
41	5 25·3	5 26·1	5 10·4	4·1	1·5	10·1	3·6	16·1	5·8
42	5 25·5	5 26·4	5 10·7	4·2	1·5	10·2	3·7	16·2	5·8
43	5 25·8	5 26·6	5 10·9	4·3	1·5	10·3	3·7	16·3	5·8
44	5 26·0	5 26·9	5 11·1	4·4	1·6	10·4	3·7	16·4	5·9
45	5 26·3	5 27·1	5 11·4	4·5	1·6	10·5	3·8	16·5	5·9
46	5 26·5	5 27·4	5 11·6	4·6	1·6	10·6	3·8	16·6	5·9
47	5 26·8	5 27·6	5 11·9	4·7	1·7	10·7	3·8	16·7	6·0
48	5 27·0	5 27·9	5 12·1	4·8	1·7	10·8	3·9	16·8	6·0
49	5 27·3	5 28·1	5 12·3	4·9	1·8	10·9	3·9	16·9	6·1
50	5 27·5	5 28·4	5 12·6	5·0	1·8	11·0	3·9	17·0	6·1
51	5 27·8	5 28·6	5 12·8	5·1	1·8	11·1	4·0	17·1	6·1
52	5 28·0	5 28·9	5 13·1	5·2	1·9	11·2	4·0	17·2	6·2
53	5 28·3	5 29·1	5 13·3	5·3	1·9	11·3	4·0	17·3	6·2
54	5 28·5	5 29·4	5 13·5	5·4	1·9	11·4	4·1	17·4	6·2
55	5 28·8	5 29·7	5 13·8	5·5	2·0	11·5	4·1	17·5	6·3
56	5 29·0	5 29·9	5 14·0	5·6	2·0	11·6	4·2	17·6	6·3
57	5 29·3	5 30·2	5 14·3	5·7	2·0	11·7	4·2	17·7	6·3
58	5 29·5	5 30·4	5 14·5	5·8	2·1	11·8	4·2	17·8	6·4
59	5 29·8	5 30·7	5 14·7	5·9	2·1	11·9	4·3	17·9	6·4
60	5 30·0	5 30·9	5 15·0	6·0	2·2	12·0	4·3	18·0	6·5

Appendix F-11

POLARIS (POLE STAR) TABLES, 1970

FOR DETERMINING LATITUDE FROM SEXTANT ALTITUDE AND FOR AZIMUTH

L.H.A. ARIES	0°–9°	10°–19°	20°–29°	30°–39°	40°–49°	50°–59°	60°–69°	70°–79°	80°–89°	90°–99°	100°–109°	110°–119°
	a_0	a_0	a_0	a_0	a_0	a_0	a_0	a_0	a_0	a_0	a_0	a_0
0	0 14·2	0 10·2	0 07·6	0 06·7	0 07·4	0 09·6	0 13·4	0 18·6	0 25·0	0 32·4	0 40·7	0 49·5
1	13·7	09·8	07·5	06·7	07·5	09·9	13·9	19·2	25·7	33·2	41·5	50·4
2	13·3	09·5	07·3	06·7	07·7	10·3	14·3	19·8	26·4	34·0	42·4	51·3
3	12·8	09·2	07·2	06·7	07·9	10·6	14·8	20·4	27·1	34·8	43·3	52·2
4	12·4	09·0	07·1	06·8	08·1	11·0	15·3	21·0	27·9	35·7	44·1	53·1
5	0 12·0	0 08·7	0 07·0	0 06·8	0 08·3	0 11·3	0 15·8	0 21·7	0 28·6	0 36·5	0 45·0	0 54·0
6	11·6	08·5	06·9	06·9	08·5	11·7	16·4	22·3	29·4	37·3	45·9	54·9
7	11·2	08·2	06·8	07·0	08·8	12·1	16·9	23·0	30·1	38·1	46·8	55·8
8	10·9	08·0	06·8	07·1	09·1	12·5	17·5	23·6	30·9	39·0	47·7	56·7
9	10·5	07·8	06·7	07·2	09·3	13·0	18·0	24·3	31·7	39·8	48·6	57·6
10	0 10·2	0 07·6	0 06·7	0 07·4	0 09·6	0 13·4	0 18·6	0 25·0	0 32·4	0 40·7	0 49·5	0 58·5

Lat.	a_1	a_1	a_1	a_1	a_1	a_1	a_1	a_1	a_1	a_1	a_1	a_1
0	0·5	0·6	0·6	0·6	0·6	0·5	0·5	0·4	0·3	0·2	0·2	0·1
10	·5	·6	·6	·6	·6	·5	·5	·4	·3	·3	·2	·2
20	·5	·6	·6	·6	·6	·5	·5	·4	·4	·3	·3	·3
30	·6	·6	·6	·6	·6	·6	·5	·5	·4	·4	·4	·4
40	0·6	0·6	0·6	0·6	0·6	0·6	0·6	0·5	0·5	0·5	0·5	0·5
45	·6	·6	·6	·6	·6	·6	·6	·6	·6	·5	·5	·5
50	·6	·6	·6	·6	·6	·6	·6	·6	·6	·6	·6	·6
55	·6	·6	·6	·6	·6	·6	·6	·6	·7	·7	·7	·7
60	·6	·6	·6	·6	·6	·6	·7	·7	·7	·8	·8	·8
62	0·7	0·6	0·6	0·6	0·6	0·6	0·7	0·7	0·8	0·8	0·9	0·9
64	·7	·6	·6	·6	·6	·7	·7	·8	·8	·9	0·9	0·9
66	·7	·6	·6	·6	·6	·7	·7	·8	·9	0·9	1·0	1·0
68	0·7	0·6	0·6	0·6	0·6	0·7	0·8	0·8	0·9	1·0	1·1	1·1

Month	a_2	a_2	a_2	a_2	a_2	a_2	a_2	a_2	a_2	a_2	a_2	a_2
Jan.	0·7	0·7	0·7	0·7	0·7	0·7	0·7	0·7	0·7	0·7	0·7	0·7
Feb.	·6	·6	·7	·7	·7	·8	·8	·8	·8	·8	·8	·8
Mar.	·5	·5	·6	·6	·7	·7	·8	·8	·9	·9	·9	0·9
Apr.	0·3	0·4	0·4	0·5	0·6	0·6	0·7	0·8	0·8	0·9	0·9	1·0
May	·2	·3	·3	·4	·4	·5	·6	·6	·7	·8	·8	0·9
June	·2	·2	·2	·3	·3	·4	·4	·5	·5	·6	·7	·8
July	0·2	0·2	0·2	0·2	0·2	0·3	0·3	0·4	0·4	0·5	0·5	0·6
Aug.	·4	·3	·3	·3	·3	·3	·3	·3	·3	·3	·4	·4
Sept.	·5	·5	·4	·4	·3	·3	·3	·3	·3	·3	·3	·3
Oct.	0·7	0·7	0·6	0·6	0·5	0·4	0·4	0·3	0·3	0·3	0·3	0·2
Nov.	0·9	0·9	0·8	0·7	·7	·6	·5	·5	·4	·3	·3	·3
Dec.	1·0	1·0	1·0	0·9	0·8	0·8	0·7	0·6	0·6	0·5	0·4	0·3

Lat.	AZIMUTH											
0	0·4	0·2	0·1	359·9	359·8	359·6	359·5	359·4	359·3	359·2	359·2	359·1
20	0·4	0·3	0·1	359·9	359·8	359·6	359·5	359·4	359·2	359·2	359·1	359·1
40	0·5	0·3	0·1	359·9	359·7	359·5	359·4	359·2	359·1	359·0	358·9	358·9
50	0·6	0·4	0·1	359·9	359·7	359·4	359·2	359·0	358·9	358·8	358·7	358·7
55	0·7	0·4	0·2	359·9	359·6	359·4	359·1	358·9	358·8	358·6	358·5	358·5
60	0·8	0·5	0·2	359·9	359·6	359·3	359·0	358·8	358·6	358·4	358·3	358·3
65	0·9	0·6	0·2	359·8	359·5	359·1	358·8	358·5	358·3	358·1	358·0	357·9

Latitude = Apparent altitude (corrected for refraction) − 1° + a_0 + a_1 + a_2

The table is entered with L.H.A. Aries to determine the column to be used; each column refers to a range of 10°. a_0 is taken, with mental interpolation, from the upper table with the units of L.H.A. Aries in degrees as argument; a_1, a_2 are taken, without interpolation, from the second and third tables with arguments latitude and month respectively. a_0, a_1, a_2 are always positive. The final table gives the azimuth of *Polaris*.

TABLES FOR INTERPOLATING SUNRISE, MOONRISE, ETC.

TABLE I—FOR LATITUDE

Tabular Interval 10°	5°	2°	5ᵐ	10ᵐ	15ᵐ	20ᵐ	25ᵐ	30ᵐ	35ᵐ	40ᵐ	45ᵐ	50ᵐ	55ᵐ	60ᵐ	1ʰ 05ᵐ	1ʰ 10ᵐ	1ʰ 15ᵐ	1ʰ 20ᵐ
0 30	0 15	0 06	0	0	1	1	1	1	1	2	2	2	2	2	0 02	0 02	0 02	0 02
1 00	0 30	0 12	0	1	1	2	2	3	3	3	4	4	4	5	05	05	05	05
1 30	0 45	0 18	1	1	2	3	3	4	4	5	5	6	7	7	07	07	07	07
2 00	1 00	0 24	1	2	3	4	5	5	6	7	7	8	9	10	10	10	10	10
2 30	1 15	0 30	1	2	4	5	6	7	8	9	9	10	11	12	12	13	13	13
3 00	1 30	0 36	1	3	4	6	7	8	9	10	11	12	13	14	0 15	0 15	0 16	0 16
3 30	1 45	0 42	2	3	5	7	8	10	11	12	13	14	16	17	18	18	19	19
4 00	2 00	0 48	2	4	6	8	9	11	13	14	15	16	18	19	20	21	22	22
4 30	2 15	0 54	2	4	7	9	11	13	15	16	18	19	21	22	23	24	25	26
5 00	2 30	1 00	2	5	7	10	12	14	16	18	20	22	23	25	26	27	28	29
5 30	2 45	1 06	3	5	8	11	13	16	18	20	22	24	26	28	0 29	0 30	0 31	0 32
6 00	3 00	1 12	3	6	9	12	14	17	20	22	24	26	29	31	32	33	34	36
6 30	3 15	1 18	3	6	10	13	16	19	22	24	26	29	31	34	36	37	38	40
7 00	3 30	1 24	3	7	10	14	17	20	23	26	29	31	34	37	39	41	42	44
7 30	3 45	1 30	4	7	11	15	18	22	25	28	31	34	37	40	43	44	46	48
8 00	4 00	1 36	4	8	12	16	20	23	27	30	34	37	41	44	0 47	0 48	0 51	0 53
8 30	4 15	1 42	4	8	13	17	21	25	29	33	36	40	44	48	0 51	0 53	0 56	0 58
9 00	4 30	1 48	4	9	13	18	22	27	31	35	39	43	47	52	0 55	0 58	1 01	1 04
9 30	4 45	1 54	5	9	14	19	24	28	33	38	42	47	51	56	1 00	1 04	1 08	1 12
10 00	5 00	2 00	5	10	15	20	25	30	35	40	45	50	55	60	1 05	1 10	1 15	1 20

Table I is for interpolating the L.M.T. of sunrise, twilight, moonrise, etc., for latitude. It is to be entered, in the appropriate column on the left, with the difference between true latitude and the nearest tabular latitude which is *less* than the true latitude; and with the argument at the top which is the nearest value of the difference between the times for the tabular latitude and the next higher one; the correction so obtained is applied to the time for the tabular latitude; the sign of the correction can be seen by inspection. It is to be noted that the interpolation is not linear, so that when using this table it is essential to take out the tabular phenomenon for the latitude *less* than the true latitude.

TABLE II—FOR LONGITUDE

Long. East or West	10ᵐ	20ᵐ	30ᵐ	40ᵐ	50ᵐ	60ᵐ	1ʰ+ 10ᵐ	20ᵐ	30ᵐ	1ʰ+ 40ᵐ	50ᵐ	60ᵐ	2ʰ 10ᵐ	2ʰ 20ᵐ	2ʰ 30ᵐ	2ʰ 40ᵐ	2ʰ 50ᵐ	3ʰ 00ᵐ
0	0	0	0	0	0	0	0	0	0	0	0	0	0 00	0 00	0 00	0 00	0 00	0 00
10	0	1	1	1	1	2	2	2	2	3	3	3	04	04	04	04	05	05
20	1	1	2	2	3	3	4	4	5	6	6	7	07	08	08	09	09	10
30	1	2	2	3	4	5	6	7	7	8	9	10	11	12	12	13	14	15
40	1	2	3	4	6	7	8	9	10	11	12	13	14	16	17	18	19	20
50	1	3	4	6	7	8	10	11	12	14	15	17	0 18	0 19	0 21	0 22	0 24	0 25
60	2	3	5	7	8	10	12	13	15	17	18	20	22	23	25	27	28	30
70	2	4	6	8	10	12	14	16	17	19	21	23	25	27	29	31	33	35
80	2	4	7	9	11	13	16	18	20	22	24	27	29	31	33	36	38	40
90	2	5	7	10	12	15	17	20	22	25	27	30	32	35	37	40	42	45
100	3	6	8	11	14	17	19	22	25	28	31	33	0 36	0 39	0 42	0 44	0 47	0 50
110	3	6	9	12	15	18	21	24	27	31	34	37	40	43	46	49	0 52	0 55
120	3	7	10	13	17	20	23	27	30	33	37	40	43	47	50	53	0 57	1 00
130	4	7	11	14	18	22	25	29	32	36	40	43	47	51	54	0 58	1 01	1 05
140	4	8	12	16	19	23	27	31	35	39	43	47	51	54	0 58	1 02	1 06	1 10
150	4	8	13	17	21	25	29	33	38	42	46	50	0 54	0 58	1 03	1 07	1 11	1 15
160	4	9	13	18	22	27	31	36	40	44	49	53	0 58	1 02	1 07	1 11	1 16	1 20
170	5	9	14	19	24	28	33	38	42	47	52	57	1 01	1 06	1 11	1 16	1 20	1 25
180	5	10	15	20	25	30	35	40	45	50	55	60	1 05	1 10	1 15	1 20	1 25	1 30

Table II is for interpolating the L.M.T. of moonrise, moonset and the Moon's meridian passage for longitude. It is entered with longitude and with the difference between the times for the given date and for the preceding date (in east longitudes) or following date (in west longitudes). The correction is normally *added* for west longitudes and *subtracted* for east longitudes, but if, as occasionally happens, the times become earlier each day instead of later, the signs of the corrections must be reversed.

Appendix G-1

DECLINATION SAME NAME AS LATITUDE

Lat. 34°

22° 30' Alt. / Az.	23° 00' Alt. / Az.	23° 30' Alt. / Az.	H.A.
78 30.0 1.0 03 180.0	79 00.0 1.0 04 180.0	79 30.0 1.0 04 180.0	00
78 28.0 1.0 10 175.4	78 57.9 1.0 10 175.2	79 27.8 1.0 11 175.0	1
78 22.0 99 16 170.8	78 51.7 99 17 170.4	79 21.3 99 18 170.0	2
78 12.1 98 23 166.3	78 41.4 98 24 165.8	79 10.6 97 24 165.2	3
77 58.5 96 28 162.0	78 27.3 96 30 161.3	78 56.0 95 31 160.5	4
77 41.4 94 34 157.8	78 09.6 94 35 157.0	78 37.6 93 36 156.1	05
77 21.0 92 39 153.8	77 48.5 91 40 152.9	78 15.8 90 42 151.9	6
76 57.6 89 44 150.1	77 24.3 89 45 149.0	77 50.8 88 46 147.9	7
76 31.5 87 48 146.5	76 57.4 86 49 145.4	77 23.0 85 50 144.2	8
76 02.8 84 52 143.2	76 28.0 83 53 142.0	76 52.8 82 54 140.8	9
75 31.9 82 55 140.0	75 56.3 81 56 138.9	76 20.3 79 57 137.6	10
74 59.0 79 58 137.1	75 22.6 78 59 135.9	75 45.8 77 60 134.6	1
74 24.3 77 61 134.4	74 47.1 75 62 133.2	75 09.5 74 63 131.9	2
73 48.0 74 63 131.8	74 10.1 73 64 130.6	74 31.8 71 65 129.3	3
73 10.3 72 65 129.5	73 31.7 71 66 128.2	73 52.7 69 67 127.0	4
72 31.2 70 67 127.2	72 52.0 69 68 125.9	73 12.4 67 69 124.8	15
71 51.1 68 69 125.2	72 11.3 66 70 124.0	72 31.0 65 70 122.7	6
71 10.0 66 70 123.2	71 29.5 65 71 122.0	71 48.7 63 72 120.8	7
70 27.9 64 71 121.4	70 47.0 63 72 120.2	71 05.6 61 73 119.0	8
69 45.0 63 73 119.7	70 03.6 61 73 118.5	70 21.7 60 74 117.3	9

Lat. 35°

H.A.	24° 00' Alt. / Az.	24° 30' Alt. / Az.
00	79 00.0 1.0 03 180.0	79 30.0 1.0 04 180.0
1	78 57.9 1.0 10 175.2	79 27.9 1.0 11 175.0
2	78 51.8 99 17 170.5	79 21.5 99 18 170.1
3	78 41.8 98 23 165.9	79 11.0 97 24 165.3
4	78 27.9 96 29 161.4	78 56.6 95 30 160.7
05	78 10.5 94 35 157.1	78 38.6 93 36 156.3
6	77 49.8 91 40 153.1	78 17.1 91 41 152.1
7	77 26.1 89 44 149.2	77 52.6 88 45 148.1
8	76 59.6 86 48 145.6	77 25.3 85 50 144.4
9	76 30.6 84 52 142.2	76 55.5 82 53 141.0
10	75 59.5 81 55 139.1	76 23.6 80 57 137.8
1	75 26.3 78 58 136.1	75 49.6 77 59 134.8
2	74 51.4 76 61 133.4	75 13.9 74 62 132.1
3	74 14.9 73 63 130.8	74 36.7 72 64 129.5
4	73 37.0 71 65 128.4	73 58.2 70 66 127.1
15	72 57.9 69 67 126.2	73 18.4 67 68 124.9
6	72 17.6 67 69 124.1	72 37.6 65 70 122.9
7	71 36.6 65 70 122.2	71 55.9 64 71 120.9
8	70 54.5 63 71 120.3	71 13.3 62 72 119.1
9	70 11.8 62 72 118.6	70 30.0 60 73 117.4
20	69 28.3 60 73 117.0	69 46.1 59 74 115.8
1	68 44.2 59 74 115.5	69 01.6 57 75 114.3
2	67 59.6 57 75 114.0	68 16.6 56 76 112.9
3	67 14.4 56 76 112.7	67 31.1 55 76 111.6
4	66 28.9 55 77 111.4	66 45.2 54 77 110.3
25	65 42.9 54 77 110.2	65 58.9 53 78 109.1

Lat. 35°

H.A.	12° 00' Alt. / Az.	12° 30' Alt. / Az.	13° 00' Alt. / Az.
00	67 00.0 1.0 02 180.0	67 30.0 1.0 02 180.0	68 00.0 1.0 02 180.0
1	66 58.9 1.0 05 177.5	67 28.9 1.0 05 177.4	67 58.9 1.0 05 177.4
2	66 55.7 1.0 09 175.0	67 25.6 1.0 09 174.9	67 55.5 1.0 09 174.8
3	66 50.4 99 12 172.5	67 20.2 99 13 172.4	67 50.0 99 13 172.2
4	66 42.9 99 16 170.1	67 12.6 99 16 169.9	67 42.3 99 16 169.7
05	66 33.4 98 19 167.6	67 02.9 98 20 167.4	67 32.4 98 20 167.2
6	66 21.9 98 23 165.2	66 51.2 98 23 165.0	67 20.4 97 23 164.7
7	66 08.4 97 26 162.9	66 37.4 97 26 162.6	67 06.4 97 27 162.2
8	65 52.9 96 29 160.5	66 21.7 96 29 160.2	66 50.5 96 30 159.8
9	65 35.6 95 32 158.3	66 04.1 95 32 157.9	66 32.6 95 33 157.5
10	65 16.6 94 35 156.0	65 44.7 94 35 155.6	66 12.8 94 36 155.2
1	64 55.7 93 37 153.9	65 23.6 93 38 153.4	65 51.4 92 39 153.0
2	64 33.3 92 40 151.7	65 00.8 92 41 151.3	65 28.2 91 41 150.8
3	64 09.2 91 43 149.7	64 36.4 90 43 149.2	65 03.4 90 44 148.7
4	63 43.7 89 45 147.7	64 10.5 89 46 147.2	64 37.1 89 46 146.6

Lat. 33°

22° 30' Alt. / Az.	23° 00' Alt. / Az.	23° 30' Alt. / Az.	H.A.
79 30.0 1.0 04 180.0	80 00.0 1.0 04 180.0	80 30.0 1.0 04 180.0	00
79 27.8 1.0 11 174.9	79 57.7 1.0 12 174.7	80 27.6 1.0 12 174.5	1
79 21.2 99 18 170.0	79 50.8 99 19 169.5	80 20.3 98 20 169.0	2
79 10.3 97 25 165.1	79 39.4 97 26 164.4	80 08.4 97 27 163.7	3
78 55.3 95 31 160.4	79 23.8 95 32 159.6	79 52.2 94 34 158.7	4
78 36.6 93 37 155.9	79 04.4 92 38 155.0	79 32.0 92 40 153.9	05
78 14.4 90 42 151.7	78 41.4 89 44 150.6	79 08.1 89 45 149.4	6
77 49.0 87 47 147.8	78 15.1 86 48 146.6	78 40.9 85 50 145.3	7
77 20.8 85 51 144.1	77 46.0 83 53 142.8	78 10.9 82 54 141.5	8
76 50.1 82 55 140.6	77 14.4 80 56 139.3	77 38.3 79 58 137.9	9
76 17.0 79 58 137.4	76 40.5 78 60 136.1	77 03.5 76 61 134.7	10
75 42.0 76 61 134.5	76 04.7 75 63 133.1	76 26.8 73 64 131.7	1
75 05.3 74 64 131.7	75 27.1 72 65 130.4	75 48.5 70 66 129.0	2
74 27.0 71 66 129.2	74 48.1 69 67 127.8	75 08.6 68 68 126.4	3
73 47.3 69 68 126.8	74 07.7 67 69 125.5	74 27.5 65 70 124.1	4
73 06.5 66 70 124.6	73 26.2 65 71 123.3	73 45.4 63 72 122.0	15
72 24.6 64 71 122.6	72 43.6 63 72 121.3	73 02.2 61 73 120.0	6
71 41.7 62 73 120.7	72 00.2 61 74 119.4	72 18.2 59 75 118.1	7
70 58.0 61 74 118.9	71 16.0 59 75 117.7	71 33.5 57 76 116.4	8
70 13.6 59 75 117.2	70 31.1 57 76 116.0	70 48.1 56 77 114.8	9

Lat. 36°

H.A.	56° 30' Alt. / Az.	57° 00' Alt. / Az.
65	42 45.3 06 55 42.9	42 46.7 06 54 42.3
6	42 12.2 07 55 42.9	42 14.0 06 54 42.2
7	41 39.2 08 55 42.9	41 41.4 07 54 42.2
8	41 06.2 09 55 42.9	41 08.9 09 54 42.2
9	40 33.3 11 55 42.8	40 36.4 10 54 42.1
70	40 00.4 12 55 42.7	40 03.8 12 54 42.0
1	39 27.5 13 55 42.6	39 31.5 13 54 42.0
2	38 54.7 15 54 42.5	38 59.1 14 54 41.9
3	38 22.0 16 54 42.3	38 26.7 15 54 41.7
4	37 49.4 17 54 42.2	37 54.5 17 54 41.6

Appendix G-2

DECLINATION CONTRARY NAME TO LATITUDE

Lat. 33°

21° 30' Alt.	Δd Δt	Az.	22° 00' Alt.	Δd Δt	Az.	22° 30' Alt.	Δd Δt	Az.	23° 00' Alt.	Δd Δt	Az.	23° 30' Alt.	Δd Δt	Az.	H.A.
35 30.0	1.00 01	180.0	35 00.0	1.00 01	180.0	34 30.0	1.00 01	180.0	34 00.0	1.00 01	180.0	33 30.0	1.00 01	180.0	00
35 29.5	1.00 02	178.9	34 59.5	1.00 02	178.9	34 29.5	1.00 02	178.9	33 59.5	1.00 02	178.9	33 29.5	1.00 02	178.9	1
35 28.0	1.00 04	177.7	34 58.0	1.00 04	177.7	34 28.0	1.00 04	177.8	33 58.1	1.00 04	177.8	33 28.1	1.00 04	177.8	2
35 25.5	1.00 06	176.6	34 55.5	1.00 06	176.6	34 25.6	1.00 06	176.6	33 55.6	1.00 06	176.7	33 25.7	1.00 06	176.7	3
35 22.0	1.00 08	175.4	34 52.1	1.00 07	175.5	34 22.1	1.00 07	175.5	33 52.2	1.00 07	175.6	33 22.3	1.00 07	175.6	4
35 17.5	1.00 09	174.3	34 47.6	1.00 09	174.4	34 17.7	1.00 09	174.4	33 47.8	1.00 09	174.5	33 17.9	1.00 09	174.5	05
35 12.0	99 11	173.2	34 42.2	99 11	173.2	34 12.3	99 11	173.3	33 42.5	99 10	173.4	33 12.7	99 10	173.4	6
35 05.5	99 12	172.0	34 35.7	99 12	172.1	34 06.0	99 12	172.2	33 36.2	99 12	172.3	33 06.4	99 12	172.3	7
34 58.0	99 14	170.9	34 28.3	99 14	171.0	33 58.6	99 14	171.1	33 28.9	99 14	171.2	32 59.2	99 14	171.2	8
34 49.6	99 16	169.8	34 20.0	99 16	169.9	33 50.4	99 15	170.0	33 20.7	99 15	170.1	32 51.1	99 15	170.2	9

Lat. 35°

22° 30' Alt.	Δd Δt	Az.	23° 00' Alt.	Δd Δt	Az.	H.A.
32 30.0	1.00 01	180.0	32 00.0	1.00 01	180.0	00
32 29.5	1.00 02	178.9	31 59.6	1.00 02	178.9	1
32 28.1	1.00 04	177.8	31 58.2	1.00 04	177.8	2
32 25.8	1.00 06	176.7	31 55.8	1.00 06	176.8	3
32 22.5	1.00 07	175.6	31 52.6	1.00 07	175.7	4
32 18.3	1.00 08	174.5	31 48.4	1.00 08	174.6	05
32 13.2	99 10	173.4	31 43.3	99 10	173.5	6
32 07.1	99 12	172.3	31 37.3	99 12	172.4	7
32 00.1	99 13	171.3	31 30.3	99 13	171.4	8
31 52.2	99 15	170.2	31 22.5	99 14	170.3	9
31 43.4	99 16	169.1	31 13.8	99 16	169.2	10
31 33.7	98 18	168.1	31 04.1	98 17	168.2	1
31 23.0	98 19	167.0	30 53.6	98 19	167.1	2
31 11.5	98 21	166.0	30 42.2	98 20	166.1	3
30 59.1	97 22	164.9	30 29.9	97 22	165.0	4
30 45.9	97 23	163.8	30 16.8	97 23	164.0	15
30 31.8	97 25	162.9	30 02.8	97 25	163.0	6
30 16.8	96 26	161.8	29 48.0	96 26	161.9	7
30 01.0	96 28	160.8	29 32.3	96 27	160.9	8
29 44.4	96 29	159.7	29 15.8	96 29	159.9	9
29 27.0	96 30	158.7	28 58.5	96 30	158.9	20
29 08.8	94 32	157.7	28 40.5	94 31	157.9	1
28 49.7	94 33	156.7	28 21.6	94 33	156.9	2
28 29.9	93 34	155.7	28 02.0	93 34	156.0	3
28 09.4	92 35	154.8	27 41.5	92 35	155.0	4
27 48.1	92 37	153.8	27 20.4	92 36	154.0	25
27 26.0	91 38	152.8	26 58.5	91 38	153.1	6
27 03.2	90 39	151.9	26 35.9	90 39	152.1	7
26 39.7	89 40	150.9	26 12.6	89 40	151.2	8
26 15.5	89 41	150.0	25 48.5	89 41	150.3	9
25 50.6	89 43	149.1	25 23.9	89 42	149.4	30
25 25.0	88 44	148.3	24 58.4	88 43	148.5	1
24 58.8	88 45	147.3	24 32.5	88 44	147.6	2
24 31.9	87 46	146.4	24 05.8	87 45	146.7	3
24 04.4	86 47	145.5	23 38.5	86 46	145.8	4

Lat. 33°

H.A.	24° 00' Alt.	Δd Δt	Az.	24° 30' Alt.	Δd Δt	Az.
00	33 00.0	1.00 01	180.0	32 30.0	1.00 01	180.0
1	32 59.5	1.00 02	178.9	32 29.5	1.00 02	178.9
2	32 58.1	1.00 04	177.8	32 28.1	1.00 04	177.8
3	32 55.7	1.00 06	176.7	32 25.7	1.00 06	176.8
4	32 52.4	1.00 07	175.6	32 22.4	1.00 07	175.7
05	32 48.1	1.00 09	174.6	32 18.2	1.00 09	174.6
6	32 42.8	99 10	173.5	32 13.0	99 10	173.5
7	32 36.6	99 12	172.4	32 06.9	99 12	172.5
8	32 29.5	99 13	171.3	31 59.8	99 13	171.4
9	32 21.5	99 15	170.3	31 51.8	99 15	170.4
10	32 12.5	99 16	169.2	31 42.9	99 16	169.3
1	32 02.6	98 18	168.1	31 33.1	98 18	168.2
2	31 51.8	98 20	167.1	31 22.4	98 19	167.2
3	31 40.1	98 21	166.0	31 10.8	98 21	166.2
4	31 27.5	97 22	165.0	30 58.4	97 22	165.1
15	31 14.0	97 24	163.9	30 45.0	97 24	164.1

Appendix H

MECHANICS OF "ERROR FINDING" IN SIGHT REDUCTION BY HO 214

It is not unusual for a student of celestial navigation to make frequent errors in solving for a line of position; hence the following table illustrates the mechanics of "error finding."

A. If t exceeds values given in HO 214—

1. Check date, ZD, and GMT
2. Check longitude. East λ is added and west λ subtracted in the step between GHA and LHA.
3. Check conversion of LHA to t.
4. Check GHA in Nautical Almanac.
5. If working a star sight, check SHA and insure that the GHA as taken from the Almanac is the GHA of Υ.
6. Search for arithmetical error.

B. If Ht differs from Ho (or Hs) by several degrees—

1. Check declination. Note whether latitude and declination are of same name or of contrary name.
2. Check assumed latitude.
3. Assume possible error in t.
4. Search for arithmetical error.

C. If Hc differs from Ho by 1 or 2 degrees ("a" exceeds 60 mi.)—

1. Check assumed longitude.
2. Check Greenwich date.
3. Check GMT.
4. If correction to Hs is large (as in a moon sight) check sign of correction.
5. Check sign of correction to Ht.
6. Check values copied from HO 214.
7. Search for arithmetical error.

D. If results fail to plot favorably—

1. Check labels and try to isolate LOP (or LOP's) in error. Keep in mind your DR position, and possible set and drift. Then carry out steps 2 to 9 for sights isolated.
2. Check conversion of WT to ZT.
3. Check AP's and their advance.
4. Check conversion of azimuth angle to azimuth.
5. Check label of intercept.
6. Check correction to Ht and the sign of that correction.
7. Check the sign of correction applied to Hs to obtain Ho.
8. Check sextant altitude corrections.
9. Check the accuracy of your plot.
10. Search for arithmetical error.

Appendix I-1

LAT 40°N

LHA T	Hc	Zn	Hc	Zn	Hc	Zn	Hc	Zn	Hc	Zn	Hc	Zn
	CAPELLA		ALDEBARAN		Diphda		ALTAIR		VEGA		Kochab	
0	34 40	056	26 53	091	31 00	168	26 22	259	29 39	298	27 49	348
1	35 18	056	27 39	091	31 08	170	25 37	260	28 58	298	27 40	348
2	35 57	057	28 25	092	31 16	171	24 51	260	28 18	298	27 31	349
3	36 35	057	29 11	093	31 23	172	24 06	261	27 37	299	27 22	349
4	37 14	057	29 57	093	31 29	173	23 21	262	26 57	299	27 13	349
5	37 52	058	30 43	094	31 35	174	22 35	262	26 17	300	27 04	349
6	38 31	058	31 29	095	31 39	175	21 50	263	25 37	300	26 56	350
7	39 10	058	32 14	095	31 42	176	21 04	264	24 58	301	26 47	350
8	39 49	059	33 00	096	31 45	177	20 18	264	24 18	301	26 39	350
9	40 29	059	33 46	097	31 47	178	19 32	265	23 39	302	26 32	350
10	41 08	059	34 31	097	31 48	180	18 47	266	23 00	302	26 24	351
11	41 48	059	35 17	098	31 47	181	18 01	266	22 21	303	26 17	351
12	42 27	060	36 02	099	31 46	182	17 15	267	21 43	303	26 09	351
13	43 07	060	36 48	100	31 45	183	16 29	268	21 04	304	26 02	351
14	43 47	060	37 33	100	31 42	184	15 43	268	20 26	304	25 56	352
	CAPELLA		ALDEBARAN		Diphda		Alpheratz		DENEB		Kochab	
15	44 27	061	38 18	101	31 38	185	74 20	229	43 10	299	25 49	352
16	45 07	061	39 03	102	31 34	186	73 45	231	42 30	299	25 43	352
17	45 47	061	39 48	103	31 28	187	73 09	233	41 50	299	25 37	353
18	46 27	061	40 33	103	31 22	188	72 31	236	41 10	300	25 31	353
19	47 08	062	41 18	104	31 15	190	71 53	237	40 30	300	25 25	353
20	47 48	062	42 02	105	31 07	191	71 14	239	39 50	300	25 20	353
21	48 29	062	42 46	106	30 58	192	70 34	241	39 10	301	25 15	354
22	49 09	062	43 31	107	30 48	193	69 53	243	38 31	301	25 10	354
23	49 50	063	44 14	108	30 37	194	69 12	244	37 52	301	25 05	354
24	50 31	063	44 58	108	30 26	195	68 31	246	37 12	302	25 00	355
25	51 12	063	45 42	109	30 13	196	67 48	247	36 33	302	24 56	355
26	51 53	063	46 25	110	30 00	197	67 06	248	35 54	302	24 52	355
27	52 34	063	47 08	111	29 46	198	66 23	250	35 16	303	24 48	355
28	53 15	064	47 51	112	29 31	199	65 40	251	34 37	303	24 45	356
29	53 56	064	48 33	113	29 16	200	64 56	252	33 59	303	24 41	356
	CAPELLA		BETELGEUSE		RIGEL		Diphda		Alpheratz		DENEB	
30	54 38	064	28 51	106	24 26	126	29 00	201	64 12	253	33 20	304
31	55 19	064	29 35	106	25 03	127	28 42	202	63 28	254	32 42	304
32	56 00	064	30 19	107	25 39	128	28 24	203	62 44	255	32 04	304
33	56 42	064	31 03	108	26 16	129	28 06	204	61 59	256	31 26	305
34	57 23	065	31 47	109	26 51	129	27 46	205	61 14	257	30 49	305
35	58 05	065	32 30	110	27 27	130	27 26	206	60 29	258	30 11	306
36	58 46	065	33 13	110	28 01	131	27 05	207	59 44	259	29 34	306
37	59 28	065	33 56	111	28 36	132	26 44	208	58 59	260	28 57	306
38	60 10	065	34 39	112	29 10	133	26 22	209	58 14	261	28 20	307
39	60 51	065	35 21	113	29 43	134	25 59	210	57 28	262	27 43	307
40	61 33	065	36 04	114	30 16	135	25 35	211	56 43	263	27 07	308
41	62 15	065	36 46	115	30 48	136	25 11	212	55 57	263	26 31	308
42	62 55	065	37 27	116	31 20	137	24 46	213	55 11	264	25 54	308
43	63 38	065	38 08	116	31 51	138	24 21	214	54 26	265	25 18	309
44	64 20	065	38 49	117	32 21	139	23 54	215	53 40	266	24 43	309
	Dubhe		POLLUX		BETELGEUSE		RIGEL		Alpheratz		DENEB	
45	22 41	026	31 45	078	39 30	118	32 51	140	52 54	266	24 07	310
46	23 01	026	32 30	079	40 10	119	33 21	141	52 08	267	23 32	310
47	23 22	027	33 15	079	40 50	120	33 49	142	51 22	268	22 57	311
48	23 43	027	34 00	080	41 30	121	34 17	143	50 36	268	22 22	311
49	24 04	027	34 45	080	42 09	122	34 45	144	49 50	269	21 47	311
50	24 25	028	35 31	081	42 48	123	35 11	145	49 04	270	21 13	312
51	24 47	028	36 16	082	43 26	124	35 37	146	48 18	270	20 39	312
52	25 09	028	37 01	082	44 04	125	36 02	147	47 33	271	20 05	313
53	25 31	029	37 47	083	44 41	126	36 27	148	46 47	272	19 31	313
54	25 53	029	38 33	083	45 18	127	36 50	150	46 01	272	18 58	314
55	26 15	029	39 18	084	45 54	129	37 13	151	45 15	273	18 25	314
56	26 38	030	40 04	084	46 29	130	37 35	152	44 29	273	17 52	315
57	27 01	030	40 50	085	47 04	131	37 56	153	43 43	274	17 19	315
58	27 24	030	41 36	086	47 39	132	38 17	154	42 57	275	16 47	316
59	27 47	031	42 21	086	48 13	133	38 36	155	42 11	275	16 15	316
	Dubhe		POLLUX		PROCYON		SIRIUS		RIGEL		Alpheratz	
60	28 11	031	43 07	087	30 19	110	21 46	138	38 55	157	41 26	276
61	28 35	031	43 53	087	31 02	111	22 17	138	39 13	158	40 40	276
62	28 59	032	44 39	088	31 45	112	22 47	139	39 30	159	39 54	277
63	29 23	032	45 25	089	32 27	113	23 17	140	39 46	160	39 09	277
64	29 47	032	46 11	089	33 09	114	23 46	141	40 01	162	38 23	278
65	30 11	032	46 57	090	33 51	115	24 15	142	40 15	163	37 38	279
66	30 36	033	47 43	090	34 33	115	24 43	143	40 28	164	36 52	279
67	31 01	033	48 29	091	35 14	116	25 10	144	40 40	165	36 07	280
68	31 26	033	49 15	092	35 55	117	25 37	145	40 51	167	35 22	280
69	31 51	033	50 01	092	36 35	118	26 03	146	41 01	168	34 36	281
70	32 17	034	50 47	093	37 16	119	26 28	147	41 10	169	33 51	281
71	32 42	034	51 33	094	37 56	120	26 53	148	41 18	171	33 05	282
72	33 08	034	52 18	095	38 36	121	27 18	149	41 25	172	32 21	282
73	33 34	034	53 04	095	39 15	122	27 41	150	41 31	173	31 36	283
74	34 00	035	53 50	096	39 54	123	28 04	151	41 36	174	30 52	283
	Dubhe		REGULUS		PROCYON		SIRIUS		ALDEBARAN		Hamal	
75	34 26	035	18 02	089	40 32	124	28 26	152	65 45	196	49 39	259
76	34 52	035	18 48	090	41 10	125	28 48	153	65 31	198	48 54	260
77	35 18	035	19 34	090	41 47	126	29 08	154	65 16	200	48 09	261
78	35 45	035	20 20	091	42 24	127	29 28	155	65 00	202	47 23	261
79	36 12	036	21 05	092	43 01	128	29 48	156	64 42	204	46 38	262
80	36 38	036	21 51	092	43 37	129	30 06	157	64 22	206	45 52	263
81	37 05	036	22 37	093	44 12	130	30 24	158	64 01	209	45 07	264
82	37 32	036	23 23	094	44 47	131	30 41	159	63 38	211	44 21	264
83	37 59	036	24 09	094	45 21	133	30 57	160	63 14	212	43 35	265
84	38 26	036	24 55	095	45 54	134	31 12	161	62 49	214	42 49	266
85	38 54	037	25 41	096	46 27	135	31 27	162	62 22	216	42 03	266
86	39 21	037	26 26	096	46 59	136	31 41	163	61 55	218	41 18	267
87	39 49	037	27 12	097	47 31	137	31 53	164	61 26	220	40 32	268
88	40 16	037	27 58	098	48 02	139	32 05	165	60 56	221	39 46	268
89	40 41	037	28 43	098	48 32	140	32 16	167	60 25	223	39 00	269

LAT 40°N

LHA T	Hc	Zn	Hc	Zn	Hc	Zn	Hc	Zn	Hc	Zn	Hc	Zn
	Dubhe		REGULUS		PROCYON		SIRIUS		ALDEBARAN		Hamal	
90	41 12	037	29 29	099	49 01	141	32 27	168	59 53	225	38 14	270
91	41 39	037	30 14	100	49 29	143	32 36	169	59 20	226	37 28	270
92	42 07	037	30 59	101	49 56	144	32 45	170	58 47	228	36 42	271
93	42 35	037	31 44	101	50 23	145	32 52	171	58 12	229	35 56	272
94	43 03	038	32 29	102	50 49	147	32 59	172	57 37	231	35 10	272
95	43 31	038	33 14	103	51 13	148	33 05	173	57 01	232	34 24	273
96	43 59	038	33 59	104	51 37	150	33 10	174	56 24	233	33 38	274
97	44 27	038	34 44	104	51 59	151	33 14	176	55 47	235	32 52	274
98	44 56	038	35 28	105	52 21	153	33 17	177	55 09	236	32 07	275
99	45 24	038	36 12	106	52 42	154	33 19	178	54 31	237	31 21	275
100	45 52	038	36 56	107	53 01	156	33 20	179	53 52	238	30 35	276
101	46 20	038	37 40	107	53 19	157	33 20	180	53 13	240	29 49	277
102	46 48	038	38 24	108	53 36	159	33 20	181	52 33	241	29 04	277
103	47 17	038	39 08	109	53 52	161	33 18	182	51 52	242	28 18	278
104	47 45	038	39 51	110	54 07	162	33 16	184	51 12	243	27 33	278
	Dubhe		REGULUS		PROCYON		SIRIUS		ALDEBARAN		CAPELLA	
105	48 13	038	40 34	111	54 20	164	33 12	185	50 31	244	69 47	296
106	48 41	038	41 17	112	54 32	166	33 08	186	49 49	245	69 05	296
107	49 09	038	41 59	113	54 43	167	33 03	187	49 07	246	68 24	295
108	49 37	038	42 42	114	54 52	169	32 57	188	48 25	247	67 42	295
109	50 05	038	43 24	115	55 00	171	32 50	189	47 43	248	67 01	295
110	50 33	037	44 05	115	55 07	172	32 42	190	47 00	249	66 19	295
111	51 01	037	44 47	116	55 12	174	32 33	192	46 17	250	65 37	295
112	51 29	037	45 28	117	55 16	176	32 24	193	45 33	251	64 56	295
113	51 57	037	46 08	118	55 19	178	32 13	194	44 50	252	64 14	295
114	52 25	037	46 48	119	55 20	179	32 02	195	44 06	253	63 32	295
115	52 52	037	47 28	121	55 19	181	31 50	196	43 22	253	62 51	295
116	53 20	037	48 08	122	55 18	183	31 36	197	42 38	254	62 09	295
117	53 47	036	48 47	123	55 15	185	31 22	198	41 54	255	61 27	295
118	54 14	036	49 25	124	55 10	186	31 08	199	41 09	256	60 46	295
119	54 41	036	50 03	125	55 04	188	30 52	200	40 25	257	60 04	295
	Dubhe		REGULUS		PROCYON		BETELGEUSE		ALDEBARAN		CAPELLA	
120	55 08	036	50 40	126	54 57	190	46 47	230	39 40	258	59 22	295
121	55 35	036	51 17	127	54 48	192	46 12	231	38 55	258	58 41	295
122	56 02	035	51 53	129	54 39	193	45 36	232	38 10	259	57 59	295
123	56 28	035	52 29	130	54 27	195	44 59	233	37 25	260	57 18	295
124	56 54	035	53 04	131	54 15	197	44 22	234	36 39	261	56 36	296
125	57 20	034	53 38	133	54 01	198	43 45	235	35 54	261	55 55	296
126	57 46	034	54 12	134	53 46	200	43 07	236	35 08	262	55 13	296
127	58 12	034	54 44	135	53 30	202	42 28	237	34 23	263	54 32	296
128	58 37	033	55 16	137	53 12	203	41 50	238	33 37	263	53 51	296
129	59 02	033	55 47	138	52 53	205	41 10	239	32 52	264	53 10	296
130	59 27	032	56 18	140	52 34	206	40 31	240	32 06	265	52 28	297
131	59 51	032	56 47	141	52 13	208	39 50	241	31 20	265	51 47	297
132	60 15	031	57 15	143	51 51	209	39 10	242	30 34	266	51 06	297
133	60 39	031	57 42	144	51 28	211	38 29	243	29 48	267	50 26	297
134	61 02	030	58 09	146	51 04	212	37 48	244	29 02	268	49 45	297
	Kochab		ARCTURUS		REGULUS		PROCYON		BETELGEUSE		CAPELLA	
135	38 51	020	20 59	082	58 34	148	50 39	214	37 06	245	49 04	298
136	39 06	020	21 44	082	58 58	149	50 13	215	36 25	246	48 23	298
137	39 22	020	22 30	083	59 21	151	49 46	216	35 43	247	47 43	298
138	39 39	020	23 15	084	59 42	153	49 18	218	35 00	248	47 02	298
139	39 55	021	24 01	084	60 02	155	48 49	219	34 18	248	46 72	299
140	40 11	021	24 47	085	60 21	157	48 20	220	33 35	249	45 42	299
141	40 27	021	25 33	085	60 39	159	47 50	222	32 52	250	45 01	299
142	40 43	021	26 18	086	60 55	160	47 19	223	32 08	251	44 21	299
143	40 59	021	27 04	087	61 09	162	46 47	224	31 25	252	43 41	300
144	41 15	021	27 50	087	61 22	164	46 14	225	30 41	252	43 02	300
145	41 32	021	28 36	088	61 34	166	45 41	227	29 57	253	42 22	300
146	41 48	021	29 22	089	61 44	168	45 08	228	29 13	254	41 42	301
147	42 04	021	30 08	089	61 52	171	44 33	229	28 29	255	41 03	301
148	42 20	021	30 54	090	61 59	173	43 58	230	27 45	255	40 23	301
149	42 36	021	31 40	090	62 04	175	43 23	231	27 00	256	39 44	302
	Kochab		ARCTURUS		SPICA		REGULUS		PROCYON		CAPELLA	
150	42 53	021	32 26	091	20 42	126	62 08	177	42 46	232	39 05	302
151	43 09	021	33 12	092	21 19	126	62 10	179	42 10	233	38 26	302
152	43 25	021	33 58	092	21 56	127	62 10	181	41 33	234	37 47	302
153	43 41	021	34 44	093	22 32	128	62 08	183	40 55	235	37 08	303
154	43 57	020	35 30	094	23 08	129	62 05	185	40 17	236	36 30	303
155	44 13	020	36 15	094	23 44	130	62 00	187	39 38	237	35 51	303
156	44 29	020	37 01	095	24 19	131	61 53	189	38 59	238	35 13	304
157	44 45	020	37 47	096	24 54	132	61 45	191	38 20	239	34 35	304
158	45 01	020	38 33	097	25 28	132	61 35	193	37 40	240	33 57	304
159	45 17	020	39 18	097	26 02	133	61 24	195	37 00	241	33 19	305
160	45 33	020	40 04	098	26 35	134	61 11	197	36 20	242	32 42	305
161	45 49	020	40 49	099	27 07	135	60 57	199	35 39	243	32 04	306
162	46 04	020	41 35	100	27 40	136	60 41	201	34 58	244	31 27	306
163	46 20	020	42 20	100	28 11	137	60 23	203	34 16	245	30 50	306
164	46 35	020	43 05	101	28 42	138	60 05	205	33 35	246	30 13	307
	Kochab		ARCTURUS		SPICA		REGULUS		POLLUX		CAPELLA	
165	46 51	020	43 50	102	29 13	139	59 45	207	48 03	269	29 36	307
166	47 06	019	44 35	103	29 43	140	59 23	209	47 17	270	28 59	307
167	47 21	019	45 20	103	30 12	141	59 01	210	46 31	271	28 23	308
168	47 36	019	46 04	104	30 41	142	58 37	212	45 45	271	27 47	308
169	47 51	019	46 49	105	31 09	143	58 12	214	44 59	272	27 11	309
170	48 06	019	47 33	106	31 36	144	57 46	215	44 13	272	26 35	309
171	48 21	019	48 17	107	32 03	145	57 19	217	43 27	273	25 59	309
172	48 35	018	49 01	108	32 29	146	56 50	219	42 41	274	25 24	310
173	48 50	018	49 45	109	32 55	147	56 21	220	41 56	274	24 49	310
174	49 04	018	50 28	110	33 19	148	55 51	222	41 10	275	24 14	311
175	49 18	018	51 11	111	33 43	149	55 20	223	40 24	275	23 39	311
176	49 32	018	51 54	112	34 06	150	54 48	225	39 38	276	23 05	311
177	49 46	017	52 37	113	34 29	151	54 16	226	38 52	277	22 30	312
178	50 00	017	53 19	114	34 51	152	53 42	227	38 07	277	21 56	312
179	50 13	017	54 01	115	35 12	154	53 08	229	37 21	278	21 22	313

Appendix I-2

LAT 40°N

LHA T	Hc	Zn	Hc	Zn	Hc	Zn	Hc	Zn	Hc	Zn	Hc	Zn
	VEGA		ARCTURUS		SPICA		REGULUS		POLLUX		CAPELLA	
180	18 03	054	54 43	116	35 32	155	52 33	230	36 36	278	20 49	313
181	18 41	055	55 24	117	35 51	156	51 58	231	35 50	279	20 15	314
182	19 18	055	56 05	118	36 09	157	51 22	232	35 05	279	19 42	314
183	19 56	056	56 45	119	36 27	158	50 45	234	34 20	280	19 09	315
184	20 34	056	57 25	121	36 43	159	50 07	235	33 34	280	18 37	315
185	21 12	057	58 04	122	36 59	160	49 30	236	32 49	281	18 04	316
186	21 51	057	58 43	123	37 14	162	48 51	237	32 04	282	17 32	316
187	22 29	058	59 21	124	37 28	163	48 12	238	31 19	282	17 00	316
188	23 08	058	59 59	126	37 41	164	47 33	239	30 34	283	16 29	317
189	23 47	058	60 36	127	37 53	165	46 53	240	29 49	283	15 58	317
190	24 27	059	61 12	129	38 05	167	46 13	241	29 05	284	15 27	318
191	25 06	059	61 47	130	38 15	168	45 33	242	28 20	284	14 56	318
192	25 46	060	62 22	132	38 24	169	44 52	243	27 36	285	14 26	319
193	26 26	060	62 56	134	38 32	170	44 10	244	26 51	285	13 56	319
194	27 06	061	63 28	135	38 40	171	43 29	245	26 07	286	13 26	320
	VEGA		ARCTURUS		SPICA		REGULUS		POLLUX		Dubhe	
195	27 46	061	64 00	137	38 46	173	42 47	246	25 23	286	61 40	331
196	28 26	062	64 31	139	38 51	174	42 05	247	24 39	287	61 17	330
197	29 07	062	65 01	141	38 56	175	41 22	248	23 55	288	60 54	330
198	29 47	063	65 29	143	38 59	177	40 39	249	23 11	288	60 30	329
199	30 28	063	65 56	145	39 01	178	39 56	250	22 28	289	60 06	328
200	31 09	063	66 22	147	39 03	179	39 13	251	21 44	289	59 42	328
201	31 51	064	66 47	149	39 03	180	38 29	252	21 01	290	59 18	328
202	32 32	064	67 10	151	39 02	182	37 46	252	20 18	290	58 53	327
203	33 13	065	67 31	153	39 00	183	37 02	253	19 34	291	58 28	327
204	33 55	065	67 51	156	38 58	184	36 18	254	18 52	291	58 02	326
205	34 37	066	68 09	158	38 54	185	35 33	255	18 09	292	57 37	326
206	35 19	066	68 25	161	38 49	187	34 49	256	17 26	292	57 11	326
207	36 01	066	68 39	163	38 43	188	34 04	256	16 44	293	56 45	325
208	36 43	067	68 52	166	38 36	189	33 20	257	16 02	294	56 19	325
209	37 25	067	69 02	168	38 29	190	32 35	258	15 20	294	55 52	325
	DENEB		VEGA		ARCTURUS		SPICA		REGULUS		Dubhe	
210	21 12	048	38 08	068	69 11	171	38 20	192	31 50	259	55 25	324
211	21 46	049	38 50	068	69 17	173	38 10	193	31 05	259	54 59	324
212	22 21	049	39 33	068	69 21	176	38 00	194	30 19	260	54 32	324
213	22 56	049	40 16	069	69 23	179	37 48	195	29 34	261	54 04	324
214	23 31	050	40 59	069	69 23	181	37 35	196	28 49	262	53 37	323
215	24 06	050	41 42	070	69 21	184	37 22	198	28 03	262	53 10	323
216	24 42	051	42 25	070	69 16	187	37 07	199	27 18	263	52 42	323
217	25 17	051	43 08	071	69 10	189	36 52	200	26 32	264	52 15	323
218	25 53	052	43 52	071	69 01	192	36 36	201	25 46	264	51 47	323
219	26 29	052	44 35	071	68 51	195	36 19	202	25 00	265	51 19	323
220	27 06	052	45 19	072	68 38	197	36 01	204	24 15	266	50 51	323
221	27 42	053	46 02	072	68 24	200	35 42	205	23 29	266	50 23	322
222	28 19	053	46 46	073	68 07	202	35 22	206	22 43	267	49 55	322
223	28 56	054	47 30	073	67 49	204	35 02	207	21 57	268	49 27	322
224	29 33	054	48 14	073	67 29	207	34 41	208	21 11	268	48 59	322
	DENEB		VEGA		ALTAIR		ANTARES		ARCTURUS		Dubhe	
225	30 10	054	48 58	074	19 13	095	20 38	159	67 08	209	48 31	322
226	30 48	055	49 42	074	19 59	095	20 54	160	66 45	211	48 03	322
227	31 25	055	50 27	075	20 45	096	21 09	161	66 20	213	47 35	322
228	32 03	056	51 11	075	21 31	097	21 24	162	65 54	215	47 06	322
229	32 41	056	51 55	075	22 16	097	21 38	163	65 27	217	46 38	322
230	33 19	056	52 40	076	23 02	098	21 51	164	64 58	219	46 10	322
231	33 57	057	53 24	076	23 47	099	22 03	165	64 29	221	45 42	322
232	34 36	057	54 09	076	24 33	099	22 15	166	63 58	223	45 14	322
233	35 14	057	54 54	077	25 18	100	22 26	167	63 26	225	44 45	322
234	35 53	058	55 39	077	26 03	101	22 36	168	62 53	227	44 17	322
235	36 32	058	56 23	078	26 48	102	22 46	169	62 19	228	43 49	322
236	37 11	058	57 08	078	27 33	102	22 54	170	61 44	230	43 21	322
237	37 50	059	57 53	078	28 18	103	23 02	171	61 09	231	42 53	322
238	38 30	059	58 38	079	29 03	104	23 09	171	60 33	233	42 25	323
239	39 09	059	59 24	079	29 47	105	23 16	172	59 56	234	41 57	323
	DENEB		VEGA		ALTAIR		ANTARES		ARCTURUS		Dubhe	
240	39 49	060	60 09	080	30 32	105	23 22	173	59 18	236	41 29	323
241	40 28	060	60 54	080	31 16	106	23 26	174	58 40	237	41 02	323
242	41 08	060	61 39	080	32 00	107	23 31	175	58 01	238	40 34	323
243	41 48	061	62 25	081	32 44	108	23 34	176	57 22	240	40 06	323
244	42 28	061	63 10	081	33 28	108	23 36	177	56 42	241	39 39	323
245	43 09	061	63 56	082	34 11	109	23 38	178	56 01	242	39 11	323
246	43 49	061	64 41	082	34 54	110	23 39	179	55 20	243	38 44	324
247	44 29	062	65 27	083	35 37	111	23 39	180	54 39	244	38 17	324
248	45 10	062	66 12	083	36 20	112	23 39	181	53 58	245	37 49	324
249	45 51	062	66 58	083	37 03	113	23 37	182	53 16	246	37 22	324
250	46 31	063	67 44	084	37 45	113	23 35	183	52 33	247	36 55	324
251	47 12	063	68 29	084	38 27	114	23 32	184	51 51	248	36 29	324
252	47 53	063	69 15	085	39 09	115	23 28	185	51 08	249	36 02	325
253	**48 34**	**063**	**70 01**	**085**	**39 50**	**116**	**23 24**	**186**	**50 25**	**250**	**35 35**	**325**
254	**49 15**	**064**	**70 47**	**086**	**40 31**	**117**	**23 19**	**187**	**49 41**	**251**	**35 09**	**325**
	DENEB		ALTAIR		Nunki		ANTARES		ARCTURUS		Dubhe	
255	49 57	064	41 12	118	18 39	153	23 13	188	48 58	252	34 42	325
256	50 38	064	41 52	119	18 59	154	23 06	189	48 14	253	34 16	325
257	51 19	064	42 32	120	19 19	155	22 58	190	47 30	254	33 50	326
258	52 01	065	43 12	121	19 38	156	22 50	191	46 45	255	33 24	326
259	52 42	065	43 51	122	19 56	157	22 41	192	46 01	256	32 58	326
260	53 24	065	44 30	123	20 13	158	22 31	193	45 16	257	32 33	326
261	54 06	065	45 08	124	20 30	159	22 20	194	44 31	257	32 07	326
262	54 48	065	45 46	125	20 47	160	22 09	195	43 46	258	31 42	327
263	55 29	066	46 23	126	21 02	161	21 57	196	43 01	259	31 17	327
264	56 11	066	47 00	127	21 17	162	21 44	197	42 16	260	30 52	327
265	56 53	066	47 36	129	21 31	162	21 31	198	41 31	261	30 27	327
266	57 35	066	48 12	130	21 45	163	21 16	198	40 46	261	30 03	328
267	58 17	066	48 47	131	21 58	164	21 01	199	40 00	262	29 38	328
268	58 59	066	49 21	132	22 10	165	20 46	200	39 15	263	29 14	328
269	59 42	067	49 55	133	22 21	166	20 29	201	38 29	263	28 50	329

LAT 40°N

LHA T	Hc	Zn	Hc	Zn	Hc	Zn	Hc	Zn	Hc	Zn	Hc	Zn
	DENEB		ALTAIR		Nunki		Rasalhague		ARCTURUS		Kochab	
270	60 24	067	50 28	135	22 31	167	61 57	194	37 43	264	49 24	342
271	61 06	067	51 00	136	22 41	168	61 45	196	36 57	265	49 10	342
272	61 48	067	51 32	137	22 50	169	61 32	198	36 12	266	48 56	342
273	62 30	067	52 02	139	22 59	170	61 17	200	35 26	266	48 41	342
274	63 13	067	52 32	140	23 06	171	61 00	202	34 40	267	48 27	341
275	63 55	067	53 01	142	23 13	172	60 42	204	33 54	268	48 12	341
276	64 37	067	53 29	143	23 19	173	60 23	206	33 08	268	47 57	341
277	65 20	067	53 56	145	23 24	174	60 02	208	32 22	269	47 42	341
278	66 02	067	54 23	146	23 29	175	59 40	209	31 36	270	47 27	341
279	66 44	067	54 48	148	23 32	176	59 17	211	30 50	270	47 12	341
280	67 27	067	55 12	149	23 35	177	58 53	213	30 04	271	46 57	341
281	68 09	067	55 35	151	23 37	178	58 27	215	29 18	271	46 41	340
282	68 51	067	55 57	152	23 39	179	58 00	216	28 32	272	46 26	340
283	69 33	067	56 17	154	23 39	180	57 33	218	27 46	273	46 10	340
284	70 16	066	56 37	156	23 39	181	57 04	219	27 01	273	45 55	340
	DENEB		Alpheratz		ALTAIR		Rasalhague		ARCTURUS		Kochab	
285	70 58	066	27 47	074	56 55	157	56 34	221	26 15	274	45 39	340
286	71 40	066	28 31	075	57 12	159	56 04	222	25 29	275	45 23	340
287	72 21	066	29 15	075	57 28	161	55 32	224	24 43	275	45 08	340
288	73 03	065	30 00	076	57 42	163	55 00	225	23 57	276	44 52	340
289	73 45	065	30 45	076	57 55	165	54 27	227	23 12	276	44 36	340
290	74 26	064	31 29	077	58 06	166	53 53	228	22 26	277	44 20	340
291	75 08	064	32 14	078	58 16	168	53 18	229	21 40	278	44 04	340
292	75 49	063	32 59	078	58 25	170	52 43	231	20 55	278	43 48	339
293	76 29	062	33 44	079	58 32	172	52 07	232	20 09	279	43 31	339
294	77 10	061	34 29	079	58 38	174	51 31	233	19 24	279	43 15	339
295	77 50	060	35 14	080	58 42	176	50 54	234	18 39	280	42 59	339
296	78 29	059	36 00	080	58 45	178	50 16	236	17 53	281	42 43	339
297	79 09	058	36 45	081	58 46	180	49 38	237	17 08	281	42 27	339
298	79 47	056	37 30	081	58 45	182	48 59	238	16 23	282	42 11	339
299	80 25	054	38 16	082	58 43	183	48 20	239	15 38	282	41 54	339
	Schedar		Alpheratz		ALTAIR		Rasalhague		VEGA		Kochab	
300	43 06	045	39 01	082	58 40	185	47 40	240	73 41	272	41 38	339
301	43 39	046	39 47	083	58 35	187	47 00	241	72 55	273	41 22	339
302	44 12	046	40 33	084	58 28	189	46 20	242	72 09	273	41 06	339
303	44 44	046	41 18	084	58 20	191	45 39	243	71 23	274	40 49	339
304	45 17	046	42 04	085	58 11	193	44 58	244	70 37	274	40 33	339
305	45 50	046	42 50	085	58 00	195	44 16	245	69 51	275	40 17	339
306	46 24	046	43 36	086	57 48	196	43 34	246	69 05	275	40 01	339
307	46 57	046	44 22	087	57 34	198	42 52	247	68 20	276	39 45	340
308	47 30	046	45 07	087	57 19	200	42 10	248	67 34	276	39 29	340
309	48 03	046	45 53	088	57 02	202	41 27	249	66 48	277	39 13	340
310	48 36	046	46 39	088	56 45	204	40 44	250	66 03	277	38 57	340
311	49 09	046	47 25	089	56 26	205	40 01	251	65 17	278	38 41	340
312	49 43	046	48 11	090	56 05	207	39 17	251	64 32	278	38 25	340
313	50 16	046	48 57	090	55 44	209	38 34	252	63 46	278	38 09	340
314	50 49	046	49 43	091	55 22	210	37 50	253	63 01	279	37 53	340
	Schedar		Alpheratz		FOMALHAUT		ALTAIR		VEGA		Kochab	
315	51 23	046	50 29	092	15 12	154	54 58	212	62 15	279	37 38	340
316	51 56	046	51 15	092	15 32	155	54 33	213	61 30	280	37 22	340
317	52 29	046	52 01	093	15 51	156	54 07	215	60 45	280	37 07	340
318	53 02	046	52 47	094	16 09	157	53 41	216	59 59	280	36 51	340
319	53 35	046	53 33	094	16 27	158	53 13	218	59 14	281	36 36	340
320	54 09	046	54 19	095	16 44	159	52 44	219	58 29	281	36 20	341
321	54 42	046	55 04	096	17 01	159	52 15	221	57 44	282	36 05	341
322	55 15	046	55 50	097	17 16	160	51 45	222	56 59	282	35 50	341
323	55 48	046	56 36	097	17 32	161	51 13	223	56 14	282	35 35	341
324	56 21	046	57 21	098	17 46	162	50 41	225	55 29	283	35 20	341
325	56 53	045	58 07	099	18 00	163	50 09	226	54 44	283	35 05	341
326	57 26	045	58 52	100	18 13	164	49 35	227	54 00	284	34 50	341
327	57 59	045	59 37	101	18 26	165	49 01	228	53 15	284	34 35	341
328	58 31	045	60 22	102	18 38	166	48 27	230	52 31	284	34 21	342
329	59 03	045	61 07	102	18 49	166	47 51	231	51 46	285	34 06	342
	CAPELLA		Alpheratz		FOMALHAUT		ALTAIR		VEGA		Kochab	
330	17 05	044	61 52	103	18 59	167	47 15	232	51 02	285	33 52	342
331	17 37	044	62 37	104	19 09	168	46 39	233	50 17	286	33 38	342
332	18 09	045	63 21	105	19 18	169	45 02	234	49 33	286	33 24	342
333	18 41	045	64 05	107	19 26	170	45 24	235	48 49	286	33 10	342
334	19 14	045	64 49	108	19 34	171	44 46	236	48 05	287	32 56	343
335	19 47	046	65 33	109	19 41	172	44 07	238	47 21	287	32 42	343
336	20 20	046	66 16	110	19 47	173	43 28	239	46 37	288	32 29	343
337	20 53	047	66 59	111	19 53	174	42 49	240	45 53	288	32 15	343
338	21 27	047	67 42	113	19 57	175	42 09	241	45 10	288	32 02	343
339	22 01	048	68 24	114	20 01	176	41 29	242	44 26	289	31 49	343
340	22 35	048	69 06	115	20 04	176	40 48	243	43 43	289	31 36	344
341	23 09	049	69 47	117	20 07	177	40 07	243	42 59	290	31 23	344
342	23 44	049	70 28	119	20 09	178	39 26	244	42 16	290	31 10	344
343	**24 19**	**049**	**71 08**	**120**	**20 10**	**179**	**38 45**	**245**	**41 33**	**290**	**30 57**	**344**
344	**24 54**	**050**	**71 47**	**122**	**20 10**	**180**	**38 03**	**246**	**40 50**	**291**	**30 45**	**344**
	CAPELLA		ALDEBARAN		FOMALHAUT		ALTAIR		VEGA		Kochab	
345	25 29	050	15 26	081	20 09	181	37 20	247	40 07	291	30 33	345
346	26 04	051	16 12	082	20 08	182	36 38	248	39 24	292	30 21	345
347	26 40	051	16 57	083	20 06	183	35 55	249	38 41	292	30 09	345
348	27 16	051	17 43	083	20 04	184	35 12	250	37 59	292	29 57	345
349	27 52	052	18 29	084	20 00	185	34 29	250	37 16	293	29 45	345
350	28 28	052	19 14	084	19 56	186	33 46	251	36 34	293	29 34	345
351	29 04	053	20 00	085	19 51	187	33 02	252	35 52	294	29 23	346
352	29 41	053	20 46	086	19 45	187	32 18	253	35 10	294	29 11	346
353	30 18	053	21 32	086	19 39	188	31 34	254	34 28	295	29 01	346
354	30 55	054	22 18	087	19 32	189	30 50	254	33 46	295	28 50	347
355	31 32	054	23 03	087	19 24	190	30 06	255	33 05	295	28 39	347
356	32 09	054	23 49	088	19 16	191	29 21	256	32 23	296	28 29	347
357	32 47	055	24 35	089	19 06	192	28 37	257	31 42	296	28 19	347
358	33 24	055	25 21	089	18 56	193	27 52	257	31 01	297	28 09	348
359	34 02	056	26 07	090	18 46	194	27 07	258	30 20	297	27 59	348

Appendix J-1

65°, 295° L.H.A. **LATITUDE SAME NAME AS DECLINATION** N. Lat. {L.H.A. greater than 180° ...... Zn=Z; L.H.A. less than 180° ...... Zn=360°−Z}

	30°			31°			32°			33°		
Dec.	Hc	d	Z	Hc	d	Z	Hc	d	Z	Hc	d	Z
°	° ′	′	°	° ′	′	°	° ′	′	°	° ′	′	°
0	21 28.1	+32.1	103.1	21 14.3	+33.0	103.5	21 00.1	+33.9	103.9	20 45.5	+34.9	104.3
1	22 00.2	31.8	102.2	21 47.3	32.8	102.6	21 34.0	33.7	103.0	21 20.4	34.5	103.4
2	22 32.0	31.5	101.3	22 20.1	32.4	101.7	22 07.7	33.3	102.1	21 54.9	34.3	102.5
3	23 03.5	31.1	100.4	22 52.5	32.1	100.8	22 41.0	33.1	101.2	22 29.2	33.9	101.6
4	23 34.6	30.8	99.4	23 24.6	31.7	99.9	23 14.1	32.7	100.3	23 03.1	33.7	100.7
5	24 05.4	+30.5	98.5	23 56.3	+31.5	98.9	23 46.8	+32.4	99.4	23 36.8	+33.3	99.8
6	24 35.9	30.1	97.6	24 27.8	31.1	98.0	24 19.2	32.0	98.5	24 10.1	33.0	98.9
7	25 06.0	29.8	96.6	24 58.9	30.7	97.1	24 51.2	31.8	97.5	24 43.1	32.7	98.0
8	25 35.8	29.3	95.6	25 29.6	30.4	96.1	25 23.0	31.3	96.6	25 15.8	32.4	97.1
9	26 05.1	29.0	94.7	26 00.0	30.0	95.2	25 54.3	31.0	95.6	25 48.2	31.9	96.1
10	26 34.1	+28.6	93.7	26 30.0	+29.5	94.2	26 25.3	+30.6	94.7	26 20.1	+31.6	95.2
11	27 02.7	28.1	92.7	26 59.5	29.2	93.2	26 55.9	30.2	93.7	26 51.7	31.3	94.2
12	27 30.8	27.7	91.7	27 28.7	28.8	92.2	27 26.1	29.8	92.8	27 23.0	30.8	93.3
13	27 58.5	27.3	90.7	27 57.5	28.3	91.2	27 55.9	29.4	91.8	27 53.8	30.4	92.3
14	28 25.8	26.8	89.7	28 25.8	27.9	90.2	28 25.3	28.9	90.8	28 24.2	30.0	91.3
15	28 52.6	+26.4	88.7	28 53.7	+27.5	89.2	28 54.2	+28.5	89.8	28 54.2	+29.5	90.3
16	29 19.0	25.9	87.7	29 21.2	26.9	88.2	29 22.7	28.1	88.8	29 23.7	29.1	89.3
17	29 44.9	25.4	86.6	29 48.1	26.5	87.2	29 50.8	27.5	87.8	29 52.8	28.6	88.3
18	30 10.3	24.9	85.6	30 14.6	26.0	86.2	30 18.3	27.1	86.7	30 21.4	28.2	87.3
19	30 35.2	24.4	84.5	30 40.6	25.5	85.1	30 45.4	26.6	85.7	30 49.6	27.7	86.3
20	30 59.6	+23.8	83.5	31 06.1	+25.0	84.1	31 12.0	+26.1	84.7	31 17.3	+27.1	85.3
21	31 23.4	23.4	82.4	31 31.1	24.4	83.0	31 38.1	25.5	83.6	31 44.4	26.7	84.2
22	31 46.8	22.7	81.3	31 55.5	23.9	81.9	32 03.6	25.0	82.5	32 11.1	26.1	83.2
23	32 09.5	22.2	80.2	32 19.4	23.3	80.8	32 28.6	24.5	81.5	32 37.2	25.6	82.1
24	32 31.7	21.7	79.1	32 42.7	22.8	79.7	32 53.1	23.9	80.4	33 02.8	25.0	81.0
25	32 53.4	+21.0	78.0	33 05.5	+22.2	78.6	33 17.0	+23.3	79.3	33 27.8	+24.4	79.9
26	33 14.4	20.4	76.9	33 27.7	21.5	77.5	33 40.3	22.7	78.2	33 52.2	23.9	78.8
27	33 34.8	19.8	75.8	33 49.2	21.0	76.4	34 03.0	22.1	77.1	34 16.1	23.2	77.7
28	33 54.6	19.2	74.6	34 10.2	20.3	75.3	34 25.1	21.5	75.9	34 39.3	22.7	76.6
29	34 13.8	18.5	73.5	34 30.5	19.7	74.1	34 46.6	20.8	74.8	35 02.0	22.0	75.5
30	34 32.3	+17.9	72.3	34 50.2	+19.0	73.0	35 07.4	+20.2	73.7	35 24.0	+21.3	74.3
31	34 50.2	17.2	71.2	35 09.2	18.4	71.8	35 27.6	19.5	72.5	35 45.3	20.7	73.2
32	35 07.4	16.6	70.0	35 27.6	17.7	70.7	35 47.1	18.9	71.3	36 06.0	20.0	72.0
33	35 24.0	15.8	68.8	35 45.3	17.0	69.5	36 06.0	18.2	70.2	36 26.0	19.3	70.9
34	35 39.8	15.2	67.6	36 02.3	16.3	68.3	36 24.2	17.4	69.0	36 45.3	18.6	69.7
35	35 55.0	+14.4	66.4	36 18.6	+15.6	67.1	36 41.6	+16.7	67.8	37 03.9	+17.9	68.5
36	36 09.4	13.7	65.2	36 34.2	14.8	65.9	36 58.3	16.1	66.6	37 21.8	17.2	67.3
37	36 23.1	13.0	64.0	36 49.0	14.2	64.7	37 14.4	15.2	65.4	37 39.0	16.4	66.1
38	36 36.1	12.2	62.8	37 03.2	13.3	63.5	37 29.6	14.5	64.2	37 55.4	15.7	64.9
39	36 48.3	11.5	61.6	37 16.5	12.6	62.3	37 44.1	13.8	63.0	38 11.1	14.9	63.6
40	36 59.8	+10.7	60.4	37 29.1	+11.9	61.0	37 57.9	+13.0	61.7	38 26.0	+14.1	62.4
41	37 10.5	9.9	59.1	37 41.0	11.0	59.8	38 10.9	12.1	60.5	38 40.1	13.3	61.2
42	37 20.4	9.2	57.9	37 52.0	10.3	58.6	38 23.0	11.4	59.2	38 53.4	12.5	59.9
43	37 29.6	8.4	56.7	38 02.3	9.5	57.3	38 34.4	10.6	58.0	39 05.9	11.7	58.7
44	37 38.0	7.6	55.4	38 11.8	8.7	56.1	38 45.0	9.8	56.7	39 17.6	10.9	57.4
45	37 45.6	+6.8	54.2	38 20.5	+7.8	54.8	38 54.8	+8.9	55.4	39 28.5	+10.0	56.1
46	37 52.4	6.0	52.9	38 28.3	7.1	53.5	39 03.7	8.1	54.2	39 38.5	9.2	54.8
47	37 58.4	5.1	51.6	38 35.4	6.2	52.3	39 11.8	7.3	52.9	39 47.7	8.4	53.6
48	38 03.5	4.4	50.4	38 41.6	5.3	51.0	39 19.1	6.4	51.6	39 56.1	7.4	52.3
49	38 07.9	3.5	49.1	38 46.9	4.6	49.7	39 25.5	5.6	50.3	40 03.5	6.6	51.0
50	38 11.4	+2.8	47.8	38 51.5	+3.7	48.4	39 31.1	+4.7	49.0	40 10.1	+5.8	49.7
51	38 14.2	1.9	46.6	38 55.2	2.9	47.1	39 35.8	3.8	47.7	40 15.9	4.8	48.4
52	38 16.1	1.0	45.3	38 58.1	2.0	45.9	39 39.6	3.0	46.5	40 20.7	4.0	47.1
53	38 17.1	+0.3	44.0	39 00.1	1.1	44.6	39 42.6	2.1	45.2	40 24.7	3.1	45.8
54	38 17.4	−0.6	42.7	39 01.2	+0.4	43.3	39 44.7	1.3	43.9	40 27.8	2.2	44.4
55	38 16.8	−1.4	41.5	39 01.6	−0.6	42.0	39 46.0	+0.3	42.6	40 30.0	+1.3	43.1
56	38 15.4	2.2	40.2	39 01.0	1.3	40.7	39 46.3	−0.5	41.3	40 31.3	+0.4	41.8
57	38 13.2	3.1	38.9	38 59.7	2.3	39.4	39 45.8	1.3	40.0	40 31.7	−0.5	40.5
58	38 10.1	3.9	37.7	38 57.4	3.0	38.1	39 44.5	2.3	38.7	40 31.2	1.4	39.2
59	38 06.2	4.7	36.4	38 54.4	3.9	36.9	39 42.2	3.1	37.4	40 29.8	2.3	37.9
60	38 01.5	−5.5	35.1	38 50.5	−4.8	35.6	39 39.1	−3.9	36.1	40 27.5	−3.2	36.6
61	37 56.0	6.3	33.9	38 45.7	5.6	34.3	39 35.2	4.9	34.8	40 24.3	4.1	35.2
62	37 49.7	7.1	32.6	38 40.1	6.4	33.0	39 30.3	5.7	33.5	40 20.2	4.9	33.9
63	37 42.6	7.9	31.3	38 33.7	7.2	31.7	39 24.6	6.5	32.2	40 15.3	5.8	32.6
64	37 34.7	8.7	30.1	38 26.5	8.1	30.5	39 18.1	7.4	30.9	40 09.5	6.7	31.3
65	37 26.0	−9.5	28.8	38 18.4	−8.8	29.2	39 10.7	−8.2	29.6	40 02.8	−7.6	30.0
66	37 16.5	10.3	27.6	38 09.6	9.7	28.0	39 02.5	9.1	28.3	39 55.2	8.4	28.7
67	37 06.2	11.0	26.4	37 59.9	10.5	26.7	38 53.4	9.9	27.1	39 46.8	9.3	27.4
68	36 55.2	11.8	25.1	37 49.4	11.2	25.5	38 43.5	10.7	25.8	39 37.5	10.1	26.2
69	36 43.4	12.5	23.9	37 38.2	12.0	24.2	38 32.8	11.5	24.5	39 27.4	11.0	24.9
70	36 30.9	−13.3	22.7	37 26.2	−12.8	23.0	38 21.3	−12.3	23.3	39 16.4	−11.8	23.6
71	36 17.6	14.0	21.5	37 13.4	13.6	21.7	38 09.0	13.0	22.0	39 04.6	12.6	22.3
72	36 03.6	14.7	20.3	36 59.8	14.3	20.5	37 56.0	13.9	20.8	38 52.0	13.4	21.1
73	35 48.9	15.5	19.1	36 45.5	15.0	19.3	37 42.1	14.6	19.6	38 38.6	14.2	19.8
74	35 33.4	16.1	17.9	36 30.5	15.8	18.1	37 27.5	15.4	18.3	38 24.4	15.0	18.6
75	35 17.3	−16.8	16.7	36 14.7	−16.4	16.9	37 12.1	−16.1	17.1	38 09.4	−15.7	17.4
76	35 00.5	17.5	15.5	35 58.3	17.2	15.7	36 56.0	16.9	15.9	37 53.7	16.5	16.1
77	34 43.0	18.2	14.4	35 41.1	17.9	14.5	36 39.1	17.5	14.7	37 37.2	17.3	14.9
78	34 24.8	18.8	13.2	35 23.2	18.5	13.4	36 21.6	18.3	13.5	37 19.9	18.0	13.7
79	34 06.0	19.4	12.1	35 04.7	19.2	12.2	36 03.3	18.9	12.4	37 01.9	18.7	12.5
80	33 46.6	−20.1	10.9	34 45.5	−19.8	11.0	35 44.4	−19.6	11.2	36 43.2	−19.4	11.3
81	33 26.5	20.6	9.8	34 25.7	20.5	9.9	35 24.8	20.3	10.0	36 23.8	20.1	10.1
82	33 05.9	21.3	8.7	34 05.2	21.1	8.8	35 04.5	21.0	8.9	36 03.7	20.7	9.0
83	32 44.6	21.9	7.5	33 44.1	21.7	7.6	34 43.5	21.5	7.7	35 43.0	21.4	7.8
84	32 22.7	22.4	6.4	33 22.4	22.4	6.5	34 22.0	22.2	6.6	35 21.6	22.1	6.7
85	32 00.3	−23.0	5.3	33 00.0	−22.8	5.4	33 59.8	−22.8	5.5	34 59.5	−22.7	5.5
86	31 37.3	23.5	4.3	32 37.2	23.5	4.3	33 37.0	23.4	4.4	34 36.8	23.3	4.4
87	31 13.8	24.1	3.2	32 13.7	24.0	3.2	33 13.6	24.0	3.3	34 13.5	23.9	3.3
88	30 49.7	24.6	2.1	31 49.7	24.6	2.1	32 49.6	24.5	2.2	33 49.6	24.5	2.2
89	30 25.1	25.1	1.1	31 25.1	25.1	1.1	32 25.1	25.1	1.1	33 25.1	25.1	1.1
90	30 00.0	−25.6	0.0	31 00.0	−25.6	0.0	32 00.0	−25.6	0.0	33 00.0	−25.6	0.0
	30°			31°			32°			33°		

34°			35°			36°			37°			
Hc	d	Z	Hc	d	Z	Hc	d	Z	Hc	d	Z	Dec.
° ′	′	°	° ′	′	°	° ′	′	°	° ′	′	°	°
20 30.6	+35.7	104.6	20 15.3	+36.5	105.0	19 59.6	+37.4	105.3	19 43.5	+38.3	105.7	0
21 06.3	35.4	103.8	20 51.8	36.3	104.1	20 37.0	37.2	104.5	20 21.8	38.0	104.9	1
21 41.7	35.2	102.9	21 28.1	36.1	103.3	21 14.2	36.9	103.7	20 59.8	37.8	104.0	2
22 16.9	34.8	102.0	22 04.2	35.8	102.4	21 51.1	36.6	102.8	21 37.6	37.5	103.2	3
22 51.7	34.6	101.1	22 40.0	35.4	101.5	22 27.7	36.4	102.0	22 15.1	37.3	102.4	4
23 26.3	+34.3	100.2	23 15.4	+35.2	100.7	23 04.1	+36.1	101.1	22 52.4	+37.0	101.5	5
24 00.6	34.0	99.3	23 50.6	34.9	99.8	23 40.2	35.8	100.2	23 29.4	36.7	100.6	6
24 34.6	33.6	98.4	24 25.5	34.6	98.9	24 16.0	35.5	99.3	24 06.1	36.4	99.8	7
25 08.2	33.3	97.5	25 00.1	34.3	98.0	24 51.5	35.2	98.5	24 42.5	36.1	98.9	8
25 41.5	33.0	96.6	25 34.4	33.9	97.1	25 26.7	34.9	97.6	25 18.6	35.8	98.0	9
26 14.5	+32.5	95.7	26 08.3	+33.5	96.2	26 01.6	+34.5	96.7	25 54.4	+35.4	97.1	10
26 47.0	32.3	94.7	26 41.8	33.2	95.2	26 36.1	34.1	95.7	26 29.8	35.1	96.2	11
27 19.3	31.8	93.8	27 15.0	32.8	94.3	27 10.2	33.8	94.8	27 04.9	34.8	95.3	12
27 51.1	31.4	92.8	27 47.8	32.5	93.4	27 44.0	33.5	93.9	27 39.7	34.4	94.4	13
28 22.5	31.0	91.9	28 20.3	32.0	92.4	28 17.5	33.0	92.9	28 14.1	34.0	93.5	14
28 53.5	+30.6	90.9	28 52.3	+31.6	91.4	28 50.5	+32.6	92.0	28 48.1	+33.6	92.5	15
29 24.1	30.1	89.9	29 23.9	31.2	90.5	29 23.1	32.2	91.0	29 21.7	33.2	91.6	16
29 54.2	29.7	88.9	29 55.1	30.7	89.5	29 55.3	31.8	90.1	29 54.9	32.8	90.6	17
30 23.9	29.3	87.9	30 25.8	30.3	88.5	30 27.1	31.3	89.1	30 27.7	32.4	89.7	18
30 53.2	28.7	86.9	30 56.1	29.8	87.5	30 58.4	30.9	88.1	31 00.1	31.9	88.7	19
31 21.9	+28.3	85.9	31 25.9	+29.3	86.5	31 29.3	+30.4	87.1	31 32.0	+31.5	87.7	20
31 50.2	27.7	84.8	31 55.2	28.9	85.5	31 59.7	29.9	86.1	32 03.5	30.9	86.7	21
32 17.9	27.2	83.8	32 24.1	28.3	84.4	32 29.6	29.4	85.1	32 34.4	30.5	85.7	22
32 45.1	26.7	82.7	32 52.4	27.8	83.4	32 59.0	28.9	84.0	33 04.9	30.0	84.7	23
33 11.8	26.2	81.7	33 20.2	27.2	82.3	33 27.9	28.3	83.0	33 34.9	29.4	83.6	24
33 38.0	+25.5	80.6	33 47.4	+26.7	81.2	33 56.2	+27.8	81.9	34 04.3	+28.9	82.6	25
34 03.5	25.0	79.5	34 14.1	26.1	80.2	34 24.0	27.2	80.8	34 33.2	28.4	81.5	26
34 28.5	24.4	78.4	34 40.2	25.5	79.1	34 51.2	26.7	79.8	35 01.6	27.7	80.4	27
34 52.9	23.8	77.3	35 05.7	25.0	78.0	35 17.9	26.0	78.7	35 29.3	27.2	79.4	28
35 16.7	23.1	76.2	35 30.7	24.3	76.9	35 43.9	25.5	77.6	35 56.5	26.6	78.3	29
35 39.8	+22.5	75.0	35 55.0	+23.6	75.7	36 09.4	+24.8	76.4	36 23.1	+25.9	77.1	30
36 02.3	21.9	73.9	36 18.6	23.0	74.6	36 34.2	24.1	75.3	36 49.0	25.4	76.0	31
36 24.2	21.1	72.7	36 41.6	22.3	73.4	36 58.3	23.5	74.2	37 14.4	24.6	74.9	32
36 45.3	20.5	71.6	37 03.9	21.7	72.3	37 21.8	22.9	73.0	37 39.0	24.0	73.7	33
37 05.8	19.8	70.4	37 25.6	20.9	71.1	37 44.7	22.1	71.8	38 03.0	23.3	72.6	34
37 25.6	+19.1	69.2	37 46.5	+20.3	69.9	38 06.8	+21.4	70.7	38 26.3	+22.5	71.4	35
37 44.7	18.3	68.0	38 06.8	19.5	68.7	38 28.2	20.6	69.5	38 48.8	21.9	70.2	36
38 03.0	17.6	66.8	38 26.3	18.7	67.5	38 48.8	20.0	68.3	39 10.7	21.1	69.0	37
38 20.6	16.8	65.6	38 45.0	18.0	66.3	39 08.8	19.1	67.1	39 31.8	20.3	67.8	38
38 37.4	16.0	64.4	39 03.0	17.2	65.1	39 27.9	18.4	65.8	39 52.1	19.6	66.6	39
38 53.4	+15.3	63.1	39 20.2	+16.5	63.9	39 46.3	+17.6	64.6	40 11.7	+18.8	65.4	40
39 08.7	14.5	61.9	39 36.7	15.6	62.6	40 03.9	16.8	63.3	40 30.5	17.9	64.1	41
39 23.2	13.6	60.6	39 52.3	14.8	61.3	40 20.7	16.0	62.1	40 48.4	17.2	62.9	42
39 36.8	12.9	59.4	40 07.1	14.0	60.1	40 36.7	15.1	60.8	41 05.6	16.3	61.6	43
39 49.7	12.0	58.1	40 21.1	13.1	58.8	40 51.8	14.3	59.5	41 21.9	15.4	60.3	44
40 01.7	+11.1	56.8	40 34.2	+12.2	57.5	41 06.1	+13.4	58.3	41 37.3	+14.6	59.0	45
40 12.8	10.3	55.5	40 46.4	11.5	56.2	41 19.5	12.5	57.0	41 51.9	13.6	57.7	46
40 23.1	9.4	54.2	40 57.9	10.5	54.9	41 32.0	11.7	55.7	42 05.5	12.8	56.4	47
40 32.5	8.6	52.9	41 08.4	9.6	53.6	41 43.7	10.7	54.3	42 18.3	11.9	55.1	48
40 41.1	7.6	51.6	41 18.0	8.7	52.3	41 54.4	9.8	53.0	42 30.2	10.9	53.8	49
40 48.7	+6.8	50.3	41 26.7	+7.9	51.0	42 04.2	+8.9	51.7	42 41.1	+10.0	52.4	50
40 55.5	5.9	49.0	41 34.6	6.9	49.7	42 13.1	8.0	50.4	42 51.1	9.1	51.1	51
41 01.4	4.9	47.7	41 41.5	6.0	48.4	42 21.1	7.0	49.0	43 00.2	8.1	49.7	52
41 06.3	4.1	46.4	41 47.5	5.0	47.0	42 28.1	6.1	47.7	43 08.3	7.1	48.4	53
41 10.4	3.1	45.0	41 52.5	4.2	45.7	42 34.2	5.2	46.3	43 15.4	6.2	47.0	54
41 13.5	+2.3	43.7	41 56.7	+3.2	44.3	42 39.4	+4.1	45.0	43 21.6	+5.1	45.6	55
41 15.8	1.3	42.4	41 59.9	2.2	43.0	42 43.5	3.2	43.6	43 26.7	4.2	44.3	56
41 17.1	+0.4	41.1	42 02.1	1.3	41.7	42 46.7	2.3	42.3	43 30.9	3.2	42.9	57
41 17.5	−0.5	39.7	42 03.4	+0.4	40.3	42 49.0	1.3	40.9	43 34.1	2.2	41.5	58
41 17.0	1.5	38.4	42 03.8	−0.6	39.0	42 50.3	+0.3	39.5	43 36.3	1.3	40.1	59
41 15.5	−2.3	37.1	42 03.2	−1.5	37.6	42 50.6	−0.7	38.2	43 37.6	+0.2	38.8	60
41 13.2	3.3	35.7	42 01.7	2.5	36.3	42 49.9	1.6	36.8	43 37.8	−0.8	37.4	61
41 09.9	4.2	34.4	41 59.2	3.4	34.9	42 48.3	2.6	35.4	43 37.0	1.8	36.0	62
41 05.7	5.1	33.1	41 55.8	4.3	33.6	42 45.7	3.6	34.1	43 35.2	2.8	34.6	63
41 00.6	6.0	31.8	41 51.5	5.3	32.2	42 42.1	4.5	32.7	43 32.4	3.7	33.2	64
40 54.6	−6.9	30.5	41 46.2	−6.2	30.9	42 37.6	−5.5	31.4	43 28.7	−4.8	31.9	65
40 47.7	7.8	29.1	41 40.0	7.1	29.6	42 32.1	6.5	30.0	43 23.9	5.7	30.5	66
40 39.9	8.7	27.8	41 32.9	8.1	28.2	42 25.6	7.4	28.7	43 18.2	6.8	29.1	67
40 31.2	9.5	26.5	41 24.8	8.9	26.9	42 18.2	8.3	27.3	43 11.4	7.6	27.8	68
40 21.7	10.4	25.2	41 15.9	9.8	25.6	42 09.9	9.2	26.0	43 03.8	8.7	26.4	69
40 11.3	−11.3	23.9	41 06.1	−10.8	24.3	42 00.7	−10.2	24.7	42 55.1	−9.6	25.0	70
40 00.0	12.1	22.7	40 55.3	11.6	23.0	41 50.5	11.1	23.3	42 45.5	10.5	23.7	71
39 47.9	12.9	21.4	40 43.7	12.4	21.7	41 39.4	11.9	22.0	42 35.0	11.5	22.4	72
39 35.0	13.8	20.1	40 31.3	13.3	20.4	41 27.5	12.9	20.7	42 23.5	12.4	21.0	73
39 21.2	14.6	18.8	40 18.0	14.2	19.1	41 14.6	13.7	19.4	42 11.1	13.3	19.7	74
39 06.6	−15.3	17.6	40 03.8	15.0	17.8	41 00.9	14.6	18.1	41 57.8	−14.1	18.4	75
38 51.3	16.2	16.4	39 48.8	15.8	16.6	40 46.3	15.5	16.8	41 43.7	15.1	17.1	76
38 35.1	16.9	15.1	39 33.0	16.6	15.3	40 30.8	16.2	15.6	41 28.6	15.9	15.8	77
38 18.2	17.7	13.9	39 16.4	17.4	14.1	40 14.6	17.1	14.3	41 12.7	16.8	14.5	78
38 00.5	18.5	12.7	38 59.0	18.2	12.9	39 57.5	17.9	13.0	40 55.9	17.6	13.2	79
37 42.0	−19.1	11.5	38 40.8	−18.9	11.6	39 39.6	−18.7	11.8	40 38.3	−18.4	12.0	80
37 22.9	19.9	10.3	38 21.9	19.7	10.4	39 20.9	19.4	10.6	40 19.9	19.3	10.7	81
37 03.0	20.6	9.1	38 02.2	20.4	9.2	39 01.5	20.3	9.3	40 00.6	20.0	9.5	82
36 42.4	21.2	7.9	37 41.8	21.1	8.0	38 41.2	20.9	8.1	39 40.6	20.7	8.3	83
36 21.2	22.0	6.8	37 20.7	21.8	6.8	38 20.3	21.7	6.9	39 19.9	21.6	7.0	84
35 59.2	−22.6	5.6	36 58.9	−22.5	5.7	37 58.6	−22.3	5.8	38 58.3	−22.2	5.8	85
35 36.6	23.2	4.5	36 36.4	23.1	4.5	37 36.3	23.1	4.6	38 36.1	23.0	4.6	86
35 13.4	23.9	3.3	36 13.3	23.8	3.4	37 13.2	23.8	3.4	38 13.1	23.7	3.5	87
34 49.5	24.4	2.2	35 49.5	24.4	2.2	36 49.4	24.4	2.3	37 49.4	24.4	2.3	88
34 25.1	25.1	1.1	35 25.1	25.1	1.1	36 25.0	25.0	1.1	37 25.0	25.0	1.1	89
34 00.0	−25.6	0.0	35 00.0	−25.7	0.0	36 00.0	25.7	0.0	37 00.0	−25.7	0.0	90
34°			35°			36°			37°			

65°, 295° L.H.A. **LATITUDE SAME NAME AS DECLINATION**

Appendix J-2

INTERPOLATION TABLE

Dec. Inc.	Altitude Difference (d): Tens 10'	20'	30'	40'	50'	Decimals	Units 0'	1'	2'	3'	4'	5'	6'	7'	8'	9'	Double Second Diff. and Corr.
16.0	2.6	5.3	8.0	10.6	13.3	.0	0.0	0.3	0.5	0.8	1.1	1.4	1.6	1.9	2.2	2.5	
16.1	2.7	5.3	8.0	10.7	13.4	.1	0.0	0.3	0.6	0.9	1.1	1.4	1.7	2.0	2.2	2.5	
16.2	2.7	5.4	8.1	10.8	13.5	.2	0.1	0.3	0.6	0.9	1.2	1.4	1.7	2.0	2.3	2.5	1.0 / 0.1
16.3	2.7	5.4	8.1	10.9	13.6	.3	0.1	0.4	0.6	0.9	1.2	1.5	1.7	2.0	2.3	2.6	3.0 / 0.2
16.4	2.7	5.5	8.2	10.9	13.7	.4	0.1	0.4	0.7	0.9	1.2	1.5	1.8	2.0	2.3	2.6	4.9 / 0.3
16.5	2.8	5.5	8.3	11.0	13.8	.5	0.1	0.4	0.7	1.0	1.2	1.5	1.8	2.1	2.3	2.6	6.9 / 0.4
16.6	2.8	5.5	8.3	11.1	13.8	.6	0.2	0.4	0.7	1.0	1.3	1.5	1.8	2.1	2.4	2.6	8.9 / 0.5
16.7	2.8	5.6	8.4	11.2	13.9	.7	0.2	0.5	0.7	1.0	1.3	1.6	1.8	2.1	2.4	2.7	10.8 / 0.6
16.8	2.8	5.6	8.4	11.2	14.0	.8	0.2	0.5	0.8	1.0	1.3	1.6	1.9	2.1	2.4	2.7	12.8 / 0.7
16.9	2.9	5.7	8.5	11.3	14.1	.9	0.2	0.5	0.8	1.1	1.3	1.6	1.9	2.2	2.4	2.7	14.8 / 0.8 / 16.7 / 0.9
17.0	2.8	5.6	8.5	11.3	14.1	.0	0.0	0.3	0.6	0.9	1.2	1.5	1.7	2.0	2.3	2.6	18.7 / 1.0
17.1	2.8	5.7	8.5	11.4	14.2	.1	0.0	0.3	0.6	0.9	1.2	1.5	1.8	2.1	2.4	2.7	20.7 / 1.1
17.2	2.8	5.7	8.6	11.4	14.3	.2	0.1	0.3	0.6	0.9	1.2	1.5	1.8	2.1	2.4	2.7	22.7 / 1.2
17.3	2.9	5.8	8.6	11.5	14.4	.3	0.1	0.4	0.7	1.0	1.3	1.5	1.8	2.1	2.4	2.7	24.6 / 1.3
17.4	2.9	5.8	8.7	11.6	14.5	.4	0.1	0.4	0.7	1.0	1.3	1.6	1.9	2.2	2.4	2.7	26.6 / 1.4
17.5	2.9	5.8	8.8	11.7	14.6	.5	0.1	0.4	0.7	1.0	1.3	1.6	1.9	2.2	2.5	2.8	28.6 / 1.5
17.6	2.9	5.9	8.8	11.7	14.7	.6	0.2	0.5	0.8	1.0	1.3	1.6	1.9	2.2	2.5	2.8	30.5 / 1.6
17.7	3.0	5.9	8.9	11.8	14.8	.7	0.2	0.5	0.8	1.1	1.4	1.7	2.0	2.2	2.5	2.8	32.5 / 1.7
17.8	3.0	6.0	8.9	11.9	14.9	.8	0.2	0.5	0.8	1.1	1.4	1.7	2.0	2.3	2.6	2.9	34.5
17.9	3.0	6.0	9.0	12.0	15.0	.9	0.3	0.6	0.8	1.1	1.4	1.7	2.0	2.3	2.6	2.9	
18.0	3.0	6.0	9.0	12.0	15.0	.0	0.0	0.3	0.6	0.9	1.2	1.5	1.8	2.2	2.5	2.8	
18.1	3.0	6.0	9.0	12.0	15.1	.1	0.0	0.3	0.6	1.0	1.3	1.6	1.9	2.2	2.5	2.8	0.9 / 0.1
18.2	3.0	6.0	9.1	12.1	15.1	.2	0.1	0.4	0.7	1.0	1.3	1.6	1.9	2.2	2.5	2.8	2.8 / 0.2
18.3	3.0	6.1	9.1	12.2	15.2	.3	0.1	0.4	0.7	1.0	1.3	1.6	1.9	2.3	2.6	2.9	4.6 / 0.3
18.4	3.1	6.1	9.2	12.3	15.3	.4	0.1	0.4	0.7	1.0	1.4	1.7	2.0	2.3	2.6	2.9	6.5 / 0.4
18.5	3.1	6.2	9.3	12.3	15.4	.5	0.2	0.5	0.8	1.1	1.4	1.7	2.0	2.3	2.6	2.9	8.3 / 0.5
18.6	3.1	6.2	9.3	12.4	15.5	.6	0.2	0.5	0.8	1.1	1.4	1.7	2.0	2.3	2.7	3.0	10.2 / 0.6
18.7	3.1	6.3	9.4	12.5	15.6	.7	0.2	0.5	0.8	1.1	1.4	1.8	2.1	2.4	2.7	3.0	12.0 / 0.7
18.8	3.2	6.3	9.4	12.6	15.7	.8	0.2	0.5	0.9	1.2	1.5	1.8	2.1	2.4	2.7	3.0	13.9 / 0.8
18.9	3.2	6.3	9.5	12.6	15.8	.9	0.3	0.6	0.9	1.2	1.5	1.8	2.1	2.4	2.7	3.1	15.7 / 0.9 / 17.6 / 1.0
19.0	3.1	6.3	9.5	12.6	15.8	.0	0.0	0.3	0.6	1.0	1.3	1.6	1.9	2.3	2.6	2.9	19.4 / 1.1
19.1	3.2	6.3	9.5	12.7	15.9	.1	0.0	0.4	0.7	1.0	1.3	1.7	2.0	2.3	2.6	3.0	21.3 / 1.2
19.2	3.2	6.4	9.6	12.8	16.0	.2	0.1	0.4	0.7	1.0	1.4	1.7	2.0	2.3	2.7	3.0	23.1 / 1.3
19.3	3.2	6.4	9.6	12.9	16.1	.3	0.1	0.4	0.7	1.1	1.4	1.7	2.0	2.4	2.7	3.0	25.0 / 1.4
19.4	3.2	6.5	9.7	12.9	16.2	.4	0.1	0.5	0.8	1.1	1.4	1.8	2.1	2.4	2.7	3.1	26.8 / 1.5
19.5	3.3	6.5	9.8	13.0	16.3	.5	0.2	0.5	0.8	1.1	1.5	1.8	2.1	2.4	2.8	3.1	28.7 / 1.6
19.6	3.3	6.5	9.8	13.1	16.3	.6	0.2	0.5	0.8	1.2	1.5	1.8	2.1	2.5	2.8	3.1	30.5 / 1.7
19.7	3.3	6.6	9.9	13.2	16.4	.7	0.2	0.6	0.9	1.2	1.5	1.9	2.2	2.5	2.8	3.2	32.3 / 1.8
19.8	3.3	6.6	9.9	13.2	16.5	.8	0.3	0.6	0.9	1.2	1.6	1.9	2.2	2.5	2.9	3.2	34.2
19.9	3.4	6.7	10.0	13.3	16.6	.9	0.3	0.6	0.9	1.3	1.6	1.9	2.2	2.6	2.9	3.2	
20.0	3.3	6.6	10.0	13.3	16.6	.0	0.0	0.3	0.7	1.0	1.4	1.7	2.0	2.4	2.7	3.1	
20.1	3.3	6.7	10.0	13.4	16.7	.1	0.0	0.4	0.7	1.1	1.4	1.7	2.1	2.4	2.8	3.1	0.9 / 0.1
20.2	3.3	6.7	10.1	13.4	16.8	.2	0.1	0.4	0.8	1.1	1.4	1.8	2.1	2.5	2.8	3.1	2.6 / 0.2
20.3	3.4	6.8	10.1	13.5	16.9	.3	0.1	0.4	0.8	1.1	1.5	1.8	2.2	2.5	2.8	3.2	4.4 / 0.3
20.4	3.4	6.8	10.2	13.6	17.0	.4	0.1	0.5	0.8	1.2	1.5	1.8	2.2	2.5	2.9	3.2	6.2 / 0.4
20.5	3.4	6.8	10.3	13.7	17.1	.5	0.2	0.5	0.9	1.2	1.5	1.9	2.2	2.6	2.9	3.2	7.9 / 0.5
20.6	3.4	6.9	10.3	13.7	17.2	.6	0.2	0.5	0.9	1.2	1.6	1.9	2.3	2.6	2.9	3.3	9.7 / 0.6
20.7	3.5	6.9	10.4	13.8	17.3	.7	0.2	0.6	0.9	1.3	1.6	1.9	2.3	2.6	3.0	3.3	11.4 / 0.7
20.8	3.5	7.0	10.4	13.9	17.4	.8	0.3	0.6	1.0	1.3	1.6	2.0	2.3	2.7	3.0	3.3	13.2 / 0.8
20.9	3.5	7.0	10.5	14.0	17.5	.9	0.3	0.6	1.0	1.3	1.7	2.0	2.4	2.7	3.0	3.4	14.9 / 0.9 / 16.7 / 1.0
21.0	3.5	7.0	10.5	14.0	17.5	.0	0.0	0.4	0.7	1.1	1.4	1.8	2.1	2.5	2.9	3.2	18.5 / 1.1
21.1	3.5	7.0	10.5	14.0	17.6	.1	0.0	0.4	0.8	1.1	1.5	1.8	2.2	2.5	2.9	3.3	20.2 / 1.2
21.2	3.5	7.0	10.6	14.1	17.6	.2	0.1	0.4	0.8	1.1	1.5	1.9	2.2	2.6	2.9	3.3	22.0 / 1.3
21.3	3.5	7.1	10.6	14.2	17.7	.3	0.1	0.5	0.8	1.2	1.5	1.9	2.3	2.6	3.0	3.3	23.7 / 1.4
21.4	3.6	7.1	10.7	14.3	17.8	.4	0.1	0.5	0.9	1.2	1.6	1.9	2.3	2.7	3.0	3.4	25.5 / 1.5 / 27.3 / 1.6
21.5	3.6	7.2	10.8	14.3	17.9	.5	0.2	0.5	0.9	1.3	1.6	2.0	2.3	2.7	3.0	3.4	29.0 / 1.7
21.6	3.6	7.2	10.8	14.4	18.0	.6	0.2	0.6	0.9	1.3	1.6	2.0	2.4	2.7	3.1	3.4	30.8 / 1.8
21.7	3.6	7.3	10.9	14.5	18.1	.7	0.3	0.6	1.0	1.3	1.7	2.0	2.4	2.8	3.1	3.5	32.5 / 1.9
21.8	3.7	7.3	10.9	14.6	18.2	.8	0.3	0.6	1.0	1.4	1.7	2.1	2.4	2.8	3.2	3.5	34.3
21.9	3.7	7.3	11.0	14.6	18.3	.9	0.3	0.7	1.0	1.4	1.8	2.1	2.5	2.8	3.2	3.5	
22.0	3.6	7.3	11.0	14.6	18.3	.0	0.0	0.4	0.7	1.1	1.5	1.9	2.2	2.6	3.0	3.4	
22.1	3.7	7.3	11.0	14.7	18.4	.1	0.0	0.4	0.8	1.2	1.5	1.9	2.3	2.7	3.0	3.4	0.8 / 0.1
22.2	3.7	7.4	11.1	14.8	18.5	.2	0.1	0.4	0.8	1.2	1.6	1.9	2.3	2.7	3.1	3.4	2.5 / 0.2
22.3	3.7	7.4	11.1	14.9	18.6	.3	0.1	0.5	0.9	1.2	1.6	2.0	2.4	2.7	3.1	3.5	4.2 / 0.3
22.4	3.7	7.5	11.2	14.9	18.7	.4	0.1	0.5	0.9	1.3	1.6	2.0	2.4	2.8	3.1	3.5	5.9 / 0.4 / 7.6 / 0.5
22.5	3.8	7.5	11.3	15.0	18.8	.5	0.2	0.6	0.9	1.3	1.7	2.1	2.4	2.8	3.2	3.6	9.3 / 0.6
22.6	3.8	7.5	11.3	15.1	18.8	.6	0.2	0.6	1.0	1.3	1.7	2.1	2.5	2.8	3.2	3.6	11.0 / 0.7
22.7	3.8	7.6	11.4	15.2	18.9	.7	0.3	0.6	1.0	1.4	1.8	2.1	2.5	2.9	3.3	3.6	12.7 / 0.8
22.8	3.8	7.6	11.4	15.2	19.0	.8	0.3	0.7	1.0	1.4	1.8	2.2	2.5	2.9	3.3	3.7	14.4 / 0.9
22.9	3.9	7.7	11.5	15.3	19.1	.9	0.3	0.7	1.1	1.5	1.8	2.2	2.6	3.0	3.3	3.7	16.1 / 1.0 / 17.8 / 1.1
23.0	3.8	7.6	11.5	15.3	19.1	.0	0.0	0.4	0.8	1.2	1.6	2.0	2.3	2.7	3.1	3.5	19.5 / 1.2
23.1	3.8	7.7	11.5	15.4	19.2	.1	0.0	0.4	0.8	1.2	1.6	2.0	2.4	2.8	3.2	3.6	21.2 / 1.3
23.2	3.8	7.7	11.6	15.4	19.3	.2	0.1	0.5	0.9	1.3	1.6	2.0	2.4	2.8	3.2	3.6	22.8 / 1.4
23.3	3.9	7.8	11.6	15.5	19.4	.3	0.1	0.5	0.9	1.3	1.7	2.1	2.5	2.9	3.3	3.6	24.5 / 1.5
23.4	3.9	7.8	11.7	15.6	19.5	.4	0.2	0.5	0.9	1.3	1.7	2.1	2.5	2.9	3.3	3.7	26.2 / 1.6 / 27.9 / 1.7
23.5	3.9	7.8	11.8	15.7	19.6	.5	0.2	0.6	1.0	1.4	1.8	2.2	2.5	2.9	3.3	3.7	29.6 / 1.8
23.6	3.9	7.9	11.8	15.7	19.7	.6	0.2	0.6	1.0	1.4	1.8	2.2	2.6	3.0	3.4	3.8	31.3 / 1.9
23.7	4.0	7.9	11.9	15.8	19.8	.7	0.3	0.7	1.1	1.4	1.8	2.2	2.6	3.0	3.4	3.8	33.0 / 2.0
23.8	4.0	8.0	11.9	15.9	19.9	.8	0.3	0.7	1.1	1.5	1.9	2.3	2.7	3.1	3.4	3.8	34.7
23.9	4.0	8.0	12.0	16.0	20.0	.9	0.4	0.7	1.1	1.5	1.9	2.3	2.7	3.1	3.5	3.9	
	10'	20'	30'	40'	50'		0'	1'	2	3'	4'	5'	6'	7'	8'	9'	

Dec. Inc.	Altitude Difference (d): Tens 10'	20'	30'	40'	50'	Decimals	Units 0'	1'	2'	3'	4'	5'	6'	7'	8'	9'	Double Second Diff. and Corr.
24.0	4.0	8.0	12.0	16.0	20.0	.0	0.0	0.4	0.8	1.2	1.6	2.0	2.4	2.9	3.3	3.7	0.8 / 0.1
24.1	4.0	8.0	12.0	16.0	20.1	.1	0.0	0.4	0.9	1.3	1.7	2.1	2.5	2.9	3.3	3.7	2.5 / 0.2
24.2	4.0	8.0	12.1	16.1	20.1	.2	0.1	0.5	0.9	1.3	1.7	2.1	2.5	2.9	3.3	3.8	4.1 / 0.3
24.3	4.0	8.1	12.1	16.2	20.2	.3	0.1	0.5	0.9	1.3	1.8	2.2	2.6	3.0	3.4	3.8	5.8 / 0.4
24.4	4.1	8.1	12.2	16.3	20.3	.4	0.2	0.6	1.0	1.4	1.8	2.2	2.6	3.0	3.4	3.8	7.4 / 0.5 / 9.1 / 0.6
24.5	4.1	8.2	12.3	16.3	20.4	.5	0.2	0.6	1.0	1.4	1.8	2.2	2.7	3.1	3.5	3.9	10.7 / 0.7
24.6	4.1	8.2	12.3	16.4	20.5	.6	0.2	0.7	1.1	1.5	1.9	2.3	2.7	3.1	3.5	3.9	12.3 / 0.8
24.7	4.1	8.3	12.4	16.5	20.6	.7	0.3	0.7	1.1	1.5	1.9	2.3	2.7	3.1	3.6	4.0	14.0 / 0.9
24.8	4.2	8.3	12.4	16.6	20.7	.8	0.3	0.7	1.1	1.6	2.0	2.4	2.8	3.2	3.6	4.0	15.6 / 1.0
24.9	4.2	8.3	12.5	16.6	20.8	.9	0.4	0.8	1.2	1.6	2.0	2.4	2.8	3.2	3.6	4.0	17.3 / 1.1 / 18.9 / 1.2
25.0	4.1	8.3	12.5	16.6	20.8	.0	0.0	0.4	0.8	1.3	1.7	2.1	2.5	3.0	3.4	3.8	20.6 / 1.3
25.1	4.2	8.3	12.5	16.7	20.9	.1	0.0	0.5	0.9	1.3	1.7	2.2	2.6	3.0	3.4	3.9	22.2 / 1.4
25.2	4.2	8.4	12.6	16.8	21.0	.2	0.1	0.5	0.9	1.4	1.8	2.2	2.6	3.1	3.5	3.9	23.9 / 1.5
25.3	4.2	8.4	12.6	16.9	21.1	.3	0.1	0.6	1.0	1.4	1.8	2.3	2.7	3.1	3.5	4.0	25.5 / 1.6
25.4	4.2	8.5	12.7	16.9	21.2	.4	0.2	0.6	1.0	1.4	1.9	2.3	2.7	3.1	3.6	4.0	27.2 / 1.7
25.5	4.3	8.5	12.8	17.0	21.3	.5	0.2	0.6	1.1	1.5	1.9	2.3	2.8	3.2	3.6	4.0	28.8 / 1.8
25.6	4.3	8.5	12.8	17.1	21.3	.6	0.3	0.7	1.1	1.5	2.0	2.4	2.8	3.2	3.7	4.1	30.4 / 1.9
25.7	4.3	8.6	12.9	17.2	21.4	.7	0.3	0.7	1.1	1.6	2.0	2.4	2.8	3.3	3.7	4.1	32.1 / 2.0
25.8	4.3	8.6	12.9	17.2	21.5	.8	0.3	0.8	1.2	1.6	2.0	2.5	2.9	3.3	3.7	4.2	33.7 / 2.1
25.9	4.4	8.7	13.0	17.3	21.6	.9	0.4	0.8	1.2	1.7	2.1	2.5	2.9	3.4	3.8	4.2	35.4
26.0	4.3	8.6	13.0	17.3	21.6	.0	0.0	0.4	0.9	1.3	1.8	2.2	2.6	3.1	3.5	4.0	0.8 / 0.1
26.1	4.3	8.7	13.0	17.4	21.7	.1	0.0	0.5	0.9	1.4	1.8	2.3	2.7	3.1	3.6	4.0	2.4 / 0.2
26.2	4.3	8.7	13.1	17.4	21.8	.2	0.1	0.5	1.0	1.4	1.9	2.3	2.7	3.2	3.6	4.1	4.0 / 0.3
26.3	4.4	8.8	13.1	17.5	21.9	.3	0.1	0.6	1.0	1.5	1.9	2.3	2.8	3.2	3.7	4.1	5.7 / 0.4
26.4	4.4	8.8	13.2	17.6	22.0	.4	0.2	0.6	1.1	1.5	1.9	2.4	2.8	3.3	3.7	4.2	7.3 / 0.5 / 8.9 / 0.6
26.5	4.4	8.8	13.3	17.7	22.1	.5	0.2	0.7	1.1	1.5	2.0	2.4	2.9	3.3	3.8	4.2	10.5 / 0.7
26.6	4.4	8.9	13.3	17.7	22.2	.6	0.3	0.7	1.1	1.6	2.0	2.5	2.9	3.4	3.8	4.2	12.1 / 0.8
26.7	4.5	8.9	13.4	17.8	22.3	.7	0.3	0.8	1.2	1.6	2.1	2.5	3.0	3.4	3.8	4.3	13.7 / 0.9
26.8	4.5	9.0	13.4	17.9	22.4	.8	0.4	0.8	1.2	1.7	2.1	2.6	3.0	3.4	3.9	4.3	15.4 / 1.0
26.9	4.5	9.0	13.5	18.0	22.5	.9	0.4	0.8	1.3	1.7	2.2	2.6	3.0	3.5	3.9	4.4	17.0 / 1.1 / 18.6 / 1.2
27.0	4.5	9.0	13.5	18.0	22.5	.0	0.0	0.5	0.9	1.4	1.8	2.3	2.7	3.2	3.7	4.1	20.2 / 1.3
27.1	4.5	9.0	13.5	18.0	22.6	.1	0.0	0.5	1.0	1.4	1.9	2.3	2.8	3.3	3.7	4.2	21.8 / 1.4
27.2	4.5	9.0	13.6	18.1	22.6	.2	0.1	0.5	1.0	1.5	1.9	2.4	2.8	3.3	3.8	4.2	23.4 / 1.5
27.3	4.5	9.1	13.6	18.2	22.7	.3	0.1	0.6	1.1	1.5	2.0	2.4	2.9	3.3	3.8	4.3	25.1 / 1.6
27.4	4.6	9.1	13.7	18.3	22.8	.4	0.2	0.6	1.1	1.6	2.0	2.5	2.9	3.4	3.8	4.3	26.7 / 1.7
27.5	4.6	9.2	13.8	18.3	22.9	.5	0.2	0.7	1.1	1.6	2.1	2.5	3.0	3.4	3.9	4.4	28.3 / 1.8
27.6	4.6	9.2	13.8	18.4	23.0	.6	0.3	0.7	1.2	1.6	2.1	2.6	3.0	3.5	3.9	4.4	29.9 / 1.9
27.7	4.6	9.3	13.9	18.5	23.1	.7	0.3	0.8	1.2	1.7	2.2	2.6	3.1	3.5	4.0	4.4	31.5 / 2.0
27.8	4.7	9.3	13.9	18.6	23.2	.8	0.4	0.8	1.3	1.7	2.2	2.7	3.1	3.6	4.0	4.5	33.1 / 2.1
27.9	4.7	9.3	14.0	18.6	23.3	.9	0.4	0.9	1.3	1.8	2.2	2.7	3.2	3.6	4.1	4.5	34.7
28.0	4.6	9.3	14.0	18.6	23.3	.0	0.0	0.5	0.9	1.4	1.9	2.4	2.8	3.3	3.8	4.3	0.8 / 0.1
28.1	4.7	9.3	14.0	18.7	23.4	.1	0.0	0.5	1.0	1.5	1.9	2.4	2.9	3.4	3.8	4.3	2.4 / 0.2
28.2	4.7	9.4	14.1	18.8	23.5	.2	0.1	0.6	1.0	1.5	2.0	2.5	2.9	3.4	3.9	4.4	4.0 / 0.3
28.3	4.7	9.4	14.1	18.9	23.6	.3	0.1	0.6	1.1	1.6	2.0	2.5	3.0	3.5	3.9	4.4	5.6 / 0.4
28.4	4.7	9.5	14.2	18.9	23.7	.4	0.2	0.7	1.1	1.6	2.1	2.6	3.0	3.5	4.0	4.5	7.2 / 0.5 / 8.8 / 0.6
28.5	4.8	9.5	14.3	19.0	23.8	.5	0.2	0.7	1.2	1.7	2.1	2.6	3.1	3.6	4.0	4.5	10.4 / 0.7
28.6	4.8	9.5	14.3	19.1	23.8	.6	0.3	0.8	1.2	1.7	2.2	2.7	3.1	3.6	4.1	4.6	12.0 / 0.8
28.7	4.8	9.6	14.4	19.2	23.9	.7	0.3	0.8	1.3	1.8	2.2	2.7	3.2	3.7	4.1	4.6	13.6 / 0.9
28.8	4.8	9.6	14.4	19.2	24.0	.8	0.4	0.9	1.3	1.8	2.3	2.8	3.2	3.7	4.2	4.7	15.2 / 1.0
28.9	4.9	9.7	14.5	19.3	24.1	.9	0.4	0.9	1.4	1.9	2.3	2.8	3.3	3.8	4.2	4.7	16.8 / 1.1 / 18.4 / 1.2
29.0	4.8	9.6	14.5	19.3	24.1	.0	0.0	0.5	1.0	1.5	2.0	2.5	2.9	3.4	3.9	4.4	20.0 / 1.3
29.1	4.8	9.7	14.5	19.4	24.2	.1	0.0	0.5	1.0	1.5	2.0	2.5	3.0	3.5	4.0	4.5	21.6 / 1.4
29.2	4.8	9.7	14.6	19.4	24.3	.2	0.1	0.6	1.1	1.6	2.1	2.6	3.0	3.5	4.0	4.5	23.2 / 1.5
29.3	4.9	9.8	14.6	19.5	24.4	.3	0.1	0.6	1.1	1.6	2.1	2.6	3.1	3.6	4.1	4.6	24.8 / 1.6
29.4	4.9	9.8	14.7	19.6	24.5	.4	0.2	0.7	1.2	1.7	2.2	2.7	3.1	3.6	4.1	4.6	26.4 / 1.7
29.5	4.9	9.8	14.8	19.7	24.6	.5	0.2	0.7	1.2	1.7	2.2	2.7	3.2	3.7	4.2	4.7	28.0 / 1.8
29.6	4.9	9.9	14.8	19.7	24.7	.6	0.3	0.8	1.3	1.8	2.3	2.8	3.2	3.7	4.2	4.7	29.6 / 1.9
29.7	5.0	9.9	14.9	19.8	24.8	.7	0.3	0.8	1.3	1.8	2.3	2.8	3.3	3.8	4.3	4.8	31.2 / 2.0
29.8	5.0	10.0	14.9	19.9	24.9	.8	0.4	0.9	1.4	1.9	2.4	2.9	3.3	3.8	4.3	4.8	32.8 / 2.1
29.9	5.0	10.0	15.0	20.0	25.0	.9	0.4	0.9	1.4	1.9	2.4	2.9	3.4	3.9	4.4	4.9	34.4
30.0	5.0	10.0	15.0	20.0	25.0	.0	0.0	0.5	1.0	1.5	2.0	2.5	3.0	3.6	4.1	4.6	0.8 / 0.1
30.1	5.0	10.0	15.0	20.0	25.1	.1	0.1	0.6	1.1	1.6	2.1	2.6	3.1	3.6	4.1	4.6	2.4 / 0.2
30.2	5.0	10.0	15.1	20.1	25.1	.2	0.1	0.6	1.1	1.6	2.1	2.6	3.2	3.7	4.2	4.7	4.0 / 0.3
30.3	5.0	10.1	15.1	20.2	25.2	.3	0.2	0.7	1.2	1.7	2.2	2.7	3.2	3.7	4.2	4.7	5.6 / 0.4
30.4	5.1	10.1	15.2	20.3	25.3	.4	0.2	0.7	1.2	1.7	2.2	2.7	3.3	3.8	4.3	4.8	7.2 / 0.5 / 8.8 / 0.6
30.5	5.1	10.2	15.3	20.3	25.4	.5	0.3	0.8	1.3	1.8	2.3	2.8	3.3	3.8	4.3	4.8	10.4 / 0.7
30.6	5.1	10.2	15.3	20.4	25.5	.6	0.3	0.8	1.3	1.8	2.3	2.8	3.4	3.9	4.4	4.9	12.0 / 0.8
30.7	5.1	10.3	15.4	20.5	25.6	.7	0.4	0.9	1.4	1.9	2.4	2.9	3.4	3.9	4.4	4.9	13.6 / 0.9
30.8	5.2	10.3	15.4	20.6	25.7	.8	0.4	0.9	1.4	1.9	2.4	2.9	3.5	4.0	4.5	5.0	15.2 / 1.0
30.9	5.2	10.3	15.5	20.6	25.8	.9	0.5	1.0	1.5	2.0	2.5	3.0	3.5	4.0	4.5	5.0	16.8 / 1.1 / 18.4 / 1.2
31.0	5.1	10.3	15.5	20.6	25.8	.0	0.0	0.5	1.0	1.6	2.1	2.6	3.1	3.7	4.2	4.7	20.0 / 1.3
31.1	5.2	10.3	15.5	20.7	25.9	.1	0.1	0.6	1.1	1.6	2.2	2.7	3.2	3.7	4.3	4.8	21.6 / 1.4
31.2	5.2	10.4	15.6	20.8	26.0	.2	0.1	0.6	1.2	1.7	2.2	2.7	3.3	3.8	4.3	4.8	23.2 / 1.5
31.3	5.2	10.4	15.6	20.9	26.1	.3	0.2	0.7	1.2	1.7	2.3	2.8	3.3	3.8	4.4	4.9	24.8 / 1.6
31.4	5.2	10.5	15.7	20.9	26.2	.4	0.2	0.7	1.3	1.8	2.3	2.8	3.4	3.9	4.4	4.9	26.4 / 1.7
31.5	5.3	10.5	15.8	21.0	26.3	.5	0.3	0.8	1.3	1.8	2.4	2.9	3.4	3.9	4.5	5.0	28.0 / 1.8
31.6	5.3	10.5	15.8	21.1	26.3	.6	0.3	0.8	1.4	1.9	2.4	2.9	3.5	4.0	4.5	5.0	29.6 / 1.9
31.7	5.3	10.6	15.9	21.2	26.4	.7	0.4	0.9	1.4	1.9	2.5	3.0	3.5	4.0	4.6	5.1	31.2 / 2.0
31.8	5.3	10.6	15.9	21.2	26.5	.8	0.4	0.9	1.5	2.0	2.5	3.0	3.6	4.1	4.6	5.1	32.8 / 2.1
31.9	5.4	10.7	16.0	21.3	26.6	.9	0.5	1.0	1.5	2.0	2.6	3.1	3.6	4.1	4.7	5.2	34.4
	10'	20'	30'	40'	50'		0'	1'	2	3'	4'	5'	6'	7'	8'	9'	

Double Second Difference correction (Corr.) is always to be added to the tabulated altitude

U.S.
NAVY
NAVIGATION
WORKBOOK

U.S.S._____

PERIOD

_____19__ TO _____19__

OPNAV FORM 3530/1 and 1A thru 1J (Rev. 7-71)

ENCLOSURE (1)

Appendix K-2

NAVIGATION WORKBOOK

U.S. Navy Regulations require the navigator to "Maintain record books of all observations and computations made for the purpose of navigating the ship, with results and dates involved. Such books shall form a part of the ship's official records." This publication has been printed to meet a recognized need for a standard computation book. In addition to providing a standard record, the format is intended to provide optimum utility, economy and flexibility, by providing strip inserts to assist the navigator in the below computations: (Strip inserts, marked to size for cut out, are printed on the back pages of this book. An envelope, suitable for stowing inserts when not in use, is attached to the inside back cover.)

CELESTIAL SIGHTS and LORAN

Place proper Computation Strip beside a blank column, and align so that entries will correspond with information on strip. Insure name of celestial body or "LORAN" is entered at top, and that the Fix is entered for appropriate celestial sights or LORAN LOPs.

AZIMUTH, LAN, SUNRISE/SUNSET, TIDES, CURRENTS, etc.

Place proper Computation Strip beside a blank column. Insure top of column is labeled to identify the type of computation.

MODIFICATION OF COMPUTATION STRIPS

This workbook is to serve navigators, and strip forms may be used to suit individual preference. Note: Any modified strip form is to become an official part of this record.

NAVIGATOR'S SIGNATURE

Space is provided at the bottom of each page for required signature of the navigator.

Appendix K-3

NAVIGATION WORKBOOK
OPNAV FORM 3530/1 (Rev. 7-71)

DATE OR POSIT	DATE OR POSIT	DATE OR POSIT	DATE OR POSIT	DATE OR POSIT

USN, NAVIGATOR

187

OPNAV FORM 3530/1A (7-71)	OPNAV FORM 3530/1B (7-71)	OPNAV FORM 3530/1C (7-71)	OPNAV FORM 3530/1D (7-71)	OPNAV FORM 3530/1E (7-71)	OPNAV FORM 3530/1F (7-71)	OPNAV FORM 3530/1G (7-71)
HO 214	HO 249 VOL I	HO 229	LATITUDE BY POLARIS	LAN (TIME)	AZIMUTH BY HO 214	AZIMUTH BY HO 229
Body	Body	Body	Body (Polaris)	Sun (UL, LL)	Body	Body
GMT	GMT	GMT	GMT	DRλ	GMT	GMT
IC (±)	IC (±)	IC (±)	IC (±)	LMT	DR Lat	DR Lat
Dip (–)	Dip (–)	Dip (–)	Dip (–)	λ arc to time	GHA*	GHA*
hs	hs	hs	hs	GMT	Increment (+)	Increment (+)
Sum	Sum	Sum	Sum	ZD (rev)	Total GHA	GHA
ha	ha	ha	ha	ZT (first est)	DRλ (+E,–W)	DRλ (+E,–W)
R	R	R	R	DRλ (at first est)	LHA	LHA
Corr'n	Corr'n	Corr'n	Corr'n	LMT	t (E or W)	Tab Dec
Ho	Ho	Ho	Ho	λ arc to time	Tab Dec	d corr'n (±)
GHA*	GHA*	GHA*		GMT	d corr'n (±)	True Dec
Increment (+)	Increment (+)	Increment (+)	GHA*	ZD (rev)	True Dec	LHA Inc × Z diff
SHA or v corr'n	Total GHA*	SHA or v corr'n	Increment (+)	ZT (2nd est)		Dec Inc × Z diff
Total GHA	aλ (+E,–W)	Total GHA	Total GHA*		t corr'n	Lat Inc × Z diff
aλ (+E,–W)	LHA*	aλ (+E,–W)	DRλ (+E,–W)	LAN (Lat)	Dec corr'n	Total Corr'n
LHA		LHA	LHA*	IC (±)	Lat corr'n	Tab Z
t (E or W)	aLat	Tab Dec		Dip (–)	Tab Az	Exact Z
Tab Dec	Hc	d corr'n (±)	Ho	hs	Exact Az	Exact Zn
a corr'n (±)	Ho	True Dec	a0 (+)	Sum	Zn	Gyro Brg
True Dec	a (T or A)	a Dec	a1 (+)	ha	Gyro Brg	GE (E or W)
a Dec	Zn	Dec Inc	a2 (+)	R	GE (E or W)	
Dec Diff		d (±)	Sum	Ho	time	time
Δd (±)	Fix L	Hc (Tab)	–1°00'	Tab Dec		
Dec Diff × Δd (±)	A	Dec Inc × d (±)	Latitude	d corr'n (±)		
hr	Precession Corr'n	DSD		True Dec		
Hc	time	Hc				
Ho		Ho		90 Ho		
a (T or A)		a (T or A)		True Dec		
L (Az) t		Z		Lat		
Zn		Zn		time		
Fix L		Fix L				
A		A				
time		time				

Appendix K-5

OPNAV FORM 3530/1H (7-71)	OPNAV FORM 3530/1I (7-71)	OPNAV FORM 3530/1J (7-71)	
LORAN	SUNRISE/SET TWILIGHT	MOONRISE/SET	
Date	Date	Date	
DR Lat	DR Lat	DR Lat	
DRλ	TABLE I:	TABLE I:	
TG/TS	Tab Interval	Tab Interval	
Sys Corr'n	Lat diff	Lat Diff	
Skywave corr'n	Time diff	Time Diff	
TG	Time Corr'n	Time Corr'n	
Lat/Lon for T	Tab LMT	Tab LMT	
J from Table	LMT	LMT	
TG	DRλ .	DRλ	
TG – T (±)	λ arc to time	TABLE II.	
(TG – T)(Δλ±)	LMT	Tab LMT today	
Tab Lat/Lon	GMT	LMT (preceding/ following)	
Adj Lat/Lon	ZD (rev.)	time Difference	
	ZT (1st est.)	time corr'n	
	DRλ (1st est.)	LMT	
Fix Lat	LMT	LMT actual	
	λ arc to time	λ arc to time	
time	GMT	GMT	
	ZD (rev)	ZD (rev)	
	ZT (2nd est.)	ZT (1st est)	
		DRλ (1st est)	
		λ arc to time	
		LMT Actual	
		GMT	
		ZD (rev)	
		ZT (2nd est)	

189

Appendix L-1

		W ⟋ ◯ ⟍ E	W ⟋ ◯ ⟍ E	W ⟋ ◯ ⟍ E	W ⟋ ◯ ⟍ E
LOCAL DATE: _____ COURSE ____ °T SPEED ____					
DR:	LAT. LONG.				
BODY					
Z.T. Z.D.					
GMT Gr. Date					
GHA (hrs) GHA (m & s) v corr. or SHA*					
GHA a Long.		E/W	E/W	E/W	E/W
LHA t (H.A.)					
Dec. Tab. d. corr. (±)		( )	( )	( )	( )
Dec.		N/S	N/S	N/S	N/S
ENTER H.O. 214	Dec. t (H.A.) a Lat.	N/S E/W N/S	N/S E/W N/S	N/S E/W N/S	N/S E/W N/S
d. diff. d (+ or –)					
Ht corr.					
Hc Az		N/S E/W	N/S E/W	N/S E/W	N/S E/W
		+ –	+ –	+ –	+ –
I.C. Dip Main Corr. Add'l					
SUMS					
Hs Corr.					
Ho Hc					
a Zn		T/A °T	T/A °T	T/A °T	T/A °T
Advance					

An alternate form for multiple sight computations

190

Appendix L-2

PREDICTING TIME OF SUNS MERIDIAN PASSAGE (LAN)

S. M.				S. M.			
← + W		− E →		← + W		− E →	

* DLo BTN STANDARD MERIDIAN & DR LONGITUDE | DLo BTN STANDARD MERIDIAN & DR LONGITUDE

1200 DR LAT			1200 DR LAT	
DR LONG			DR LONG	
LOCAL DATE			LOCAL DATE	
LMT OF MER PASS			LMT OF MER PASS	
* DLo (IN TIME)			DLo (IN TIME)	
PREDICTED ZT OF MER PASS			PREDICTED ZT OF MER PASS	

SOLUTION FOR LATITUDE			SOLUTION FOR LATITUDE	
ACT ZT OF MER PASS			ACT ZT OF MER PASS	
ZD (+W) (−E)			ZD (+W) (−E)	
GMT			GMT	
GR DATE			GR DATE	
TAB DEC			TAB DEC	
d CORR ( ) $\pm$			d CORR ( ) $\pm$	
TOTAL DEC			TOTAL DEC	

	+	−			+	−
I. C.			L & D SAME L + (L − D + ZD)	I. C.		
DIP			L & D SAME D + (L − D − ZD)	DIP		
MAIN CORR			L & D CONTRARY (L − ZD − D)	MAIN CORR		
SUMS (+)				SUMS (+)		
SUMS (−)			Z	SUMS (−)		
TOTAL CORR				TOTAL CORR		
HS				HS		
HO				HO		
ZENITH	8 9°−6 0. 0'		Z	ZENITH	8 9°− 6 0. 0'	
ZEN DIST				ZEN DIST		
TOTAL DEC				TOTAL DEC		
LATITUDE				LATITUDE		

Appendix L-3

LATITUDE = CORRECTED SEXTANT ALTITUDE - 1° + a_0 + a_1 + a_2

DATE (LOCAL)			DATE (LOCAL)		
DR LATITUDE			DR LATITUDE		
DR LONGITUDE			DR LONGITUDE		
ZT			ZT		
ZD (+W) (-E)			ZD (+W) (-E)		
GMT			GMT		
GR DATE			GR DATE		
GHA ARIES (hrs)			GHA ARIES (hrs)		
GHA ARIES (m&s)			GHA ARIES (m&s)		
TOTAL GHA ARIES			TOTAL GHA ARIES		
DR LONG (+E) (-W)			DR LONG (+E) (-W)		
LHA ARIES			LHA ARIES		
	+	-		+	-
IC			IC		
DIP	///		DIP	///	
MAIN CORR	///		MAIN CORR	///	
a_0 (LHA)		///	a_0 (LHA)		///
a_1 (LAT)		///	a_1 (LAT)		///
a_2 (MONTH)		///	a_2 (MONTH)		///
ADD'L	///	6 0. 0'	ADD'L	///	6 0. 0'
SUMS (+)			SUMS (+)		
SUMS (-)			SUMS (-)		
TOTAL CORR			TOTAL CORR		
Hs			Hs		
LATITUDE		N	LATITUDE		N

192

Appendix L-4

SUNRISE, SUNSET & LHA ARIES

S. M.

← + W   - E →

** Dlo BTN STANDARD MERIDIAN & DR LONGITUDE

DATE _____ SUN	
DR LATITUDE _____	
DR LONGITUDE _____	
STANDARD MERIDIAN	
** DIFF IN LONGITUDE	
SUN ____ LAT _____ ( )	
SUN ____ LAT _____ ( )	
1° LAT = _____	
DIFF IN LAT = ____ X _____	
DIFF IN LONG = _____ X 4m =	
TOTAL CORR	
BASETIME	
ZT OF SUN _____	
TWILIGHT CORR EVE (+30m) MORN (-45m)	
ZT OF TWILIGHT	
ZD (+W) (-E)	
GMT OF TWILIGHT	
GHA ARIES (hrs)	
GHA ARIES (m&s)	
TOTAL GHA ARIES	
DR LONG (+E) (-W)	
LHA ARIES	

PLANET INFORMATION

PLOT RIGHT ASCENSION (RA) AND DECLINATION OF PLANET

$RA = 360° - SHA$ OF PLANET

BODY	VENUS	MARS
	3 6 0	3 6 0
SHA (-)		
RA		
DEC		

BODY	JUPITER	SATURN
	3 6 0	3 6 0
SHA (-)		
RA		
DEC		

BODY	AZIMUTH	ALTITUDE

1. SELECT TEMPLATE TO CORRESPOND TO DR LATITUDE.
2. PLACE TEMPLATE ON STARBASE TO CORRESPOND TO LATITUDE (NORTH or SOUTH).
3. SET ARROW ON TEMPLATE TO CORRESPOND TO LHA ARIES

INDEX

Printed in the United States
74500LV00005B/145